Y0-DWO-940

International Studies in Educational Achievement

VOLUME 4

The IEA Classroom
Environment Study

International Studies in Educational Achievement

Other titles in the Series include:

GORMAN, PURVES & DEGENHART

The IEA Study of Written Composition: The International Writing Tasks and Scoring Scales

TRAVERS & WESTBURY

The IEA Study of Mathematics I: International Analysis of Mathematics Curricula

ROBITAILLE & GARDEN

The IEA Study of Mathematics II: Contexts and Outcomes of School Mathematics

The IEA Classroom Environment Study

Edited by

L. W. ANDERSON
University of South Carolina, U.S.A.

D. W. RYAN
University of New Brunswick, Canada

and

B. J. SHAPIRO
Ontario Ministry of Education, Canada

Published for the International Association for the
Evaluation of Educational Achievement by

PERGAMON PRESS
Member of Maxwell Macmillan Pergamon Publishing Corporation
OXFORD · NEW YORK · BEIJING · FRANKFURT
SÃO PAULO · SYDNEY · TOKYO · TORONTO

U.K.	Pergamon Press plc, Headington Hill Hall, Oxford OX3 0BW, England.
U.S.A.	Pergamon Press, Inc., Maxwell House, Fairview Park, Elmsford, New York 10523, U.S.A.
PEOPLE'S REPUBLIC OF CHINA	Pergamon Press, Room 4037, Qianmen Hotel, Beijing, People's Republic of China
FEDERAL REPUBLIC OF GERMANY	Pergamon Press GmbH, Hammerweg 6, D-6242 Kronberg, Federal Republic of Germany
BRAZIL	Pergamon Editora Ltda, Rua Eça de Queiros, 346, CEP 04011, Paraiso, São Paulo, Brazil
AUSTRALIA	Pergamon Press Australia Pty. Ltd., P.O. Box 544, Potts Point, N.S.W. 2011, Australia
JAPAN	Pergamon Press, 5th Floor, Matsuoka Central Building, 1-7-1 Nishishinjuku, Shinjuku-ku, Tokyo 160, Japan
CANADA	Pergamon Press Canada Ltd., Suite No. 271, 253 College Street, Toronto, Ontario, Canada M5T 1R5

First edition 1989

Library of Congress Cataloging in Publication Data
The IEA classroom environment study/edited by
L. W. Anderson, D. W. Ryan and B. J. Shapiro.
p. cm. — (International studies in educational
achievement; v.4)
1. Classroom environment — Cross-cultural studies.
I. Anderson, Lorin W. II. Ryan, D. W. III. Shapiro,
Barbara J. IV. International Association for the Evaluation
of Educational Achievement. V. Series.
LB3013.13 1989   371.1'02—dc20   89-33431

British Library Cataloguing in Publication Data
The IEA classroom environment study. - (International
studies in educational achievement; v.4).
1. Schools. Teaching. Research
I. Anderson, L. W. II. Ryan, D. W. III. Shapiro, B.J.
IV. International Association for the Evaluation of
Educational Achievement
371.1'02'072

ISBN 0-08-037268-6

Printed in Great Britain by B.P.C.C. Wheatons Ltd., Exeter

Contents

Foreword

The International Association for the Evaluation of Educational Achievement (IEA) was founded in 1959 for the purpose of comparing the educational performance of school students in various countries and systems of education around the world. Its aim was to look at achievement against a wide background of school, home, student, and societal factors in order to use the world as an educational laboratory so as to instruct policymakers at all levels about alternatives in educational organization and practice. IEA has grown over the years from a small number of nations and systems of education to a group of over forty. Its studies have covered a wide range of topics, and have contributed to a deeper understanding of education and of the nature of teaching and learning in a variety of school subjects.

This particular study of the classroom environment was somewhat of a departure from other IEA studies in that it involved not the usual survey of student achievement but an attempt to examine in detail those instructional variables that effect successful learning. The study is to be seen, therefore, as a set of replications in different countries of intensive classroom observation coupled with a pretest and a posttest. Like all IEA studies this one is a cooperative venture. Each of the participating systems contributes all local costs as well as a portion of the international costs, particularly travel and meeting costs. IEA is a unique international organization in that it has virtually no international overhead, and is truly a cooperative venture in finance, planning, and execution. Each participant contributes to all phases of the study.

The international costs of the study were supported by grants from a number of agencies: Canadian International Development Research Center, Ford Foundation, German Unilever Foundation, and IEA. The Ontario Institute for Studies in Education (OISE) donated a great deal of space and support as well as direct financial aid to the international coordinating center. To each of these agencies, those involved in the project and the General Assembly of IEA are extremely grateful. We are also well aware of the support given the researchers by their own institutions, support that is almost impossible to itemize.

This volume represents the efforts of the many people involved in the study to clarify the domain and its assessment. As the editors note, many people were involved in the preparation of the volume. I should like to express the gratitude of IEA to the editorial committee and in particular to Professor Richard Wolf of Teachers College, Columbia University, its chairman, for his shepherding of the manuscript. This volume was reviewed for the editorial committee by two people, whose comments were particularly useful to the editors: Michael J. Dunkin, University of Sydney, Australia, and T. Neville Postlethwaite, University of Hamburg, Federal Republic of Germany, who reviewed the report in his capacity as Chairman of IEA. We are also grateful to Pergamon Press, and its publisher Mr. Robert Maxwell for his kindness in supporting the IEA publications program.

ALAN C. PURVES
Chairman IEA

Preface

The initial planning for the Classroom Environment Study began ten years ago. Many educators (including the editors and authors at times) would likely think that a decade is more than enough time to plan, conduct, and report on a study of classroom teaching and school learning. Nonetheless, during the lengthy process of writing this volume, we discovered that other studies and projects had, in fact, required a decade to complete.

For example, A. S. Barr, one of the earliest American educators to conduct research on classroom teaching, described the time frame for a series of reports linked with a single major study which were published in the *Journal of Experimental Education* in two consecutive issues (September and December 1945).

> The project was initiated during the academic year of 1934-35. Throughout this year a group of some twenty persons representing the State Department of Public Instruction; the Department of Education, University of Wisconsin; and a number of local school systems, met every other Saturday morning to discuss possible approaches to a systematic study of the problem of teacher evaluation. The result of this year's work was a statement of the problem and a tentative formulation of the procedure to be followed in this study. During the academic year of 1935-36, this tentative formulation was turned over to a graduate seminar in Education for their critical analysis and revision. ... The procedure as then formulated provided the general pattern for the series of investigations here reported. The data ... were collected for the most part during the academic years of 1936-1938. The statistical analysis of the data consumed the greater part of the period intervening from 1938 and 1944 (Barr 1945, p.1).

Quite remarkably, the timeline of the Classroom Environment Study parallels that of Barr's study quite closely. The planning phase lasted about three years (from 1978 through 1981). The data collection phase lasted about two years (from 1981 through 1983, although one country, Canada Quebec, began this phase somewhat earlier than the others). The data analysis phase lasted approximately four years (from 1983 through 1987).

We offer as additional evidence in support of the reasonableness of a ten-year period of time for the completion of classroom research studies, the ORACLE project, which was funded by the British Social Science Research Council and was conducted by faculty of the University of Leicester 1975 to 1980 (Delamont and Galton 1986). That is, the preparation and data collection lasted the better part of five years. To date, five volumes have been published, the latest carrying a 1986 copyright.

ix

Rather, therefore, than apologize for the length of time between inception and completion, we would like to suggest that such time is, in fact, needed if quality classroom research is to be conducted and reported. Further, we offer two additional considerations.

First, classroom research is labor-intensive. Judged by any standard, the Classroom Environment Study is "large scale." Observations were conducted in 429 classrooms in 275 schools located in eight countries (with three replications in Canada). Across all countries the median number of observations per classroom was about seven. Thus, some 3,000 observation periods took place during the study. Since each observation period lasted at least 40 minutes, the data compiled for the study were collected during approximately 120,000 minutes (or 2,000 hours) that observers spent in these classrooms. Moreover, prior to the actual observations, observers had to be trained and certified, permissions to conduct the observations had to be secured from school administrators, and schedules had to be prepared. Following completion of the observations in most countries, the observers' records had to be transformed into a format appropriate for computer reading and analyses.

Second, proper analysis, interpretation, and display of the results of classroom research are not trivial matters. Large-scale data sets are unusually "messy." Codings for variables appear in improper places on the data records and sometimes exceed the range of possible or appropriate numerical values. Data on important variables (e.g., classroom identification number) are omitted. As a consequence, the task of producing a complete, valid data set is difficult, often frustrating.

In view of the nature of classroom research, the data analytic process can best be described as both interactive, involving an often intimate relationship between the data analyst and the data, and iterative, involving multiple "passes" through the data. Those readers well versed in experimental research methodology, in which most decision rules are stated *a priori* and decisions are made by simply "following the rules," will likely find the data analytic process involved in classroom research somewhat "subjective." Data analysts make decisions based on what "makes sense," "seems reasonable," or "is consistent with the variables as measured or the conceptual model as specified."

Multiple printouts of each data set must be examined, each based on revisions made based on the prior printouts. Data pertaining to individuals are combined, modified, or deleted. Ultimately, the process of data analysis must come to an end, but even the end is determined by the data analyst, not by the data.

Finally, proper displays of the data must be considered. Pages upon pages of frequency counts or correlation coefficients may be complete, but are not necessarily communicative. Rather, the objective is for simple tables, charts, and graphs, coupled with clear, concise prose to convey the message of the completed study. The format of the displays must be determined, and the specific data to include in the various displays must be selected from the mass of data available for inclusion.

Thus, we quite obviously have a number of people to thank for their time and effort in all phases of the study. We would like to express our appreciation to all of the National Research Coordinators for contributing to the organizing framework of the study, conducting the training program for the observers in their countries, supervising the data collection, and preparing and submitting the data for international analysis. In this regard, we would also like to thank all of the classroom observers (unknown to us personally) who spent the many hours in the actual classroom settings.

We owe, as well, a great debt of gratitude to Garrett Mandeville and Norbert Sellin for their yeoman work in the cleaning, editing, and analyses of the data. The precision of their efforts and the professionalism of their demeanor can serve as models for us all.

We would also like to thank Beatrice Avalos, Sid Bourke, and Angela Hildyard for participating in countless discussions about the study and the manuscript, and for contributing substantial portions to the various chapters. In addition, we are most appreciative of the work of Richard Wolf in preparing all of the figures which appear in Chapter 4. Finally, we would like to thank Betty Benayon and Catherine Schachner for typing the various drafts of the manuscript, a number too painful to remember.

At its very least, the Classroom Environment Study represents a large-scale, cross-national study designed to increase our understanding of the nature of classroom teaching and school learning by looking "behind the classroom door" (Goodland, Klein, and associates 1970). Many of the results to be presented in this volume are intriguing, if for no other reason than to provide a set of baseline data to use in developing and monitoring instructional improvement efforts. In addition, many lessons were learned concerning the design and conduct of large-scale classroom observational studies (see, for example, Ryan and Anderson 1984).

Undoubtedly, many readers will be disappointed with the study and its results. Some will criticize the design and methodology. Others will criticize the flexibility given to the countries in implementing the study. Still others, seeking a series of variables that can be manipulated so that improved learning will be virtually guaranteed, will be particularly disappointed. Although most of us as educators wish for simple, straightforward solutions to complex problems, such solutions are not to be found in this volume. In fact, much of the credibility of the results of the study resides in their complexity.

Our attempt in this volume will be to present the study "warts and all" in an academically honest manner. In this way, readers can decide for themselves the value of the study and the nature of its contribution to the field of classroom research.

1

An Introduction to the Classroom Environment Study

The behaviors teachers use in their classrooms to achieve a variety of instructional and management purposes have been the focus of considerable research, and suggestions about what teachers should and should not do in their classrooms, based at least in part on this research, are often included in the content of teacher training courses. This book describes an international study that attempted to discover similarities and differences across countries in terms of rather typical teaching behaviors, and to identify, within each country, those behaviors associated with differences in student cognitive and affective learning.

The Emergence of a Research Plan

In 1970 the first results were emerging from a series of international and comparative studies of student achievement conducted under the auspices of the International Association for the Evaluation of Educational Achievement (IEA). The results of the first three of six subject areas—reading comprehension (Thorndike 1973), literature (Purves 1973), and science (Comber and Keeves 1973)—suggested that only 40 to 50 percent of the achievement differences among students could be explained by the host of variables included in the studies. The results for the final three subject areas—English as a second language (Lewis 1975), French as a second language (Carroll 1975), and civic education (Farnen, Marklund, Oppenheim, and Torney 1976)—supported this general conclusion.

Researchers involved in these studies, however, voiced concerns about two deficiencies. First, the studies were cross-sectional, not longitudinal. Second, no measures of actual teaching were included. If only, it was argued, longitudinal studies could be designed in which achievement was measured at two or more points in time, and teacher behaviors were observed during the time period(s) between those achievement measures, we would then be in a much better position to explain additional variation in student achievement.

This chapter was written by Lorin W. Anderson, with the assistance of T. Neville Postlethwaite and Bernard J. Shapiro.

2   *Lorin W. Anderson, T. Neville Postlethwaite, Bernard J. Shapiro*

Furthermore, we would gain far more knowledge about school-related factors that actually contribute to differences in what students do and do not learn.

In view of the disagreements among researchers as to whether such a study was either possible or useful, IEA convened a meeting of interested and concerned researchers in Stockholm in 1972 to discuss its merit. A proposal for a study was prepared, but it lay dormant for several years. During these years, however, a number of research activities and publications led to renewed interest in the direct study of classroom teaching. Thus, for example, the *Second Handbook of Research on Teaching* (Travers 1973) included several chapters pertaining to models, methods, and results of such studies. Further, Neville Bennett reported the initial findings of his teaching style research (Bennett et al. 1976), and the results of a reanalysis of these data were reported some five years later (Aitkin et al. 1981). In addition, the results of a meta-analysis of studies based on the ideas expressed by Benjamin Bloom in his development of "mastery learning" were quite positive (Block and Burns 1976). Finally, the results of experimental studies based largely on the results of prior correlational work involving observed teacher behaviors (e.g., Anderson, Evertson, and Brophy 1979; Crawford, Gage, Corno, Stayrook, Mitman, Schunk, and Stallings 1978; Good and Grouws 1979; and Stallings, Needels and Stayrook 1979) were beginning to be known outside of the United States. The basis for these studies lay in the derivation of teaching practices from the results of studies examining the relationship between observed teaching behaviors and residualized student achievement gain. Once such practices were identified, they were used in experimental studies in which one group of teachers was trained to use the practices and a similar group was not trained. If the students of the trained group of teachers demonstrated greater achievement than those of the appropriate comparison group of teachers, the superiority of the former group was attributed to the differences in the clusters of teaching behaviors that comprised the more general teaching practices. Furthermore, since one group of teachers had been successfully trained to employ the identified teaching practices, much could be learned about the nature of the training programs appropriate for both preservice and inservice teachers (cf. Gage 1972, 1978).

The results of these studies were becoming known at a time when more attention was being paid to improving the quality of teaching in developing countries. Because nearly all of the studies had been carried out in North America and England, however, questions were being asked about the generalizability of these research findings to educational practice in developing countries. In particular, there was a question about the extent to which classrooms and teaching practices were—as is anecdotally reported—similar around the world.

Therefore, in 1978, IEA brought together a small group of researchers in Israel for the purposes of discussing the various research paradigms or approaches that could be used to answer such a question. Stimulated by the work of Tamar Levin and her colleagues at Tel Aviv University on classroom environments (Levin et al. 1977; Levin 1981) and the correspondence between Levin and Arieh Lewy (also of Tel Aviv University) with individuals and research centers throughout the world, two meetings attended by researchers from interested research institutions in different countries were held. The first meeting was held in Berlin in 1979; the second in Hamburg in 1980. Finally, in 1980, a plan for the present research, the Classroom Environment Study (CES), emerged.

The Plan of the Study

As has been mentioned, this study of classroom environments was to be directed toward two major aims. First, the study was to describe the similarities and differences in the nature of teaching in classrooms in many countries. Second, the results of this descriptive inquiry were to be used to identify those teaching behaviors that were associated with greater student achievement. If such behaviors could be identified, then they could be combined to form more general teaching practices and, in an experimental mode, these practices could be taught to teachers in an effort to improve both teaching and, therefore, learning in the participating countries.

The first major problem in planning the study was to arrive at the list of teaching behaviors that would be included. A variety of potential behaviors were included in several literature reviews conducted during the 1970s (Crawford and Gage 1977; Dunkin and Biddle 1974; Levin et al. 1977; and Rosenshine 1976, 1979). Three criteria were used to select from these lists of behaviors those that would be included in the Classroom Environment Study. To be included, a teaching behavior had to:

(1) have a demonstrated relationship with student learning outcomes;
(2) be able to be taught to teachers in a relatively short period of time; and
(3) be amenable to definition, measurement, and implementation in an international study.

In order to apply the three criteria to the behaviors included in the literature reviews, two major categories of teaching behavior were identified: management practices and instructional practices. Management practices are those teaching behaviors intended to bring students into contact with relevant learning tasks. Six appropriate management practices were selected from among behaviors identified in the researches of Borg and Ascione 1979, 1982; Emmer, Evertson, and Anderson 1980; Evertson and Emmer 1982; Goldstein and Weber 1979; Peacock and Weber 1980; Sanford and Evertson 1981; and Kounin 1970. These behaviors were:

(1) provides a clear set of rules governing student conduct and routine student behavior;

(2) takes quick disciplinary action to halt misbehavior;
(3) aims disciplinary action at the student who was the source of the misbehavior;
(4) makes disciplinary action mild rather than severe, except in rare instances;
(5) monitors student behavior during assigned seatwork; and
(6) organizes and makes efficient transitions between parts or segments of the lesson or class period.

In contrast with management practices, instructional practices are those teaching behaviors that directly influence the learning processes of students during their contact with the learning tasks. Five subcategories and associated teaching behaviors for instructional practices were derived from the work of several researchers (Anderson, Evertson, and Brophy 1979; Brophy and Evertson 1976; Evertson, Anderson, Anderson, and Brophy 1980; Fisher et al. 1978; Good and Grouws 1977, 1979; McDonald et al. 1975; Crawford et al. 1978; Soar and Soar 1976; Stallings and Kaskowitz 1974; Rosenshine 1978). These subcategories and behaviors were:

1. Instructional Practices: Cues
    (a) presents learning objectives; and
    (b) emphasizes the important ideas and major points during and at the end of a lesson.

2. Instructional Practices: Questions
    (a) asks questions frequently;
    (b) asks questions whose answers require student thinking at a variety of cognitive levels;
    (c) addresses questions to specific students;
    (d) redirects questions to other students as needed; and
    (e) probes the depth of student knowledge and understanding when an answer is partially satisfactory.

3. Instructional Practices: Reactions
    (a) praises correct responses;
    (b) indicates disapproval of incorrect responses; and
    (c) accepts a variety of responses when no specific correct answer is called for.

4. Instructional Practices: Feedback and Correction
    (a) establishes clear student expectations concerning testing and grading;
    (b) uses tests for formative evaluation of student achievement of unit objectives;
    (c) acknowledges excellent performance on the formative evaluation tests; and

    (d)   provides additional instruction intended to help students correct errors and misunderstandings identified by the formative evaluation.

5. Instructional Practices: Content
    (a)   covers the content expected to be covered as indicated by the nature of the tests given to the students.

In addition, and in order to gain a more complete understanding of the context within which teachers teach and students learn, a decision was made to include in the study a set of student, school, parent, classroom and community variables, each of which is more fully described in Chapter 2.

The General Design of the Study

The study was originally designed to include both a correlational and an experimental phase. The design for the correlational study (Phase I) was to be longitudinal. Each national center was to select one or more learning units that required a specified period of time to teach to the students. The time period between the administration of the pretest at the beginning of the unit(s) and the administration of the posttest at the end of the unit(s) would then be a function of the number and type of units selected by that particular national center. Unlike previous IEA studies, all of which used internationally standardized achievement tests, this study focused on "national" pretests and posttests, each of which was constructed by the appropriate national center according to specifications given by IEA's International Coordinating Center. The pretest was, in each case, to stress general aptitude for the subject and/or specific cognitive prerequisites and/or prior knowledge of the content to be covered. Where possible, the pretest and posttest were to be identical or overlap substantially, but in all cases, the posttest was to include a direct measure of what was contained in the learning unit(s). An internationally standardized measure of student attitude toward the subject being taught was, however, to be administered as both pretest and posttest to students in each participating country.

During the time that elapsed between the pretest and posttest, each classroom included in the study would be observed from six to ten times at regular intervals. Data pertaining to instructional and management practices employed by teachers would be gathered during these observations. Finally, multivariate analyses would be carried out to determine the nature and extent of the relationship between these observed practices and students' achievement and attitudes within the context of the community, school, classroom, parent, teacher and student variables referred to earlier and more fully described in Chapter 2. Eventually, these findings were to provide the basis for Phase II (the experimental phase) of the CES by (i) identifying teaching practices that were strongly related to student learning and (ii) then using these practices as program elements in the training of teachers whose relative effect on student learning could then be assessed. The specifics of Phase II design were, however, to be left for a later date. The details that follow, therefore, relate entirely to Phase I, the correlational study.

Target Populations and Sampling

Observational studies require a great deal of coordination and cooperation among observers, teachers of the selected classes and school principals. Thus, although a probability sample of teachers and classrooms would clearly have been desirable for the Classroom Environment Study, the strong probability of obtaining only a volunteer sample or sample of convenience was recognized. Since the use of volunteer or convenience samples precludes the calculation of sampling errors, a decision was made to include within the CES a two-step procedure for examining the representativeness of the participating teachers *vis-à-vis* the general population of teachers. First, a set of "marker" variables was to be identified so that by comparing the actual sample with the population at large on these variables, one could reasonably test the alternative hypotheses that the actual sample did or did not represent the general population. Second, once such "marker" variables were identified and because data on these variables were not currently available, items pertaining to them were included on two questionnaires: (1) the Initial Teacher Questionnaire (ITQ) to be given to the participating teachers; and (2) the Teacher Survey Questionnaire (TSQ) to be given to a probability sample of the population of similar grade level and subject matter teachers in each participating country.

The question as to the number of classrooms to include in the study was raised several times during the planning meetings. With some 200 variables (as identified in Chapter 2), the vast majority pertaining to classes or teachers (rather than to individual students), approximately 2,000 classrooms would be needed within each country to obtain highly reliable results. If one could assume that the 200 variables could be organized around approximately ten primary constructs, then some 100 classrooms would be sufficient. More precisely, the number of classrooms required depends on the complexity of the models being built and tested. If the complexity is reduced to a series of bivariate zero-order correlations between individual teacher behaviors and student achievement, then a smaller number of classrooms can be included. If, on the other hand, the interrelationships among the predictor variables is of some interest, then it should be recognized that one needs approximately ten times as many classrooms as predictor variables.

In the early planning meetings a conflict arose between the number of classrooms "needed" and the number of classrooms that could feasibly be included in the actual samples. Representatives from several national centers pointed out the enormous expense in terms of both time and money of observing in so many classrooms. Eventually, a compromise position was reached when it was deemed possible to do some analyses with a minimum of forty classrooms within any specific country. If certain national centers opted to include fewer than forty classrooms (see Chapter 3 for the actual sampling results), they were to recognize that their data could be used at the international level in the univariate descriptive analyses but probably not in the more complex testing of multivariate models.

Instrument Construction

Although, as mentioned above, the achievement tests for the Classroom Environment Study were constructed nationally, the majority of the other data collection instruments were developed internationally, and the specific instruments actually so developed are described in Chapter 2. In general the construction of these international instruments followed a standard series of steps. First, an initial set of questions would be written by an international committee. Second, this set would be field tested in several of the participating countries representing a range of different cultures. Third, appropriate univariate statistics (including classical item and factor analyses) would be computed. Fourth, revisions in the questions would be made in accordance with the data obtained during the field testing. Fifth, depending on the magnitude of the revisions, each instrument would either be finalized or subjected to a second field test.

Since the national instruments were the sole source of student aptitude and achievement prior to the study, and student achievement at the end of the study, they were critical. The national centers had two options: they could construct the instruments or they could use existing instruments provided these instruments were appropriate. If the former option was selected, the instruments were to be constructed in accordance with a series of steps and a set of criteria determined jointly by the national center and the International Coordinating Center. If the latter option was chosen, evidence of the appropriateness of the instruments for inclusion in the study had to be submitted to and endorsed by the International Coordinating Center. Again, descriptions of the actual construction of each instrument and its final psychometric properties are given in Chapter 2.

Data Collection and Data Recording

Once the number and length of learning units to be included in the study was determined, each national center was to draw up a plan for conducting the study. The plan was to include the dates on which the pretest and initial questionnaires were to be administered, the six to ten classroom observations were to take place, and the posttest and final questionnaires were to be given. Since a different sample of teachers was involved, it was agreed that the

8   *Lorin W. Anderson, T. Neville Postlethwaite, Bernard J. Shapiro*

Teacher Survey Questionnaire could be administered at any time agreeable to both the national center and the International Coordinating Center.

Since questionnaires and achievement tests had been used in previous IEA studies, these instruments were not expected to be especially problematic. The collection of the observational data, on the other hand, was seen as a major problem. As a consequence, a great deal of effort was spent on providing proper training for those responsible for conducting the observations. A two-stage approach to observer training was developed. In the first stage, one or two key persons from each national center would be brought together to receive training in the observation system designed for the CES from a person with extensive experience in training classroom observers. In the second stage, these key people would return to their own countries and provide the training for those responsible for conducting the observations in those countries.

Great care also was to be exercised in the recording of all the data for use in the study. International code books were written, each specifying precisely how each bit of data was to be readied for the international analyses. Missing data rules were written at the International Data Processing Center as soon as the data were received and the preliminary examination of the data was completed, although some rough guidelines for establishing the final missing data rules were consensually determined prior to this time. The first guidelines suggested a variable would be eliminated within a country if more than 15 percent of the data relating to that variable was missing. The second guideline suggested that a student would be eliminated within a country if data on more than 20 percent of the variables pertaining to that student were missing. The third guideline suggested that an entire class of students would be eliminated within a country if data on more than 20 percent of the variables aggregated at the class level were missing. Some variables (e.g., those on the initial and final teacher and student questionnaires) were believed to be of great importance to the overall aim of the study. If students did not complete both student questionnaires, they were eliminated from the study. Finally, if teachers did not complete both teacher questionnaires the entire class was eliminated from the study. The actual data editing procedures and problems are described more fully in Chapters 3 and 6.

Data Analysis

Apart from the analyses required for proper instrument construction and initial data editing, several other general guidelines for data analysis were prepared. Standard errors of sampling (including the calculation of the design effect) were to be calculated for all probability samples. Univariate statistics were to be used to summarize the data pertaining to the activities, behaviors, perceptions, and interactions occurring in the classrooms. Multivariate analyses were to be used to examine the influence of student variables on student learning outcomes and to examine the influence of school, classroom, and teaching variables on student learning outcomes.

Unfortunately, no general theoretical framework to encompass all of these considerations existed at the outset of the study. Thus, the choice of variables (and, to a certain extent, the choice of instruments related to these variables) was based on an atheoretical review of past research and on the collective wisdom of those participating in the study. Thus, a collection of rather discrete variables, rather than an integrated and cohesive set of constructs, lay at the heart of the Classroom Environment Study. As will be seen later, this lack of an initial organizing framework was a serious omission.

The Execution of the Study

The purpose of this section is to address, in a general way, issues concerning funding and participation in Phase I of the CES as well as the roles of the various organizational units set up by IEA in relationship to the Classroom Environment Study. Finally, brief references will be made to the varying contexts in which each of the national centers carried out its work for the CES.

Participation in the Study

The IEA did not select countries for participation in the Classroom Environment Study. Rather, the IEA informed its member countries of the pending study and the head of each national center decided whether or not to participate. Spain, Belgium, Hong Kong, Malaysia and Indonesia each suggested initially that they would participate. However, Belgium and Hong Kong withdrew for lack of adequate funding; the government of Malaysia decided not to join IEA; and Indonesia collected the data for the CES but for undisclosed reasons decided not to have these data analyzed either nationally or internationally. Spain decided to withdraw from the IEA study, but they began a replication of the study in 1985. The countries which did participate fully in the CES correlational study (the experimental study was to be a related but independent inquiry) were Australia, Canada, Hungary, Israel, the Republic of Korea, the Netherlands, Nigeria, and Thailand.[1] More details concerning these participating countries including, in each case, the participating national center, the name of the head of each center, and the name of the person within each center assigned to serve as the National Research Coordinator (NRC) for the CES are given in Chapter 3.

---

[1] Three replications of the study were conducted in Canada. In the province of Ontario separate studies were conducted in English-speaking and French-speaking classrooms. The third replication was conducted in the province of Quebec (also in French-speaking classrooms). The Federal Republic of Germany also participated in the CES, but began its national study too late to be included in the international analyses.

10   *Lorin W. Anderson, T. Neville Postlethwaite, Bernard J. Shapiro*

Funding

Once national centers had indicated an interest in participating in the study, the funding for the study had to be raised nationally and internationally. Each national center was responsible for raising the money to cover all costs for planning and conducting the study within its country plus the costs of sending the NRCs (and other key study personnel) to international meetings. Typically, funds were raised from ministries of education or major national grant-giving agencies. Examples of national expenditures relative to the CES correlational study are Canada Ontario at US$160,000, Australia at US$195,000, and Canada Quebec at US$300,000.

The international costs had to be raised from grant-giving agencies of multilateral agencies. These monies were needed to cover the salaries of those who staffed the International Coordinating Center and the International Data Processing Center, costs of computerized data processing, and costs of arranging and conducting international training sessions and meetings. Raising sufficient funds to cover the international costs proved extremely difficult. The actual amount of international funding eventually secured from the Canadian International Development Research Center, supplemented with grants from the Ford Foundation, German Unilever, the Ontario Institute for Studies in Education (OISE), and IEA itself, was US$197,900. Although this support was much appreciated and of great value, it was not, in fact, sufficient. Thus, throughout the conduct of the CES, there was a need to rely both on the goodwill and efforts of many individuals involved in the CES at the international effort and on the indirect institutional subsidies from OISE, Auburn University, the University of Hamburg, and the University of South Carolina.

The CES International Coordinating Center

Whereas much of the preparatory work for the CES had been carried out in Tel Aviv by Arieh Lewy and Tamar Levin, the IEA considered it desirable for both communication and funding reasons to establish the International Coordinating Center (ICC) at the Ontario Institute for Studies in Education (OISE) in Toronto. Doris Ryan of the OISE faculty was appointed as international coordinator for the study. Beatrice Avalos of University College, Cardiff, was appointed as assistant international coordinator. Avalos, Ryan, and a part-time secretary constituted the entire ICC staff. As its name implies, the International Coordinating Center was responsible for coordinating all of the work involved in conducting the Classroom Environment Study. In addition, the ICC was responsible for the completion of several technical tasks, either by doing them directly or seeing that they were properly undertaken.[2]

[2]Accordingly, several other persons accepted international responsibilities. Clare Burstall of NFER was to approve the achievement tests to be used in each country. George Henry of the University of Liege was to approve the sampling plans. Angela Hildyard of OISE served as the International Observation Coordinator. Initially, Bernhard Treiber of the Federal Republic of Germany coordinated the plans for data preparation and analysis.

The International Project Council

Within the IEA organizational framework, the International Project Council (IPC) has the overall policy responsibility for the conduct of a study, and it is the IPC which reports directly to the IEA General Assembly. With respect to the CES, the IPC consisted of the heads of all participating national centers (see Chapter 3) or their designated representatives. During the conduct of the CES, the IPC met annually. Professor N. L. Gage of Stanford University was the first chairperson of the IPC. When it proved impossible to raise the funding needed to conduct a replication of the study in the United States, Gage left the IPC and Bernard Shapiro, Director of OISE, became the IPC chairperson.

The CES Steering Committee

Within the IEA framework, a Project Steering Committee is appointed for each study, consisting of a small number of recognized experts in the field of the study. During the various phases of the CES, the CES Steering Committee was reconstituted several times. During the final years of the study, the Steering Committee was composed of Doris Ryan and Bernard Shapiro of OISE, Egbert Warries of the Netherlands, Lorin Anderson of the University of South Carolina, Clare Burstall of the National Foundation for Education Research in England and Wales, and Arieh Lewy of Tel Aviv. The Committee delegated responsibility for overseeing data editing and analysis and report writing to a "work group," consisting of Ryan, Anderson, Sid Bourke then of the Australian Council for Educational Research, Garrett Mandeville of the University of South Carolina, Norbert Sellin then of the University of Hamburg, and Angela Hildyard of OISE.

The CES International Data Processing Center

Due to funding difficulties and personnel changes at the international level, the location of the International Data Processing Center (IDPC) changed several times during the planning and conduct of the CES. Initially, the IDPC was to have been located at the Max-Planck Institut für Psychologische Forschung in Munich, Federal Republic of Germany. Next, there were to be two IDPCs: one housed at Auburn University (with James Wilmoth doing the data editing and computation of univariate statistics) and one housed at the University of Hamburg (with Norbert Sellin and Manfred Glang performing the multivariate analyses). Ultimately, the responsibilities of the IDPC were divided between two data analysts located at two universities. Garrett Mandeville of the University of South Carolina performed the basic editing of the CES data and produced the initial univariate statistics. Norbert Sellin conducted additional data editing and performed all relevant multivariate analyses at the University of Hamburg. Ideally, of course, the IDPC should have been located within the ICC, but financial difficulties made this impossible.

The National Research Coordinators: Meetings and Training

As has been mentioned, a National Research Coordinator (NRC) for the CES was appointed within each national center. The NRCs were responsible for agreeing on the details of the study design, instruments, data collection procedures, and the like. The NRCs met as a group on four occasions: in Hamburg, Germany (1979); in Liege, Belgium (1981); in Auburn, Alabama (1982); and in Columbia, South Carolina (1983). In addition, the majority of the NRCs met in Enschede, the Netherlands (1980) to receive initial training in the use of the observation instruments. NRCs from Thailand, Indonesia and Malaysia met in Jakarta, Indonesia, in the same year to receive their training. Further training for most of the NRCs was provided as part of the meeting in Liege in 1981.

During the NRC meetings held in Belgium and the United States, the emphasis was on the design of instruments, international coding requirements, data editing procedures, the unit of analysis, appropriate causal modeling techniques, and the possible interpretation of results. Issues were presented and discussed, and, quite typically, consensus among all participating NRCs was attained.

During the meetings held in Enschede, Liege, and Jakarta, Margaret Needels, then of SRI, provided training in the understanding and proper use of the observational instruments. Procedures for estimating inter-observer agreement were discussed and illustrated. As has been mentioned, the NRCs were to return to their own countries following these meetings and train the observers who would actually be collecting the data in their individual replications of the CES.

CES National Center Work

Upon return to their national centers, the NRCs had to arrange for the appointment of a national committee and a research staff. The national committee was to consist of scholars in the relevant fields, and its function was to consider the soundness of the CES within the context of each country, to decide on issues labeled as "national options" (e.g., to decide whether to expand the study by including additional variables and/or more frequent observations), and to make recommendations to the CES Project Steering Committee and IPC for the improvement of the study in general. The research staff was to consist of persons with sufficient research and technical skill to enable the study to be carried out successfully. The staff was responsible for the field testing of the instruments, the selection of samples, the training of observers, the collection and recording of data, the dispatch of internationally-required data in proper form to the University of South Carolina, the analyses of all country-unique data, and the preparation of a national report.[3]

The CES National Replications

A more complete description of the nature of the CES studies as designed and executed in the participating countries is provided in Chapter 3 which, among other things, includes information about the various grade levels (grade 5, grade 6, or grade 8), subject matters (mathematics, physics, history, or science), sample sizes (from twenty-two to eighty-seven classes) and time periods (from two to nine months). The beginning time for the various national studies also varied, from 1980 in Canada Quebec to 1982 in the Republic of Korea.

In examining the results of the CES presented in subsequent chapters, the reader is asked to keep in mind these and other between-country differences in the execution of the CES national replications. In addition, the reader is reminded of the differences in the validity of the achievement tests that are likely to exist among the various classrooms in those countries in which there is no centralized curriculum. Estimates of the differential validity of the achievement tests in several of these countries are possible using the Opportunity to Learn (OTL) instrument available for use in the CES. In all cases, as shall be seen in subsequent chapters, the range of students' opportunity to learn within these countries was quite large.

General Comment and Organization of the Report

Phase I of the Classroom Environment Study was conceived as a needed next step in a series of IEA-sponsored studies. An observational study of the instructional and management practices of teachers was seen as necessary if similarities and differences in the nature of teaching across countries were to be examined. Ultimately, an increased understanding of such similarities and differences could be expected to contribute to a more complete understanding of school-related factors that influence cognitive and affective achievement.

From its inception, however, the CES correlational study has been plagued with a series of problems. Several key personnel moved in and out of the study, and both IPC and Project Steering Committee membership changed over time. Partly as a result of these personnel changes, the study lacked an overall conceptual framework within which to relate the major variables. Several organizing frameworks were developed during the actual conduct of the study, but all were constrained by decisions concerning the inclusion or exclusion of variables made earlier. Finally, the project suffered from

---

[3] A list of the available reports is given in Appendix A.

insufficient funding. This lack of adequate funding contributed to an in-adequately staffed International Coordinating Center, the absence of a consolidated International Data Processing Center, and fewer meetings of the international and national researchers than would have been desirable.

Despite these and other problems, the CES was completed, largely because of the hard work of a number of people. What follows is the result of their dedication. Seven chapters remain in this volume. These chapters describe the variables, models, and instruments (Chapter 2); the participating countries and national replications (Chapter 3); the results pertaining to instructional practices, classroom activities, and teacher behavior (Chapter 4); the results concerning the structure of the observed lessons (Chapter 5); the findings derived from the multivariate analyses relating student variables directly to learning outcomes (Chapter 6); and the results of the multivariate analyses linking "schooling" variables to learning outcomes (Chapter 7). Chapter 8 provides a summary and concluding statement.

2

Variables, Models, and Instruments

As mentioned in Chapter 1, variables included in the study were derived primarily from several reviews of previous research on classroom teaching and learning. Demographic variables pertaining to communities, schools, teachers, and students were added by the Project Steering Committee and the National Research Coordinators to provide a more complete description of the studies' samples and settings.

Once the list of variables had been drawn up, two major tasks became apparent. First, because of the large number of variables, some type of framework had to be developed if they were to be organized in some logical manner. Second, instruments that could be used to gather data on the variables had to be selected or designed.

This chapter, organized around these two tasks, begins with a discussion of groupings of the variables into what are termed *constructs*. The constructs are defined and the associated variables identified. Next, the hypothesized interrelationships among the constructs are displayed in what is referred to as the *core model* and a rationale for the core model is presented. In the third section, the instruments used to collect the data are described in terms of (1) their development and structure, (2) their format, (3) the number of questions or items, (4) whether use was required or optional, (5) when during the study they were administered or used, and (6) their technical quality (e.g., reliability) when such data were available. The chapter concludes with a summary table illustrating the relationships of the constructs, variables, and instruments.

Constructs and Variables

The conceptualization of a study of this magnitude was not an easy task, one that fell to the Steering Committee, National Research Coordinators, and several consultants. They were to formulate a reasonable, workable conceptual framework for the study based on their collective experience and their knowledge of studies of teaching conducted in their countries.

This chapter was written by Sid Bourke, Angela Hildyard, and Lorin W. Anderson.

15

The variables included in the study were thought to be important for descriptive or predictive purposes. Variables were included for predictive purposes if they were hypothesized to influence student achievement or student attitude either directly or indirectly. Variables were believed to indirectly influence achievement or attitude if they directly influenced other variables with hypothesized direct influences on these outcomes.

Variables were associated with fifteen constructs. Five constructs included variables traditionally referred to as demographic variables. These constructs were labeled "community," "school," "teacher," "home," and "student" characteristics. As mentioned, the primary purpose of these constructs was to provide a description of samples of teachers and students, as well as the community and school settings within which the study was undertaken. Secondarily, they permitted differences in teaching and learning in different settings to be examined.

Another five constructs included classroom behavior variables. These variables were associated with constructs based on the function they served (or were expected to serve) in the classroom. The function of some of the variables was to teach knowledge and skills. These variables were associated with the construct "teaching students." The function of other variables was to determine how well students had learned and/or to judge the quality or amount of that learning. These variables were associated with the construct "assessing and evaluating students." Similar clusters of variables produced the constructs "orienting students" (where the function was to ensure that students understood what to do and learn, as well as how to do and learn it), "managing students" (where the function was to get students to behave in appropriate ways), and "student participation" (where the function from the student's perspective was to become and remain actively involved in the classroom activities).

Two constructs included variables pertaining to ways in which teachers and students viewed one another and their classrooms. These constructs were labeled "teacher perceptions" and "student perceptions."

Two constructs included variables concerning the nature of the classroom itself and the type and amount of instruction students received there. These constructs were labeled "classroom context" and "quantity of instruction."

The final construct included two variables: student achievement and student attitude toward the subject. This construct, labeled "student outcomes," contained the study's dependent variables.

In certain portions of this book, variables are termed "manifest variables" (since they were directly observed or measured). Constructs may be referred to as "latent variables" (since their existence is hypothetical and inferred).

Community Characteristics

"Community characteristics" was associated with a single manifest variable, school location. Four types of communities were identified: rural, suburban, urban (that is, smaller cities), and metropolitan (that is, larger cities).

School Characteristics

"School characteristics" was associated with four manifest variables: the type of school students attended (e.g., public comprehensive, selective, or parochial), the grade level organization of the school (e.g., elementary, secondary, or both), the size of the school, and the number of hours the subject matter included in the study was taught during an entire school year. With the possible exception of the last manifest variable, this construct is defined in terms of the demographic factors typically included in a description of a school.

Teacher Characteristics

"Teacher characteristics" is a combination of traditional demographic teacher variables and variables associated with the teachers' working conditions. The five demographic variables are the sex and age of the teacher, years of teaching experience, type of certification held by the teacher (e.g., elementary, secondary, or both), and the extent of the training received by the teacher in the subject matter included in the study. The three variables associated with the teachers' working conditions are the number of hours per week the teacher teaches the subject matter included in the study, the number of additional subject areas taught during the week, and the total number of hours per week the teacher spends teaching, regardless of the subject area taught.

Home Characteristics

"Home characteristics" was associated with four variables: father's education, father's occupation, mother's education, and the similarity of the language used in the home with the language of instruction in the school. Thus, this construct is defined in terms of what traditionally is referred to as the students' socio-economic status (SES).

Student Characteristics

This construct includes variables that permit an accurate description of the students prior to the beginning of the study. Two of the variables, sex and age, are traditional demographic variables. A third variable, pretest, provides information as to the extent of the student's knowledge of the subject matter prior to the study. The final three variables are attitudinal in nature. These variables pertain to (1) the extent to which students aspire to higher levels of education, (2) the extent to which students enjoy school in general, and (3) the extent to which they enjoy the subject being taught during the study. These three variables are referred to as aspirations, attitude toward school, and attitude toward subject, respectively.

Classroom Context

"Classroom context" is defined in terms of the setting or situation in which teachers are expected to teach and students are expected to learn. Nine variables are included in this construct. Two variables pertain to the use of grouping of students within classrooms. The first concerns the typical use of various grouping configurations (e.g., whole class, small groups, individualized) as reported by the teacher. The second concerns the observed use of grouping during the study.

Another two variables pertain to the availability and use of various instructional materials by teachers and students. The first concerns the extent to which teachers make use of certain types of instructional materials (e.g., textbooks, workbooks, audio-visual materials). The second concerns whether students have access to textbooks out of school.

Two of the variables in the construct are concerned with the nature of the lessons given to the students. The first, lesson emphasis, refers to the general purpose of the lesson. Was the lesson intended to introduce students to new knowledge or skills? Was the lesson intended to help students master knowledge or skills previously introduced? Was the lesson intended to be a review of knowledge and skills previously taught? If so, was the review intended to remind students of knowledge and skills they once had mastered, or to correct errors and misunderstandings of knowledge and skills apparently not mastered?

The second variable dealing with the nature of lessons was type of objective being pursued. This variable focused on the type of learning outcome students were expected to achieve. Were students expected to develop an understanding of an important concept? Were they expected to develop skill in applying important rules? Were they expected to acquire problem solving skills and strategies? Or, was the objective non-academic (e.g., social, emotional)?

The final three variables associated with this construct identified the membership of the classroom. These variables are (1) the number of students enrolled, (2) the number of students attending the class on a given day, and (3) the number of adults in the classroom (e.g., teachers, aides, parent volunteers).

Teacher Perceptions

"Teacher perceptions" address the views that teachers have concerning the decisions they are able to make with respect to curriculum and instruction, and the ability of the class of students they teach. The three variables included within this construct are (1) teacher autonomy, (2) teacher judgment of the relative ability of the class as a whole, and (3) teacher judgment of the percent of students in the class who are in need of remedial instruction or reteaching.

Quantity of Instruction

Stated simply, "quantity of instruction" has to do with the amount of instruction and teaching students receive. Specifically, the variables associated with this construct pertain to (1) the amount of instruction students receive that is related to the knowledge and skills included on the test (i.e., the students' opportunity to learn), (2) the total amount of time per day that is allocated to providing instruction in the subject matter included in the study, (3) the percent of the time allocated to the subject matter that is actually spent on instruction, (4) the number of homework assignments given to the students per week, and (5) the total amount of time that students are expected to spend on homework assignments.

Orienting Students

"Orienting students" refers to what teachers say or do to ensure that students understand what they are to learn about a subject in a given amount of time (e.g., a lesson, a class period). The variables associated with the construct have to do with (1) the extent to which teachers inform students of the objectives of lessons or class period, and (2) the extent to which teachers review related knowledge and skills previously taught.

Teaching Students

"Teaching students" refers to what teachers say and do to facilitate or foster the academic learning of their students. Twenty-six variables are associated with this construct. Because of the large number of variables they will be discussed in clusters.

General teacher-student interaction. Six variables are concerned with the relationship of the teachers with their students in the classroom. Are teachers directly involved in instructing the students (referred to as "teacher interacting")? Or, are teachers supervising and monitoring students' work (termed "teacher monitoring")? When teachers are supervising and monitoring their students, do they do so while students are working individually (i.e., monitoring individual seatwork) or in groups (i.e., monitoring groupwork)? What is the direction of the verbal interchange between teachers and students—from teacher to student or students, or from student or students to teacher (labeled "direction of verbal interaction")? To what extent is there an absence of talking in the classroom (labeled "silence"). This last variable is frequently observed when students are working individually or collectively on their assignments.

Instructional format. Six of the variables associated with this construct pertain to the general format within which the instruction is delivered. The formats used in the study are: (1) lecture, (2) discourse/discussion, (3) oral practice/drill, (4) reading at seats, (5) written seatwork, and (6) laboratory work.[1]

Nature of teacher-student interaction. Another six variables are concerned with the nature of the verbal interactions between teachers and students. These variables are the extent to which the teachers (1) provide cues to structure the learning of their students, (2) provide directions to their students as to what they are to do to learn or to complete an assignment, (3) explain things to their students, (4) use instructional materials to aid their explanations, (5) demonstrate for students what they are expected to do or learn, and (6) use examples to illustrate the major points of their explanations.

Remedial help. Five of the variables associated with this construct are concerned with the extent to which teachers provide help to those students who apparently need it. These variables pertain to (1) the frequency of extra help, (2) the number of students receiving such help, (3) when the help is provided (i.e., the timing of teacher assistance), (4) the format of the help (e.g., groups or individual students), and (5) the type of help provided (e.g., workbooks, tutorials, alternate textbooks).

Student-initiated interactions. The final three variables associated with this construct have to do with the influence of the students on the classroom environment. These three variables are the extent to which students (1) engage in social interactions, (2) make substantive contributions to the academic discussion, and (3) ask questions.

Assessing and Evaluating Students

This construct includes variables associated with ways that teachers find out how well students are learning so that judgments as to the quality or

---

[1] A seventh instructional format, review, was associated with the construct "orienting students." An eighth format, composite management activities, was aligned with the construct "managing students."

extent of their learning can be made. The nature of assessment and evaluation can be divided into more and less formal approaches. The majority of the variables in this construct are related to informal assessment; namely, the questions that teachers ask, the nature of the students' responses, and the ways in which teachers react to student responses to the questions.

Seven of the variables are concerned with the kinds of questions that teachers ask. These variables are the extent to which teachers (1) indicate they engage in informal assessment, (2) ask questions that require students to remember what they have learned, (3) ask questions that require students to think about their answers to questions (so-called "higher-order questions"), (4) ask questions that require students to express and defend their opinions, (5) ask questions as to whether the explanations they give have been understood by the students, (6) address their questions to individual students, or (7) address their questions to groups of students.

Three variables pertain to the way in which students respond to teacher questions. Specifically, do they (1) give short answers, (2) give extended responses, or (3) not answer the question at all?

Nine variables are concerned with the way in which teachers react to students' responses to their questions. How long do they wait for a student to respond to a question (i.e., "wait time")? Does the teacher indicate an answer is right or wrong (i.e., "positive acknowledgment" or "says answer wrong")? If the answer is correct, does the teacher repeat the answer for the class? If the answer is incorrect, does the teacher redirect the question to another student, or does the teacher give the correct answer? Does the teacher follow up student responses (either correct or incorrect) with probes as to the depth of understanding or the nature of the misunderstanding? If so, does the teacher direct the probes to individual students or groups?

The final two variables associated with this construct have to do with two different uses of formal assessment or tests. Specifically, to what extent do teachers use tests for evaluating or grading students? In addition, to what extent do teachers use tests to diagnose specific learning deficiencies of the students?

Managing Students

This construct includes variables associated with teacher behaviors directed toward student conduct or classroom behavior. These five variables deal with several key aspects of classroom management: (1) the lack of involvement of the teacher with the students (i.e., "uninvolved teacher"), (2) the estimated time spent on disciplinary activities, (3) the estimated time spent on procedural or "housekeeping" activities (such as making general announcements, taking attendance), (4) the estimated time spent in transitions from one instructional format or classroom activity to another, and (5) the estimated time spent on routine administration matters or general management activities.

Student Perceptions

This construct includes the way in which students view three key aspects of classroom life. First, students were asked to express their opinions as to whether their classroom was a business-like and academically-oriented environment. Second, students were asked to express their views as to the nature of the instruction they received. Specifically, they were asked about the structure their teachers provided for their learning. As used in the study, "structure" refers to the clarity and completeness of the teachers' explanations, the appropriateness and relevance of the teachers' examples, and the ability of teachers to clarify the distinction between what is important and unimportant. Students also were asked to give their opinions concerning the feedback they received as to the adequacy or appropriateness of their learning or performance. Third, students were asked about their teachers' classroom management techniques and abilities.

Student Participation

This construct was defined simply in terms of the extent to which students in the classroom paid attention or were actively engaged in the process of learning.

Student Outcomes

As has been mentioned, two kinds of learning outcomes were included in the study. The first was the level of academic achievement attained by the students as a result of the instruction they had received. The second was the attitude of the students toward the subject matter taught during the study.

The Core Model

Once all of the variables had been associated with, or nested within, the fifteen constructs, the expected relationships among the constructs were considered. Once again, prior research results were examined in an effort to identify defensible relationships. An initial set of hypothetical relationships was set forth and submitted to the National Research Coordinators at one of their training sessions. Based on the discussion that took place at that time several changes were made resulting in what was labeled as the core model (see Fig. 2.1).

The arrows in the core model represent the hypothesized causal relationships among the fifteen constructs. In many ways the relationships are easier to understand if the model is examined from *right to left* (that is, "backwards"). For example, ten constructs are hypothesized to have a *direct* influence on student learning outcomes: home characteristics, student characteristics,

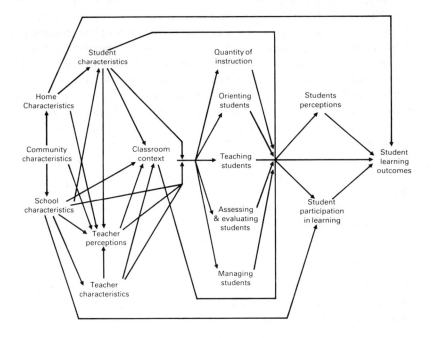

FIG. 2.1   The Core Model.

classroom context, quantity of instruction, orienting students, teaching students, assessing and evaluating students, managing students, student perceptions, and student participation in learning. Three constructs are hypothesized to have an *indirect* influence on student learning outcomes by virtue of their *direct* influence on one or more of the aforementioned ten constructs. For example, teacher perceptions are hypothesized to have a direct effect on classroom context, quantity of instruction, orienting students, teaching students, assessing and evaluating students, and managing students. All of these constructs, in turn, are hypothesized to have a direct effect on student learning outcomes. As a consequence, teacher perceptions are hypothesized to have an indirect effect on student learning outcomes.

Some constructs are hypothesized to have both a direct and an indirect effect on student learning outcomes. Consider "teaching students," for example. As had been mentioned, teaching students is hypothesized to have a direct influence on student learning outcomes. In addition, however, teaching students is hypothesized to have an indirect influence on student learning outcomes by virtue of its hypothesized direct effect on student perceptions and student participation in learning. The *total effect* of constructs such as teaching students in student learning outcomes, then, is some combination of the direct and indirect effects.

As can be seen in Fig. 2.1 the core model is quite complex. This level of complexity results from the inclusion of a large number of constructs and a fairly intricate set of relationships among the constructs. The complexity is further increased because of the large number of manifest variables associated with many of the constructs, particularly those pertaining to teaching and classroom management. The consensus among the designers of the study and the National Research Coordinators, however, was that the complexity of the core model mirrored the complexity of the classroom environment.

In the end the core model served three functions within the context of the study. First, the discussion involved in the development of the model helped all participants in the study gain a better understanding of the nature and complexity of the study being undertaken. Second, the model provided an organizing framework within which to present and interpret the descriptive data collected during the study. Third, the model provided a starting point for the multivariate analysis, which was to focus on the interrelationships among the constructs and associated variables.

Instruments

Fifteen instruments were selected or designed for use in the study. Because of time constraints in the design and implementation of the study, available instruments were selected whenever possible.

The instruments can be organized in several ways. One way is consider the person or persons responsible for completing the instruments. Using this organization criterion, there are four categories of instruments: those completed by the National Research Coordinators, those completed by the teachers who participated in the study, those completed by the students who participated in the study, and those completed by trained observers. Table 2.1 summarizes the instruments according to these four categories.

As can be seen in Table 2.1, the National Research Coordinators completed but a single instrument, the National Description Report (NDR).The teachers completed five instruments: the Initial Teacher Questionnaire (ITQ), the Opportunity to Learn Form (OTL), the Teacher Interview (TI), the Pre-Observation Interview (POI), and the Final Teacher Questionnaire (FTQ). The students completed four instruments: the Initial Student Questionnaire (ISQ), the Pretest (PRETEST), the Final Student Questionnaire (FSQ), and the Posttest (POSTTEST). Finally, the observers completed five instruments: the Classroom Identification and Information Form (CIIF), the Snapshot (SNAP), the Five-Minute Interaction Form (FMI), the Individual Activity Record (IAR), and the Classroom Rating Scale (CRS).

A second way of organizing the instruments is to consider the time during the study at which the instruments were completed. Table 2.2 displays the instruments organized in this manner. As can be seen in Table 2.2, five instruments were to be completed prior to the study: the National Description

TABLE 2.1 *Summary of instruments included in the study*
(organized by person or persons completing the instrument)

Person completing	Instrument	Abbreviation
National Research Coordinator	National Description Report	NDR
Teachers	Initial Teacher Questionnaire	ITQ
	Opportunity to Learn	OTL
	Teacher Interview	TI
	Pre-Observation Interview	POI
	Final Teacher Questionnaire	FTQ
Students	Initial Student Questionnaire	ISQ
	Pretest	PRETEST
	Final Student Questionnaire	FSQ
	Posttest	POSTTEST
Observers	Classroom Identification and Information Form	CIIF
	Snapshot	SNAP
	Five-Minute Interaction Form	FMI
	Individual Activity Record	IAR
	Classroom Rating Scale	CRS

TABLE 2.2 *Summary of instruments included in the study*
(organized by time administered or completed)

Time completed	Instrument	Abbreviation
Prior to the study	National Description Report	NDR
	Initial Teacher Questionnaire	ITQ
	Teacher Interview	TI
	Initial Student Questionnaire	ISQ
	Pretest	PRETEST
Before each observation	Pre-Observation Interview	POI
During each observation	Classroom Identification and Information Form	CIIF
	Snapshot	SNAP
	Five-Minute Interaction Form	FMI
	Individual Activity Record	IAR
	Classroom Rating Scale	CRS
At end of study	Opportunity to Learn	OTL
	Final Teacher Questionnaire	FTQ
	Final Student Questionnaire	FSQ
	Posttest	POSTTEST

Report, the Initial Teacher Questionnaire, the Teacher Interview, the Initial Student Questionnaire, and the Pretest. Prior to each observation the Pre-Observation Interview was completed. During each observation five instruments were completed: the Classroom Identification and Information Form, the Snapshot, the Five-Minute Interaction Form, the Individual Activity Record, and the Classroom Rating Scale. At or near the end of the study the final four instruments were completed; the Final Teacher Questionnaire, the Opportunity to Learn Form, the Final Student Questionnaire, and the Posttest.

In the following sections these instruments are discussed in some detail. The discussion begins with the National Description Report, proceeds to the teacher instruments, then to the student instruments, and concludes with the observation instruments.

National Description Report (NDR)

The NDR contained open-ended questions to be completed by the National Research Coordinator. The questions were to be answered with reference to the subject and grade or age level included in the study. The questions were divided into five major areas: (1) identification information (e.g., the country, state, or province to be included; the subject matter and grade or age level to be included), (2) structure of the education system (e.g., legislation and regulations relevant to the curriculum included; administrative units for the provision of schooling; types of schools in country as well as those to be included in the study), (3) student admission policies (e.g., years of compulsory full-time schooling, length of school year and school day), (4) governance and decision-making structures related to the curriculum (e.g., extent of participation of various groups in the decision-making process), and (5) teacher information (e.g., education level, training, and qualifications). The NDR contained thirteen questions to be answered and two tables to be completed, and was required in all participating countries.

Initial Teacher Questionnaire (ITQ)

The ITQ contained thirty-two questions; some open-ended, others multiple-choice. The ITQ included four sections: (1) "your background and responsibilities" (nine questions), (2) "about your school" (five questions), (3) "about your class" (nine questions), and (4) "your decision-making" (one question divided into nine types of decisions that teachers may or may not make). Table 2.3 gives an overview of the contents of the ITQ. The ITQ was required in all participating countries.

TABLE 2.3 *Summary of the contents of the Initial Teacher Questionnaire*

Section	Questions	Sample items
Teacher Background and Responsibilities	9	Teacher Age and Sex Years of Teaching Experience Type of Formal Certification Special Training in Subject? Hours/Weeks Teaching Number of Subjects Taught
School Characteristics	5	School Location (e.g., rural or metropolitan) Size of School (No. of Students) Type of School (e.g., public or private)
Class Characteristics	9	Class Size Number of Periods per Week in Target Subject Average Length of Class Period Overall Class Ability (e.g., higher or lower ability than most of the students of similar grade or age) Need for Remediation (e.g., few or most of the students in class need remedial help)
Autonomy in Decision Making	9	Selection of Topics Selection of Materials Type of Class Organization Amount of Homework

Final Teacher Questionnaire (FTQ)

The FTQ included sixteen primarily multi-part questions. Fifteen of the questions are accompanied with a set of modified Likert-style response options (e.g., rarely or never, sometimes, usually, always); the other question required teachers to approximate the number of weeks they spent on a variety of curricular topics. The multi-part questions dealt with issues such as frequency of use of various instructional materials, use of various tests and projects for assigning grades or diagnosing learning deficiencies, and use of various teaching methods and styles. A summary of the contents of the Final Teacher Questionnaire is presented in Table 2.4. Like the ITQ, the FTQ was required in all participating countries.

Teacher Interview (TI)

The TI was intended to gather information concerning the general approaches to classroom instruction and classroom management used by the teacher. Brief vignettes describing six different management approaches and five different instructional approaches were read by the teacher. After reading

TABLE 2.4 *Summary of the contents of the Final Teacher Questionnaire*

Section	Questions	Sample items
Use and Availability of Materials	2	Use of Published Textbooks Use of Workbooks Use of Individualized Materials Use of Teacher Worksheets Use of Audiovisual Materials Can Textbook be taken Home?
Use of Tests for Grading and Diagnostic Purposes	2	Use of Objective Tests Use of Essay-Type Tests Use of Oral Tests Use of Homework
Time Spent on Instructional Activities	1	Teaching New Content to Whole Class or Small Groups Reviewing Content Asking and Answering Questions Monitoring Class Work Disciplinary Activities Routine Administrative Tasks
Specify Lesson Objectives and Use of Questions	2	Specify Lesson Objectives Never, Seldom, Usually, or Always? Use of Recall Questions Use of Opinion Questions Use of Higher Order Questions
Homework Assignments and Marking	3	Number of Homework Assignments Time Needed by Typical Student to Complete Homework Time Spent on Marking Papers
Feedback and Remedial Help	5	Tendency to Individualize Remedial Help Extent to Which Additional Help was Given to Students in the Target Class Number of Students Receiving Additional Instruction Use of Different Types of Remedial Instruction (e.g., Whole Class Instruction, Peer Tutoring, Suggestions for Reviewing New Materials)
Time Spent on Curricular Topics	1	List of Topics or Contents as appropriate for Subject Tested

each approach the teacher was to indicate the extent to which their classroom practices were consistent with the approach. After reading all of the approaches the teacher was to indicate which single management approach and which single instructional approach were closest to the approaches used in the classroom.

The TI was required in all participating countries. Based on the results of the preliminary analysis of the data, however, a decision was made to eliminate the TI from additional analyses because of severe inconsistencies of the teacher responses to the various descriptions. Although the descriptions were intended to reflect mutually exclusive approaches, teachers apparently had great difficulty differentiating one general approach from another, a difficulty so severe that the validity of the data was questionable.

Pre-Observation Interview (POI)

The POI was to be administered prior to each observed lesson and consisted of multiple-choice questions. The first question asked teachers to select the statement that best described the main emphasis of the lesson to be observed (e.g., introduction of new material, expansion of new material, or review of material previously taught). The second question was to be answered only if the answer to the first question was the review of material previously taught. This question focused on the purpose of the review, and offered two options: (1) refreshing past learning of material, or (2) correcting pupils' errors of misunderstandings that appeared in homework, class assignments, or tests. The third question asked teachers about their major intention or objective for the lesson to be observed (e.g., comprehension of a concept, applying a rule to routine problems or tasks, solving a novel problem, or developing social learning or interpersonal skills). The POI was required in all participating countries.

Opportunity to Learn (OTL)

The OTL instrument was intended to get teacher judgments of the extent to which their students received instruction related to the knowledge and skills assessed by the various items on the posttest. Based on their examinations of the test items, teachers were asked three questions about each item. First, what percentage of their students (in the class included in the study) would be expected to answer the item correctly without guessing? Second, during the school year, did they (the teachers) teach or review the content necessary to answer the item correctly? Third, if during the school year they did not teach or review the content, why did they choose not to do so? Response options to this last question were: (1) it had been taught prior to this school year, (2) it will be taught later, (3) it is not in the school curriculum at all, and (4) other reasons. Based on decisions made early in the discussion of the study, the use of the OTL instrument within participating countries was optional.

Initial Student Questionnaire (ISQ)

The ISQ consisted of three sections. The first section involved ten questions related to basic student variables such as student sex, father's and mother's occupation and education, and aspirations for further education. The students were also asked to indicate whether the language of school instruction was the same as the language usually spoken at home. The second section involved a set of eight items which were intended to measure the extent to which the students liked being in school. Each item involved a statement expressing an opinion or sentiment about school (e.g., "I enjoy everything about school") and the students were asked to indicate whether they strongly agreed, agreed, were undecided, disagreed, or strongly disagreed with the statement. The third section of the ISQ involved twelve questions related to student self-perceptions and attitudes toward the target subject. Self-perceptions were measured by statements such as "I usually understand what is taught in class" while attitudes were measured by statements expressing liking and enjoyment of studying the target subject. The response options offered with each statement were the same as those associated with the items related to enjoyment of being in school.

Final Student Questionnaire (FSQ)

The FSQ contained thirty-six statements. For the first twenty-six statements students were asked to indicate whether they strongly agreed, agreed, were undecided, disagreed, or strongly disagreed with the opinion or sentiment expressed. Ten of these statements were identical to those included on the ISQ.

For the remaining ten statements included on the FSQ students were asked to indicate whether they believed the statement was true or false. The FSQ was required in all participating countries.

Table 2.5 displays the internal consistency reliability estimates for the attitude and perception scales included on the ISQ and the FSQ. Attitude toward school and initial attitude toward the subject (Subject 1) were measured by the ISQ. Finally, attitude toward the subject (Subject 2), perceptions of task-orientation (Task), instruction (Instruct), and management (Manage) were measured by the FSQ. All of the estimates are Cronbach's alphas.

Several comments on the data shown in Table 2.5 are in order. First, the internal consistency estimates of the scales vary widely across countries. In fact, in Nigeria and Thailand the estimates are sufficiently low that the use of these instruments in these countries is questionable.

Second, the internal consistency estimates for the perception measures are lower than those for the attitude measures. In fact, the estimate for at least one of the perception measures is lower than 0.500 in all countries except Canada Ontario-English and the Netherlands. Estimates below 0.500 suggest that more than one-half of the variation in students' scores on these measures *can neither be explained by nor attributed to* the perception being measured. In view of this finding, the perception variables were reconstituted before they were included in the multivariate analysis (see Chapter 6).

TABLE 2.5 *Coefficient alphas for the student attitude and perception scales*

Country	Attitude toward			Perceptions of		
	School (8)	Subject 1 (10)	Subject 2 (10)	Task (10)	Instruct (8)	Manage (8)
Australia (*n* = 1,812)	0.83	0.74	0.64	0.43	0.59	0.44
Canada Ontario-English (*n* = 642)	0.80	0.78	0.76	0.54	0.52	0.58
Canada Ontario-French (*n* = 363)	0.79	0.73	0.62	0.52	0.61	0.41
Canada Quebec (*n* = 531)	0.80	0.72	0.82	na	na	na
Hungary (*n* = 1,099)	0.70	0.78	0.75	0.56	0.49	0.07
Israel (*n* = 578)	0.67	0.66	0.64	0.36	0.44	0.14
Korea (*n* = 2,323)	0.67	0.55	0.53	0.49	0.68	0.27
Netherlands (*n* = 1,068)	0.66	0.72	0.70	0.62	0.60	0.68
Nigeria (*n* = 813)	0.52	0.60	0.42	0.48	0.66	0.00
Thailand (*n* = 2,380)	0.41	0.34	0.21	0.48	0.55	0.19

Notes: The numbers in parentheses at the top of the table indicate the number of items associated with each variable on the instruments administered to the students. The sample size (*n*) given for each country is the minimum number of students who responded to all of the items associated with a particular scale. There were small differences in the number of students who completed each instrument. Finally, the perception scales were not administered in Canada Quebec.

Pretest

The pretest was intended to determine the extent of each student's knowledge and skills prior to the beginning of the study. To increase its validity, the pretest was developed in each country under the direction of the National Research Coordinators. The National Research Coordinators had two options in constructing the pretest. First, they could design or select a single test to be used as both the pretest and the posttest. Such an approach seems reasonable when, prior to the study, students already possessed some of the knowledge and skills that were to be taught during the study. In this case, achievement differences among students prior to the study could be taken into consideration when interpreting their posttest performances.

Second, the National Research Coordinators could design or select a test of general knowledge of the subject matter (termed an aptitude test) to be used as the pretest and, then, design or select a more focused, content-valid test to be used as the posttest. This option would seem logical when students were expected to have little knowledge or few skills pertaining to the specific content being taught during the study. The first option was selected in five countries (Australia, Canada Ontario-English, the Republic of Korea, Nigeria, and Thailand), while the second option was selected in the others.

Posttest

The posttest was intended to assess the amount of learning that students had acquired during the study. In each country, then, a test was to be designed that would validly assess the knowledge and skills taught during the study in the various classrooms.

The procedure used in Australia is illustrative of the general approach that National Research Coordinators used in developing the posttest. Initially, structured discussions were held with fifteen to twenty upper primary teachers (that is, years 5 and 6) at the end of the school year that preceded the study. These teachers, none of whom were included in the study, were asked about the major topics they would teach during the time period in which the study was to be conducted. They also were asked to indicate the approximate number of weeks they would spend on each topic.

Based on these discussions, the only topics on which all teachers intended to devote a significant amount of time during the study period were the four basic arithmetic operations as applied to whole numbers. Particular emphasis was to be given to the multiplication of whole numbers. The twenty-five-item posttest, then, included only those items which tested students' knowledge and skills in adding, subtracting, multiplying, and dividing whole numbers. The percentage of test items associated with each of these skills reflected differences in emphasis as suggested by the teachers.

Towards the end of the study the seventy-five teachers who participated in the study were asked to submit fifteen items that best represented what they had been teaching. Sixty-five of the teachers submitted a total of 1,237 items. Approximately one-fourth of the items submitted tested the four arithmetic operations applied to whole numbers. Of these 311 items, 33 percent tested addition, 29 percent tested multiplication, 27 percent tested subtraction, and 11 percent tested division. Because these percentages were quite similar to those obtained from the initial sample of teachers, the numbers of items on the posttest pertaining to addition, multiplication, subtraction, and division reflected these percentages.

A summary of the test lengths and internal consistency estimates for the pretests and posttests is shown in Table 2.6. The test lengths ranged from twenty-five to fifty items on the pretests, and from fifteen to fifty items on the posttests.

The internal consistency estimates for the pretests ranged from 0.45 in Nigeria to 0.88 in Australia, with a median of 0.72. For the posttests, the

TABLE 2.6   *Summary of the internal consistency estimates*
for Pretests and Posttests

	Pretest		Posttest	
Country	No. items	KR20	No. items	KR20
Australia	25	0.88	25	0.88
Canada Ontario-English	40	0.82	40	0.87
Canada Ontario-French	40	0.72	35	0.88
Canada Quebec	25	0.74	23	0.61
	23	0.75	17	0.60
Hungary	25	0.72	15	0.68
Israel	30	0.78	42	0.81
Korea	25	0.67	25	0.82
Netherlands	20	0.57	20	0.70
Nigeria	50	0.45	50	0.59
Thailand	35	0.71	35	0.83

Notes: Based on some preliminary analyses of the pretest and post-test data in Canada Quebec, a few items were excluded from the final data analyses. KR20 estimates for the initial and revised tests are included in the table. No item data were available for the Canada Ontario-French replication. As a consequence, the reliability estimates in the table were computed using the KR21 formula. Finally, it should be recalled that different tests were used as pretests and posttests in Canada Ontario-French, Canada Quebec, Hungary, Israel, and the Netherlands.

range was from 0.59 in Nigeria to 0.88 in Australia and Canada Ontario-French, with a median of 0.815. In five countries (including two of the three Canadian replications), the internal consistencies for the posttests were greater than 0.80.

Classroom Identification and Information Form (CIIF)

The CIIF was completed by the observers upon entering the classrooms. On the CIIF, observers were to record the total student enrollment and attendance, the number of adults present, and the time instruction began and ended.

Snapshot (SNAP)

The three primary observation instruments were the Snapshot (SNAP), Five-Minute Interaction (FMI), and the Individual Activity Record (IAR). The first two instruments were required for use in all countries; the IAR was a country option. These instruments were modifications of ones developed by Stallings (1976) and used extensively in several program evaluations (e.g., Stallings and Kaskowitz 1974) and large-scale research studies (e.g., Goodlad 1984). In the CES, the instruments were employed in a fixed sequence—SNAP, then FMI, then IAR—five times during each observation period. For observation periods lasting 40 minutes, then, there would be five SNAP-FMI-IAR sequences, each lasting eight minutes. Five of these eight minutes would be spent by observers using the FMI. The SNAP and IAR were to fit into the remaining three minutes.

The Snapshot provided data on the general class activity or activities in which students were expected to be engaged, the numbers of students who were in fact engaged in the activity or activities, and the teacher's role in the classroom. When using the Snapshot, the classroom activity or activities were first coded into one or more of ten categories: lecture, review, discussion, oral practice or drill, testing, reading at seats, written seatwork, laboratory work, management or non-academic, and other. The "other" category was used for activities not fitting into one of the nine categories.

After coding the classroom activity or activities, the attention of the observers shifted to the students. A count was made of the number of students who were and were not engaged in the activity or activities. If the activity was a lecture, for example, students listening to the lecture were coded as engaged. Those obviously not listening (e.g., asleep, engaged in some other activity) were coded as being not engaged.

Finally, the teacher's role was coded into one of three categories: interacting, monitoring, or uninvolved. These categories basically represent "talking with," "watching," or "absent from" the students. When multiple groups were present in a classroom, then multiple activities were coded, the engagement of students was coded separately for each group, and the role of the teacher *vis-à-vis* the students in each group was noted. Table 2.7 provides an overview of the Snapshot instrument.

Five-Minute Interaction (FMI)

After a Snapshot was completed, observers coded teacher-student interactions for a five-minute period on the FMI form. Each interaction was coded in terms of three dimensions: context, direction, and nature. Six "context" categories were included: large group, small group, private interaction, monitoring, transition, and uninvolved.

Five "direction" categories were included. They were teacher to individual student, teacher to group, individual student to teacher, group to teacher, and teacher to other adult (or other adult to teacher) (see Table 2.8).

Finally, five global "nature" categories were included: instructional, questioning, responding, feedback, and management. Twenty-eight distinct coding categories were included in these five categories (e.g., uses examples, asks opinion questions, gives short response, says answer is wrong, and disciplines a student) (see Table 2.9).

TABLE 2.7   *Summary of the contents of the classroom snapshot (SNAP)*

Category	Contents
Class Activities	Listening to Lecture/Explanation/ Demonstration
	Review of Previously Taught Content
	Discourse or Discussion
	Oral Practice or Drill
	Seatwork on Tests
	Seatwork Reading
	Seatwork on Written Assignments
	Laboratory Work
	Classroom Management
	Other Activities
Student Engagement	Number of Students Engaged in Activity
	Number of Students Not Engaged in Activity
Teacher Role	Teacher Interacting
	Teacher Monitoring
	Teacher Uninvolved

TABLE 2.8   *Summary of the contents of the FMI dimensions context and direction*

Dimension	Observational category
Context	Large Group
	Small Group
	Private Interaction
	Monitoring
	Transition
	Uninvolved
Direction	Teacher to Student
	Teacher to Group or Class
	Student to Teacher
	Group or Class to Teacher
	Teacher to Other Adult or Other Adult to Teacher

TABLE 2.9   *Summary of the contents of the FMI dimensions reflecting the nature of interactions*

Dimension	Observational categories
Instructional	Verbal Lecture
	Lecture with Materials
	Non-Verbal Lecture/Demonstration
	Use of Examples
	Structuring Cues
	Directives
	Probes
Questioning	Higher-Order Questions
	Recall/Recognition Questions
	Opinion Questions
	Redirecting Questions
Responding	Teacher or Student Response
	Recitation
	Extended Response
	Respondent says "Don't Know"
	Statement
Feedback	Acknowledgment of Correct Answer
	Teacher says Answer Wrong
	Physical Punishment
	Repeat Answer
	Give Correct Answer
	Effectiveness Questions
Management/	Discipline
Non-Academic	Procedural
	Silence
	Social Interaction
	Observer Could Not Hear Interaction

The FMI data belonging to the observational categories displayed in Tables 2.8 and 2.9 were used to derive seventeen composites that were intended to reflect more complex interactions. It is useful to classify these composites in terms of the operations necessary to arrive at the corresponding data. In this regard, the FMI composites can be organized into two broader classes, namely (1) composites derived from FMI codes belonging to just one interaction, and (2) composites derived from FMI codes belonging to several interactions which occurred in a prescribed sequential order. Table 2.10 summarizes the seventeen FMI categories using this classification scheme.

The derivation of the first type of FMI composites was fairly simple. For example, the composite category "teacher to student questions" was derived from the joint occurrence of the direction code "teacher to group interaction" and one of the various types of questions listed in Table 2.9 above. A somewhat more difficult task was to derive the data for the composite categories which involved some specified sequence of interactions. This task was to be

TABLE 2.10   *Summary of composite categories*
derived from the FMI by type of composite

Type of composite	Composite categories
One Interaction	Teacher to Group Questions
	Teacher to Student Questions
	Teacher to Group Probes
	Teacher to Student Probes
	Student Questions
	Student Qualitative Contribution
	Positive Feedback to Students
	Negative Feedback to Students
	Noise
Sequence of Interactions	Teacher Lectures with Stress
	Teacher Stresses Cues and Objectives
	Teacher Gives Example and Student then Asks Questions
	Students Unable to Answer Question
	Teacher Gives Answer to Student Question
	Probes after Higher Level Questions
	Probes after Recall Questions
	Teacher Waits for Student Response

accomplished under the direction of the National Research Coordinators who also worked out the details of obtaining the data related to the FMI composites. For example, in order to obtain the data related to the category "probes for higher level questions" the recorded FMI interactions had to be examined for all occurrences of "teacher to group" or "teacher to student" interactions in conjunction with higher level questions which were followed by the joint occurrence of "teacher to group" or "teacher to student" interactions and probes. In some cases, the data for the FMI composites were obtained with the aid of a computer using some suitable algorithms to identify specific sequences of interactions. In other cases, the identification of interaction sequences was left to the observers who noted the appropriate codes on the FMI form when the observed lesson was finished.

It should be noted that four of the composite categories displayed in Table 2.10 involved "emphasis" as one component. These composites were "teacher lectures with stress," "teacher stresses cues and objectives," "positive acknowledgment," and "negative acknowledgment." When the FMI data were finally available and examined it turned out, however, that the "emphasis" category was quite rarely coded in all participating countries. Thus, the ensuing composite categories usually had almost no variance so that they were useless for further analyses.

Observers were instructed to record the interactions occurring in the class-room at least every five seconds, or each time the nature of the interactions changed. Thus, a minimum number of sixty codings for each of the dimensions context, direction, and nature were made during each five minute period.

Individual Activity Record (IAR)

The coding categories and the format of the IAR and the SNAP were identical. The difference between these two instruments concerned the focus of the observer. The SNAP focused on the whole class or on groups of students if the class was divided into separate groups. The IAR focused on eight randomly selected students and was to be coded for each of these students. The observers watched each student and noted the activity to which the student was assigned, the engagement of the student in this activity, and the role of the teacher.

Classroom Rating Scale (CRS)

The Classroom Rating Scale was to be completed by the observers immediately after each observed lesson. It contained a variety of high-inference ratings of the instructional processes that occurred in the classroom. The instrument included rating dimensions such as the teacher effectiveness in the use of specific behavioral class rules, the timing of instructional behaviors and actions, avoidance of target errors (e.g., misdirected disciplinary activities), and managerial skills. As was the case for the Opportunity to Learn Rating (OTL) instrument, the use of the Classroom Rating Scale was optional. The instrument was not used in any of the participating countries so that no data were available for further analyses.

Observers' Qualifications and Training

The quality of the data in any observational study rests primarily with the qualifications and training of those doing the observing. National Research Coordinators were encouraged to seek out individuals with prior teaching experience since such individuals would likely be (1) afforded greater credibility by teachers being observed, and (2) more skilled in interpreting classroom events in terms of the variety of categories included on the observation instruments.

In order to ensure quality training, the following procedures were followed. Two international training sessions were held; the first at the Technische Hogeschool Twente in Enschede, the Netherlands, in the summer of 1980, and the second at the Universite de Liege au Sart Tilman in Liege, Belgium, in the summer of 1981. Each country was to send at least one person, referred to as the National Observation Coordinator, to these training sessions. Because of travel difficulties or the time at which countries chose to participate in the study, two additional training sessions were held. One session was held in Jakarta, Indonesia, and was attended by representatives from Indonesia, Thailand, and Malaysia. (At the time, both Indonesia and Malaysia were participating in the study.) The second session was held in Seoul, Korea, for representatives from the Republic of Korea.

The training methods at all sites were modifications on those developed by Jane Stallings. Detailed training manuals incorporating those methods were prepared by N. L. Gage and Margaret Needels.

Each training session lasted seven consecutive days. The major emphases of the session were the familiarity with the instruments and skill in using them. Participants had to learn the definitions of the coding categories and their location on the instruments. They had to recognize verbal and visual examples of each category, so they could accurately code them in the time available. Written transcripts and videotapes of actual classrooms, primarily North American elementary classrooms in which mathematics and science were taught, were used as part of the training. Finally, at least two classroom visits were arranged during the workshop. During these visits pairs of observers coded behaviors and activities using the instruments and compared their results. In this way, misunderstanding could be identified and discussed and, ultimately, consensus gained.

Following the training sessions, the National Observation Coordinators returned home and trained a cadre of observers for the study in their countries. The same format and materials were used in this training.

Observer Agreement

All National Observation Coordinators were required to achieve an acceptable level of agreement during the international training sessions (defined as 80 percent). Beginning with the second day of training and continuing throughout the sessions, each Coordinator coded a series of videotaped classroom segments. The codings were compared with those made by the international observer trainer. Coordinators achieving less than an overall 80 percent agreement were provided with additional training and assistance.

The manual prepared for use within each country contained scripts of rather lengthy dialogues between teachers and students, similar to those that occur in natural classroom settings. In addition, a "scoring key" for each script was included in the manual. Trainees with less than an overall 80 percent agreement with these keys received assistance.

Furthermore, checks on each observer's proficiency were to be made on three occasions within each country using videotapes of classrooms in that country. The first check occurred on the final day of training. The second took place one week after the completion of training (but prior to the beginning of the study). Finally, the third occurred midway through the study, when observers had completed approximately one-half of their observations.

The Supervision of Observers

National Observation Coordinators were expected to maintain regular contact with the observers throughout the study. Observers were to report to the Coordinators daily during the first three observations. In addition, observers were to send their coding sheets to the Coordinators during the first several weeks of the study. Coordinators were to examine these sheets and discuss illogical or inconsistent patterns with the observers.

During the remainder of the study Coordinators were to maintain weekly contacts with observers. The primary responsibility of Coordinators during this time was to listen to observers' problems and discuss possible solutions with them. A secondary responsibility was to maintain the enthusiasm of the observers as the observational task became routine.

Summary

In this chapter a great deal of information concerning the constructs, variables, and instruments has been presented. The core model illustrating the hypothesized relationships among the constructs has been displayed and explained. Issues pertaining to the selection, training, and supervision of observers have been raised and discussed.

In an attempt to integrate much of the information contained in this chapter, Table 2.11 has been prepared. This table displays the relationships among all of the constructs, variables, and instruments included in the study. The table is organized around the fifteen major constructs. The variables associated with each construct are nested within construct. Computer labels for specific manifest variables (e.g., TYPESC for "type of school") also are included. Finally, the abbreviations of the instruments used to gather information on each of the variables are listed in the right-hand column of Table 2.11.

TABLE 2.11   *Constructs, variables, and instruments*

Construct/Variables	Instruments
COMMUNITY CHARACTERISTICS	
School Location	ITQ
SCHOOL CHARACTERISTICS	
Type of School (TYPESC)	ITQ
Grade Level Organization	ITQ
Size of School	ITQ
Time Allocated to Subject (per year)	ITQ

contd...

Table 2.11 *(continued)*

Construct/Variables	Instruments
TEACHER CHARACTERISTICS	
Sex (SEXT)	ITQ
Age (AGET)	ITQ
Years of Experience (YRS)	ITQ
Certification	ITQ
Subject Area Training	ITQ
Subject Contact Hours (per week)	ITQ
Number of Additional Subjects Taught	ITQ
Total Contact Hours (per week)	ITQ
HOME CHARACTERISTICS	
Father's Education	ISQ
Mother's Education	ISQ
Father's Occupation	ISQ
Language Used in Home	ISQ
STUDENT CHARACTERISTICS	
Sex (SEXS)	ISQ
Age (AGES)	ISQ
Pretest (PRETEST)	PRETEST
Aspirations (ASPIRATION)	ISQ
Attitude Toward School (ATTSCH)	ISQ
Attitude Toward Subject (PREATTSUBJ)	ISQ
CLASSROOM CONTEXT	
Typical Use of Grouping	ITQ
Observed Use of Grouping	FMI
Use of Types of Materials	ITQ
Student Access to Books Outside School	ITQ
Lesson Emphasis	POI
Lesson Objective	POI
Class Size	CIIF
Number of Adults Per Classroom	CIIF
Student Attendance	CIIF
TEACHER PERCEPTIONS	
Teacher Autonomy	ITQ
Relative Class Ability Level	ITQ
Percent of Students Needing Remediation	ITQ
QUANTITY OF INSTRUCTION	
Amount of Homework	ITQ
Time for Homework	ITQ
Opportunity to Learn	OTL
Allocated Time	CIIF
Instructional Time	FMI
ORIENTING STUDENTS	
Specifying Objectives	ITQ
Reviewing Content	SNAP
TEACHING STUDENTS	
Teacher Interacting	SNAP
Teacher Monitoring	SNAP
Monitoring Individual Seatwork	ITQ
Monitoring Groupwork	ITQ
Lecture	SNAP
Discourse/Discussion	SNAP

Contd...

Table 2.11 *(continued)*

Construct/Variables	Instruments
Oral Practice/Drill	SNAP
Reading at Seats	SNAP
Written Seatwork	SNAP
Laboratory Work	SNAP
Direction of Verbal Interactions	FMI
Explanation	FMI
Explanation Using Materials	FMI
Demonstration	FMI
Use of Examples	FMI
Structuring Cues	FMI
Directives	FMI
Student Questions	FMI
Student Contributions	FMI
Social Interactions	FMI
Silence (Absence of Verbal Interactions)	FMI
Frequency of Extra Help	FTQ
Number Receiving Extra Help	FTQ
Timing of Extra Help	FTQ
Format of Extra Help	FTQ
Type of Extra Help	FTQ
ASSESSING & EVALUATING STUDENTS	
Questioning Student	FMI
Questioning Group	FMI
Asks Recall Questions	FMI
Asks Higher-Order Questions	FMI
Asks Opinion Questions	FMI
Asks Effectiveness Questions	FMI
Amount of Questioning	FTQ
Waits for Student(s) Response	FMI
Student Short Response	FMI
Student Recitation	FMI
Student Extended Response	FMI
Student Doesn't Answer	FMI
Positive Acknowledgement	FMI
Says Answer Wrong	FMI
Repeats Answer	FMI
Redirects Question	FMI
Gives Answer	FMI
Probes	FMI
Probes to Student	FMI
Probes to Group	FMI
Tests for Grading Purposes	FTQ
Diagnostic Testing	FTQ
MANAGING STUDENTS	
Management & Routine Administration	FTQ, SNAP
Procedural Interactions	FMI
Transitional Interactions	FMI
Disciplinary Actions	FTQ, FMI
Uninvolved Teacher	SNAP

Contd...

Table 2.11 *(continued)*

Construct/Variables	Instruments
STUDENT PERCEPTIONS	
Task Orientation (TASK)	FSQ
Structure of Lesson (STRUCTURE)	FSQ
Teacher Feedback (FEEDBACK)	FSQ
STUDENT PARTICIPATION	
Percent of Students Engaged in Learning (ENGPCT)	IAR, SNAP
STUDENT OUTCOMES	
Student Achievement (POSTTEST)	POSTTEST
Attitude Toward Subject (POSTATTSUBJ)	FSQ

3

Descriptions of the Participating Countries

Ten replications of the study were conducted, each replication being the direct responsibility of a National Research Coordinator (NRC). Each NRC was affiliated with a research center located in that country. The name and address of each research center, its head at the time of the study, and the person who served as the NRC for the study are displayed in Table 3.1.

As can be seen, the research centers were in eight countries, which in turn were located on five continents. As a consequence, the study was replicated in culturally diverse settings. Throughout the volume the three replications. conducted in Canada will be referred to as Canada Ontario-English for the study conducted in the English-speaking classrooms in the province of Ontario, Canada Ontario-French for the study conducted in the French-speaking classrooms in the province of Ontario, and Canada Quebec for the study conducted in the province of Quebec. Finally, throughout this volume the Republic of Korea will be referred to in tables and figures as Korea (ROK).

In this chapter, basic information concerning the schools, teachers, students' homes, and the students themselves will be presented. To help the reader make sense of the variety of information to be presented, the chapter begins with an overview of the design and execution of the study in each country. Next, the initial methods used to prepare the data for analyses are presented. The data are then summarized in two ways. First, they are summarized on a country-by-country basis. This summarization provides a fairly detailed description of the settings in which the study was conducted. Second, the data are summarized on a construct-by-construct basis (that is, school characteristics, teacher characteristics, home characteristics, and student characteristics). This summarization permits cross-country comparisons on the variety of variables associated with each construct. The chapter concludes with a brief summary.

This chapter was written by Lorin W. Anderson, Beatrice Avalos, and Garrett K. Mandeville.

TABLE 3.1   *Participating countries, research centers, head of centers, and National Research Coordinator (NRC) for the study*

Country/Center/Address	Head of Center	NRC
AUSTRALIA		
Australian Council for Educational Research	J. P. Keeves (until 1985)	S. Bourke
P.O. Box 210	B. McGaw	
Hawthorn, Victoria, Australia	(after 1985)	
CANADA ONTARIO		
Ontario Institute for Studies in Education	B. J. Shapiro	D. Ryan & A. Hildyard (English);
252 Bloor Street West		S. Churchill
Toronto, Ontario		(French)
Canada		
CANADA QUEBEC		
L'Institut National de Recherche Scientifique	M. Leclerc	M. Leclerc & R. Bertrand
2383 Chemin Ste-Foy Quebec, Quebec, Canada		
HUNGARY		
Orszagos Pedagogical Intezet	Z. Bathory	A. Joo
Gorkij Fasor 17-21		
H-1071 Budapest		
Hungary		
ISRAEL		
School of Education	D. Nevo (Tel Aviv)	L. Kremer (Haifa)
University of Haifa		
Haifa, Israel		
KOREA (REPUBLIC OF)		
Korean Educational Development Institute	Y. S. Kim	U. Huh
20-1 Umyeon-Dong		
Gangnam-Gu		
Seoul, Korea		
NETHERLANDS		
Technische Hogeschool Twente	E. Warries	W. Tomic & H. Krammer
Vakgroup Onderwijskunde		
Postbus 217		
NL-7500 AE Enschede		
The Netherlands		

Contd...

Table 3.1 (continued)

Country/Center/Address	Head of Center	NRC
NIGERIA International Center for Educational Evaluation University of Ibadan Ibadan, Nigeria	E. A. Yoloye	I. Chacko
THAILAND National Education Commission Sukhothai Road Bangkok 10300 Thailand	P. Sapianchai	M. Nitsaisook

Notes: The Federal Republic of Germany conducted the study two years later than the other countries, with design variations based on the preliminary results from other countries. As a consequence, this study is not included in this volume. The interested reader is encouraged to read Helmke A., Schneider W., and Weinert, F. E. 1986 Quality of instruction and classroom learning outcomes: The German contribution to the Classroom Environment Study of the IEA, *Teaching and Teacher Education. 2: 1-18.* The address for the national center is the Max-Planck-Institute for Psychological Research, Leopoldstrasse 14, D-8000 Munich, Federal Republic of Germany. The head of the center is F. E. Weinert and the NRC for the study was A. Helmke.

Overview of Studies in the Participating Countries

For a variety of reasons, countries differed in the design and execution of the study. NRCs were asked to make certain choices concerning elements of the design such as subject matter, grade level, and number of teachers. They were also asked whether or not they wished to administer or use the instruments that were not required in all participating countries. For example, the instrument used to estimate opportunity to learn was a "national option."

Many of the decisions appeared to be based on feasibility considerations. In view of the amount of funding and the cost of observations, for example, how many classrooms could be observed on how many occasions? Furthermore, were the classrooms accessible in light of travel time and the willingness of administrators and teachers to give their permission? Because of such practical constraints, probability samples could not be drawn in any country. The reader is asked to remember these between-country differences in the design and execution of the study when examining the results.

Table 3.2 includes a brief overview of the study as designed and executed in each country. Data are presented on grade level and subject matter; number of schools, classes, and students; length of the study; and number of observations conducted in each classroom. As can be seen in Table 3.2, mathematics was the preferred subject, being included in seven of the ten studies. Science and history were the other two subjects included in the studies.

TABLE 3.2   *Overview of the execution of the
Classroom Environment Study*

Country	Grade level	Subject matter	No. of schools	No. of classes	No. of students	Study length	No. of observations
Australia	5	Maths	39	75	1,963	3 mos.	8 – 10
Canada Ontario-Engl	8	Maths	18	27	751	7 mos.	8
Canada Ontario-French	8	Maths	14	18	420	6 mos.	8
Canada Quebec	7 – 8	Maths	9	30	749	6 mos.	10
Hungary	5	Physics	40	40	1,180	—	5
Israel	6	History	11	22	671	4 mos.	1 – 5
Korea (ROK)	5	Science	15	45	2,400	2 mos.	8
Netherlands	8	Maths	17	50	1,125	7 mos.	8
Nigeria	8	Maths	35	35	1,416	—	4
Thailand	5	Maths	77	87	2,572	9 mos.	6

Notes: The number of classes shown in this table represent those classes in which at least one observation was conducted. As a result of various editing procedures and the application of missing data rules, the numbers of classes (and hence the numbers of students) included in each analysis are typically lower than those shown in this table. Finally, in Hungary and Nigeria the study length was not provided by the NRCs.

In terms of grade level, fifth grade students were included in four of the replications; eighth grade students also were included in four. Sixth grade students were included in one replication, while seventh and eighth grade students were included in another.

The number of schools in which the studies were conducted ranged from 9 to 77 (with more than one-half of the replications involving fewer than 20 schools). The number of classrooms (which is identical to the number of teachers) ranged from 18 to 87 (with a median between 35 and 40). The number of students ranged from 420 to 2,572 (with a median between 1,100 and 1,200). The actual length of the studies (that is, the time between the collection of the first and last data) ranged from two to nine months. Finally, the number of times each classroom was observed ranged from 1 to 10 (with a median and mode of 8). In two of the countries (Australia and Israel) not all classrooms were observed the same number of times.

As has been mentioned, in no country were probability samples of schools or classrooms selected for the study. In Australia, for example, state and private schools were selected within the Melbourne metropolitan area. In Canada, the Ontario English schools were within two hours travel time from Toronto. Similarly, the schools in Quebec were located within a 25-mile radius of Sainte-Foy. In Israel, schools had to meet two criteria before they were included. First, they had to be located in or around the city of Haifa. Second, the teachers had to teach a unit on Ancient Greece during the time that observers would be in their classrooms. Similarly, in the Republic of Korea, schools in which students were studying a specific unit of natural science were selected. In the Netherlands, the schools selected were those preparing students for university-level education. Thus, students tended to be of higher abilities or come from higher SES homes. In addition, these schools could not be participating in the IEA Second Mathematics Study. Furthermore, teachers in these schools must have been teaching from one of three textbook series. In Nigeria, schools were located in the state of Oyo, near the University of Ibadan. Finally, in Thailand, schools in various parts of the country were selected.

Despite the fact that the schools were not selected randomly, there was an interest on the part of those who designed the study in generalizing the results beyond those specific schools and included. As a consequence, a decision was made to identify a set of variables (referred to in Chapter 1 as marker variables) that could be used to compare the schools and classrooms included in the study with national probability samples. Examples of such variables were type of school, class size, and years of teaching experience.

Questions pertaining to these variables were included both on the Initial Teacher Questionnaire (ITQ), administered to teachers whose classrooms were observed, and the Teacher Survey Questionnaire (TSQ), which was to be administered to a probability sample of teachers. Because of financial and practical constraints, however, true probability samples of teachers for the TSQ were not drawn in any of the countries (although the samples drawn in some countries came closer to this ideal than did those in others).

In general, the samples of teachers to whom the TSQ was administered were considerably larger than those to whom the ITQ was administered. Nonetheless, it was not known whether the TSQ samples were any more representative of the teacher populations in the countries. Thus, although comparisons of the two samples on the pre-selected variables were possible, proper interpretations of differences between the two samples would have been difficult if not impossible. As a consequence, data gathered from the TSQ are not presented in this volume. Those interested in the data obtained from this instrument are invited to consult Avalos (1983) as well as the various national reports included in Appendix A.

Overview of Data Cleaning, Editing, and Preparation

As might be expected in view of the vast amounts of data collected in each country, the cleaning and editing of the data represented major undertakings. Initially, numerical values outside the range of possible numerical values for a given variable were identified. Such was the case, for example, when a numerical value of "3" appeared in a column corresponding with a dichotomous variable such as student sex which was coded "1" for male and "2" for female. These "impossible" numerical values were either corrected (when it appeared that such corrections were justified) or replaced with a blank space, thus resulting in missing data. Data also were classified as "missing" when students or teachers failed to respond to one or more of the items associated with a specific variable. In some cases, no responses were made to an entire instrument.

In anticipation of problems caused by missing data, the Project Steering Committee established five rules for dealing with missing data. First, a *variable* was eliminated from the data set in a country when more than 15 percent of the data pertaining to that variable was missing. Second, a *student* was eliminated from the data set in a country when data on more than 20 percent of the variables pertaining to that student were missing. Third, a *student* was eliminated from the data set in a country when he or she had failed to complete any of four instruments: the Initial Student Questionnaire (ISQ), the Final Student Questionnaire (FSQ), the aptitude or achievement pretest (PRETEST), or the achievement posttest (POSTTEST). Fourth, an entire *class* was eliminated in a country when the data pertaining to more than 20 percent of the variables aggregated to the classroom level were missing. Fifth, a *teacher* (and subsequently the teacher's class) was eliminated in a country when he or she had not completed either of two instruments: the Initial Teacher Questionnaire (ITQ) or the Final Teacher Questionnaire (FTQ).

Once the data had been properly cleaned and edited, three data sets were created for each country: a student-level data set, a classroom-level data set, and a country-level data set. The student-level data set was created as follows. For each variable on the four student instruments (that is, ISQ, PRETEST, FSQ, and POSTTEST—see Table 2.1), each student was assigned his or her unique response (coded numerically) or total score. For each variable on the four teacher instruments (that is, ITQ, TI, POI, and FTQ—see Table 2.1), each student was assigned a numerical value corresponding to the response given by his or her teacher. Thus, all students in a classroom were assigned the same numerical value for all variables on the four teacher instruments. For each variable included on the observation instruments (that is, CIIF, SNAP, FMI, and IAR—see Table 2.1), all students in a particular classroom were assigned the same numerical value. This numerical value was typically in the percent metric (e.g., the percent of all activities which involved written seatwork, or the percent of all interactions in which the teacher was talking with groups of students).

In many countries the classroom mean for a specific activity included on the Snapshot, for example, would be based on 40 numerical values (that is, 8 observed lessons times 5 uses of the Snapshot during each lesson). Each of these 40 numerical values would be coded "0" if the activity was not observed or "1" if it was observed. The mean for that activity, then, would represent the percent of the 40 numerical values that were coded as "1." This mean, representing the percentage of all activities that were of a particular type (e.g., written seatwork), would then be assigned to all of the students in that classroom. This same approach was used for variables on the IAR.

In general, the means for those variables included on the FMI represent the mean percent of all five-second time intervals in each classroom during which each variable was observed to occur. Finally, the means for the variables included on the CIIF referred to actual numbers of students or minutes, not percents. Once again, the class mean was assigned to each student in the classroom.

The classroom-level data set was the same as the student-level data set except for the treatment of those variables included on the student instruments. For these variables, the mean response or score for all students in each classroom was assigned to that classroom. For categorical variables such as father's education, the percentages of students responding in each category (that is, higher education, secondary education, primary education, and little or no education) were entered into the classroom-level data set.

Finally, in order to describe the variables within each country and to examine similarities and differences across countries, country-level data sets were formed. For the variables on the teacher and observation instruments, the data in the classroom-level data set were simply aggregated across classrooms. For the variables on the student instruments, the data in the student-level data set were directly aggregated to the country level. That is, student data were entered directly into the country-level data sets regardless of their classroom membership. The country-level data sets provided the primary data presented in this chapter and the next.

Descriptions of the Study Settings

The data pertaining to the variables associated with school, teacher, home, and student characteristics are shown in Table 3.3. The number of schools, teachers, and students are indicated in parentheses to the right of the major construct labels. Since students provided the information on their home backgrounds, the sample sizes for the variables associated with the home characteristics are identical to those for the variables associated with the student characteristics.

Virtually all of the data displayed in Table 3.3 are presented in a percent metric (that is, the percent of schools located in rural areas). Exceptions to this generalization are school size (for which the data represent actual enrollment categories), and attitudes toward school and subject matter (both of which are presented as mean scores on a five-point scale, with five being most positive). Finally, with the exception of the student achievement data, all percentages are rounded to the nearest whole number, resulting in some totals which are slightly less or more than 100 percent.

TABLE 3.3   Summary of data for school, teacher, home, and school variables

Variables	Country									
	Australia	COE	COF	CQ	Hungary	Israel	ROK	Netherlands	Nigeria	Thailand
	(n = 39)	(n = 18)	(n = 14)	(n = 9)	(n = 40)	(n = 11)	(n = 15)	(n = 17)	(n = 35)	(n = 77)
SCHOOLS										
School Location										
Rural	0	26	33	5	0	0	18	30	0	37
Suburban	0	11	11	81	26	20	31	20	14	43
Urban	0	22	56	14	54	80	24	28	43	13
Metropolitan	100	41	0	0	21	0	27	22	43	8
School Type										
Public Comprehensive	84	67	0	38	100	5	93	10	45	84
Selective	0	0	0	62	0	95	0	44	40	0
Parochial	13	33	100	0	0	0	0	18	15	16
Other	3	0	0	0	0	0	7	28	0	0
Grade Levels										
Elementary Only	100	96	100	*	95	95	100	0	95	85
Elementary & Secondary	0	4	0	*	3	5	0	0	0	14
Secondary Only	0	0	0	*	3	0	0	100	0	1
Other	0	0	0	*	0	0	0	0	5	0
School Size										
Median	<501	501-600	<501	501-600	601-700	501-600	1,501-2,000	1,001-1,500	901-1,000	<501
Minimum	<501	<501	<501	<501	<501	<501	<501	<501	601-700	<501
Maximum	901-1,000	1,001-1,500	2,001-2,500	1,501-2,000	1,501-2,000	901-1,000	>5,000	1,501-2,000	1,001-1,500	4,001-5,000

Contd...

Table 3.3 *(continued)*

					Country					
Variables	Australia	COE	COF	CQ	Hungary	Israel	ROK	Netherlands	Nigeria	Thailand
Subject Hours/Year										
40 or fewer	0	0	*	0	0	67	0	2	0	0
41-80	1	0	*	0	100	33	0	2	16	0
81-120	3	54	*	10	0	0	0	68	58	0
121-160	43	29	*	80	0	0	100	26	26	0
161-200	36	13	*	10	0	0	0	2	0	19
201 or more	18	4	*	0	0	0	0	0	0	81
TEACHERS	(n = 75)	(n = 27)	(n = 18)	(n = 30)	(n = 40)	(n = 22)	(n = 45)	(n = 50)	(n = 35)	(n = 87)
Sex										
Male	41	59	50	57	18	100	67	90	70	31
Female	59	41	50	43	82	0	33	10	30	69
Age (years)										
25 or Younger	23	0	0	0	8	0	20	10	19	7
26-35	52	62	29	38	31	57	44	48	67	49
36-45	15	24	53	43	44	24	20	22	14	40
46-55	8	10	18	14	15	10	16	12	0	3
56 or Older	1	5	0	5	3	10	0	8	0	0

Contd...

Table 3.3 (continued)

					Country					
Variables	Australia	COE	COF	CQ	Hungary	Israel	ROK	Netherlands	Nigeria	Thailand
Experience (years)										
10 or Fewer	67	21	17	14	36	20	56	60	78	49
11-20	24	58	39	62	38	60	24	22	17	38
21 or More	9	21	44	24	26	20	20	18	4	13
Certification										
Elementary Only	100	54	100	5	82	86	91	*	0	72
Elementary & Secondary	0	0	0	43	8	14	2	*	57	23
Secondary Only	0	46	0	52	10	0	7	*	43	4
Subject Matter Training										
Specialist's Degree	*	48	65	21	38	75	84	*	5	15
Major Component	*	43	35	37	0	0	0	*	14	59
Minor Component	*	9	0	37	41	0	16	*	59	9
Neither Major nor Minor	*	0	0	5	21	25	0	*	23	16
Subject Contact Hrs/Week										
10 or Fewer	100	88	94	5	45	100	100	18	37	56
11-20	0	8	6	95	47	0	0	24	63	43
21 or More	0	4	0	0	8	0	0	58	0	1

Contd....

Table 3.3 *(continued)*

						Country				
Variables	Australia	COE	COF	CQ	Hungary	Israel	ROK	Netherlands	Nigeria	Thailand
Additional Subjects Taught										
2 or Fewer	*	39	18	100	100	5	3	100	100	65
3-4	*	22	47	0	0	19	6	0	0	12
5 or More	*	39	35	0	0	76	91	0	0	22
Total Class Contact Hours/Week										
10 or Fewer	36	0	0	0	10	10	0	12	10	0
11-20	9	13	0	95	13	5	0	16	85	56
21-30	54	87	94	5	67	86	51	72	5	43
31-40	1	0	6	0	3	0	44	0	0	1
41 or More	0	0	0	0	7	0	5	0	0	0
HOME										
Father's Education										
Higher Education	*	40	28	*	*	34	28	33	41	7
Secondary Education	*	36	39	*	*	42	45	54	21	19
Primary Education	*	17	29	*	*	18	24	11	20	62
Little or No Education	*	6	4	*	*	6	3	2	18	11
Mother's Education										
Higher Education	*	32	30	*	*	29	14	13	22	5
Secondary Education	*	46	50	*	*	51	48	70	26	12
Primary Education	*	17	20	*	*	16	30	15	22	65
Little or No Education	*	6	2	*	*	4	7	2	29	18
Father's Occupational Status										
Upper Class	22	22	29	*	21	30	3	21	35	0
Middle Class	41	56	53	*	21	54	44	57	26	28
Working Class	37	22	18	*	58	17	53	22	39	72

Contd....

Table 3.3 *(continued)*

	Country									
Variables	Australia	COE	COF	CQ	Hungary	Israel	ROK	Netherlands	Nigeria	Thailand
Use of Language in Home										
Always	70	64	44	91	97	66	100	87	3	36
Usually	7	11	30	7	3	9	0	9	21	17
Sometimes	16	17	21	1	0	22	0	3	48	17
Never	7	8	6	1	0	3	0	1	28	27
STUDENT	(n=1,963)	(n=715)	(n=396)	(n=569)	(n=1,104)	(n=606)	(n=2,396)	(n=1,067)	(n=855)	(n=2,563)
Sex										
Male	55	50	49	43	49	46	50	51	54	51
Female	45	50	51	57	51	54	50	49	46	49
Aspirations										
Stay in School	49	96	83	79	49	79	88	77	88	49
Pursue Higher	32	85	60	62	39	72	50	55	**	41
Pretest										
Mean (percent correct)	57.6	42.0	32.2	59.0	59.7	66.3	44.8	64.5	39.3	37.1
Minimum	0.0	10.0	7.5	8.7	16.0	20.7	8.0	25.0	13.2	2.9
Maximum	100.0	95.0	82.5	100.0	96.0	100.0	96.0	100.0	78.9	91.4
Attitude to School (5=most positive)										
Mean	3.3	3.3	3.4	3.1	2.7	3.4	3.6	2.8	4.2	3.6
S.D.	0.8	0.6	0.8	0.7	0.5	0.6	0.6	0.5	0.6	0.5
Attitude to Subject (5=most positive)										
Mean	3.7	3.7	3.9	3.7	3.7	3.5	3.4	3.2	3.8	3.5
S.D.	0.6	0.6	0.6	0.5	1.0	0.6	0.5	0.6	0.6	0.4

Notes: The sum of the percentages within variable categories do not always sum to 100 because of rounding errors. A single asterisk (*) indicates that data for that variable were not collected. A double asterisk (**) indicates the validity of that variable is questionable. The country abbreviations are COE for Canada Ontario-English, COF for Canada Ontario-French, CQ for Canada Quebec, and ROK for the Republic of Korea.

Before discussing the data for each country, one comment on the school data reported in Table 3.3 is in order. Data on the school variables were provided by the teachers. As a consequence, the numbers in the cells of the table represent the *percent of teachers* who responded in a particular way, not the *percent of schools.* The only condition under which these two percents would be identical is when equal numbers of teachers in all schools were included in the study.

Consider, for example, the data on school location in Canada Ontario-French. The study was conducted in 14 schools and included 18 teachers. Thus, in at least some of the schools multiple teachers were included in the study. Of these 18 teachers, 6 (or 33 percent) reported teaching in rural schools, 2 (or 11 percent) reported teaching in suburban schools, while the remaining 10 (or 56 percent) reported teaching in urban schools. These data do not imply that one-third of the schools were located in rural areas. Quite obviously, one-third of 14 is not a whole number.

In each of the following subsections, the data concerning school, teacher, home, and student variables are summarized. Following these summaries, comparisons among the countries will be made in a separate section of the chapter.

Australia

In Australia, the study was conducted primarily in fairly small public comprehensive schools located in the Melbourne area. Most of the teachers were less than 35 years old and had been teaching for 10 or fewer years. Few teachers were older than 56 years or had been teaching for more than 20 years. About three-fifths of the teachers were female. All were generalist elementary teachers, with more than one-half teaching between 21 or 30 hours per week. About one-third were more senior teachers who taught fewer than 10 hours per week.

Students were fairly equally divided among upper, middle, and working class homes. In 7 of 10 homes, English (the language of instruction) was always spoken. In fewer than 1 in 10 homes English was never spoken. About one-half of the students intended to stay in school beyond the age of compulsory attendance, while one-third of the students intended to pursue some form of higher education.

The average student answered about 6 of 10 items correctly on the pretest, some students answered no items correctly while others answered all of them correctly. Finally, the average student's attitude toward school was slightly positive (that is, slightly above 3 on a 5-point scale, with higher numbers indicating more positive attitudes), while this student's attitude toward mathematics was quite positive (that is, almost 4 on a 5-point scale).

Canada Ontario-English

In Canada Ontario-English, the study was conducted in a variety of metropolitan, urban, and rural elementary schools of moderate size. Two-thirds of the schools were public comprehensive; the remainder were parochial. Teachers in all schools reported that their students received at least 81 hours of mathematics instruction; about one-half of the teachers reported that their students received more than 120 hours per year of mathematics instruction.

Teachers held either elementary or secondary certification, but not both. Furthermore, the proportion of teachers holding elementary or secondary certification was quite similar. In general, teachers had an undergraduate major or a specialist's degree in mathematics. Almost 60 percent of the teachers were men. The vast majority taught mathematics for 10 or fewer hours per week, although the number of additional subjects taught varied greatly. Almost 90 percent taught a total of 21 to 30 hours per week.

The vast majority of students' fathers and mothers had achieved either a secondary or some form of higher education. Slightly more than one-half of the students came from working class homes, with the remaining students equally divided between middle and upper class homes. English (the language of instruction) was always spoken in almost two-thirds of the homes. In fewer than 1 home in 10 was English never spoken.

Ninety-six percent of the students said they would stay in school beyond the age of compulsory attendance, while 85 percent intended to pursue some form of higher education. On the achievement pretest, the average student answered about 4 of 10 items correct with a range from 0 to 95 percent correct. Finally, the average student's attitude toward school was slightly positive and his or her attitude toward mathematics was quite positive.

Canada Ontario-French

In Canada Ontario-French, the study was conducted primarily in small schools operated by Catholic Separate School Boards. All teachers held elementary certification, with over 80 percent having taught for a minimum of 10 years. As will be seen later, these teachers were among the oldest and most experienced in the study. Furthermore, all teachers either had an undergraduate major or a specialist's degree in mathematics. Almost all teachers taught mathematics for 10 or fewer hours per week and a total of 21 to 30 hours per week, while most teachers taught 3 or more additional subjects.

A roughly equal proportion of students' fathers had received some primary, secondary, and higher education, with a majority employed in working class occupations. Interestingly, a higher percentage of students' mothers in comparison to students' fathers had received at least some secondary or higher education. In less than one-half of the homes was French (the language of instruction) always spoken, although in approximately one-half of the homes French was either "usually" or "sometimes" spoken.

Over 4 students in 5 stated that they intended to stay beyond the age of compulsory attendance. About three-fifths of the students intended to pursue some form of higher education. The average student answered fewer than one-third of the items on the achievement pretest correctly, with the highest scoring student answering 82.5 percent correctly. Finally, the average student's attitude toward school was slightly positive, while this student's attitude toward mathematics was very positive.

Canada Quebec

In Canada Quebec, the study was conducted primarily in suburban elementary schools of moderate size. Two of every 3 teachers taught in selective schools, with the remainder teaching in public comprehensive schools. All of the students reportedly received a minimum of 81 hours of mathematics instruction per year, with the vast majority receiving from 81 to 120 hours of mathematics teaching per year.

The vast majority of teachers were between 26 and 45 years of age and had been teaching for at least 11 years. Almost 3 of every 5 teachers were male. Virtually all teachers were certified to teach at the secondary school level (either only at that level or at both the elementary and secondary level). About 3 teachers in 4 had either an undergraduate major or minor in mathematics. Most of the teachers taught only mathematics, teaching a total of 11 to 20 hours per week.

French (the language of instruction) was always spoken in virtually all homes. Almost 4 of every 5 students indicated a willingness to stay in school beyond the age of compulsory attendance, while over 3 of 5 students stated their intention to pursue some form of higher education. The average student answered approximately 3 of every 5 items correctly on the pretest. Finally, the average student's attitude toward school was fairly neutral; his or her attitude toward mathematics was fairly positive.

Hungary

In Hungary, the study was conducted in public comprehensive elementary schools of moderate size. While a majority of the teachers taught in schools located in urban areas, fairly equal percentages taught in suburban and metropolitan schools. All teachers reported spending from 121 to 160 hours per year teaching physics.

All teachers held elementary school certification; about 4 of every 5 were women. The teachers varied widely in their ages, years of experience, and subject matter training. With respect to training, teachers either had received a specialist's degree in physics or had received little if any specific training in this subject field. All of the teachers reported teaching 2 or fewer additional subjects. Two-thirds taught a total of 21 to 30 hours per week, with few teaching physics for more than 20 hours per week.

Almost 60 percent of the students came from working class homes, with the remainder equally divided between upper and middle class homes. In almost all homes, Hungarian (the language of instruction) was always spoken.

Slightly under one-half of the students reported they would stay in school beyond the age of compulsory attendance; almost 40 percent intended to pursue some form of higher education. On the pretest the average students answered 6 of 10 items correctly. The lowest score was 16 percent correct; the highest was 96 percent. Finally, the average student's attitude toward school was slightly negative (that is, below 3 on a 5-point scale), while his or her attitude toward physics was fairly positive.

Israel

In Israel, the study was conducted primarily in selective elementary schools of moderate size. Eight of every 10 teachers taught in schools located in an urban area; the remainder taught in suburban schools. Approximately two-thirds of the teachers reported spending 40 or fewer hours per year teaching history. No teacher reported spending more than 80 hours per year teaching this subject.

All of the teachers were men. A majority ranged in ages from 26 to 35 years and had been teaching for more than 10 but fewer than 21 years. The vast majority held specialist's degrees in history and were certified to teach at the elementary school level only. All teachers taught history for 10 or fewer hours per week. Over 90 percent taught 5 or more additional subjects; almost 90 percent taught a total of 21 to 30 hours per week.

The vast majority of students' fathers and mothers had received either secondary or some form of higher education. The majority of students came from middle class homes, with almost one-third coming from upper class homes. In approximately two-thirds of the homes Hebrew (the language of instruction) was always spoken.

Almost 80 percent of the students reported they would stay in school beyond the age of compulsory attendance; almost three-fourths indicated they planned to pursue some form of higher education. On the pretest, the average student answered about 2 of every 3 items correctly. The lowest scoring student answered 1 of 5 items correctly, while the highest scoring student answered all correctly. Finally, the average student's attitude toward school and toward history was slightly positive.

Korea (ROK)

In the Republic of Korea, the study was conducted primarily in large public comprehensive elementary schools located in metropolitan, urban, suburban, and rural areas. All teachers reported that their students received from 121 to 160 hours of science instruction per year.

The vast majority of teachers held elementary school certification and a specialist's degree in science. Two-thirds of the teachers were men. The ages of the teachers varied widely, although a majority had been teaching for 10 years or fewer. All teachers reported teaching science for 10 or fewer hours per week, while over 90 percent reported teaching 5 or more additional subjects. All teachers taught at least a total of 21 hours per week.

Almost all of the students came from either working class or middle class homes; homes in which Korean (the language of instruction) was always spoken. Approximately three-fourths of the students' fathers and three-fifths of the students' mothers had achieved at least a secondary education.

The vast majority of students intended to stay in school beyond the compulsory attendance age. One-half intended to pursue some form of higher education. On the achievement pretest, the average student answered slightly less than one-half of the items correctly. The lowest scoring student answered 8 percent of the items correctly; the highest scoring student answered 96 percent correctly. Finally, the average student's attitudes toward school and toward science were slightly positive.

Netherlands

In the Netherlands, the study was conducted in various types of schools (e.g., comprehensive, selective) in a variety of locations (e.g., rural, urban). The diversity of school types and school locations was greater in the Netherlands than in any other country. More than two-thirds of the teachers reported that their students received between 81 and 120 hours of mathematics instruction. The remaining teachers reported students spending more than 120 hours on mathematics.

Nine of every 10 teachers were men, and all taught 2 additional subjects or fewer. The teachers differed widely in their ages, although the majority had been teaching for fewer than 11 years and almost all had been teaching for 20 years or less. Over one-half of the teachers taught mathematics for 21 hours or more per week, while almost three-fourths of the teachers had a total of 21 or more contact hours. Coupled with the fact that all teachers reported teaching 2 or fewer additional subjects, one can conclude that most teachers taught only mathematics.

The vast majority of parents had received at least a secondary education. The majority of students reported coming from middle class homes. In almost 90 percent of the homes, Dutch (the language of instruction) was always spoken.

Almost 80 percent of the students intended to stay in school beyond the compulsory attendance age; somewhat more than one-half planned to pursue some form of higher education. On the pretest, the average student answered about two-thirds of the items correctly. The lowest scoring student answered about one-fourth of the items correctly, while the highest scoring student answered all items correctly. Finally, the average student's attitude toward school was slightly negative (with a mean of less than 3 on a 5-point scale), while his or her attitude toward mathematics was slightly positive.

Nigeria

At least two caveats must be stated prior to discussing the Nigeria data. First, for virtually all of the variables, missing data exceeded 20 percent. That is, more than 20 percent of the teachers did not respond to items pertaining to the school or teacher variables. Similarly, more than 20 percent of the students did not respond to items pertaining to the home or student variables.

Second, with respect to students' aspirations, the percent of students indicating they intended to pursue higher education was greater than the percent of students indicating that they intended to stay in school beyond the compulsory attendance age. Since the two questions pertaining to these variables were presented in sequence, with the second question to be answered only by those answering "Yes" to the first question, an increase in the percentage of students who responded positively to these two questions is impossible. Despite these difficulties and because data on Nigerian schools, teachers, and students appear only in this chapter and the next, it seems important to include the Nigerian contribution to the study in the volume.

In Nigeria, the study was conducted primarily in urban and metropolitan areas. The schools in which the study was conducted were fairly large elementary schools. The vast majority were either public comprehensive or selective. The majority of teachers reported that their students received from 81 to 120 hours of mathematics instruction per year.

More than two-thirds of the teachers were men between 26 and 35 years of age, having taught for 10 or fewer years. Almost 60 percent held both elementary and secondary certification, with the remainder holding secondary certification only. All teachers taught 2 or fewer additional subjects, with the majority teaching from 11 to 20 hours of mathematics and a total of 11 to 20 teaching hours per week.

The education level of the parents was fairly equally distributed among the four basic categories (i.e., higher, secondary, primary, or little or none) as was their socio-economic status (i.e., upper class, middle class, and working class). In only three percent of the homes was English (the language of instruction) always spoken in the homes. In 3 of every 4 homes English was "sometimes" or "never" spoken.

Almost 90 percent of the students intended to stay in school beyond the age of compulsory attendance. On the pretest, the average student answered about 4 of 10 items correctly. The lowest scoring student answered about 1 of 7 items correctly, while the highest scoring student answered almost 4 of 5 items correctly. Finally, the average student's attitude toward school was quite positive (over 4 on a 5-point scale) and his or her attitude toward mathematics was fairly positive (almost 4 on a 5-point scale).

Thailand

In Thailand, the study was conducted primarily in rural and suburban public comprehensive elementary schools. In general, these schools were fairly small. All teachers reported that their students received at least 161 hours of mathematics instruction per year, with 4 of 5 teachers reporting 201 or more hours of mathematics instruction.

Almost 7 of every 10 teachers were men and held elementary school certification only. Almost 90 percent of the teachers were between 26 and 45 years of age, and had been teaching for 20 years or less. Three-fifths of the teachers had an undergraduate major in mathematics; another 15 percent held specialist's degrees in mathematics. The majority of the teachers taught mathematics for 10 or fewer hours per week, taught a total of 11 to 20 hours per week, and taught two or fewer additional subjects.

About three-fourths of the parents had received a primary school education or less. Similarly, about three-fourths of the students reported coming from working class homes. No students reported coming from upper class homes. In approximately one-third of the homes the language of instruction was always spoken. On the other hand, the language of instruction was never spoken in more than one-fourth of the homes.

Almost one-half of the students said they planned to stay in school beyond the age of compulsory attendance; about 2 of every 5 students intended to pursue some form of higher education. On the pretest, the average student answered about 3 of 8 items correctly. The lowest scoring student answered about 1 item correctly, while the highest scoring student answered more than 9 of 10 items correctly. Finally, the average student's attitudes toward school and toward mathematics were fairly positive.

Comparisons Among the Study Settings

Even a cursory examination of the country descriptions included in the previous section will result in an awareness of the diversity of the study settings. While all of Australia's teachers taught in metropolitan schools, 80 percent of the Israeli teachers taught in urban schools, and 81 percent of the Canada Quebec teachers taught in suburban schools. In contrast to these countries, 30 percent or more of the teachers in Canada Ontario-French, the Netherlands, and Thailand taught in rural schools.

Similarly, differences in the amount of instruction that students received in the subject matter also were evident. Two-thirds of the students in Israel received instruction in history for 40 or fewer hours per year. All of the students in Hungary received instruction in physics for 41 to 80 hours per year. Two-thirds of the students in the Netherlands received instruction in mathematics for 81 to 120 hours per year. All of the Korean students received instruction in science for 121 to 160 hours per year. Finally, all of the students in Thailand received instruction in mathematics for a minimum of 161 hours per year.

In order to examine more carefully the between-country differences, a summary table comparing and contrasting the countries on the various school, teacher, home, and student variables was prepared (see Table 3.4). For each variable included in Table 3.4 the median, minimum, and maximum are presented, typically in a percent metric. Most typically, the median is half-way between the two middle countries. The country or countries responsible for the maximum values are shown in parentheses to the right of the maximum values.

TABLE 3.4   *Cross-country comparison of school, teacher,*
home, and student variables

Variables	Median	Minimum	Maximum
SCHOOLS			
School Location			
Rural	11.5	0	37 (Thailand)
Suburban	20.0	0	81 (CQ)
Urban	26.0	0	80 (Israel)
Metropolitan	21.5	0	100 (Australia)
School Type			
Public Comprehensive	56.0	0	100 (Hungary)
Selective	0.0	0	95 (Israel)
Parochial	14.0	0	100 (COF)
Other	0.0	0	28 (Netherlands)
Grade Levels			
Elementary Only	95.5	85	100 (More Than 1)
Elementary & Secondary	1.5	0	14 (Thailand)
Secondary Only	0.0	0	3 (Hungary)
Other	0.0	0	5 (Nigeria)
School Size			
Median	501-600	<501	1,501-2,000 (ROK)
Subject Hours			
40 or Fewer	0.0	0	67 (Israel)
41-80	1.0	0	100 (Hungary)
81-120	5.0	0	68 (Netherlands)
121-160	26.0	0	100 (ROK)
161-200	1.0	0	19 (Thailand)
201 or More	0.0	0	100 (Thailand)
TEACHERS			
Sex			
Male	58.0	18	100 (Israel)
Female	42.0	0	82 (Hungary)
Age (years)			
25 or Younger	7.5	0	23 (Australia)
26-35	48.5	29	67 (Nigeria)
36-45	24.0	14	53 (COF)
46-55	11.0	0	18 (COF)
56 or Older	2.0	0	10 (Israel)

Contd...

TABLE 3.4 *(continued)*

Variables	Median	Minimum	Maximum
Experience (years)			
10 or Fewer	42.5	14	78 (Nigeria)
11-20	38.0	17	62 (CQ)
21 or More	20.0	4	44 (COF)
Certification			
Elementary Only	77.0	0	100 (More Than 1)
Elementary & Secondary	11.0	0	57 (Nigeria)
Secondary Only	8.5	0	52 (CQ)
Subject Matter Training			
Specialist's Degree	43.0	5	84 (ROK)
Major Component	24.5	0	59 (Thailand)
Minor Component	12.5	0	59 (Nigeria)
Neither Major Nor Minor	10.5	0	25 (Israel)
Subject Contact Hrs/Week			
10 or Fewer	56.0	0	100 (More Than 1)
11-20	24.0	0	95 (CQ)
21 or More	0.0	0	58 (Netherlands)
Total Class Contact Hrs/Wk			
10 or Fewer	10.0	0	51 (ROK)
11-20	13.0	0	95 (CQ)
21-30	67.0	0	94 (COF)
31-40	0.0	0	44 (ROK)
41 or More	0.0	0	7 (Hungary)
Additional Subjects Taught			
2 or Fewer	65.0	3	100 (More Than 1)
3-4	6.0	0	47 (COF)
5 or More	32.0	0	91 (ROK)
HOME			
Father's Education			
Higher Education	33.0	7	41 (Nigeria)
Secondary Education	39.0	19	54 (Netherlands)
Primary Education	20.0	11	62 (Thailand)
Little or No Education	6.0	2	18 (Nigeria)
Mother's Education			
Higher Education	22.0	5	32 (More Than 1)
Secondary Education	48.0	12	70 (Netherlands)
Primary Education	22.0	15	65 (Thailand)
Little or No Education	6.0	2	29 (Nigeria)
Father's Occupational Status			
Upper Class	22.0	3	35 (Nigeria)
Middle Class	44.0	21	57 (Netherlands)
Working Class	37.0	17	72 (Thailand)
Use of Language in Home			
Always	67.0	3	100 (ROK)
Usually	10.0	0	30 (COF)
Sometimes	14.0	0	48 (Nigeria)
Never	4.5	0	28 (Nigeria)

Contd...

66   *Lorin W. Anderson, Beatrice Avalos, and Garrett K. Mandeville*

TABLE 3.4 *(continued)*

Variables	Median	Minimum	Maximum
STUDENT			
Sex			
Male	50.0	43	55 (Australia)
Female	50.0	45	57 (CQ)
Aspirations			
Stay in School	79.0	49	96 (COE)
Pursue Higher Education	55.0	32	85 (COE)
Pretest			
Mean (% Correct)	51.2	32.2	66.3 (Israel)
Attitude to School			
Mean (1 to 5 Scale)	3.35	2.7	4.2 (Nigeria)
Attitude to Subject			
Mean (1 to 5 Scale)	3.7	3.2	3.9 (COF)

Notes: All data are in terms of percentages except school size (which is a median), and pretest, attitude toward school, and attitude toward subject (which are means). Canada Ontario-English is abbreviated COE, Canada Ontario-French is abbreviated COF, Canada Quebec is abbreviated CQ, and the Republic of Korea is abbreviated ROK.

School Variables

As has been pointed out, the countries differed widely on the school location variable. In no country did the majority of teachers teach in rural schools. Nonetheless, a sizeable minority of teachers in Canada Ontario-French, the Netherlands, and Thailand did teach in such schools. Only in Australia did the majority of teachers teach in metropolitan schools. In Canada Ontario-French, Hungary, and Israel, the majority of teachers taught in urban schools. Only in Canada Quebec did the majority of teachers teach in suburban schools. In all remaining countries (Canada Ontario-English, the Republic of Korea, the Netherlands, Nigeria, and Thailand) fairly large proportions of teachers taught in three or more school locations.

Most of the schools in the studies were public comprehensive schools. Two-thirds of the schools in Australia, Canada Ontario-English, Hungary, the Republic of Korea, and Thailand were public comprehensive schools. Three-fifths of the schools in Canada Quebec and almost all of the schools in Israel, however, were selective schools. Furthermore, all of the schools in Canada Ontario-French were parochial schools. Finally, in the Netherlands and Nigeria the schools were distributed across three or four of the school types.

The median school size across countries was between 501 and 600 students. In Australia, Canada Ontario-French, and Thailand the average school size was less than 501 students. In contrast, the average school size in the Netherlands was between 1,001 and 1,500 students, while that of Korea was between 1,501 and 2,000 students.

As has been mentioned earlier, the countries differed greatly in terms of the number of hours of instruction per year in the subject matter provided to the students. In Hungary and Israel students received 80 or fewer hours of instruction in physics and history, respectively. In most elementary schools, these subjects would be classified as "minor" subjects and, hence, the lower number of hours seems reasonable and appropriate. In the Republic of Korea, in contrast, students received from 121 to 160 hours of instruction per year in science. They also were elementary students.

Those countries in which mathematics was taught also varied in the number of hours of instruction in mathematics provided to their students. In Nigeria, for example, approximately three-fourths of the students received less than 120 hours of instruction in mathematics per year. Students in the Netherlands received a similar number of hours of mathematics instruction per year. In contrast, 90 percent of the students in Canada Quebec received more than 120 hours of mathematics instruction annually, while all of the students in Thailand received at least 120 hours of instruction per year in mathematics. Finally, the largest within-study variation occurred in Canada Ontario-English and Nigeria.

Teacher Variables

On the average, slightly more male than female teachers were included in the study. More than two-thirds of the teachers in Israel, the Republic of Korea, the Netherlands, and Nigeria were men. In contrast, more than two-thirds of the teachers in Hungary and Thailand were women.

The countries also differed in terms of the age and experience of the teachers. In Australia, the Republic of Korea, and Nigeria, about one of five teachers was younger than 26 years. In Israel and the Netherlands, however, one in five teachers was older than 45 years. The majority of teachers in Australia, Canada Ontario-English, Israel, and Nigeria were between 26 and 35 years of age. Large within-country variation in teachers' ages also was evident in most countries.

The majority of teachers in Australia, the Republic of Korea, the Netherlands, and Nigeria had taught for fewer than 11 years. In contrast, most teachers in Canada Ontario-English, Canada Quebec, and Israel had been teaching for more than 11 but less than 20 years. In no country had a majority of teachers been teaching for more than 20 years, although 44 percent of the teachers in Canada Ontario-French had been teaching that long.

Differences between countries in teacher certification tended to mirror the differences in the grade levels at which the studies were conducted. In those countries in which grades 5 and 6 students were included, the vast majority of teachers held elementary school certification only. Most of the other teachers in these countries held both elementary and secondary school certification.

68   *Lorin W. Anderson, Beatrice Avalos, and Garrett J. Mandeville*

In contrast, the vast majority of teachers in Canada Quebec (grades 7 and 8) and Nigeria (grade 8) held either secondary school or combined elementary and secondary certification. Approximately one-half of the teachers in Canada Ontario-English and the Netherlands and all of the teachers in Canada Ontario-French held *elementary school certification* only. It must be remembered, however, that the vast majority of the seventh and eighth grade students included in various replications were housed in elementary schools.

Teachers in the various countries also differed in their preparation for teaching the subject matter. In Canada Ontario-French, Israel, and the Republic of Korea, three-fifths or more of the teachers held specialist's degrees in the subject matter. In Nigeria and Thailand, fewer than one in five teachers had attained this level of training. On the other end of the scale, more than one-fourth of the teachers in Hungary, Israel, and Nigeria had little specialized training in the subject matter being taught.

The vast majority of the teachers in Canada Ontario-English and Canada Ontario-French and all of the teachers in Israel and the Republic of Korea reported teaching these subjects for 10 or fewer hours per week. In Canada Quebec and Nigeria, the majority of teachers taught the subjects for more than 11 but less than 20 hours per week. Only in the Netherlands did the majority of teachers teach the same subject for more than 20 hours per week. Finally, large within-country differences in time spent teaching the subject existed in Hungary and Thailand.

All teachers in Canada Quebec, Hungary, the Netherlands, and Nigeria taught two or fewer additional subjects. In all of these countries except Hungary, seventh or eighth grade students were included in the study. And, in Hungary, the subject matter was physics. In Thailand, almost two-thirds of the teachers taught two or fewer additional subjects. In contrast, more than three-fourths of the teachers in Israel (grade 6) and the Republic of Korea (grade 5) taught five or more additional subjects. Large within-country differences in the number of additional subjects taught existed in the two remaining replications (Canada Ontario-English and Canada Ontario-French) in which data on this variable were collected. The majority of teachers in seven of the replications had a total teaching load of more than 21 but less than 30 hours. In Canada almost all teachers reported a total teaching load of more than 11 but less than 20 hours. The majority of teachers in Nigeria and Thailand had a similar teaching load.

Home Variables

In most countries in which data were collected, three-fifths or more of the students' parents had attained a secondary school education or some level of higher education. Exceptions occurred in Thailand (in which 70 percent or more of the parents received no higher than a primary education) and in Nigeria (where slightly more than one-half of the mothers had received no higher than a primary education). Data on parents' education were not collected in Australia or Canada Quebec.

The majority of students in Canada Ontario-English, Canada Ontario-French, Israel, and the Netherlands reported coming from middle class homes. In Hungary, the Republic of Korea, and Thailand, the majority of students reported coming from working class homes. Finally, within-country variation in social class was quite large in Australia and Nigeria (with data on this variable not collected in Canada Quebec).

The language of instruction was always used in the homes of almost all students in Canada Quebec, Hungary, the Republic of Korea, and the Netherlands. In contrast, for more than one-fourth of the students in Canada Ontario-English, Canada Ontario-French, Israel, and Thailand, the language of instruction was used in the home either "sometimes" or "never." In Nigeria, as has been mentioned, almost four of five students reported the language of instruction was "sometimes" or "never" spoken in the home.

Student Variables

In almost all countries, about one-half of the students were male; one-half were female (plus or minus seven percent). About one-half or more of the students in all countries intended to stay in school beyond the age of compulsory attendance. In Canada Ontario-English, Canada Ontario-French, Canada Quebec, Israel, the Republic of Korea, the Netherlands, and Nigeria, this figure exceeded 75 percent. One-half or more of the students in these countries (with the exception of Nigeria) also planned to pursue some form of higher education. Nevertheless, the percent of students planning to pursue a higher education ranged from less than one-third in Australia to more than four-fifths in Canada Ontario-English.

Data pertaining to the pretests cannot be directly compared since tests administered to the students in each country were unique. Similarly, although the attitudinal data were collected using similar instruments, the means on the attitude toward school and attitude toward subjects are not directly comparable since the meaning of individual items may differ according to the culture and language of the students who responded to those items (as has been mentioned in Chapter 2).

Summary

In this chapter the settings within which the studies were conducted were described and the differences between the countries in terms of school, teacher, home, and student characteristics were explicated. The countries differed widely in terms of school location, school type, and school size. They also differed in terms of the number of hours of instruction per year devoted to the subject matter included in the study. The vast majority of schools in each country, however, housed only elementary students.

The participating countries also differed in the predominant sex of the teachers, and their age and years of experience. Within most countries, however, differences among the teachers in age and years of experience also were notable. The vast majority of teachers included in the study were certified at the elementary school level. Those certified at the secondary school level were exceptions (even for the teachers of seventh and eighth grade students).

Teachers in the various countries also differed in their subject matter training, the number of hours per week spent teaching the subject matter, and the number of additional subjects taught. Fairly large within-country differences in subject matter training also existed. The vast majority of teachers in all countries taught a total of 11 to 30 hours per week.

Large within-country differences also existed in terms of the educational level of the parents and the occupation level of the father. With the exceptions of the Republic of Korea and Thailand, between-country differences on these variables were fairly small.

Differences between countries in terms of the percentage of students who received their instruction in the same language as that predominantly spoken in the home were quite large. Within-country variations on this variable also were evident.

Finally, comparisons among the students themselves were minimally useful. Roughly equal proportions of boys and girls were included in each country. Between-country comparisons of pretest and attitudinal scores were fraught with hazard. Furthermore, within-country differences on the pretest and attitudinal measures were quite large.

The only between-country differences worth noting concerned the educational aspirations of the students. Countries differed greatly in the number of students intending to remain in school beyond the age of compulsory attendance and the number of students who planned to pursue some form of higher education.

The general picture that emerges from this analysis is one of diversity, both between and within countries. Such diversity is important in two respects. Between-country diversity helps us better understand the nature of the settings within which the various studies were conducted. Within-country diversity, on the other hand, helps to identify those variables which may be associated with student and classroom differences in achievement and attitude in particular countries. As we move to Chapter 4, then, we shall examine the extent to which these between- and within-country differences in school, teacher, home, and student characteristics are reflected in the perceptions and classroom behaviors of both teachers and students.

4

Description of Classroom Teaching and School Learning

One of the major purposes of the Classroom Environment Study was to provide descriptions of the similarities and differences in the nature of classroom teaching and school learning in the participating countries. Using the country as the unit of analysis, this chapter provides summary descriptions of the context and process of teaching and learning from three perspectives: that of the classroom teacher, that of trained observers, and that of the students in the classroom.

The chapter addresses four primary questions. To what extent did teachers in the various countries experience similar constraints on their instructional practices, classroom activities, and teaching behaviors? How similar were the instructional practices reported by the teachers? How similar were the classroom activities and teaching behaviors recorded by the observers? Finally, how similar were students' perceptions of their classrooms, their participation in the activities of the classroom, and their achievement?

Each of these four primary questions is addressed in one of the major sections of this chapter. The first section presents data concerning the classrooms within which the teaching and learning occurred, and the extent to which school and classroom factors were believed to act as constraints on teachers' decision-making. The second section reports the data on reported instructional practices, while the third section includes data on observed classroom activities and teaching behaviors. The fourth section includes data on student perceptions of their classrooms, their participation in classroom activities, as well as their achievement. The final section presents a summary of findings with respect to the four questions posed above. Wherever possible, between-country and within-country differences are identified, and the perceptions of teachers, observers, and students are compared.

It should be noted that available data from all participating countries are reported in this chapter. In some cases, large amounts of missing data were evident. Where missing data exceeded 20 percent, a notation is made in the tables or figures included in the chapter.

This chapter was written by Doris W. Ryan, Angela Hildyard, and Sid Bourke, with the assistance of Richard Wolf.

72   *Doris W. Ryan, Angela Hildyard, and Sid Bourke*

Classroom Contexts

In all countries teachers are generally assigned by school administrators to teach specified subject matters to particular groups of students for certain lengths of time. Variations in these contextual aspects of instruction—class size, classroom organization, materials supportive of teaching, and time schedules—result less from teacher choice than from organizational constraints and the availability of resources.

As we shall see, teachers in the various studies taught in classrooms which differed in the sheer number of students as well as in the heterogeneity of those students. The time allocated for teaching and learning the specified subject matter also varied, particularly from one country to the next. Finally, teachers reported different levels of autonomy in making a variety of curricular and instructional decisions. These differences were evident both from country to country (that is, between-countries) and for teachers within the same country (that is, within-country).

Class Size

Class size and pupil-adult ratio in the classroom are commonly believed to affect the nature of the teaching-learning process. In very large classes, for example, teachers may find it difficult to use small group practices or interact frequently with individual students. Data on class size were collected by the classroom observers and are summarized in Fig. 4.1.

As can be seen, teachers in the different countries were confronted with quite varying class sizes. For example, elementary science teachers in Hungary had classes of 30 students, on the average, while those in the Republic of Korea had classes of more than 50 students. The smallest average class sizes were about 24 students in Canada Ontario-French and about 25 students in the Netherlands. The largest average class sizes were about 41 in Nigeria and approximately 54 in the Republic of Korea. In the remaining countries average class sizes were approximately 30.

Quite large within-country differences in class sizes also were evident. The smallest within-country range was from 24 to 33 in Canada Quebec, while the largest within-country range was from 17 to 57 in Thailand. Differences of 20 students or more between the smallest and largest classes existed in almost all countries.

The number of students that teachers are expected to manage and teach on any given day may be less than the official class size because of student absences. As can be seen in Fig. 4.1, however, absenteeism was small in all countries. In Israel, the Republic of Korea, and the Netherlands, no more than one student was absent on a typical day. In Canada Ontario-English, Nigeria, and Thailand, the rates averaged from 2 to 3 students per day. Other countries were somewhere between these two extremes.

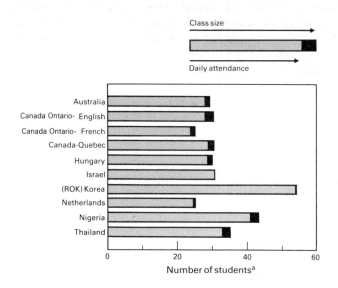

FIG. 4.1   Average class size and daily attendance.[b]
[a] The horizontal axis represents the mean number of students enrolled in, and attending, classes over all observations.
[b] Source: CIIF.

Finally, the impact of class size on teaching may be decreased by placing additional adults in the classroom. However, in virtually all classrooms in every country only one adult (the teacher) was present; few, if any, teaching assistants or aides were noted by observers.

In summary, then, both between-country and within-country differences in class size were found to exist. The "official" class size appears to be a valid indicator of the number of students for whom teachers are responsible since (1) absence rates were uniformly low across classes and countries, and (2) additional adults were almost never observed in any classes.

Class Ability/Achievement Levels

Teachers may adjust their instructional approach or teaching style to the ability or achievement levels of their students. For example, teachers may assign more independent work to higher achieving students, while feeling the need to supervise quite closely the work of less able students. As can be seen in Fig. 4.2, teachers in the various countries perceived the ability levels of their classes somewhat differently.

As also can be seen in Fig. 4.2, between 20 and 30 percent of the teachers in Canada Quebec and the Netherlands stated that their classes of students had *higher* ability levels than did other similar classes. In contrast, between 30 and 40 percent of the teachers in Australia, Canada Ontario-English, and Thailand perceived the ability levels of their classes of students to be *lower than* those of similar classes (that is, classes of same-age students studying the same subject matter). As expected, the majority of teachers in all countries (with the possible exception of Canada Ontario-English) reported the ability level of their classes to be "about average."

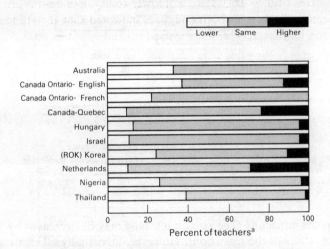

FIG. 4.2   Teachers' perceptions of relative class ability level.[b]
[a] The horizontal axis represents the percentage of teachers who perceived the ability level of their students, compared with same-age students in the same subject matter, to be (respectively) lower, the same, or higher.
[b] Source: ITQ.

Several differences between the countries also were evident in teachers' perceptions of the number of their students who were in need of remedial instruction at the beginning of the school (see Fig. 4.3). Over 30 percent of the teachers in Nigeria and Thailand reported that most or all of their students were in need of such remediation. In contrast, 90 percent or more of the teachers in Canada Quebec, Hungary, and the Netherlands stated that none or few of their students needed remedial instruction. In fact, the most frequent response given by teachers in all countries except Nigeria and Thailand was that none or few of their students required remedial instruction.

Thus far the data displayed in Fig. 4.3 have been examined from a between-country perspective. The data also can be perused from a within-country point of view. Consider the perceptions of relative class ability level reported by the teachers in Canada Quebec or the Republic of Korea. In Canada Quebec approximately 10 percent of the teachers reported teaching students who, as a class, were of lower ability than most other classes. At the same time, however, somewhat more than 20 percent of these teachers said they taught students who, as a class, were of higher ability than most other classes. In the Republic of Korea, the situation was almost exactly the opposite. Approximately 10 percent of the teachers reported teaching students who, as a class, were of higher ability than most other classes. At the same time, however, somewhat more than 20 percent of the Korean teachers said they taught students who, as a class, were of lower ability than most other classes. The remaining teachers in both countries indicated that the students they taught were, on the average, quite typical of students in general.

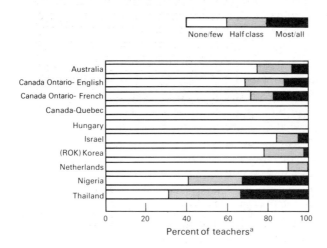

FIG. 4.3   Teachers' perceptions of students' need for remediation.[b]
[a] The horizontal axis represents the percentage of teachers, respectively, who perceived that none/few, half the class, or most/all of their students were in need of remedial work in their subject matter at the beginning of the school year/term.
[b] Source: ITQ.

In Thailand, teachers were almost equally divided into those who reported that few if any students needed remedial instruction, those who reported that about half of the class needed remedial instruction, and those who reported that most or all of the class needed remedial instruction. In contrast, consider the relative homogeneity of the classes in Hungary and Israel. In both of these countries, the vast majority of teachers reported their class ability levels to be fairly typical, with few if any students in need of remedial instruction.

Furthermore, as expected, a relationship exists across countries between the teachers' perceptions of relative class ability level and the teachers' perceptions of their students' need for remediation. The Spearman rank order correlation of the proportion of teachers who perceived their classes to be of lower-than-average ability and the proportion of teachers who perceived that at least one-half of the students in their classes would need remedial instruction was 0.79. Thus, in those countries (technically countries and provinces) in which more teachers perceived their classes to be of lower-than-average ability, more teachers also perceived that a greater percentage of their students required remediation.

As can be seen, then, both between-country and within-country differences existed in the class ability and achievement levels of the students as reported by their teachers. While the between-country differences are potentially interesting, they may well simply indicate differences in the sampling plan used in the various countries. Since, for example, the estimates of class ability level are made relative to the other classes in the school, it seems reasonable that most of the classes in any school are viewed as "typical" with a few seen as "above average" and a few seen as "below average." Thus, patterns such as those found in Canada Quebec and the Republic of Korea are expected. In the remaining countries, particular types of classes (e.g., high ability, low ability) may have been oversampled.

While the between-country differences are interesting and expected, the within-country differences are both unexpected and problematic. These differences were unexpected in that the original study design called for the inclusion of classes enrolling students of similar ability levels. These differences are problematic in that similar teaching practices and teacher behaviors are unlikely to be effective for students differing widely in ability and prior achievement levels. Furthermore, because of the well-established linkage between entering ability or prior achievement and subsequent achievement, these initial differences in class ability levels are likely to be reflected in end-of-study differences in class achievement levels regardless of the type or quality of instruction presented and received.

The data reported thus far in this section were collected from teacher reports. Prior to the beginning of the study, however, students were administered tests either of their knowledge of the content to be taught during the study or their general aptitude for learning the subject matter. The mean for each class in each country was computed, as was a mean of the class means. These country means, the means for the lowest and highest scoring classes, and the number of items on the tests are displayed in Table 4.1.

Because the tests differed in the number of items, the range of scores between the highest and lowest scoring classes in each country was standardized by dividing by the test length. These standardized ranges, shown in the far right-hand column, represent the proportion of the total number of items reflected in the differences between the highest and lowest scoring classes. Thus, for example, this difference in Australia and Thailand is slightly more than one-half of the items included on the test.

As can be seen in Table 4.1, the differences between the means of the highest and lowest scoring classes are substantial in most countries. The largest differences are those in Australia and Thailand, as mentioned. The smallest differences are those in Canada Ontario-French and Nigeria. These differences are approximately 17 and 21 percent of the items, respectively. Quite interestingly, the standardized ranges shown in Table 4.1 parallel the perceived differences among classes presented in Fig. 4.2. The rank order correlation of the standardized ranges and the percentage of teachers who perceived the ability levels of their classes to be atypical (that is, either above or below average) is 0.65.

In summary, large between-class differences in ability and achievement existed within virtually every country. These differences were evident both from teachers' reports and from class mean scores on the pretests.

TABLE 4.1   *Number of items, overall means, class minimums,*
and class maximums on cognitive pretests

Country	Items	Mean	Minimum	Maximum	Range	Range/Items
Australia	25	14.2	6.8	20.4	13.6	0.54
COE	40	15.8	8.6	24.0	15.4	0.39
COF	40	12.9	9.2	16.0	6.8	0.17
CQ	25	14.3	10.3	20.3	10.0	0.40
Hungary	25	14.8	10.6	18.2	7.6	0.30
Israel	30	18.8	14.2	23.5	9.3	0.31
Korea (ROK)	25	11.0	8.3	14.7	6.4	0.26
Netherlands	20	12.7	9.2	16.4	7.2	0.36
Nigeria	50	14.4	11.8	22.2	10.3	0.21
Thailand	35	12.3	5.2	23.7	18.5	0.53

Notes: The three Canadian replications are abbreviated as COE (Canada Ontario-English), COF (Canada Ontario-French), and CQ (Canada Quebec). The standardized ranges in the far right-hand column represent the range (that is, the maximum class mean minus the minimum class mean) divided by the total number of items included on the test. Thus, a standardized range of 0.40 (as in the case of Canada Quebec) indicates that the difference between the highest and lowest scoring classes was equal to 40 percent of the total number of items on the pretest.

Time Allocated for Teaching and Subject Matter

The nature of teaching and learning may differ according to the amount of time teachers have to teach and students have to learn the subject matter. For example, it seems fairly obvious that students can be exposed to more of the subject matter when more time is allocated to its study. The data with respect to time allocation, displayed in Fig. 4.4, were collected by the classroom observers.

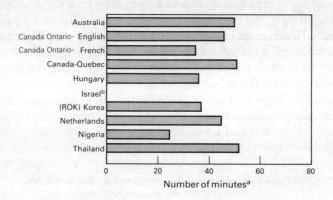

FIG. 4.4   Average length of observed lessons (allocated time).[c]
[a] The horizontal axis represents the mean length, in minutes, of all observed lessons per teacher, averaged over all teachers per sample.
[b] Data not reported.
[c] Source: CIIF.

As can be seen in Fig. 4.4, between-country differences on this variable were quite large. Some of these differences can be explained, at least partially, by variation in the subject matters included in the studies. The fifth and sixth grade science lessons in Hungary and Korea, for example, lasted an average of 36 or 37 minutes, while the fifth grade mathematics lessons in Australia and Thailand were approximately 50 minutes long.

Other differences appear to be between-country differences. Five replications included teachers of eighth grade mathematics in the study. The average length of mathematics lessons within these replications varied considerably, from slightly over 20 minutes in Nigeria to slightly over 50 minutes in Canada Quebec. The average length of the eighth grade mathematics lessons in Canada Ontario-English and the Netherlands was approximately 45 minutes, while the average in Canada Ontario-French was approximately 35 minutes.

Within-country variation in allocated time across lessons was surprisingly large. Differences between the shortest and longest lessons observed ranged from just over 12 minutes in the Republic of Korea to over 50 minutes in Canada Quebec. Differences of 20 minutes or more occurred in the majority of the countries.

Because these data were collected by classroom observers, it is possible that on a few occasions the observers left before the lesson had been completed. Differences between the longest lesson and the average lesson, however, support the diversity of lesson length. The median difference in length of the longest lesson and the average lesson across all countries was approximately 10 minutes.

Teacher Autonomy

Because of differences in class size, class ability level, and allocated time, it seems reasonable to assume that teachers in the various countries operated within different organizational constraints. Do such constraints impact on curriculum and instruction? Could, for example, teachers decide whether to assign homework, and, if so, how much homework to assign? Similarly, could teachers determine the nature and frequency of their contacts with parents? From the point of view of this study, one could assume that classroom activities and teaching behaviors would be more similar in those countries in which teachers reported less autonomy in terms of curricular and instructional decisions.

To answer these questions teachers were asked to indicate the extent to which they were able to make a variety of curricular and instructional decisions that may impact on their ability to teach and the way in which they did, in fact, teach. Figure 4.5 displays the responses made by the teachers in each study in terms of the percentages of teachers who reported being "fully free" or "free to a large extent" to make decisions in the various areas.

Across all countries, teachers generally reported the least freedom to make decisions concerning the selection of topics to be taught (TS) and interactions with parents (PI). In contrast, they generally reported the highest levels of autonomy with respect to decisions about the assignment of homework (HW), the manner in which their classrooms are organized (CO), and the use of achievement tests (AT). With respect to the other four decision-making areas, the majority of teachers in about one-half of the studies reported having a great deal of autonomy, while the majority of teachers in the other half reported having less autonomy.

Despite this general teacher consensus across countries in many of these areas, there were wide ranges between the extreme cases in virtually each area. For example, while none of the Canada Quebec teachers reported they were fully or to a large extent responsible for selecting the topics they taught, one-half or more of the teachers in Australia and Israel said they were either fully or largely responsible for this decision.

Australia   Canada Ontario-English[a]   Canada Ontario-French   Canada-Quebec

Hungary   Israel   Korea (ROK)   Netherlands

Nigeria[b]   Thailand

Percent of teachers reporting
levels of autonomy for:

TS: Topic selections
MS: Materials selection
SQ: Learning sequencing
CO: Classroom organization
AT: Use of achievement tests
MP: Minimum promotion requirements
HW: Homework assigned
PR: Parent reports
PI: Parent interactions-meetings

100%
Not at all
To some extent
To a large extent
Fully

FIG. 4.5 Teacher autonomy: perceptions of responsibility
for curricular and instructional decisions.[c,d]
[a] PR and PI not reported.
[b] Missing data exceeded 20 percent.
[c] The maximum percentage represented by a single bar is 100 percent,
e.g., for Canada Ontario-English, category SQ.
[d] Source: ITQ.

Even more striking is the difference between the Canada Quebec and Hungary teachers with regard to their role in making decisions about classroom organization. The vast majority of the Canada Quebec teachers said they were fully responsible for these decisions, while the vast majority of the Hungarian teachers said they were not at all responsible for such decisions.

Finally, the different heights of the nine shaded bars within each country illustrate the extent to which teachers differentiate their autonomy in terms of the various curricular and instructional decisions. Bars of similar heights indicate little differentiation, while bars of different heights indicate a great deal of differentiation. Once again, this analysis focuses on within-country differences.

In Australia and Israel, for example, teachers perceived themselves as having decision-making authority in all nine areas. In Canada Quebec, Hungary, Nigeria, and Thailand, on the other hand, teachers seem to clearly differentiate those curricular and instructional areas in which they do and do not have the authority for making decisions. In Canada Quebec, Nigeria, and Thailand, for example, teachers are in general agreement that their autonomy in making decisions concerning topic selection and minimum promotion requirements is quite limited. In Hungary, teacher autonomy is reported to be limited in the areas of topic selection, material selection, and classroom organization.

Interestingly, teachers in most countries disagreed as to the extent to which they had autonomy for decision-making in all of the areas included on the list. In the Netherlands, for example, an almost equal percentage of teachers reported having complete autonomy, a large amount of autonomy, limited autonomy, and no autonomy at all in the area of parent meetings. Thus, like class size, class ability level (both perceived and actual), and time allocated for the subject matter under study, perceptions of teacher autonomy in curricular and instructional matters tended to vary both between and within countries.

Instructional Practices

On the Initial Teacher Questionnaire, teachers were asked to report on their typical practices in a variety of curricular and instructional areas. These areas included instructional materials, classroom organization (i.e., whole class, small groups, and individualized), teacher roles and typical behaviors (e.g., monitoring, disciplining, questioning, providing student help), and homework and tests. Summaries of their reported practices in these areas are included in this section.

Using Various Instructional Materials

In Fig. 4.6, the relative heights of the bars in each country indicate the

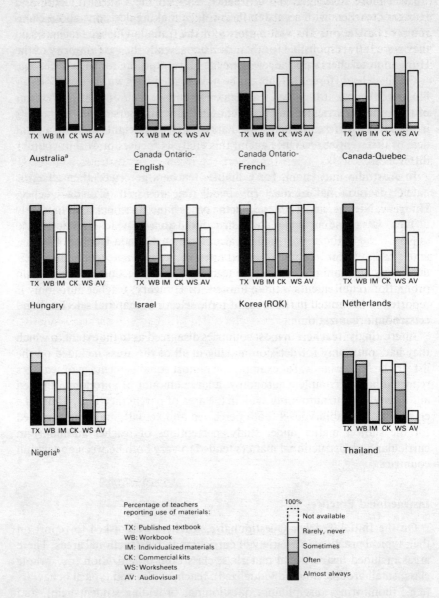

FIG. 4.6 Teacher reports of use of types of materials.[c,d]
[a] WB not available.
[b] Missing data exceeded 20 percent.
[c] The maximum percentage represented by a single bar is 100 percent,
e.g., for Australia, category TX.
[d] Source: FTQ.

range of materials available to teachers in each country. Thus, for example, teachers in Australia, Canada Ontario-English, Hungary, and the Republic of Korea have access to a wide variety of instructional materials. In contrast, teachers in Israel and the Netherlands have access to less of a variety. Not surprisingly, the vast majority of teachers in Nigeria and Thailand do not have access to audio-visual materials.

As can be seen in Fig. 4.6, published textbooks were reported to be the most frequently used instructional materials in virtually all countries. Large proportions of teachers in Hungary, Israel, the Republic of Korea, the Netherlands, Nigeria, and Thailand reported that they almost always used published textbooks. Exceptions were the teachers in Australia who relied somewhat more heavily on individualized and audio-visual materials, and teachers in the three Canadian replications who appeared not to have a clear preference for the use of any particular type of instructional materials.

One notable finding in Fig. 4.6 is the variation among teachers within each country in their reported use of the various instructional materials. In Israel, for example, a few teachers reported using individualized materials almost always, while equal proportions of teachers reported using such materials "often," "sometimes," and "rarely or never." Interestingly, however, a majority of the Israeli teachers indicated that individualized materials were not available to them. Similar examples can be given in virtually every country.

Finally, teachers were asked to report whether students had access to textbooks outside of school (see Fig. 4.7).

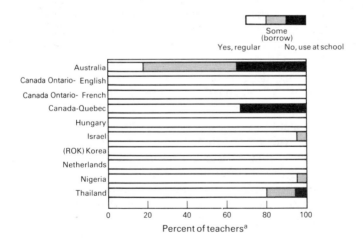

FIG. 4.7   Percent of teachers reporting student access to books to take home.[b]
[a] The horizontal axis represents the percentage of teachers, respectively, who reported that students could take books home regularly, could sometimes borrow books, or could use them only at school.
[b] Source: FTQ.

In all countries except Australia and Canada Quebec an overwhelming number of teachers indicated that students were able to take books home for out-of-school study. As has been mentioned earlier, teachers in Canada Quebec reported less frequent use of textbooks. Thus, access may be less problematic. Finally, the Australian data should be viewed somewhat tentatively since a large proportion of teachers did not respond to this question.

Organizing the Class for Instruction

As was seen in Fig. 4.5, teachers in most countries reported they were relatively free to make decisions concerning classroom organization. However, the majority of teachers in most of the countries reported that they used whole class instruction to teach new content either a "fair amount" or "great deal" of time (see Fig. 4.8). Furthermore, teachers in all countries indicated they used whole class instruction more frequently than small group instruction to review previously taught content. In fact, teachers in all countries reported spending little if any time in small group instruction. The greatest use of small group instruction was reported by teachers in Australia and Nigeria.

As a separate issue, teachers were asked to indicate the frequency with which they individualized instruction. Across all countries, few teachers responded that they individualized instruction very frequently. In fact, the modal responses were "often" in Australia, Hungary, Nigeria, and Thailand, "sometimes" in the three Canadian replications and Israel, and "rarely or never" in the Republic of Korea and the Netherlands.

Despite these modal responses, variation among the teachers within countries is once again notable. In Canada Ontario-French, Israel, Nigeria, and Thailand, for example, a sizable minority of teachers reported using individualized instruction "very frequently." At the other extreme, however, slightly larger proportions of teachers in Nigeria and Thailand and much larger proportions in Canada Ontario-French and Israel indicated they "sometimes" individualized their instruction. The most homogeneous country in this regard was the Netherlands where all teachers reported using individualized instruction sometimes, rarely, or never.

One might expect that those countries in which teachers reported more frequent formation of small groups would also be the countries in which teachers reported greater use of individualized instruction. Such was not the case, however. More than one-half of the teachers of Australia, Hungary, Israel, Nigeria, and Thailand indicated they "very frequently"or "often" individualized instruction. As can be seen in Fig. 4.8, these five countries differed widely in their formation of small groups either for teaching new content or reviewing.

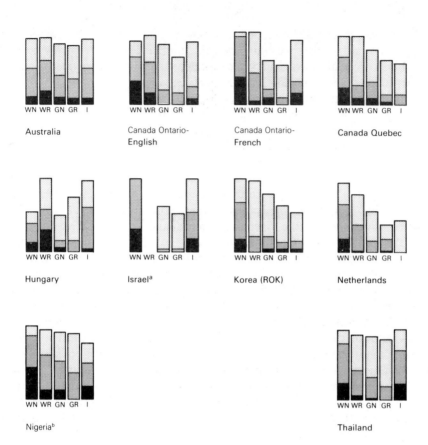

FIG. 4.8   Teachers' reports of typical use of
grouping and of individualization.[c,d]
[a] WR not reported.
[b] Missing data exceeded 20 percent.
[c] The maximum percentage represented by a single bar is 100 percent,
e.g., for Canada Ontario-French, category WN.
[d] Source: FTQ.

Spending Time in Various Instructional Activities

The data displayed in Fig. 4.8 also suggest that teachers spent at least a "fair amount" of time teaching new content or reviewing previously taught content. In addition, teachers spent at least some of their time in other instructional and classroom management activities (see Fig. 4.9).

In most countries teachers reported spending at least a "fair amount" of time in two primary activities: monitoring individual seatwork and asking questions. Teachers in Hungary, Israel, and the Republic of Korea were exceptions to this generalization. Quite interestingly, these three countries were the only ones in which mathematics was *not* taught during the study.

The vast majority of teachers in all countries except Nigeria reported spending little or no time correcting papers, engaged in disciplinary action, or involved in routine administrative activities. Once again, however, it must be noted that many of the Nigerian teachers did not repond to these questions on the Initial Teacher Questionnaire.

Two other discrepancies from the overall pattern of responses are worth noting. First, approximately forty percent of the teachers in Thailand reported spending a "great deal" or a "fair amount" of time correcting papers or engaged in disciplinary action. As will be seen, the observation data concerning the Thai teachers' use of discipline does not support these perceptions. Second, nearly one-half of the Israeli teachers indicated they spent at least a fair amount of time correcting student papers. This finding is not surprising in that history was used as the subject matter in the Israeli study.

Quite interestingly, much greater consensus among teachers within countries occurs on these variables than on the previous ones. For example, the vast majority of teachers in all countries (with the possible exception of Nigeria) reported spending little if any time on routine administration. Similar levels of consistency in teacher responses occurred with respect to correcting papers and discipline. Variation among the teachers did exist on the time reportedly spent monitoring individual seatwork, asking questions, and to a somewhat lesser extent, monitoring group seatwork.

Using Various Questioning Practices

As was mentioned in the previous section, teachers reported spending at least a "fair amount" of time questioning their students. On the Initial Teacher Questionnaire, teachers were asked to indicate the nature of the questions they typically asked their students. Specifically, teachers were asked to indicate the frequency with which they asked questions that required their students to recall previously taught information (RC), to seek answers in books (SK), to express an opinion (OP), or demonstrate by their explanation that the content had been comprehended (EX). The results are summarized in Fig. 4.10.

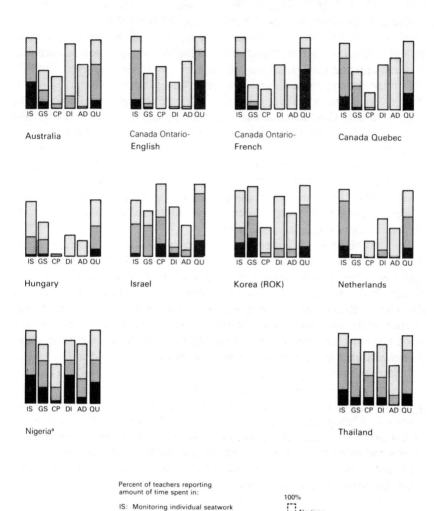

FIG. 4.9 Teacher reports of time spent apart from
presentation of new content and review.[b,c]
[a] Missing data exceeded 20 percent.
[b] The maximum percentage represented by a single bar is 100 percent,
e.g., for Canada Ontario-French, category IS.
[c] Source: FTQ.

About two-thirds of the teachers in all countries reported they "very frequently" or "often" asked recall questions. A majority of the teachers in all countries reported that they "very frequently" or "often"asked comprehension questions. In only Hungary, Israel, and the Republic of Korea, however, did the reported frequency of comprehension questions exceed that of recall questions. Once again, these were the three countries in which mathematics was *not* the subject matter included in the study.

In all countries, questions requiring students to seek answers in books were reportedly the least frequently asked. However, the variation among the countries was greatest for this type of question. A majority of the Israeli teachers reported asking such questions "often" or "very frequently." In contrast, the majority of the teachers in Canada Ontario-English, the Netherlands, and Nigeria reported asking such questions "rarely or never."

In most of the countries, opinion questions were reportedly asked less frequently than recall or comprehension questions, but somewhat more frequently than questions requiring students to seek answers from books. Exceptions occurred in Israel and the Republic of Korea where teachers indicated they asked opinion questions more frequently than they did recall questions. Once again, differences in subject matter (history and science, respectively) may account for these findings.

Finally, within-country differences among teachers are evident once again in Fig. 4.10. Somewhat more agreement among teachers existed in their reports of "answer seeking" questions. With respect to the other three types of questions, however, wide variation among teachers was evident in virtually all countries.

Providing Extra Help

Teachers were asked to indicate the extent to which they provided extra help to students who seemed to be experiencing difficulty learning or were learning poorly. Their responses are summarized in Fig. 4.11.

The majority of teachers in all countries except Israel, the Republic of Korea, and the Netherlands reported they "very frequently" or "often" provided extra help to students. However, this help was given to a small number of students in most countries, typically less than one-half of the class. Exceptions occurred in Australia and Nigeria where the majority of teachers reported providing extra help to at least one-half of the students in the class.

A comparison of these results with those pertaining to the teachers' reports of their students' needs for remediation (see Fig. 4.3) leads to a fairly predictable conclusion. In those studies in which teachers reported a greater proportion of their students in need of remediation, they also reported providing help to more of the students (rho = 0.65).

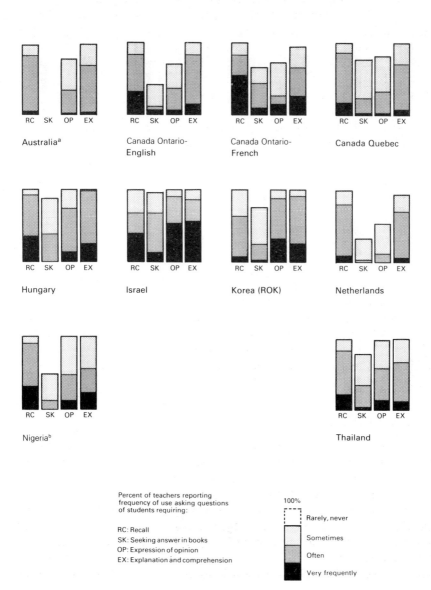

FIG. 4.10   Teacher reports of how questions are asked of students.[c,d]
[a] SK not reported.
[b] Missing data exceeded 20 percent.
[c] The maximum percentage represented by a single bar is 100 percent,
e.g., for Canada Ontario-English, category RC.
[d] Source: FTQ.

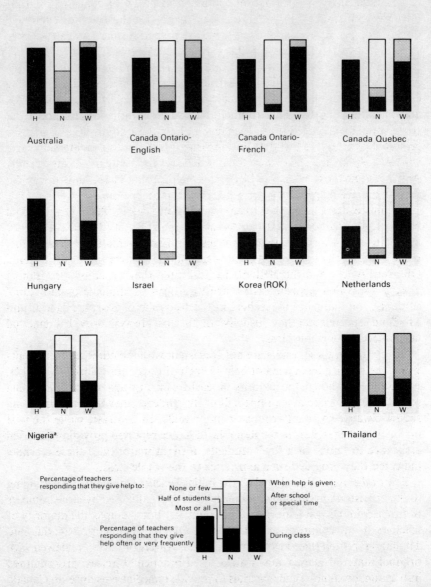

Fig. 4.11   Teacher reports of the frequency and timing of extra help
and the number of students receiving extra help.[b,c]
[a] Missing data exceeded 20 percent.
[b] The maximum percentage represented by an H bar is 98 percent,
for Thailand; the N and W bars all show 100 percent.
[c] Source: FTQ.

The final piece of information contained in Fig. 4.11 concerns the time during which teachers provided the extra help. Did they provide such help during class, or after school or at some other special time? As can be seen, the countries differed widely on this variable. In Australia, Canada Ontario-English, Canada Ontario-French, Canada Quebec, and the Netherlands, the majority of teachers reported that extra help was provided to students during class. In contrast, the majority of teachers in the Republic of Korea, Nigeria, and Thailand reported that extra help was provided either after school or at some specially arranged time. Teachers in these three countries also had the largest class sizes (see Fig. 4.1) thus making it difficult to provide individual student help during class time. Finally, teachers in Hungary seemed evenly split between those who provided extra help during class, and those who provided extra help either after school or at another time.

Finally, teachers were asked to report on the manner in which the additional help was provided to the students. As can be seen in Fig. 4.12, little consistency among teachers in the various countries exists on this matter. For example, while most of the teachers in Australia, Canada Ontario-English, Canada Ontario-French, and the Netherlands indicated they "usually" or "almost always" provided remedial assistance to groups of students or individual students, the majority of teachers in the Republic of Korea, Nigeria, and Thailand reported that they "usually" or "almost always" provided remedial assistance to the whole class.

Interestingly, these results are not consistent with the numbers of students who were reportedly in need of help in each of the countries (see Fig. 4.11). For example, although the majority of teachers in Australia reported providing remedial assistance to at least one-half of the students, they reported providing such assistance to small groups or individuals. In contrast, while the vast majority of the teachers in the Republic of Korea reported providing remedial assistance to "none or a few" students, a slight majority of these teachers indicated they provided such assistance to the whole class.

Few of the materials included on the Initial Teacher Questionnaire pertaining to the provision of remedial assistance were reportedly used by large numbers of teachers in the vast majority of the countries. For example, the majority of teachers in all countries except Canada Quebec, Hungary, Nigeria, and Thailand reported that they "sometimes" or "rarely or never" reviewed with original material or new material, or used practice exercises, programmed instruction, or audio-visual materials to provide remedial assistance. In Canada Quebec, a slight majority of the teachers indicated they conducted reviews with the original instructional materials. In Hungary and Nigeria, a majority of the teachers reportedly used practice exercises. And in Thailand a majority of the teachers said they reviewed with both original and new instructional materials as well as used practice exercises. It seems important to point out that audio-visual materials and programmed instructional materials were least likely to be used to provide remedial assistance in virtually every country.

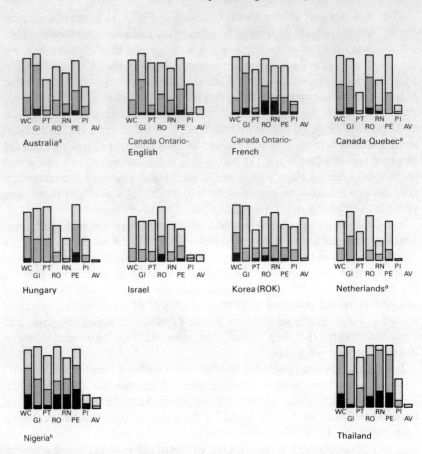

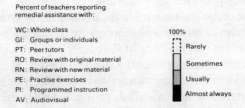

Percent of teachers reporting
remedial assistance with:

WC: Whole class
GI: Groups or individuals
PT: Peer tutors
RO: Review with original material
RN: Review with new material
PE: Practise exercises
PI: Programmed instruction
AV: Audiovisual

100%

Rarely

Sometimes

Usually

Almost always

FIG. 4.12   Teacher reports of formats and types of remedial assistance
used for their students.[c,d]
[a] AV not reported.
[b] Missing data exceeded 20 percent.
[c] The maximum percentage represented by a single bar is 100 percent,
e.g., for Australia, category GI.
[d] Source: FTQ.

Assessing and Evaluating Students

Teachers in all countries indicated they had relatively high autonomy concerning the assignment of homework. Not surprisingly, then, there were large differences within each country as to the amount of homework assigned per school week (see Fig. 4.13). In the Republic of Korea, for example, almost 20 percent of the teachers assigned no homework or one homework assignment per week of school. Approximately 40 percent assigned homework two or three times per week, while the remaining 40 percent or so assigned homework almost every school day.

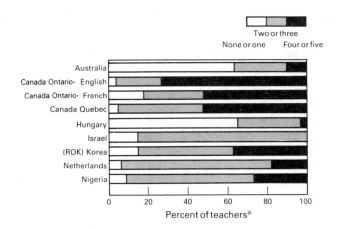

FIG. 4.13.   Teachers' estimates of the number of homework assignments
during a five-day period.[b]
[a] The horizontal axis represents the percentage of teachers who,
during a five-day period, assigned homework never or once,
two or three times, and four or five times, respectively.
[b] Source: FTQ.

Despite these within-country differences, some differences among countries also are evident. For example, daily assignments were given by the majority of the teachers in all three Canadian replications. In contrast, the majority of teachers in Australia and Hungary reported giving one or fewer homework assignments each school week. The majority of the teachers in Israel, the Netherlands, Nigeria, and Thailand indicated they gave two or three homework assignments per week. Finally, as has been mentioned, the teachers in the Republic of Korea were fairly equally divided in the frequency with which they gave such assignments to their students.

Teachers were asked to indicate the frequency with which they used particular types of assignments and tests for two primary purposes: grading students and diagnosing students' learning weaknesses. The results are summarized in Figs. 4.14 and 4.15. In considering these results the emphasis will be placed on the proportion of teachers who reported they used each type of test or assignment "very frequently" or "often."

As can be seen in the figures, countries differed in the number of different tests and assignments that were used by the teachers. For example, none of the tests or assignments were used "very frequently" or "often" for diagnostic purposes by a majority of the teachers in Israel. Similarly, none of the tests or assignments were used "very frequently" or "often" for grading purposes by a majority of teachers in Canada Quebec. On the other hand, a majority of the teachers in Nigeria and Thailand reported using four different types of tests and assignments for diagnostic purposes, and five different types for grading purposes.

In general, homework was the primary vehicle for diagnosing student weaknesses in four countries (Canada, the Republic of Korea, Nigeria, and Thailand). Oral tests (including classroom participation in a question-answer format) were used "very frequently" or "often" by the majority of teachers in Australia, Hungary, and the Netherlands. A majority of teachers in Canada Ontario-English and the Netherlands also reported frequent use of short quizzes, while a majority of teachers in the Republic of Korea reported frequent use of combined tests (i.e., tests including both objective and open-ended questions) in addition to homework. As has been mentioned, no clear preference emerged from the teachers in Israel.

In contrast to the reliance on homework for diagnostic purposes, tests were the primary vehicle for assigning grades, although the format of the tests varied from country to country. In Australia, Canada Ontario-French, and the Netherlands open-ended tests were reportedly used by the largest percentage of teachers. Objective tests were used by the largest percentage of teachers in Canada Ontario-English, oral tests by those in Hungary, and combined tests by teachers in the Republic of Korea. In Nigeria, Thailand, and Israel, homework was most used by the largest number of teachers to assign grades. Finally, no preference among teachers was evidenced in Canada Quebec.

Once again, the large within-country variation in teacher reports is present in Figs. 4.13 through 4.15. This variation has been mentioned already with respect to the assignment of homework. Similar variation in the use of the various assignments and tests for both grading and diagnostic purposes also is clear.

Some consistency does exist, however. The vast majority of teachers in most countries rarely if ever use projects or reports to assign grades to students or to diagnose their learning deficiencies (the exceptions being Hungary, Israel, and Nigeria). Similarly, teachers in the Netherlands were in high levels of agreement concerning their non-use of objective tests, combined tests, and homework for grading purposes.

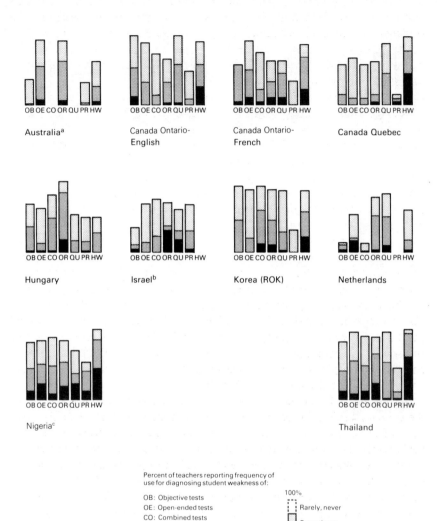

FIG. 4.14   Teacher reports of tests used for diagnosing student weaknesses.[d,e]
[a] No data for CO or QU.
[b] No data for HW.
[c] Missing data exceeded 20 percent.
[d] The maximum percentage represented by a single bar is 97 percent,
for Hungary, category OR.
[e] Source: FTQ.

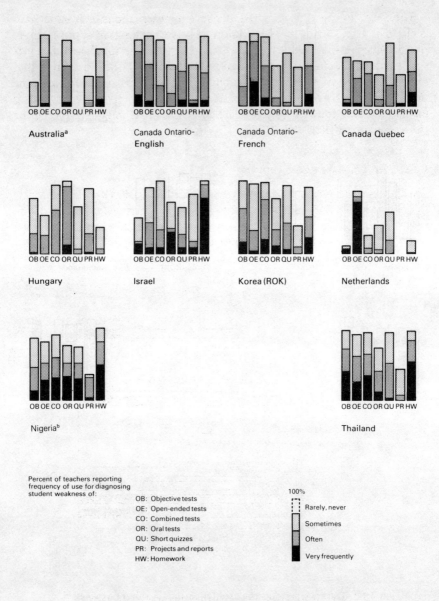

Percent of teachers reporting
frequency of use for diagnosing
student weakness of:

OB: Objective tests
OE: Open-ended tests
CO: Combined tests
OR: Oral tests
QU: Short quizzes
PR: Projects and reports
HW: Homework

100%

Rarely, never

Sometimes

Often

Very frequently

FIG. 4.15   Teacher reports of tests used for grading.[c,d]
[a] No data for CO or QU.
[b] Missing data exceeded 20 percent.
[c] The maximum percentage represented by a single bar is 100 percent,
e.g., for Canada Ontario-French, category OE.
[d] Source: FTQ.

Classroom Activities and Teacher Behaviors

The design of the study required that several observations be conducted in each classroom. During the observation, observers completed approximately five SNAP-FMI-IAR sequences (see Chapter 3). As a national option, it was suggested that teachers be interviewed briefly prior to the observation so that observers would be aware of the emphasis and objective of the lesson to be observed. The data to be reported in this section were derived from the three primary observation instruments (the SNAP, the FMI, and the IAR) and the Pre-Observation Interview (POI).

Lesson Emphases and Objectives

The Pre-Observation Interview was conducted in six of the studies. This interview yielded data related to the emphasis and intended objective of the lesson. The data were summed across both teachers and lessons producing a metric which represented the *percentage of observed lessons* with particular emphases and particular objectives (see Figs. 4.16 and 4.17).

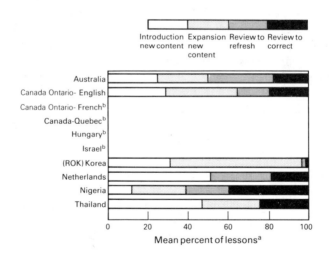

FIG. 4.16 Teachers' reports of the emphasis of observed lessons.[c]
[a] The horizontal axis represents the mean percentage of lessons, over all teachers and observed lessons, that were intended to emphasize introduction of new content, expansions of new content, review to refresh, and review to correct errors, respectively.
[b] Data not reported.
[c] Source: POI.

The portrait painted in Fig. 4.16 is one of large within-country variation in all countries except the Republic of Korea. Virtually all of the lessons in the Republic of Korea emphasized the teaching of new content, either by introducing the new content or expanding on it. One must keep in mind, however, that the observation portion of the study conducted in the Republic of Korea lasted for two consecutive weeks. Thus, it is quite possible that the teachers emphasized the learning of new content during that entire time period.

In Australia, Canada Ontario-English, and Nigeria, all four lesson emphases were in evidence, although the predominant emphasis differed in the three countries. In Australia, somewhat more of the lessons were spent helping students remember what previously had been taught. In Canada Ontario-English somewhat more of the lessons were spent on expansions of new content. Finally, in Nigeria the emphasis of almost 40 percent of the lessons was review for the purpose of correcting students' mistakes and misunderstandings.

In Australia and the Netherlands an equal number of lessons was spent on teaching new content and on reviewing previously taught content. Interestingly, in the Netherlands, all of the teaching new content lessons focused on introducing the content. No lessons were spent on expansions of the content, once introduced.

Finally, in Thailand, as in the Republic of Korea, the vast majority of the lessons emphasized the teaching of new content (both introduction and expansion). Interestingly, all of the review lessons were conducted for the purpose of correcting students' mistakes and misunderstandings. With respect to lesson emphasis, then, both within-country and between-country variations were evident.

The picture is slightly different in the Fig. 4.17. While the within-country variation is still quite obvious, the between-country variation is minimal. In no country were many lessons spent primarily on the development of social skills. Rather, in most countries the lessons were fairly equally distributed among the three major academic objectives. In the Netherlands and Nigeria a somewhat greater proportion of the lessons was spent on the use of rules. And in Australia and Thailand a somewhat greater percentage was spent on comprehending concepts. Typically, the fewest number of lessons with an academic focus addressed the objective of problem solving (although in Canada Ontario-English and the Republic of Korea almost one-third of the lessons were devoted to this objective).

It is worth noting that on the Initial Teacher Questionnaire all participating teachers were asked to estimate the frequency with which they informed their students of their instructional objectives. In all countries with the exception of the Netherlands the majority of the teachers responded that they "always" or "usually" did so. For the Netherlands teachers, however, informing students of objectives is apparently not a common practice since only about 10 percent of these teachers did so.

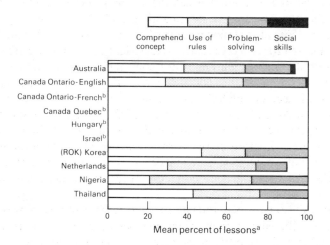

FIG. 4.17 Teachers' reports of the objective of observed lessons.[c]
[a] The horizontal axis represents the mean percentage of lessons, over all teachers and observed lessons, for which the teachers' objectives were to teach comprehension, use of rules, problem-solving, and social skills, respectively.
[b] Data not reported.
[c] Source: POI.

Classroom Activities

On the Snapshot instrument, observers recorded the nature of the class-room activity in which teachers and students were engaged. As has been mentioned, five Snapshots were "taken" during each observed lesson. The Snapshot data were summed first across the five Snapshots taken during each lesson, then across all lessons taught by each teacher, and finally across all teachers within each country. The metric for reporting the classroom activity data, then, was the percentage of Snapshots during which each activity was observed and coded.

Ten possible activities were included on the Snapshot. These activities could be separated into three categories: a teacher talk or teacher-student communication category (C), a student work category (S), and a category containing classroom management and other activities (O). Each category contained two or more activity formats (see Fig. 4.18).

In all countries except Australia formats within the communication category occurred more frequently than did formats within the student work category. In Australia the increased frequency of student work formats is quite likely

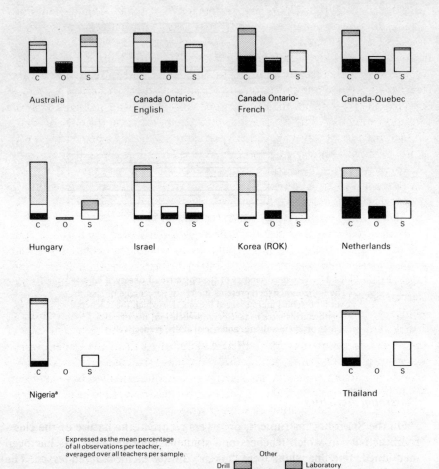

FIG. 4.18   Relative frequency of observed activity formats
related to teaching students.[b,c]
[a] Missing data exceeded 20 percent.
[b] The maximum percentage represented by bar C is 84 percent in Nigeria,
by bar O is 19 percent in Canada Quebec,
by bar S is 47 percent in Australia.
[c] Source: SNAP.

the result of several teachers who employed student-paced, individualized instruction (see Bourke 1984). Excluding Australia, the ratio of communication to student work ranged from approximately 3 to 2 in Canada Ontario-English to approximately 6 to 1 in Nigeria, with a median ratio of approximately 2 to 1 in Thailand.

In all countries, the most frequently occurring format in the communication category was either lecture or discourse. In essence, both of these formats are teacher-directed communication. In discourse, there is somewhat more opportunity for students to talk, although most of the student talk is of short duration and much is in response to a directive or question from the teacher. In fact, because observers have great difficulty predicting when teachers will stop talking and student talk will be permitted or requested, initial portions of discourse formats are often coded as lecture. Drill and review, the two formats most associated with student talk, were used infrequently in most countries with the exceptions of the Canadian replications and the Netherlands, in which the review format was used reasonably often.

Quite expectedly, the nature of student work mirrored the nature of the subject matter taught. In those countries in which mathematics was the subject matter under investigation, written seatwork predominated. Some laboratory work occurred in the mathematics classrooms in Australia. In the science classrooms, particularly in Korea and to a somewhat lesser extent in Hungary, laboratory work prevailed. Finally, the history classrooms of Israel were the only ones in which students were observed to be reading at their seats. In both Hungary and Israel about one-half of the student work was written. Finally, time spent in classroom management activities was nonexistent in Hungary, Nigeria, and Thailand, and quite small in Israel and the Republic of Korea. In fact, the vast majority of classroom time in all countries was spent in communication or student work.

One final comment must be made concerning the activity format labeled "Other." "Other" was included on the Snapshot instrument in order to avoid the potential problem of the category system influencing the results of the study. If, for example, observers had but two categories to choose from in recording a particular aspect of classroom instruction, these two categories would be coded with high frequency. Perhaps, however, if other categories were available, the frequencies with which the first two categories were coded would decrease substantially. The activity format labeled "Other" permitted activities not on the list to be recorded as they were observed.

From the data displayed in Fig. 4.18, however, it can be inferred that activities other than the nine included in the Snapshot instrument occurred extremely seldom if ever in virtually all countries. The only exception was Israel where a small percentage of activities was coded "Other."

The data presented in Fig. 4.18 tend to be inconsistent with data gleaned from teachers' reports of their instructional practices. For example, the between-country rank-order correlation of the time actually spent in activities coded as review and the frequency with which teachers reported spending time in review (Fig. 4.8) was only 0.13, despite the fact that Israel and the Republic of Korea ranked either ninth or tenth on both indicators. Similarly, the between-country rank-order correlation of the time actually spent in activities coded as review and the percentages of lessons for which teachers reported the primary emphasis to be review (Fig. 4.15) was 0.09 ($n = 6$).

The inconsistency of the teacher report data and observers' data across countries is most clearly seen, however, in terms of the classroom management. Here, the between-country rank-order correlation of the time actually spent in management activities and the frequency with which teachers reported spending time in discipline and routine administration was -0.60. To illustrate the nature of this inconsistency, teachers in Nigeria and Thailand reported the most frequent use of disciplinary action and routine administrative activities. In contrast, however, observers in these two countries recorded the least amount of time spent on classroom management activities (which included transitions from one activity to another, distributing or collecting materials, providing general "school-like" information to students, and disciplining students). On the other hand, teachers in Canada Quebec and Canada Ontario-French ranked eighth and ninth, respectively, in terms of the frequency with which they reported using discipline and routine administration. Based on the records made by the observers, however, these two Canadian replications were ranked first and second, respectively, in terms of the actual frequency with which they engaged in classroom management activities. Only in Australia and Hungary were the rankings based on teacher reports and those based on observers' records quite similar.

Teacher Roles and Behaviors

One would expect teachers to engage in different behaviors and to relate to their students in different ways during different classroom activities. Thus, for example, teachers are more likely to be directly interacting with their students during lecture, discourse, review, and drill, and to be supervising and monitoring their students' work during testing, reading, laboratory work, and written seatwork. During these latter activities teachers also may not be involved with their students at all, as when they plan for the next period or day, or correct recently completed homework assignments.

The role assumed by the teacher—interacting, monitoring, or uninvolved—was coded each time the Snapshot was used. Thus, for each activity observed, the role of the teacher was recorded. Data on teacher role were aggregated first across Snapshots within a lesson, next across lessons, and finally across teachers within each country. Thus, the numbers presented in Fig. 4.19 represent the percentage of Snapshots during which each role was observed and recorded.

As can be seen in Fig. 4.19, the role assumed most often by teachers in

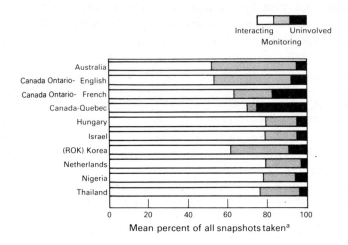

FIG. 4.19   Observed frequencies of teachers' interacting and
monitoring activities and uninvolved time.[b]
[a] The horizontal bar represents the mean percent of all Snapshots
taken (five per lesson, times the number of lessons, times the number of
teachers) over all observations and teachers in each sample.
[b] Source: SNAP.

every country was direct verbal interaction with their students. This finding
is quite expected since, as we have seen in Fig. 4.18, the majority of the
activities in most countries were of the general communication type (that is,
lecture, discourse, review, and drill). In fact, the rank-order correlation
across countries of the frequency of lecture, discourse, review and drill and
the frequency with which teachers assumed a direct verbal interaction role
with students was 0.85. As has been suggested earlier, such activities almost
require that teachers assume a very direct role with their students.

In general, the frequency with which teachers were uninvolved with their
students was quite low. Exceptions to this generalization occurred in Canada
Ontario-French and Canada Quebec. In Canada Quebec, either teachers
were directly interacting with students or they were not involved with them
at all. These teachers monitored and supervised their students' work very
infrequently. Teachers in Canada Ontario-French spent roughly equal proportions of the time monitoring students and not being involved with them.

Finally, although Australian teachers made use of seatwork activities
more frequently than communication activities, these teachers were coded as

verbally interacting with their students during slightly more than one-half of the Snapshots. This finding is quite compatible with the student-paced, individualized approach to mathematics in which teachers interact verbally with their students on a one-to-one or small group basis, while other students are engaged in seatwork.

Direction of Teacher-Student Interactions

The flow of conversation in classrooms can conceivably go in many directions: from teachers to groups of students or to individual students; from groups of students or individual students to the teachers; from students to students; and, if multiple adults are present in the classroom, from adults to adults. The data pertaining to the communication flow were collected using the Five-Minute Interaction (FMI) instrument. Since this instrument focused primarily on the teacher, student to student communication was not recorded.

Like the Snapshot data, the FMI data were first aggregated within each lesson, then across lessons, and finally across teachers within each country. As a consequence, the data represent the percentage of all observed interactions that were coded into a particular FMI category. Figure 4.20 presents the percentage of interactions that were directed from teachers to individual students, teachers to groups of students, individual students to teachers, groups of students to teachers, and teachers to other people in the classroom (e.g., aides, parents, school administrators, students carrying messages).

In Fig. 4.20, one notes immediately that communication between teachers and other people occurred very infrequently, if at all, in all countries. This finding is not surprising since, as has been mentioned earlier in this chapter, teachers were almost always the only adult in the classroom. Aides were seldom present; administrators or parents may have "dropped in" for a few minutes on one or two occasions.

Exceptions to this generalization occurred in all three Canadian replications and in Australia, where between five and ten percent of all observed teacher interactions involved another adult. It is interesting to note that the two Canadian replications with the largest percentages of "teacher-to-other" interactions were also the two studies in which teachers spent the most time not involved with their students (Canada Ontario-French and Canada Quebec).

One can examine the data displayed in Fig. 4.20 in at least two ways. First, one can compare the relative heights of the bars in the first two columns. This comparison indicates how much of the total communication was with individual students and how much was with groups. In Australia, Canada Ontario-French, Hungary, Israel, and the Netherlands, the heights of these two bars are quite similar. In these countries, then, as much commmunication occurs between teachers and individual students as between teachers and groups. In the Republic of Korea, Nigeria, and Thailand (and to a somewhat

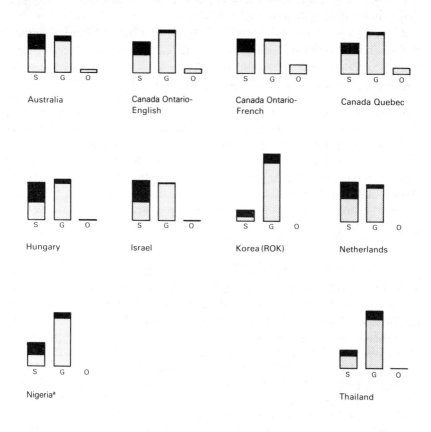

Australia

Canada Ontario-English

Canada Ontario-French

Canada Quebec

Hungary

Israel

Korea (ROK)

Netherlands

Nigeria[a]

Thailand

Expressed as the mean percent of all observed interactions per teacher, averaged across all teachers per sample.

Student to teacher   Group to teacher

Teacher to other

Teacher to student   Teacher to group

FIG. 4.20   Direction of observed interactions: who spoke to whom.[b,c]
[a] Missing data exceeded 20 percent.
[b] The maximum percentage represented by bar S is 51 percent in Israel,
by bar G is 84 percent in Korea (ROK),
by bar O is 12 percent in Canada Ontario-French.
[c] Source: FMI

lesser extent in Canada Ontario-English and Canada Quebec) far more communication occurs between teachers and groups than between teachers and individual students.

A second way of examining the data in Fig. 4.20 is to consider and compare the portions of both bars with lighter shadings (indicating teacher to student communication) with the portions with darker shading (indicating student to teacher communication). In all countries, virtually all of the communication with groups of students flowed from the teachers to the students. In several countries (e.g., Hungary, Israel, and Nigeria), however, the more personal teacher-student contact was as likely to go from the student to the teacher as from the teacher to the student. In the remaining countries, although slightly more of the one-to-one communication flowed from the teacher to the student, a fairly substantial portion flowed from the student to the teacher. As we shall see, however, most of the student-to-teacher communication involved giving fairly short answers to teacher-posed questions, rather than initiating the conversation.

Nature of Instructional Behaviors

Six of the FMI categories related to the teacher's delivery of instruction. These categories were the (1) provision of cues to structure students' learning, (2) provision of directions (e.g., Here's how to work the problems on your worksheets) and directives (e.g., Take out your homework papers from yesterday), (3) explanation of content and subject matter, (4) use of instructional materials in support of their explanations, (5) demonstrations of some procedure or skill, and (6) use of examples to illustrate major points made during the explanations. Although teachers' use of questions can be viewed as part of a teacher's instructional delivery, questioning will be addressed in the following section.

Data pertaining to these six categories of instructional delivery were collected from the FMI. Once again, the data were aggregated first within each lesson, then across lessons, and finally across teachers. The data represent the percentage of all interactions coded into each of these six categories. When interpreting these data it should be kept in mind that an average frequency of one percent is roughly equivalent to three such interactions during each 25 minutes of observed class time.

The data displayed in Fig. 4.21 are arranged into three columns for each country. The organization of the data represent three of the primary functions that teachers can accomplish as they deliver their instruction to their students. One reasonable sequence in which these three functions can be accomplished is as follows. Teachers may begin by orienting students to the objectives (e.g., Today we're going to learn how to divide fractions) and the proper behavior related to learning the objective (e.g., Open your books to page 119). In Fig. 4.21, this function is labeled SD.

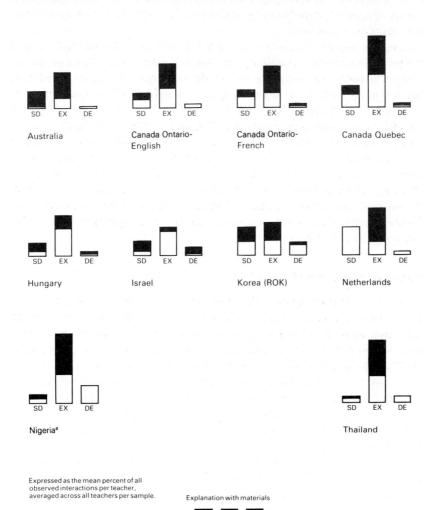

FIG. 4.21   Observed frequencies of teacher interactions coded as cues,
directions, explanations, explanations with materials,
demonstrations, and examples.[b,c]
[a] Missing data exceeded 20 percent.
[b] The maximum percentage represented by bar SD is 13 percent
in the Netherlands, by bar EX is 32 percent in Canada-Quebec,
by bar DE is 8 percent in Nigeria.
[c] Source: FMI

Teachers next may provide explanations related to the objective and focused on the specific knowledge students need for mastery (e.g., If we are to divide fractions correctly, we must understand what a "multiplicative inverse" is. In mathematics, an inverse is defined as (continues with explanation). So, when you multiply a fraction by its multiplicative inverse you always get one). During these explanations teachers may or may not make use of a variety of props (e.g., concrete objects, filmstrips, overhead projectors). In Fig. 4.21, this function is labeled EX.

Finally, teachers may use demonstrations or examples to help make the abstract knowledge more concrete for their students (e.g., The multiplicative inverse of 4/5 is 5/4. The multiplicative inverse of 1/2 is 2/1. The multiplicative inverse of 3/2 is 2/3). This function is labeled DE in Fig. 4.21.

As can be seen in Fig. 4.21, instructional delivery in virtually all countries consisted primarily of teacher explanation. Explanations accounted for more than 20 percent of all observed interactions in Canada Quebec, the Netherlands, Nigeria, and Thailand. In fact, the lowest frequency of observed use of explanations was slightly more than 13 percent.

In contrast, the use of demonstrations and examples occurred very infrequently in most countries, with the exception of the Republic of Korea and Nigeria. In the remaining countries, fewer than four percent of all observed interactions involved these two categories. Quite interestingly, examples were rarely if ever given in most countries. In view of the fact that in seven studies mathematics was the subject being taught, the infrequent use of examples is surprising, if not disturbing.

Finally, the frequency with which teachers used structuring cues, directions, and directives ranged from approximately 3 percent in Thailand to just over 15 percent in the Netherlands. In Australia, Hungary, and Israel, the majority of student orientation was provided via directions and directives. In contrast, the majority of student orientation in the three Canadian replications, the Netherlands, and Thailand was provided through structuring cues. Finally, in the Republic of Korea and Nigeria, student orientation was provided using directions, directives, and structuring cues.

Questions and Answers

Data pertaining to three aspects of teacher questioning will be presented and discussed in this section: (1) the target and type of questions, (2) the nature of students' responses to the questions, and (3) the ways in which teachers reacted to students' responses. Once again, the data were collected from the FMI and, thus, were aggregated in the typical fashion (see Fig. 4.22).

Between-country differences in the target of teacher questions are evident in Fig. 4.22. In Australia, Canada Ontario-French, and particularly the Netherlands, the majority of questions were directed to individual students. In Canada Ontario-English, Hungary, Nigeria, and Thailand, on the other

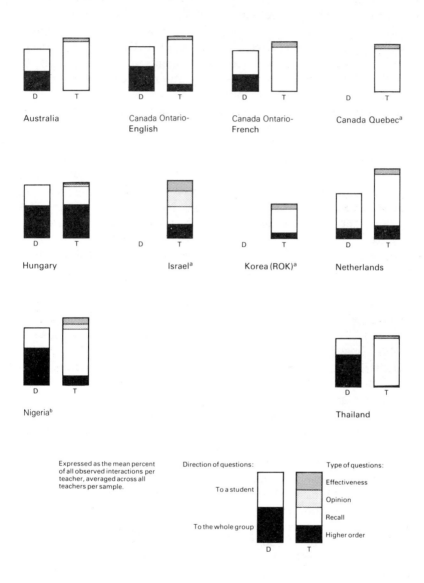

FIG. 4.22 Observed frequencies of teacher questioning practices.[c,d]
[a] Direction percentages not available.
[b] Missing data exceeded 20 percent.
[c] The maximum percentage represented by bar D is 13 percent in Nigeria,
by bar T is 16 percent in the Netherlands.
[d] Source: FMI.

hand, the majority of questions were directed to the whole class. As is indicated in Fig. 4.22, data on the target of teacher questions were not collected in Canada Quebec, Israel, and the Republic of Korea.

The most predominant type of question in the vast majority of the countries was the recall question. Exceptions occurred in Hungary and Israel. In Hungary, most of the questions required students to make inferences about what they had been taught. In Israel, the questions asked were almost equally divided among the four questioning categories.

In general, however, opinion and higher-order questions tended to be asked rarely by teachers in most countries. These findings are contrary to the teachers' self-reports (see Fig. 4.10). For example, the majority of teachers in Hungary, Israel, the Republic of Korea, Nigeria, and Thailand reported asking opinion questions "often" and "very frequently." Of these four countries, only in Israel did observers record a reasonable number of such questions. Despite their claims to the contrary, then, teachers rarely asked questions that required students to express and defend their opinions, or to integrate or evaluate the information presented to them.

Figure 4.23 presents data concerning the nature of students' responses to the questions. Four categories of responses were included on the FMI: short response, recitation, extended response, and cannot answer. As can be seen in Fig. 4.23, the vast majority of responses made by students to teacher questions (90 percent or more in most countries) were short. Only in Israel, in which history was taught during the study, did large proportions of the questions require extended responses. It should be pointed out that the frequency with which students gave short responses to questions is quite consistent with the frequency with which recall questions were asked by the teachers.

Quite interestingly, students almost always gave answers to the questions they were asked. Only in Israel was the category "cannot answer" coded at all. Finally, recitation as a questioning technique was never used in the Netherlands, and rarely used in the remaining countries.

Figure 4.24 displays the reactions of teachers to the answers given by the students. The FMI included several categories of teacher reactions. Specifically, teachers could acknowledge the answer (that is, indicate that the answer was correct), repeat the answer, indicate the answer was incorrect, or wait for an answer. The variable "waits for an answer" was defined as the extent to which teachers waited at least five seconds for students to respond before they reacted in some way. Furthermore, if an answer was not given, was incorrect or was partially correct, teachers could give the answer, redirect the question, or probe for further information. Probes can be directed either to individual students or to the whole class.

As can be seen in Fig. 4.24, the most frequent reactions of teachers to students' answers were either to indicate the answer was correct (Australia, Canada Ontario-French, Israel, and Nigeria), repeat the answer (Canada

FIG. 4.23 Observed frequencies of types of student responses
to questions asked by the teacher.[c,d]
[a] REC percentages not available.
[b] Missing data exceeded 20 percent.
[c] The maximum percentage represented by bar SR is 19 percent in Australia,
for bars REC, ER, and CNA, the maximum percentages are 5 percent,
7 percent, and 1 percent, respectively, in Israel.
[d] Source: FMI.

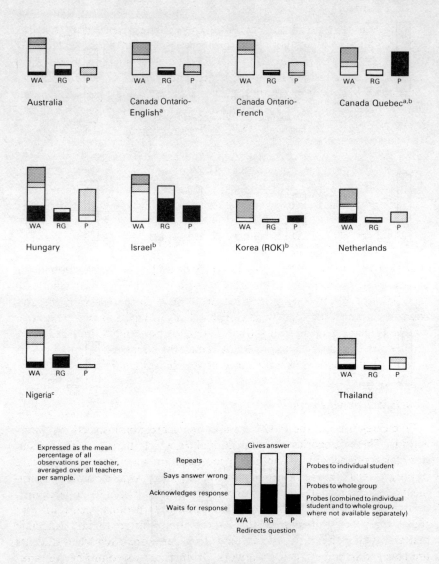

FIG. 4.24 Observed frequency of type of
teacher reactions to student responses.[d,e]
[a] Waits for response data not available.
[b] Probe to whole group and probe to individual student not available
separately, so they are presented combined.
[c] Missing data exceeded 20 percent.
[d] The maximum percentage represented by bar WA is 9 percent, for Hungary,
the maximum by bar RG is 6 percent, for Israel,
and the maximum by bar P is 5 percent, by Hungary.
[e] Source: FMI.

Ontario-English, the Republic of Korea, the Netherlands, and Thailand), or to probe the student or students (e.g., Canada Quebec and Hungary). Teachers rarely waited for student responses (with the exception of Hungary), indicated an answer was wrong (with the exceptions of Israel and Nigeria), or gave the answer. Redirecting questions to other students was a fairly common practice only in Hungary, Israel, and Nigeria.

Large within-country variation also is evident in Fig. 4.24. In Canada Ontario-French, for example, teachers were equally likely to react to students' answers by repeating the answer or by probing students. This variation seems reasonable since correct answers are more likely followed by repeated answers, while incorrect answers are more likely followed by probes. Unfortunately, the nature of the answer given by the student was not recorded on the FMI. Similar within-country variation can be seen in virtually all countries, particularly Hungary, Israel, the Netherlands, and Thailand.

Student-Initiated Interactions

As has been mentioned, the vast majority of student communication in the classroom was in response to teachers' questions, requests, and demands. In fact, student-initiated comments occurred very infrequently in the five countries in which such data were available. Only in Thailand, where approximately 14 percent of all interactions were coded as student-initiated, were such comments fairly common. In the remaining countries, no more than 3 percent of all interactions were coded as student-initiated.

Non-Instructional Interactions

Five categories on the FMI were used to record non-instructional interactions. These categories were transitional (in which there is a change from one classroom activity to another), procedural (in which teachers take care of business matters such as calling the roll or putting away laboratory equipment and materials), disciplinary (in which teachers attempt to stop inappropriate behavior), silence (in which no verbal interactions occurred), and social (in which the tone of the conversation shifted to non-academic matters). Quite obviously, silence tends to occur more often when students are engaged in some type of seatwork. In fact, across countries the rank-order correlation of the frequency with which silence was observed and the frequency with which students were engaged in laboratory work or seatwork was 0.56.

Non-instructional interactions occurred far less frequently in Canada Quebec, Israel, the Netherlands, and Nigeria, than in the other countries (see Fig. 4.25). Procedural interactions occurred quite frequently in Australia and in the two Canada Ontario replications. The majority of the non-instructional interactions in Hungary, the Republic of Korea, Nigeria, and

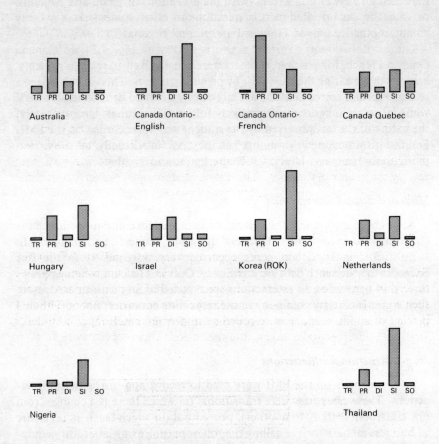

FIG. 4.25   Observed frequencies of non-instructional interactions.[a,b]
[a] The maximum percentage represented by a single bar is
24 percent, for Korea, category SI.
[b] Source: FMI.

Thailand, on the other hand, were silence. Disciplinary interactions occurred frequently only in Israel and, to a somewhat lesser extent, Australia. Social interactions occurred somewhat frequently only in Canada Quebec. Finally, transitions occurred infrequently in all countries. This last finding suggests that teachers did not shift from one classroom activity to another very often within the same lesson, or if they did so, the transition occurred very smoothly.

Student Participation, Perceptions, and Achievement

Three variables specifically dealing with students were included in the study. The first, student participation, pertained to the proportion of students observed to be engaged in learning, or on-task. The second, student perceptions, concerned the extent to which students believed their classrooms to be task-oriented, and their teachers as providing the proper classroom management and instruction. The third, student achievement, concerned student performance on end-of-study achievement tests.

Student Participation

Data on the amount of student participation was collected from the Snapshot instrument. Because the Snapshot was used approximately five times during each lesson, these data were aggregated first within each lesson, then across lessons, and finally across teachers within each country. The data displayed in Fig. 4.26, then, represent the average percentage of students who were observed to be engaged in the various classroom activities.

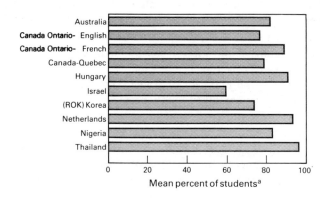

FIG. 4.26   Percentage of students observed to be engaged in assigned activities.[b]
[a] The horizontal axis represents the mean percent of students, over all observations per teacher, over all teachers in the sample, who were observed to be engaged.
[b] Source: SNAP.

Surprisingly wide variation among countries is evident in Fig. 4.26. In Thailand, for example, approximately 96 percent of the students were observed to be on-task across all lessons. In contrast, in Israel only 60 percent of the students were observed to be engaged in appropriate classroom activities. Across all countries, approximately 80 percent of the students were observed to be on-task during the study.

Student Perceptions

Data on student perceptions of the task-orientation of the classroom, their teachers' classroom management, and the nature of the instruction they were provided during the study were collected from the Final Student Questionnaire. Ten items pertained to task-orientation, and eight each to classroom management and instruction. The responses made by students to the individual items are presented in Figs. 4.27 through 4.29.

In the majority of countries, uniformly positive responses were given by students to the items concerning the task-orientation of the classrooms (see Fig. 4.25). The only exceptions occurred in Australia, Hungary, and Israel. The majority of students in Australia reported that their teachers talked about non-academic matters (i.e., "other things"). The majority of students in Hungary indicated they were not expected to do their work. Finally, the majority of students in Israel said that they were not expected to do their work *and* that their teachers talked about non-academic matters.

With respect to students' perceptions of classroom management a similar picture emerges from the data (see Fig. 4.26). In virtually every country, students reported that their teachers were able to manage their classrooms effectively "a lot" or "almost always." It should be pointed out that some of the items were written to reflect a *negative* task-orientation. Item TL, for example, asks students how frequently their teachers talk loudly because of noise in the classroom. "Almost never" would be the most positive response students could make to this item.

Quite interestingly, the majority of students in Australia and Thailand indicated that their teachers talked loudly because of noise "a lot" or "very often." Similarly, the majority of students in Australia and the two Canada Ontario replications reported that their teachers were unable to deal with misbehavior "a lot" or "almost always."

With respect to students' perceptions of their teachers' instructional practices, more variation both within and across countries is evident (see Fig. 4.29). For example, very few of the students in Australia and the Republic of Korea indicated that homework was given "a lot" or "almost always." In contrast, virtually all of the students in the Netherlands indicated that homework was given "a lot" or "almost always." Similarly, the majority of the students in Canada Ontario-French and Hungary indicated that their teachers told them what was important for them to learn "almost always."

ABCDEFGHIJ

Australia

ABCDEFGHIJ

Canada Ontario-
English

ABCDEFGHIJ

Canada Ontario-
French[a]

Canada Quebec[b]

ABCDEFGHIJ

Hungary

ABCDEFGHIJ

Israel

ABCDEFGHIJ

Korea (ROK)

ABCDEFGHIJ

Netherlands

ABCDEFGHIJ

Nigeria[c]

ABCDEFGHIJ

Thailand

Percent of students reporting TRUE (or FALSE) that:

A: Most all class time is spent on lesson
B: People are expected to do their work
C: We do talk about things beside work (FALSE)
D: Getting work done is very important
E: Most people don't do much work (FALSE)
F: We usually do what we set out to
G: Absentees have trouble catching up
H: Teacher talks about other things (FALSE)
I: We spend more time having fun than learning (FALSE)
J: Teacher sticks to work, not sidetracked

FIG. 4.27   Student perceptions of classroom task orientation.[d,e]
[a] No information for item A.
[b] Data not reported.
[c] Missing data exceeded 20 percent.
[d] The maximum percentage represented by a single bar is
98 percent, for Canada Ontario-French, category I.
[e] Source: FSQ.

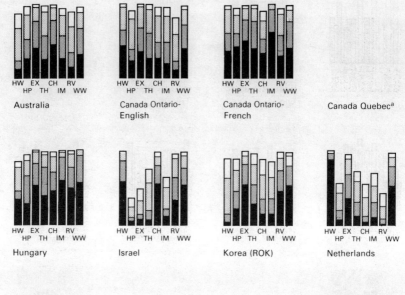

Australia   Canada Ontario-   Canada Ontario-   Canada Quebec[a]
                   English   French

Hungary   Israel   Korea (ROK)   Netherlands

Nigeria   Thailand

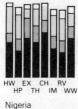

Percent of students reporting frequency
of classroom instructional practices

HW: Teacher gives us homework   100%
HP: Teacher gives me more help   Almost never
EX: Teacher explains things   Not very often
TH: Teacher gets us to think of solutions   Sometimes
CH: Teacher checks on us about completing work
IM: Teacher tells me what is important to learn   A lot
RV: Teacher reviews important things at end   Almost always
WW: Teacher tells why answers are wrong

FIG. 4.28   Student reports of classroom instructional practices.[b,c]
[a] Data not reported.
[b] The maximum percentage represented by a single bar is
100 percent, for Hungary, category EX.
[c] Source: FSQ.

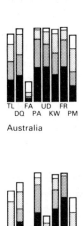
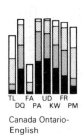
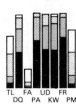

| TL | FA | UD | FR |
| DQ | PA | KW | PM |

Australia

Canada Ontario-
English

Canada Ontario-
French

Canada Quebec[a]

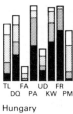
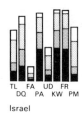
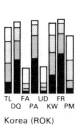
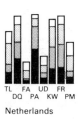

| TL | FA | UD | FR |
| DQ | PA | KW | PM |

Hungary

Israel

Korea (ROK)

Netherlands

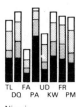
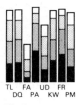

| TL | FA | UD | FR |
| DQ | PA | KW | PM |

Nigeria

Thailand

Percent of students reporting frequency of
classroom management practices

TL: Teacher talks loud because class is noisy
DQ: Teacher deals with misbehavior quickly
FA: Teacher lets the class fool around
PA: Teacher keeps the class paying attention
UD: Teacher is unable to deal with misbehavior
KW: Teacher knows what is going on in class
FR: Teacher makes us follow class rules
PM: Teacher punishes in class for minor misbehavior

100%

Almost never
Not very often
Sometimes
A lot
Almost always

FIG. 4.29 Student perceptions of classroom management practices.[b,c]
[a] Data not reported.
[b] The maximum percentage represented by a single bar is
100 percent, for Canada Ontario-French, category FR.
[c] Source: FSQ.

In contrast, almost one-half of the students in Israel and the Netherlands reported that their teachers informed them of what was important to learn "almost never" or "not very often."

The largest within-country variation across the eight items occurred in Israel and the Netherlands. In Israel, the majority of students said that their teachers gave homework, checked on their completion of work, reviewed important points at the end of the lesson, and told them why answers are wrong "a lot" or "almost always." The majority of these same students, however, reported that their teachers "almost never" or "not very often" provided extra help or explained things. In the Netherlands, the majority of students replied that their teacher assigned homework, gave explanations, and told them why their answers were wrong. In contrast, a majority of students reported that their teachers "almost never" or "not very often" provided extra help, checked on their completion of work, and reviewed important points at the end of the lessons.

Student Achievement

Table 4.2 presents for each study the mean posttest score (based on the class means, rather than individual student's scores), the mean scores of the lowest and highest achieving classes, the difference between the minimum and maximum class mean scores (the range), and the standardized range (as described earlier in this chapter) (see Table 4.1). In five of the studies the same test was used as pretest and posttest (Australia, Canada Ontario-English, the Republic of Korea, Nigeria, and Thailand). As a result, comparisons of pretest and posttest scores can be made in these studies. In the other five studies different tests were used as pretest and posttest. As a consequence, direct pretest-posttest comparisons are not possible in these studies. Finally, because of different subject matters and grade levels, cross-study comparisons of test results are inappropriate and should not be made.

At least two points can be made concerning the data displayed in Table 4.2. The first pertains to the overall student performance on the posttests. The second concerns the magnitude of the difference between the lowest and highest scoring classes.

If the mean percent correct is computed for each study, the range of these means is from 31 percent in Nigeria to 71 percent in the Republic of Korea. In four studies (including Nigeria) the mean of the class means was less than 50 percent correct. In four studies (including the Republic of Korea) the mean of the class means was 60 percent or higher. In the remaining two studies (Canada Ontario-English and the Netherlands) the mean of the class means was slightly more than 50 percent correct. Thus, in many of the classrooms in at least six of the studies, students apparently acquired one-half or less of the knowledge and skills included on the posttests.

As can be seen in Table 4.2, the differences between the lowest and highest

TABLE 4.2 *Number of items, overall means, class minimums, and class maximums on cognitive posttests*

Country	Items	Means	Minimum	Maximum	Range	Range/Items
Australia	25	15.9	6.2	21.9	15.7	0.63
COE	40	21.4	12.8	29.6	16.8	0.42
COF	35	14.4	9.4	17.6	8.2	0.23
CQ	23	9.3	6.6	13.2	6.6	0.29
Hungary	15	9.2	6.1	12.4	6.2	0.41
Israel	40	24.1	14.3	31.5	17.2	0.43
Korea (ROK)	25	17.7	12.7	22.6	9.9	0.40
Netherlands	20	11.3	6.8	16.7	9.9	0.50
Nigeria	50	15.6	12.5	23.8	11.3	0.23
Thailand	35	16.6	10.7	28.8	18.1	0.52

Notes: See notes at bottom of Table 4.1.

scoring classes were substantial in most studies. In the majority of the studies, this difference was equal to 40 percent or more of the total number of items on the posttest. In comparison to Table 4.1 (which contains the pretest data), these differences are greater in all countries except Canada Quebec and Thailand. In Thailand, the two standardized ranges are nearly identical. Thus, the variation among classes within countries was as substantial, if not somewhat more substantial, on the posttest than on the pretest. As will be seen in Chapter 7, one possible reason for this diversity among classrooms and the overall lower mean scores in most studies is that students in the various classrooms differed widely in the extent to which they had the opportunity to learn the knowledge and skills tested by the items on the posttest.

TABLE 4.3 *Mean student scores on pretests and posttests*

Country	Items	Pretest mean	S.D.	Items	Posttest mean	S.D.	Effect size
Australia	25	14.4	5.2	25	16.1	5.3	0.33
COE	40	16.0	6.5	40	21.7	7.7	0.88
Korea (ROK)	25	11.2	4.0	25	17.8	4.7	1.65
Nigeria	50	14.5	4.4	50	15.8	4.9	0.30
Thailand	35	12.7	5.0	35	17.0	6.5	0.86

Notes: Effect size is the difference between mean posttest and mean pretest in standard deviation units. The numerator is simply the mean difference; the denominator is the standard deviation of the posttest. COE is Canada Ontario-English; ROK is the Republic of Korea.

Direct comparisons of the pretest and posttest scores in the five studies in which the same test was used as pretest and posttest are shown in Table 4.3. In all five studies, the mean posttest score is higher than the mean pretest score. In general, the magnitude of these gains in test scores range from about three-tenths of a standard deviation in Nigeria to almost one and two-thirds standard deviations in the Republic of Korea. (The gains in terms of standard deviation units are listed in the column labeled "effective size." The standard deviation of the posttest was used in the denominator to compute the "effect size.")

Referring back to Table 4.2 we can see that in Australia, the minimum class mean score on the posttest is actually *lower than* that minimum class mean score on the pretest, while the maximum class mean score increased by about one and one-half items. In Canada Ontario-English, the minimum class mean score increased by approximately 4 items from pretest to posttest, while the maximum class mean score increased by approximately five and one-half items. In the Republic of Korea, the minimum class mean score increased by about four and one-half items, while the maximum class mean score increased by almost eight items. In Nigeria, the minimum class mean score increased by about one item, while the maximum class mean score increased by about one and one-half items. Finally, in Thailand, the minimum class mean score increased by approximately five and one-half items, while the maximum class mean score increased by about five items.

Summary

Four major questions were posed at the beginning of this chapter. The data presented in this chapter will be summarized in the form of answers to these questions.

Question 1—To what extent did teachers in the various countries experience similar constraints on their instructional practices, classroom activities, and teaching behaviors?

With the exception of student absences (very few) and the number of adults in the classroom (one), both within-country and between-country differences on virtually all contextual variables were found to exist. Differences in class size, class ability level, instructional time, and teacher autonomy were evident.

While the between-country differences may in fact reflect cultural or societal differences, the within-country differences are quite problematic especially given one of the primary purposes of the study: namely, to identify instructional practices, classroom activities, and teaching behaviors that are associated with, and perhaps influence, student achievement and attitudes. Large within-country differences may influence not only practices, activities, and behaviors (as has been suggested throughout this chapter), but also may directly influence the amount and quality of student learning (as hypothesized in the core model in Chapter 2). As a consequence, such within-country differences in contextual variables are likely to hide or mask possible impacts of teaching on learning.

Question 2—How similar were the instructional practices reported by teachers?

With a few exceptions, there was a great deal of similarity in the instructional practices reported by most of the teachers in the various countries. For example, the majority of teachers in virtually all countries reported making extensive use of published textbooks. Teachers also indicated that they used whole class instruction more frequently than they did small group or individualized instruction. When teachers were not presenting new content or reviewing previously taught content, they reported asking questions of the whole class or monitoring their students as they worked on individual assignments at their seats, desks, or tables.

The questions teachers reported asking were more likely to require students to recall or explain previously taught content, and less likely to require students to seek answers in books or express their opinions. Exceptions to this last generalization occurred in the three countries in which mathematics was not the subject matter under investigation (namely, Hungary, Israel, and the Republic of Korea). In these countries, opinion questions were reportedly asked almost as often as recall and comprehension questions.

The majority of teachers in most countries reported that they often or very frequently provided extra help to their students. Such help, however, was reportedly provided to only a few students, generally far less than one-half of the students in their classes. The methods used to provide this additional help varied, moreover, from country to country, as did the time at which the help was provided (e.g., during class, after school).

The frequency with which homework was assigned also varied widely from country to country, with a mode of one assignment per week in one country and one assignment per day in another. In about one-half of the countries the majority of teachers said they used homework assignments for the purpose of identifying those content areas in which their students were weak. In several of the other countries oral tests (including recitation) were reportedly used for this purpose. With respect to the grading of students, the preferred type of test or assignment used to assign grades varied from one country to the next, although for the most part written formal tests were reported to be used most frequently for this purpose.

The above generalizations focus on between-country differences in reported instructional practices. Once again, within-country differences were evident in the data gathered on most of these practices. In contrast with the discussion of the first question, however, such within-country differences are important in the light of the overall purpose of the study. Since such differences do exist, we may concern ourselves with the extent to which they are related to differences in student learning.

Question 3—How similar were the classroom activities and teaching behaviors recorded by the observers?

Several generalizations seem to follow from the data pertaining to classroom activities and teaching behavior. When considering these generalizations, however, the reader should keep in mind that there is at least one country in which virtually every one of these generalizations does not hold.

First, a substantial number of lessons emphasizing the review of previously taught content was observed in many countries. If viewed on a weekly basis, from one to three lessons per week were typically spent primarily on review.

Second, the objectives of the lessons varied greatly both within countries and across countries. At the same time, however, non-academic or social-interpersonal objectives were rarely pursued.

Third, more "talk" than "work" was observed in most countries. This generalization is supported by the data pertaining to classroom activities as well as the role of the teacher. Furthermore, teachers typically talked to groups of students using a lecture or engaging in discourse. During most of the time they were talking teachers were providing explanations to the students (with or without the use of supplementary materials such as the chalkboard). Demonstrations and the use of examples were rare. Structuring cues, directions and directives, however, occurred with reasonable frequency.

Fourth, questions were asked almost routinely in most countries. While the target of the questions (individual students or groups) differed across countries, the vast majority of them required students to recall previously taught content. Virtually all of the answers given by students were of short duration. Extended responses (and interestingly, no responses) occurred rarely if ever.

Fifth, students almost always spoke only when asked to speak. Student verbal initiations were rare in most countries. Drill and recitation also were rarely observed.

Sixth, teachers reacted to students' answers by indicating they were correct or repeating them (quite likely when they were in fact correct), or by redirecting them to other students or probing for additional information (quite likely when they were incorrect or partially correct). Teachers rarely if ever said that answers were wrong or gave the students the correct answer.

Seventh, for at least some portion of time in the classrooms, silence occurred. Quite typically, silence occurred when students were engaged in some type of work at their seats, desks, or tables. The nature of the seatwork tended to depend on the subject matter, with written seatwork used almost exclusively in mathematics and laboratory seatwork in science. Students almost never were observed to be simply reading a book or other written material at their seats.

Finally, non-instructional activities and behaviors occurred fairly frequently in many of the countries. Most of these activities and behaviors involved procedural matters (e.g., calling roll). Transitions between activities, disciplinary actions, and social interactions were kept to a minimum.

Question 4—How similar were students' perceptions, their participation, and their achievement?

Starting with the last part of this question first, no direct comparison of student achievement across countries was possible in view of the design of the study. Nonetheless, students in the various countries differed widely in terms of the percent of items they answered correctly on the posttest (from just over 30 percent to just over 70 percent). Furthermore, in those countries in which the same test was used as pretest and posttest, the magnitude of the changes differed widely (from almost one-third of a standard deviation to almost one and two-thirds of a standard deviation).

Perhaps more striking were the class mean posttest scores within countries. The median posttest score of the lowest scoring classes across all ten studies was 30 percent correct. In contrast, the median posttest scores of the highest scoring classes across all ten studies was 80.5 percent correct. Thus, across all studies, the average student in the highest achieving class answered approximately 50 percent more items correctly than the average student in the lowest achieving class. Unfortunately, but as might be expected, these differences were also evident on the pretests. As we shall see in Chapter 6, substantial correlations between students' pretest and posttest scores were found in all countries.

In the vast majority of the countries students' perceptions of their classrooms and teachers were uniformly positive. Students tended to see their classrooms as "business-like" and task-oriented. They saw their teachers as able to properly manage the classrooms and control student behavior. There was somewhat more variation, both between countries and within countries, with respect to students' perceptions of their teachers' instructional practices. Thus, although observers' records produced similar classroom activities and teaching behaviors across most classrooms, students appeared to perceive certain differences in their teachers' practices, activities, and behaviors.

In general, the vast majority of students were observed to be engaged in learning, or on-task, while they were in their classrooms. Despite quite large differences across countries, approximately 80 percent of the students were coded as being on-task. In some countries, very little variation among classrooms in terms of student engagement was evident.

All of the generalizations pertaining to observed practices, activities, and behaviors were based on data recorded during lessons, aggregated both within and across lessons, and ultimately across teachers within countries.

Such aggregation practices are consistent with those used in studies in which teachers or classrooms are the unit of analysis. Other units of analysis are possible, however, in the study of classrooms. One such unit, the lesson, is the focus of the analysis in the next chapter.

5

Descriptions of Lessons

In the previous chapter, classroom contexts, teachers' perceptions, classroom activities and behaviors, and students' perceptions and achievement have been described. In these descriptions of classroom activities and behaviors, the observational data were aggregated to the classroom/teacher level in keeping with the original intention and design of the study. Furthermore, data aggregated to this level were used in the multivariate analyses, the results of which will be presented in Chapters 6 and 7.

The rich observational data also are amenable to other types of examination and analysis. One examination focuses on portions or *segments* of the lessons as the unit of analysis. Such a focus permits an analysis of the structure of the lessons in terms of the behaviors that occur within particular types of segments and the ways in which the segments are sequenced within lessons.

Because the three observational instruments (that is, the Snapshot (SNAP), the Five-Minute Interaction instrument (FMI), and the Individual Activity Record (IAR)) were employed sequentially approximately five times during each lesson, it was possible to "look inside" each lesson and infer the primary *activity* that occurred during each segment of the lesson. For example, a lesson in which the teacher lectured to the students for the first three SNAP-FMI-IAR sequences and then gave them assignments (e.g., textbook or workbook exercises) to complete at their desks or tables for the remaining two SNAP-FMI-IAR sequences would contain two activities (lecture, written seatwork) and two segments.

As a second example consider a lesson in which the teacher engaged the students in discourse for the first SNAP-FMI-IAR sequence, supervised their work in laboratory activities for the next three SNAP-FMI-IAR sequences, and engaged them in discourse for the final SNAP-FMI-IAR sequence. Like the first example, this lesson would contain two activities (discourse, laboratory seatwork). However, this lesson would include three segments: discourse, then laboratory seatwork, then discourse.

Once lesson segments (or more simply, segments) were identified, it was then possible to describe them in terms of a number of other variables. For each type of segment (defined first in terms of its primary activity), summary statistics could be obtained for the segment duration, teacher's role, percent

This chapter was written by Garrett K. Mandeville.

of students engaged in learning, and nature of teacher behavior and teacher-student interactions.

The data describing segments were initially aggregated across all lessons (independent of the classroom in which the segments were observed). As such, they provided no direct information on the structure of the lessons themselves. Therefore, a second set of analyses were performed. These analyses focused on the sequence with which the segments occurred within lessons (e.g., the activities that typically began and ended the lessons).

The data presented in this chapter were collected in five of the studies: Canada Ontario-English, Canada Ontario-French, Hungary, the Republic of Korea, and Thailand. Data collected in the remaining studies were not included in the analysis either because (1) the IAR data were not available (Canada Quebec and the Netherlands), (2) the FMI data were already aggregated to the lesson level when they were received at the University of South Carolina (Australia), (3) there were too few observations per classroom to warrant the analysis (Israel), or (4) there were large amounts of missing data (Nigeria). Despite these omissions, the studies considered in this chapter permit interesting comparisons since they reflect educational practices in mathematics and science classrooms in North America, Eastern Europe, and the Far East.

This chapter is organized in the following manner. A brief overview of the methodology used in the analysis is included in the next two sections. The results of the analyses are presented and discussed in several sections that follow. Finally, a brief summary concludes the chapter.

The Observational Data Sets

Because this chapter relies heavily on the observational data collected during the study, the discussions of the observation instruments included in Chapter 2 and the cleaning and editing of the observational data described in Chapter 3 will be reviewed and expanded somewhat at this point in the discussion. Observers used the SNAP, FMI, and IAR in that exact sequence five times during each observed lesson. Thus, each lesson was to be divided into five equal time intervals and one SNAP-FMI-IAR sequence was to be completed during each interval. For 40 minute lessons, then, each sequence was to be completed in about eight minutes.

Of the three observation instruments, only the FMI had a time requirement (that is, five minutes). Observers were free to work out the details of coding the SNAP and IAR within each time interval. For clarity of exposition, however, it is assumed that the lessons were 40 minutes long so that the five within-lesson time intervals could be referred to unambiguously as "eight-minute intervals."

Each SNAP coding generated four data elements. These were the activity code (ten levels), the code for teacher role (three levels), and the counts of the number of students who were and were not engaged in the activity. In addition, each SNAP record included a combined school and classroom code, a code for the group within the classroom that was observed (when multiple groups were present in a single classroom), the number of that specific observation of that classroom (e.g., first, second, and the like), and a sequence number which identified the particular eight-minute interval within the observed lesson (e.g., again, first, second, and the like). Most frequently, multiple groups were not present in the classrooms; thus, only one SNAP record was made during each eight-minute interval.

Following the SNAP, the FMI was coded. Specifically, classroom context (six levels), who-to-whom (five levels), and the nature of the interaction (approximately 28 "types" depending on the particular study) were recorded approximately every five seconds for the entire five minutes. As a consequence, approximately 60 codes for each of the three major coding categories on the FMI should have been recorded during each eight-minute interval. Information pertaining to the school and class, observation number, and interval number also were included.

Coding of the IAR, which completed the eight-minute interval, was similar to the SNAP as regards activity and teacher role. Since, however, the focus of the IAR was the individual student, engagement in the activity was simply coded as a "1" (engaged) or a "0" (not engaged) for each of the eight pre-selected students. In addition to the identifying information coded on the SNAP, a unique student code was included on each IAR record.

Data from the SNAP and IAR were punched in what might be considered raw form prior to sending to the Data Editing Center at the University of South Carolina. For the FMI, however, most of the National Research Coordinators submitted data summarized for each eight-minute interval.

The normal preparation of these data for use in the Partial Least Squares (PLS) analysis (see Chapters 6 and 7) involved a series of aggregations. For the SNAP, the data were first aggregated over within-classroom groups (when more than one existed), then over the five eight-minute intervals to the lesson level, and finally across lessons to the classroom (or teacher) level. For the FMI data (which, as has been said, were typically already aggregated to the eight-minute interval level), only the last two steps in the aggregation process were necessary. For the IAR, an initial step of aggregating the data across the eight preselected students was added. Thus, the data sets used in the analysis described in this chapter (that is, those aggregated to the eight-minute interval level) were in fact created as a by-product of the overall data processing and editing.

Identifying Segments

In the process of merging the SNAP, FMI, and IAR data sets, it was necessary to eliminate records for which a complete set of five SNAP-FMI-IAR sequences were not available. Using this merged file as an input, a FORTRAN program was employed to assess the consistency of the SNAP and IAR activity codes for each eight-minute interval. If the two activity codes were consistent, it was assumed that the class was engaged in the same activity throughout the interval. Consistent activity codes for two or more consecutive eight-minute intervals were interpreted as meaning that the same activity was in place over the extended time period. Thus, a single segment could be in place for one, two, three, four, or all five eight-minute intervals.

Segments were said to change when one of three conditions was met. First, when the "management" activity on either the SNAP or IAR was coded, it was assumed that a transition from one activity to another (and hence one segment to another) had occurred. Second, when the SNAP activity code from a later eight-minute interval was different from the IAR activity code from the previous eight-minute interval, a new segment was identified. Third, when the SNAP and IAR activity codes within the same eight-minute interval were different, a new segment was said to be in place.

Included as an input parameter in the FORTRAN program was the requirement that each type of activity included on the SNAP and IAR had to account for at least three percent (3 %) of all the activities coded during the study. Because of this requirement, three types of activities were excluded from further analysis in all five studies. These activities were: testing (code 5), reading seatwork (code 6), and "other" (code 10). Since "management" (code 9) was used to signal a change in segments, it was not retained as an activity of interest.

Visual inspection of the raw data indicated that it was quite common in several studies for teachers to lecture and engage in discourse during the same eight-minute interval. Since lecture and discourse both involve a great deal of teacher talk, and since they differ primarily in the extent to which the relationship between teacher-student is one-way (lecture) or two-way (discourse), it seemed reasonable to classify those eight-minute intervals in which a lecture activity was coded on the SNAP and a discourse activity was coded on the IAR, or vice versa, as combined lecture/discourse intervals. Furthermore, since the "testing" activity had been eliminated, these intervals were assigned an activity code of 5.

During this identification process, data pertaining to the FMI were allocated to the segment during which they were observed. When the activity changed during an eight-minute interval, however, such an allocation was impossible. For purposes of estimating the duration of each activity within an interval, it was assumed that the change in activity occurred midway through the interval. Thus, two four-minute time intervals were formed, each aligned with a particular activity. All data collected on the FMI variables within the eight-minute interval were allocated on a 50-50 basis to the two four-minute time intervals. Later, the frequency counts for all FMI variables were transformed to duration estimates by assuming that records were made on the FMI every five seconds as prescribed. With this assumption, dividing the frequency counts by 12 provided a first approximation of the duration of the variables in minutes. These estimates were then adjusted in proportion to the actual length of the lesson since the FMI was only coded for 25 minutes during the lesson.

The FORTRAN program produced an output record for each segment. Each record contained identifying information pertaining to the class, observation, eight-minute interval, and estimated number of FMI codings during the interval. Data on activity, teacher role, students' engagement in activity, and FMI variables also were included. Using these records as input data, it was a relatively simple matter to generate the results presented in the body of this chapter using standard statistical procedures.

Before presenting the data, however, it should be pointed out that the method used to identify lesson segments is not likely to be completely accurate. As a consequence, three of the problems which might have led to the misidentification of segments will be mentioned briefly.

First, because activity was not coded on the FMI, it is possible that the activity may have changed during the five-minute period that the FMI was coded and then reverted back to the SNAP activity that preceded it. If such a change did occur, the activity in which the FMI variables were embedded would go undetected.

Second, the "management" code was used to signal a change in activity; that is, a transition from one activity to another. In fact, transitions were to be coded as "management" by the observers. However, disciplinary actions and social interactions also were to be coded as "management." Thus, actual changes in activities may have been overestimated slightly (although not greatly because of the infrequent coding of disciplinary actions and social interactions as was seen in Chapter 4).

Third, there is an imperfect fit between the low inference activity codes and the true structure of the lessons. For example, suppose that while students are engaged in written seatwork, a teacher stops them to briefly address the whole class on a difficulty experienced by a fairly large number of students. If the SNAP or IAR was coded at that point in time, the activity would be labeled "lecture." Immediately before or after this brief lecture, the activity would be labeled "seatwork." If anything, then, the number of "lecture" or "discourse" activities may have been overestimated. For these reasons, the data on frequency of various activities and types of segments should be interpreted with some caution.

Distribution and Duration of Segments

The number of segments identified and the number of lessons observed differed from study to study. In the Republic of Korea 1,305 segments were identified in 323 lessons. In Thailand 1,014 segments were identified in 366 lessons. Thus, there were slightly more segments per lesson in the Republic

132   *Garrett K. Mandeville*

of Korea as compared with Thailand. For the three remaining studies the
figures were as follows: Hungary, 824 segments in 160 lessons; Canada
Ontario-English, 501 segments in 173 lessons; and in Canada Ontario-
French, 349 segments in 94 lessons.

TABLE 5.1 *Percentage distribution of classroom
activities across lessons*

Activity/Code	Canada Ontario-Eng	Canada Ontario-Fr	Hungary	Korea (ROK)	Thailand
Lecture (1)	26	34	5	20	43
Review (2)	17	20	10	NA	12
Discourse (3)	10	1	37	16	1
Oral Practice (4)	NA	13	NA	NA	4
Lecture/ Discourse (5)	7	0	10	18	2
Written Seatwork (7)	40	32	25	17	38
Laboratory Seatwork (8)	NA	NA	13	29	NA
Total	100	100	100	100	100

Notes: NA indicates that the activity rarely if ever occurred. Activity code 6
initially was for reading seatwork, which rarely if ever occurred in the
countries. Activity codes are included since they will be referenced later
in the chapter.

The percentage distributions of segments by type of activity for the five
studies are shown in Table 5.1. Although these results are similar to the data
on activities presented in Chapter 4, they are not identical. The data in
Chapter 4 represent the percentage of all Snapshots during which each
activity was coded. The data in Table 5.1 represent the percentage of all
segments during which each activity was coded.

As can be seen in Table 5.1, from 35 to 54 percent of the segments across
countries were associated with lecture, discourse, or a lecture/discourse
combination. A similar percentage, from 32 to 46 percent, was associated
with seatwork, either written or laboratory. Not surprising, laboratory seatwork segments were only observed in the countries where students were
studying science. A small, but consistent, percentage of segments was
associated with review (with the Republic of Korea an exception). Finally,
oral practice segments were only observed in Canada Ontario-French
and Thailand.

The data displayed in Table 5.1 take no account of the amount of time
devoted to each type of segment. For this information, we turn to Table 5.2
which provides estimates of the mean duration of the various lesson segments.

TABLE 5.2 *Mean duration of lesson segments*
by type of activity (in minutes)

Activity	Canada Ontario-Eng	Canada Ontario-Fr	Hungary	Korea (ROK)	Thailand
Lecture	16	11	7	9	23
Review	16	12	6	NA	15
Discourse	11	NM	10	9	NM
Oral Practice	NA	9	NA	NA	12
Lecture/Discourse	27	NM	20	15	NM
Written Seatwork	15	11	6	7	18
Laboratory Seatwork	NA	NA	6	11	NA
Lesson total	45	40	45	40	55

Notes: Class periods in Hungary and Korea were of constant length; in the other studies class periods varied as follows: Canada Ontario-English (35-60 minutes); Canada Ontario-French (30-75 minutes); Thailand (45-60 minutes). For simplicity, however, duration estimates for these studies were arbitrarily expanded to accommodate to the "lesson totals" as reported in the table. The lengths reported in the "lesson total" row were quite close to the averages in each of these three studies. NA indicates that an activity was rare and not assessed by the algorithm. NM indicates that, although assessed by the algorithm, too few activities were identified for the duration estimates to be meaningful.

Before discussing the data in Table 5.2, it should be noted that the average durations for the various segments will not typically sum to the total lesson length (which is shown at the bottom of the table). The reason for any discrepancies is simple: the duration estimates were computed for segments independent of lessons and teachers. The data on total lesson length are provided to facilitate cross-study comparisons while controlling for different lesson lengths.

As can be seen in Table 5.1, most types of segments (approximately five-eighths of all segment types across countries) average from 9 to 16 minutes in length. Exceptions are combined lecture and discourse segments in Canada Ontario-English (27 minutes) and Hungary (20 minutes), and in lecture segments in Thailand (23 minutes). The combined lecture/discourse segments were also the longest of all segments in the Republic of Korea, while in Canada Ontario-French the average length of all types of segments was quite similar.

Based on the mean length of the review segments, it appears that they lasted for no more than 30 percent of a typical lesson. However, the distributions of the duration estimates for review segments tended to be positively skewed, with a few lessons consisting of a single review segment. Such lessons may have been used to prepare students for formal tests and examinations. Lessons with shorter review segments, on the other hand, may have been a regular part of the ongoing instructional process.

Lesson Segments and Teachers' Roles

The teacher's role during each type of activity was examined, and the results can be summarized rather easily. Common sense would dictate that teachers would likely assume a more direct, interactive role during review, lecture, discourse, and combination lecture/discourse segments. On the other hand, they would more likely assume a more indirect, supervisory role during written and laboratory seatwork segments. For the most part the data support this common sense.

During the lecture, discourse, and combination segments, the role of the teacher was coded as "interacting" during at least 94 percent of the segments identified in all studies except Canada Ontario-English. In this study, the teacher's role was coded as "monitoring" during 13 percent of the segments. Similarly, in the four studies in which review segments were applicable, the teacher's role during over 90 percent of the segments was coded as "interacting" in all countries except Hungary where the percentage was 83. In 15 percent of the review segments in Hungary, the teacher was coded as being "uninvolved" in the activity, perhaps indicating increased responsibility for students in conducting their own reviews.

During 92 percent of the oral practice segments in Canada Ontario-French, the teacher's role was coded as "interacting." In contrast, in Thailand the teacher's role was coded as "interacting" and "monitoring" about equally during oral practice segments.

Common sense and data were less in agreement during written and laboratory seatwork segments. In Canada Ontario-French, for example, the teacher's role was coded as "monitoring" during only 38 percent of the written seatwork segments. For the other studies, the percentages were as follows: Thailand, 51 percent; Hungary, 72 percent; Republic of Korea, 80 percent; and Canada Ontario-English, 89 percent. The data seem to suggest that the teachers in Canada Ontario-English and Thailand were more active during those segments in which the students were working on written assignments. During 80 percent of the laboratory seatwork segments, teachers in the Republic of Korea were coded as "monitoring." In contrast, in only 39 percent of the laboratory seatwork segments were teachers in Hungary coded as "monitoring."

In combination, the data suggest that the role of the teacher is quite clear during those segments that involve teacher talk or teacher-student dialogue. In contrast, however, the teacher's role is somewhat more ambiguous during seatwork segments, with some teachers in each country assuming a more active role than others.

Lesson Segments and Student Engagement

Are students likely to be more engaged in learning during different types of lesson segments? Data pertaining to this question are shown in Table 5.3. Since data on this variable were collected from both the SNAP and the IAR, both estimates are shown in Table 5.3.

TABLE 5.3 *Percentage of students academically engaged during each activity as estimated from the Snapshot and the Individual Activity Record*

Activity	Canada Ontario-Eng		Canada Ontario-Fr		Hungary		Korea (ROK)		Thailand	
	SNAP	IAR	SNAP	IAR	SNAP	IAR	SNAP	IAR	SNAP	IAR
Lecture	95	89	96	85	92	84	89	80	96	95
Review	95	85	99	90	90	71	NA	NA	97	94
Discourse	97	93	NA	NA	92	80	94	81	NA	NA
Oral Practice	NA	NA	98	89	NA	NA	NA	NA	94	93
Written SW	86	80	96	85	94	90	93	82	96	94
Laboratory SW	NA	NA	NA	NA	90	92	93	86	NA	NA

Notes: NA indicates that an activity was rare and not assessed by the algorithm.

The data are somewhat troubling. In all but one of the 21 SNAP-IAR comparisons displayed in Table 5.3, the SNAP estimate is higher than that obtained from the IAR. The median difference for the 14 comparisons involving non-seatwork segments is 9 percentage points; the overall median difference is 8 percentage points. The estimates are comparable only in Thailand.

Although the meaning of these data is unclear, one speculation is that because of a lack of focus and time pressures during the SNAP coding observers *estimated* the number of students who were engaged in the activity, rather than actually *counting* them. If so, the SNAP estimates would be biased in favor of over-reporting student engagement. Since the IAR caused observers to focus on individual students, accuracy is far more likely. This explanation, although tentative, suggests that the IAR estimates will be used in this discussion.

The data suggest that student engagement rates were quite similar across all types of segments in Canada Ontario-French, the Republic of Korea, and Thailand, with no more than a six percentage point difference being observed. The variation across types of segments was the largest in Hungary. In this study, students were most likely to be engaged during written and laboratory seatwork, and least likely to be engaged during review. In Canada Ontario-English, students were least likely to be engaged during written seatwork and most likely to be engaged during discourse.

Lesson Segments and Behaviors

As our final source of information for describing lesson segments we turn to the behaviors included on the FMI. As has been stated earlier, about 28 different behaviors were included on the FMI (depending on the study). For economy of presentation only those behaviors which accounted for a minimum of three percent of all behaviors coded during at least one type of segment will be discussed. Data on fourteen behaviors will be presented in three tables, each focused on specific segments: Table 5.4, lecture and discourse segments; Table 5.5, written and laboratory seatwork segments, and Table 5.6, review and oral practice segments. In combination, the fourteen or so behaviors not included in these tables accounted for between 5 and 10 percent of all behaviors observed during the time the FMI was coded.

Lecture and Discourse Segments

Two generalizations seem to emerge from the data displayed in Table 5.4. First, in those countries in which both lecture and discourse segments were observed, the percentages of behaviors exhibited during these two types of segments were quite similar. There are, of course, exceptions to this generalization. For example, in both Canada Ontario-English and Hungary, teachers more frequently used materials (e.g., chalkboards) while lecturing than when engaging in discourse. Also, in Hungary, teachers asked recall questions more frequently in discourse segments, and higher-order questions more frequently during lecture segments. Perhaps, the higher-order questions were rhetorical. Finally, teachers in Canada Ontario-English used structuring cues more frequently in discourse segments than in lecture segments. Other than these exceptions, however, the percentages of behaviors exhibited during lecture and discourse segments were quite similar, particularly in the Republic of Korea.

Second, the percentages of behaviors exhibited during lecture segments were quite similar across all five studies. This across-study consistency is particularly clear for teacher explanation, student short response, student extended response, teacher acknowledges response, and teacher repeats answer. Summing across similar behaviors tends to increase the consistency. If, for example, recall and higher-order questions are combined into a general questioning behavior, the range across studies is from eight percent (in the Republic of Korea) to 14 percent (in Canada Ontario-English). The difference in the percentage of all behaviors observed during lecture segments that were questions was only two percent across Canada Ontario-English, Canada Ontario-French, Hungary, and Thailand.

Before moving to the next section, it should be made clear that the presence of teacher questions and student responses within a lecture format may be disconcerting to some readers. In fact, one of the reviewers of this manuscript

TABLE 5.4 *Percentages of selected teacher and student behaviors during lecture and discourse segments*

FMI Category	Canada Ontario-Eng		Canada Ontario-Fr		Hungary		Korea (ROK)		Thailand	
	LE	DS	LE	DS	LE	DS	LE	DS	LE	DS
Explanation	12	11	9	—	12	7	9	9	13	—
Explan. w/ materials	18	10	20	—	10	0	8	8	25	—
Demonstration	3	2	1	—	2	0	7	4	5	—
Structuring cues	3	10	6	—	3	0	9	6	1	—
Directives	3	3	2	—	2	2	8	7	2	—
Higher questions	3	5	0	—	10	5	2	2	0	—
Recall questions	11	9	12	—	2	10	6	7	13	—
Short response	18	18	15	—	19	28	16	21	16	—
Extended response	1	1	1	—	0	2	1	5	2	—
Acknowledges response	3	6	3	—	3	3	1	1	1	—
Repeats answer	4	3	3	—	3	4	4	5	4	—
Probes	3	2	2	—	8	7	2	1	2	—
Procedural	7	8	13	—	11	8	9	6	3	—
Silence	4	5	4	—	6	9	13	9	5	—

Notes: Since the primary purpose of this table is to contrast behaviors and interactions manifest within the lecture and discourse segments, data on the combined lecture/discourse activity format have not been included. Because discourse was rarely coded in Canada Ontario-French and Thailand, no behavior and interaction data are presented for this activity in the table.

indicated a certain amount of confusion caused by this state of affairs. The best explanation for this state of affairs is that observers were unable to reliably differentiate lecture (or one-way communication) from discourse (or two-way communication). Since teachers talked for a large portion of the observed lesson, the differentiation needed to be made based on the number of uninterrupted minutes of teacher talk during the lesson. Different standards among observers concerning the appropriate number of minutes needed to code "lecture" are quite likely. Consistent with this argument, then, it may be wise to consider the inclusion of questions and answers during a lecture format to be an indication of observer error.

Written and Laboratory Seatwork Segments

As might be expected, silence or quiet talk (coded as "observer can't hear") predominated during seatwork segments in most of the studies, particularly Canada Ontario-English, the Republic of Korea, and Thailand. Only in Hungary did silence and quiet talk account for less than 30 percent of the total behaviors observed.

Procedural matters such as distributing and collecting papers, arranging materials, and cleaning up also were attended to frequently during seatwork segments. With the exception of the written seatwork segments in the Republic of Korea and in Thailand, procedural matters accounted for 10 percent or more of the behaviors observed during seatwork segments.

TABLE 5.5 *Percentages of selected teacher and student behaviors during written and laboratory seatwork*

FMI Category	Canada Ontario-Eng	Canada Ontario-Fr	Hungary		Korea (ROK)		Thailand
	WSW	WSW	WSW	LSW	WSW	LSW	WSW
Explanation	5	9	7	13	4	4	12
Explan. w/materials	8	8	4	9	4	8	4
Demonstration	1	0	1	0	5	4	2
Structuring cues	3	2	1	1	5	3	0
Directives	2	2	7	4	6	6	2
Higher questions	1	0	6	8	0	1	0
Recall questions	7	8	4	2	3	3	4
Short response	9	10	13	14	9	9	6
Acknowledges response	1	2	3	3	0	0	1
Probes	1	1	5	6	0	1	2
Procedural	13	20	14	15	6	10	8
Silence	34	18	23	14	49	41	51
Observer can't hear	11	12	3	3	1	1	2

Notes: WSW refers to written seatwork; LSW refers to laboratory/manipulative seatwork.

Teachers did, in fact, actively teach during seatwork segments, but not nearly as much as they did during lecture and discourse segments. Comparing the percentages of teacher explanations and explanations with materials in lecturing segments (Table 5.4) and in written seatwork segments (Table 5.5) makes this point quite nicely. The decreases in percentages range from 9 percent in the Republic of Korea to 22 percent in Thailand, with a median decrease of 12 percent. Questions also were much less frequently asked during seatwork.

Review and Oral Practice Segments

The behaviors exhibited during these segments resemble those exhibited during lecture and discourse segments (Table 5.4). In fact, the Hungarian data for discourse and review segments are virtually identical. In the remaining studies, slightly more questions were asked during review and/or oral practice segments than during the lecture and discourse segments. Also, some use of recitation (that is, rapid-fire question and answer sessions) is evident in Table 5.6 (but was not evident in either of the previous two tables).

TABLE 5.6   *Percentages of selected teacher and student*
behaviors during review and oral practice segments

FMI Category	Canada Ontario-Eng REV	Canada Ontario-Fr REV	ORAL	Hungary REV	Thailand REV	ORAL
Explanation	15	5	7	7	14	15
Explan. w/materials	12	14	10	0	15	7
Demonstration	2	0	0	0	5	9
Structuring cues	2	5	5	0	1	0
Directives	3	3	5	2	2	3
Higher questions	1	0	0	5	0	1
Recall questions	15	12	16	10	14	11
Short response	19	17	19	28	17	16
Extended response	1	2	1	2	10	8
Recitation	1	3	6	3	1	1
Acknowledges response	3	5	7	3	1	0
Repeats answer	3	3	4	4	5	4
Probes	3	3	5	10	2	3
Procedural	6	16	8	8	3	7
Silence	5	5	2	9	9	12

In summary, although differences in the frequency of behaviors in different types of segments do exist, these differences are not as large as intuition might suggest. A composite picture during lecture and discourse segments, for example, would include about 40 percent of behaviors that involved "showing and telling," and another 40 percent that involved asking and answering questions, and reacting to the answers. The remaining time in these segments is spent on a variety of behaviors (e.g., procedural, silence). This composite picture would fairly accurately describe review and oral practice segments as well, with perhaps a slight shift away from "showing and telling," and toward "asking, answering, and reacting." Finally, during seatwork, one does see a shift toward procedural matters, silence, and quiet talk, and away from behaviors in the two large categories which predominate the other segments.

The Structure of Lessons

To this point in the discussion, the emphasis has been on lesson segments and behaviors associated with various types of segments. The emphasis in the remaining sections of this chapter is on the structure of lessons. Specifically, three questions will be addressed:

1. What is the distribution of the number of segments per lesson?
2. Do typical lesson structures exist and, if so, what are they?
3. What can be said about the ways in which teachers typically begin and end lessons?

The Distribution of Lesson Segments

The data pertaining to the distribution of segments within lessons are shown in Table 5.7. As can be seen, considerable cross-study variation exists in the number of segments per lesson. Although intuition would suggest that teachers of younger children (e.g., those in Thailand) in contrast to teachers of older children (e.g., those in Canada Ontario-English) might tend to "package" their lessons into a greater number of shorter segments to provide greater variety or to accommodate more limited attention spans, the data are not generally supportive of this position. The data, however, do support a greater number of segments in science lessons than in mathematics lessons.

TABLE 5.7 *Percent distribution and selected measures of central tendency for the number of segments per lesson*

No. of Segments	Canada Ontario-Eng	Canada Ontario-Fr	Hungary	Korea (ROK)	Thailand
6 or more	10	14	42	14	6
5	4	12	23	21	6
4	16	25	15	26	12
3	14	30	8	31	20
2	39	15	8	5	44
1	17	4	4	3	12
Mean	2.9	3.7	5.2	4.0	2.8
Mode	2	3	5	3	2

The results contrast the relatively simple lesson structure in Thailand (where over half of the lessons include one or two segments), with the complex lesson structures in Hungary (where almost two-thirds of the lessons include five segments or more). Within each country, in fact, there was a reasonable degree of consistency of lesson structure in terms of the number of segments. In Canada Ontario-English, like in Thailand, over half of the lessons included one or two segments. In Canada Ontario-French, on the other hand, over half of the lessons contained three or four segments. Finally, in the Republic of Korea 78 percent of the lessons included three, four, or five segments.

Typical Lesson Structures

While the number of segments within lessons provides one indicator of the structure of lessons, more information is available when the types of segments within lessons are considered. This consideration began by assigning activity codes (see Table 5.1) to each segment and then sequencing the activity codes within each lesson. Thus, for example, a two-segment lesson consisting of a lecture (activity code = 1) followed by written seatwork (activity code = 7) would have a structure denoted by "17." Similarly, a four-segment lesson which begins with review, moves to a combination of lecture and discourse, then to laboratory seatwork, and finally to written seatwork would have a structure denoted by "2587." The position of the code numbers is used to denote the position of the segment in the lesson sequence. That is, a "71" lesson structure is different from a "17" lesson structure.

The number of unique lesson structures ranged from 60 in Canada Ontario-French to 158 in the Republic of Korea. Because the total number of lessons differed from study to study, however, a more appropriate indicator of variation in lesson structure is the ratio of the number of lessons to the number of different lesson structures. In Hungary, this ratio was 1.2 (with 160 lessons classifiable into 133 unique structures). In essence, every lesson observed in Hungary had a unique structure. In Thailand, on the other hand, the ratio was 5.1 (with 366 lessons classifiable into 72 unique structures). This ratio suggests there are some common lesson structures in place in Thailand.

TABLE 5.8 *Codes and percentages of lesson patterns which occurred during at least three percent of the observed lessons*

Canada Ontario-Eng Code	%	Canada Ontario-Fr Code	%	Hungary Code	%	Korea (ROK) Code	%	Thailand Code	%
17	14	17	14	58	4	185	8	17	35
57	10	217	8	37373	4	385	5	1	10
1	6	127	5	373	3	181	4	217	8
7	6	1217	3			585	4	1717	5
217	4	2172	3			583	3	171	4
1717	4								
Total	44		33		11		24		62

Notes: The sequences of numbers in the column "code" refer to the sequences of activity segments observed within lessons. For example, the code "17" refers to two-segment lesson which begins with a lecture ("1") and ends with written seatwork ("7"). Similarly, the code "1217" refers to a four-segment lesson consisting of an initial lecture ("1") followed by a review segment ("2") followed by another lecture ("1") and ended with written seatwork ("7"). Combined lecture/discussion segments are indicated by "5;" laboratory seatwork segments are indicated by "8." Finally, the numbers in the column "%" refer to the percentage of lessons containing a particular sequence of activity segments. Thus, for example, 14 percent of the lessons in Canada Ontario-English consisted of lectures followed by written seatwork (which was coded as "17").

The results of the overall analysis are presented in Table 5.8. Only those lesson structures accounting for a minimum of three percent of all observed lessons are included in the table.

In Thailand five lesson structures account for 62 percent of all observed lessons. Three of these structures involve various combinations of lecture and written seatwork segments. One structure includes a single lecture segment during the entire lesson. The remaining structure includes a review segment before the lecture and written seatwork segments.

In Canada Ontario-French, five lesson structures account for 33 percent of the observed lessons. Unlike Thailand, review segments are present in four of these five lesson structures (the exception being the lecture-seatwork structure also prevalent in Thailand). Interestingly, review segments occur at various times during the lesson. They begin the lesson (e.g., 217), they appear in the middle of the lesson (e.g., 127 and 1217), and they both begin and end the lesson (e.g., 2172).

In both Canada Ontario-English and the Republic of Korea, the lesson structures included in Table 5.8 account for about one-quarter of the observed lessons. The primary differences between the lesson structures in these two countries are (1) the number of segments in the lessons, (2) the type of seatwork (that is, written in Canada Ontario-English and laboratory in the Republic of Korea), and (3) the closing segment (that is, closing with seatwork in Canada Ontario-English and lecture and discourse in the Republic of Korea).

In many respects, the lesson structures in place in Canada Ontario-English are quite similar to those in place in Thailand. Four lesson structures are fairly frequently found in both studies: 17, 1, 217, and 1717. Interestingly, the rank order of these four structures is virtually identical in the two studies.

If one discounts differences between lecture and discourse in the Republic of Korea study, the lessons included in Table 5.8 have a common structure. Teachers begin the lesson by talking to or with the students, students then work on assignments in laboratory settings, and teachers close the lesson by talking to or with the students (presumably providing some type of summary or closure to the lesson).

As has been stated earlier, the lesson structures in Hungary are quite complex, typically because of the large numbers of segments within lesson. As seen in Table 5.8 one of the more common lesson structures is designated "37373." Thus, it seems in Hungary that cycles of shorter segments are the rule within lessons.

Across all studies, then, the most frequently occurring lesson structure consists of a lecture, discourse, or combination segment followed by a seatwork segment. This relatively simple two-segment lesson accounts for 35 percent of the lessons in Thailand, 24 percent of the lessons in Canada Ontario-English, 17 percent of the lessons in Canada Ontario-French, and 4 percent of the lessons in Hungary. Only in Hungary and the Republic of Korea did lessons frequently conclude with a lecture, discourse, or combination segment.

In the other three studies, lessons most frequently ended with a seatwork segment. A more detailed examination of the openings and closings of lessons will now be presented.

Lesson Openings and Closings

The data on the most frequent opening and closing segments are shown in Table 5.9. For all studies, the most frequent opening and closing segments are shown. For some studies, the second most frequent opening and/or closing segments are presented if these segments occurred as openings or closings in at least 20 percent of the lessons.

TABLE 5.9   *Popular initial and final lesson segments (estimates given in terms of both percent occurrence and duration)*

	Canada Ontario-Eng		Canada Ontario-Fr		Hungary		Korea (ROK)		Thailand	
	1st	2nd	1st	2nd	1st	2nd	1st	2nd	1st	2nd
Initial										
Activity	LEC	REV	LEC	—	DIS	REV	LEC	L/D	LEC	—
Percent	38	22	86	—	45	26	42	26	89	—
Duration	21	22	13	—	13	7	9	16	28	—
Final										
Activity	WSW	—	WSW	—	L/D	LSW	L/D	WSW	WSW	—
Percent	76	—	91	—	38	31	32	25	85	—
Duration	16	—	11	—	18	6	16	5	20	—

Notes: The "1st" column indicates the modal activity, while the "2nd" column indicates the second most popular activity. A second most popular activity is indicated only if this activity was an "initial" or "final" activity in at least 20 percent of the lessons. Single segment lessons are included in the initial segment data only. Abbreviations are as follows: lecture (LEC), discourse (DIS), composite lecture/discourse (L/D), review (REV), written seatwork (WSW), and laboratory seatwork (LSW).

The results in Table 5.9 portray a rather consistent pattern for Canada Ontario-French and Thailand. In both of these countries, the lessons typically began with a lecture segment (86 percent in Canada Ontario-French and 89 percent in Thailand) and closed with a written seatwork segment (91 percent in Canada Ontario-French and 85 percent in Thailand). In Canada Ontario-French, the opening segment lasted about 13 minutes, while in Thailand the opening segment lasted about 28 minutes. In Canada Ontario-French, the closing segment lasted about 11 minutes while in Thailand the closing segment lasted about 20 minutes. Thus, once again, we have evidence that the Canada Ontario-French lessons included a greater number of lesson segments.

In Canada Ontario-English no clear pattern concerning opening segments is evident. Sixty percent of the lessons began with either a lecture or review segment. The remaining forty percent, however, began with a discourse, lecture/discourse combination, or written seatwork segment. Over three-fourths of the lessons ended with written seatwork segments. The opening segment tended to last about 21 or 22 minutes, while the closing segment lasted for 16 minutes on the average.

In Hungary and the Republic of Korea (both studies involving science) more variation in both openings and closings is notable. In Hungary, lessons tended to begin with either discourse or review segments. They tended to end with either combined lecture/discourse or laboratory seatwork segments. In the Republic of Korea, lessons began with either lecture or combined lecture/discourse segments. They tended to end either with combined lecture/discourse or written seatwork segments. In general, the opening segments were shorter than those in the other countries, particularly if the lesson began with review in Hungary or with lecture in the Republic of Korea. If lessons in Hungary and the Republic of Korea ended with a lecture segment, the closing segment was about as long as the closing segment in the other countries. If, on the other hand, the lessons in Hungary and the Republic of Korea ended with a seatwork segment, the closing segment was quite short (i.e., about five or six minutes).

In combination, the data presented in these last three subsections present a consistent picture of the lesson structures in the studies. In Thailand, a two-segment lecture-seatwork lesson was prevalent. When lessons contained more than two segments, they typically began with a lecture segment and closed with a written seatwork segment.

In Canada Ontario-French, review segments tended to be interpersed throughout the lessons. As a result, a slightly wider range of lesson structures was present than was the case in Thailand. At the same time, however, almost ninety percent of the lessons began with a lecture segment, and slightly more than ninety percent closed with a written seatwork segment.

In the Republic of Korea and Canada Ontario-English still greater variety of lesson structures was evident. In Korea, however, three-segment lessons accounted for almost one-quarter of those observed. At the same time, however, a lesson was equally likely to close with a combined lecture/discourse segment or written seatwork segment. Despite the extensive use of laboratory seatwork, few lessons closed with such a segment. In Canada Ontario-English common lessons included from one to four segments. While lessons began with a variety of segments, more than three-fourths of them closed with a written seatwork segment.

Finally, in Hungary unique lesson structures were the rule. As was mentioned, 133 unique lesson structures were found in the 160 total lessons. Much of the variety in lesson structure would seem to stem from the inclusion of shorter segments present in a variety of sequences. At the same time, however, almost three-fourths of the lessons began with either a discourse or review segment. Finally, almost 70 percent of the lessons closed with either a combined lecture/discourse segment or a laboratory seatwork segment.

Summary

Although the data were not originally gathered for the purpose of examining the structure of lessons, the results of this examination are informative in a number of respects. First, most lessons were divided into two or more segments, lasting an average of 10 to 15 minutes each. Second, during review, oral practice, lecture, and discourse segments, teachers typically assumed a very directive, interactive role with their students. During written or laboratory seatwork segments, however, role differentiation between teachers in many countries was evident. In many seatwork segments, teachers assumed a more passive, supervisory role. In others, however, teachers engaged in what may be termed "teaching" (that is, they explained concepts and skills to their students, asked questions and reacted to their responses).

Third, teachers generally spent a great deal of time providing explanations, asking questions, and reacting to answers to those questions during the entire lesson. These behaviors were fairly common in review, oral practice, lecture, and discourse segments. Although not as predominant, these behaviors also were evident while students worked on assigned tasks at their seats. At the same time, however, with the exception of Hungary, the majority of the coded behaviors during seatwork segments involved silence, quiet talk (that is, "can't hear"), and "housekeeping" matters (that is, procedural interactions).

Fourth, students were typically engaged in the activity independent of the nature of the activity itself. That is, in general whether students were expected to attend to the teacher while he or she lectured, or work on a series of exercises at his or her seat, students complied with the expectations of the teachers. At the same time, however, the estimates of student engagement depended in part on the instrument used to provide the estimates. In general, group-focused instruments provided higher estimates than individual-focused instruments.

Fifth, and finally, the major differences among the studies lay in the structure of the lessons, not in the frequency of activities and behaviors. In some studies (e.g., Thailand), the structure of the lessons was quite simple and fairly consistent. In other countries (e.g., Hungary), the structure of the lessons was quite complex and fairly unstable. Lessons in the various studies differed in terms of (1) the average number of lesson segments, (2) the extent to which the majority of lessons possessed a similar structure, and (3) the ways in which lessons began and ended.

While these "revelations" may not surprise those involved in classroom research or research on teaching, they nonetheless began to suggest dimensions on which studies in this field may differ or be similar. Furthermore, they also suggest that the differences between studies may be related more to the subject matters studied, than the cultures in which the studies were conducted.

6

The Student Variable Model

In Chapters 4 and 5, the initial findings of the study were described. In reviewing these findings the reader quite likely has become aware of the large number of variables included in the study. A safe estimate is over 200 variables. When one considers that the number of teachers and classes in the participating countries ranged from 18 to 87 and that the smallest number of students included in any one study was 400, there was an obvious need to reduce the number of variables in order that meaningful analyses and more reliable interpretations of the data were possible.

The first attempt to classify these variables (hereafter referred to as "manifest" variables) into constructs (or "latent" variables) was made by Ryan (1981). The framework presented by Ryan contained six constructs believed to influence a seventh construct composed of student achievement and student attitude. Further discussion and consideration of the conceptual issues inherent in, the psychometric concerns with, and the data analytic consequences of the organizing work by a variety of interested educators and researchers resulted in the expansion of Ryan's six constructs into the fifteen constructs included in the model presented in Chapter 2.

Once the constructs were agreed upon, the question of the hypothesized relationships among the constructs arose. In response to this question, a causal model was developed by Anderson (1982). This model was discussed with all National Research Coordinators (NRCs) and eventually agreed upon. This model, referred to as the core model, was discussed in Chapter 2.

The core model formed the general conceptual framework for the conduct of the multivariate analyses and the empirical investigation of the relationships among the constructs and their associated manifest variables. For multivariate analyses to be feasible and to produce meaningful results, consideration must be given to a number of formal and methodological issues. These issues include the mathematical or statistical formalization of the hypotheses to be tested, the choice of appropriate statistical methods, and the preparation and selection of data to be analyzed. In this regard, some general points associated with the empirical examination of the core model must be noted.

The core model formally constitutes what is known as a recursive path model. That is, each path among the fifteen constructs represents a direct

This chapter was written by Norbert Sellin and Lorin W. Anderson.

effect of one construct on another, and all paths together form a causal chain with student achievement as the ultimate dependent variable to be predicted or "explained" in terms of various mediating and independent constructs. It is well known that this particular type of path model could, in principle, be estimated using standard path analytic procedures (see, for example, Duncan 1975). More precisely, if one makes some assumptions concerned with the residual factors associated with each dependent variable (e.g., that the residuals are uncorrelated with all explanatory variables) and with the exact form of the relationships to be examined (e.g., that the respective relationships can be formulated as linear-additive equations), the coefficients associated with each path could be estimated using Ordinary Least Squares (OLS) regression applied to each model equation separately. The validity of the hypotheses involved in the model could then be evaluated in terms of the magnitude and sign of the ensuing path coefficients. If some additional requirements are met (e.g., random sampling, and equally and normally distributed residuals), it is also possible to assess the generalizability of the various empirical relationships on the basis of inferential test statistics, such as the familiar t-tests and F-tests.

Considering the application of this data analytical approach to the core model, several difficulties and problems immediately emerge. First, as discussed in Chapter 2, the core model consists of constructs associated with multiple manifest variables. Although the variables are directly observed, the constructs are not. A straightforward application of path analytic procedures which require that directly observed variables be included in the model is thus not possible. There are, however, path analytical techniques available that can be used to examine the type of path model represented by the core model. This issue and the selection of appropriate statistical procedures for analyzing the data will be discussed later in this chapter.

Second, with the possible exception of Australia, the data sets of the various studies must be considered as being so-called "samples of convenience." That is, schools, classes, teachers, and students were not selected from well-defined populations using some probability sampling procedure. The most common reason for the use of convenience samples was that extensive class-room observation was required and, as a consequence, researchers had to rely heavily on the cooperation of teachers who voluntarily participated in the studies. Because probability samples were not available, the use of inferential statistical tests is greatly limited. It makes little sense, for example, to test whether a particular path coefficient is significantly different from zero in a population if essential sampling requirements have not been fulfilled. Yet another critical point associated with the use of conventional statistics is they typically require quite restrictive distributional assumptions, notably independence and normality of residuals.

Given the nature and distribution of the data for many of the variables included in the core model (e.g., restricted range, severe skewness), the validity of such distributional assumptions would appear questionable, if not untenable. It should be noted at this point that such difficulties do not appear to be uncommon in related research on classroom instruction (see, for example, Brophy and Good 1986 for a review). While a number of statistical techniques (e.g., multiple regression) are known to be fairly robust against departures from distributional assumptions, the absence of probability samples obviously constituted a severe constraint with regard to the use of inferential test statistics. Primarily because of the limitations of the study imposed by the sampling, then, standard significance tests were generally not used in the analysis of the data. Rather, most of the following discussion rests upon descriptive indices of statistical fit, such as R-square values indicating the relative amount of "explained" variance, or the magnitudes of particular effect estimates. To the extent possible, generalizations will be offered on the basis of some *ad hoc* criteria that were developed to evaluate the descriptive results.

Third, an important aspect associated with an empirical investigation of the core model concerns the number of cases (e.g., classes, students) in relation to the number of variables and coefficients to be examined and interpreted. The core model involves two general sets of variables, namely those reflecting properties of individual students, and those reflecting properties of the teachers, classes, and schools to which the students belong. The latter variables can be referred to as "classroom-based" variables because the corresponding data were typically aggregated to the class level. As a consequence, the number of "cases" available for an empirical examination of relationships among these variables is equal to the number of classes involved in a given data set.

As noted in Chapter 3 the number of classes included in the various studies varied from 18 to 87. The core model involves 11 "classroom-based" constructs and, depending on the use of optional instruments, at least 70 "classroom-based" manifest variables. Hence, with the exception of Australia and Thailand, the number of "classroom-based" manifest variables involved in the core model in the remaining studies is considerably larger than the number of classrooms. The ratios of "classroom-based" constructs to the number of classrooms are about 1 to 2 for the three Canadian replications and Israel, 1 to 3 for Hungary, 1 to 4 for the Republic of Korea and the Netherlands, 1 to 7 for Australia, and 1 to 8 for Thailand. These figures must be taken into account in order to assess the estimability of the core model.

Being extremely liberal, one may suppose that numerical values could be assigned to all constructs. Then, only those paths between the constructs would have to be estimated simultaneously by applying OLS regression to each model equation. As can be seen from the core model presented in Chapter 2, the construct termed "student outcomes," for example, is hypothesized to be influenced by seven "classroom-based" constructs. If a classroom to path coefficient ratio of 10 to 1 is regarded as the minimum standard for the conduct of meaningful regression analyses, only two countries, Australia and Thailand, would remain for investigating model equation linking the seven "classroom-based" constructs to "student outcomes." Stated somewhat differently, even in terms of what must be considered as being minimum standard for the conduct of meaningful analyses, it is impossible to examine the core model empirically in most of the participating countries. Quite obviously, if slightly more restrictive criteria are considered (e.g., the simultaneous estimation of more than just one equation, or a classroom to coefficient ratio of, say, 20 to 1), an examination of the core model in any of the participating countries is impossible. The number of classes would simply be too few to undertake meaningful analyses.

From the above remarks it should be evident that the multivariate analyses could not proceed with a straightforward empirical investigation of the core model. As a consequence, a submodel, termed the student variable model, was constructed. As its name implies, the student variable model was specified to include mainly "student-based" variables, that is, variables for which data were derived from student responses to questionnaires and tests. The number of "classroom-based" variables was reduced to a minimum so that the model could be tested in virtually all participating countries. Specifically, with but one exception, all variables derived from classroom observations were eliminated. These variables will be examined in Chapter 7.

The purpose of this chapter is to examine the data in terms of the student variable model. The chapter is organized into four major sections. The first three sections address major issues that must be considered and comprehended if the results of the student variable model are to be interpreted properly; namely, the preparation of the data used in multivariate analyses, the possible influence of "classroom-based" variables on student outcomes, and the content validity of the cognitive tests used in the various countries. The large fourth section describes the student variable model and presents the results. A brief summary section concludes the chapter.

Data Editing and Preparation

To be used in multivariate analyses, data must fulfill several requirements. These requirements are generally more stringent than those for univariate or descriptive analyses, especially when the multivariate analyses involve data from a number of instruments completed by different respondents (i.e., teachers, students, and observers). To compute and interpret univariate statistics, for example, missing data can be considered on a variable-by-variable or instrument-by-instrument basis and may simply be discarded in order to deal with the missing data problem. For multivariate analyses, however, the data from all instruments involved in a particular model must be sufficiently complete. It is thus necessary to examine the data to be used in multivariate analyses in terms of the amount of missing data across different instruments and different respondents. Similarly, since the cornerstone of most multivariate analyses is the simple bivariate correlation, exceedingly deviant correlations between major variables within certain groups, subgroups, or samples must be critically examined. Based on the results of this examination particular groups, subgroups, or samples may have to be deleted before a given model can be tested properly.

Prior to performing any type of multivariate analyses, then, a careful examination of the raw data is necessary. A two-step procedure was followed in this study. The first step concerned the problem of missing data; the second concerned the problem of deviant pretest-posttest relationships within classes. The purpose of this section is to describe briefly each of these steps and the decisions made based on their application.

Missing Data

Although different models (e.g., student variable model, core model) were eventually to be tested, some general criteria for selecting data for inclusion in any of the multivariate analyses were considered essential. General rules were developed for the responses of individual students and teachers as well as for the mean response rates within classes of students. While the data derived from the observational instruments were generally complete, those obtained from the teacher and student questionnaires, specifically, the Initial Student Questionnaire (ISQ), the Initial Teacher Questionnaire (ITQ), the Final Student Questionnaire (FSQ) and the Final Teacher Questionnaire (FTQ), often were not.

A listing of all variables included in each study was prepared. For each instrument teachers or students responding to fewer than fifty percent of the associated items were noted. If a teacher or student failed to respond to at least one-half of the items on an instrument, that teacher's or student's record was noted as being incomplete. The various response rates were stored in a separate computer file. A similar check was made on the students' responses to the items on the cognitive pretest and posttest. If a student failed to respond to at least one item on either test, that student's record was noted as being incomplete.

In addition to examining the responses of individual students, class mean response rates also were examined. Specifically, classes in which fewer than one-half of the students completed the ISQ or the FSQ, or failed to respond to any of the items on either the cognitive pretest or posttest were noted. The various class mean response rates were stored in a separate computer file.

The creation of separate computer files involving the response rates of teachers, students, and classes permitted an examination of the consequences of different rules for excluding particular students, teachers, and classes from the multivariate analyses. Specifically, the consequences of applying more or less restrictive criteria than the aforementioned "50 percent rule" could be investigated.

As a result of this series of examinations a total of 11 classes were eliminated from the multivariate analyses. Four of these classes were located in Hungary, two in Thailand, and one each in Australia, Israel, and the three Canadian replications (Ontario-English, Ontario-French, and Quebec). These classes were excluded because most of the students failed to respond to one or more of the questionnaires and tests. For most of these classes the mean response rates were considerably lower than 50 percent. In fact, in 6 of these classes no data at all were available for at least one of the questionnaires or tests.

Pretest-Posttest Relationships

In the second step in the editing and preparation of data for multivariate analyses the relationship between the pretest and the posttest within each classroom was examined. This step was important because cognitive achievement, as measured by the pretests and posttests used in each study, constituted the major outcome variable. Since the classroom is the unit within which teaching and learning take place, the examination of within-classroom relationships between the pretest and posttest can help identify seemingly deviant classes; that is, classes in which the pretest, posttest, or both failed to reflect cognitive achievement accurately.

Scatterplots, zero-order correlations and regression coefficients were prepared for each class in each country. Two types of deviant classes were noted. First, classes with negative correlations between the pretest and the posttest were identified. Second, in those countries in which the same test was used as the pretest and posttest, classes in which the mean posttest score was more than four points less than the mean pretest score were identified. A list of these classes was prepared for each participating country. This list, complete with the reason for each class being on it, was sent to the National Research Coordinators (NRCs). The NRCs were asked to conduct further investigations of these classes and, based on their findings, indicate whether any or all of the identified classes should be excluded from the multivariate analyses. In some cases the deviant relationship of pretest with posttest was attributed to errors in coding or data transfer. Such errors were corrected and the classes were reinstated. In other cases, however, the exceptional pretest-posttest relationships were attributed to classroom peculiarities or the lack of opportunity students had to learn the content tested. In these cases the NRCs suggested the deletion of the classes. In all, 8 classes were excluded from multivariate analyses based on the pretest-posttest relationship. Three of these classes were in the Netherlands, four in Thailand, and one in Canada Quebec.

Data Used in Subsequent Analyses

In summary, then, a total of 19 classes were excluded from the multivariate analyses; 11 because of missing data and 8 because of deviant or exceptional pretest-posttest relationships. Table 6.1 displays the number of classes and students included in the multivariate analyses, the original number of students and classes being given in parentheses. Since no additional deletion of classes or students was made based on model specific criteria, the classes and students displayed in Table 6.1 comprise the data sets for all subsequent analyses.

TABLE 6.1 *Numbers of students and classes retained for the multivariate analyses (original numbers in parentheses)*

Country	Classes		Students	
Australia	74	(75)	1,913	(1,963)
Canada Ontario-English	26	(27)	729	(751)
Canada Ontario-French	17	(18)	394	(420)
Canada Quebec	19	(21)	554	(610)
Hungary	36	(40)	1,071	(1,180)
Israel	21	(22)	639	(671)
Korea (ROK)	45	(45)	2,400	(2,400)
Netherlands	47	(50)	1,073	(1,125)
Thailand	81	(87)	2,400	(2,572)
Total	366	(385)	11,173	(11,692)
Number excluded	19		519	

Note: The number of classes and number of students in Canada Quebec is different from those shown in Table 3.2. Of the 30 classes included in the Canada Quebec study, nine were grade 7 and 21 were grade 8. Since different tests were administered to seventh and eighth grade students, only the 21 grade 8 classes were considered for inclusion in the multivariate analyses. Nigeria was excluded from all multivariate analyses because of large amounts of missing data.

For these reduced data sets the missing data rates and frequency distributions of all variables were examined once again. Recodings of and compensation for missing data (via the insertion of overall or class means) were considered and implemented where appropriate. Variables with high rates of missing data, namely more than 15 percent, were noted. Variables with highly skewed frequency distributions or extremely small variances were identified. Based on these considerations variables were eliminated on a study-by-study basis. As a final step in the data editing and in preparation for the multivariate analyses a set of figures (box and whisker plots) and tables was prepared showing the frequency distributions and missing data rates for all variables retained for further investigation. These figures and tables were referred to when models were specified and the data pertaining to these models interpreted.

Upper Bounds for the Impact of "Schooling" Variables on Student Outcomes

As evidenced by the large number of school, classroom, and teacher variables included in the Classroom Environment Study, the primary aim of the study was to examine the possible influences of what may be termed "schooling" variables (i.e., measures of school, classroom, teacher and teaching characteristics) on measures of student achievement. If students are used as units of analysis for such an investigation, the same numerical value is generally assigned to every student in a particular school or classroom for each such variable. That is, a common formal feature of "schooling" or "classroom-based" variables is that the associated numerical values are constant within classrooms or, in some cases, schools. If, for example, the variable "type of school" is coded "1" for public schools, all students enrolled in public school classes are assigned a "1" for that variable. Similarly, if a teacher indicated that his or her students had had an opportunity to learn the content associated with 80 percent of the items included on the posttest, then all students belonging to that teacher's class are assigned a value of "80" for the variable termed "opportunity to learn." Finally, if an observer recorded 25 recall questions during a particular lesson, then the value of "25" would be assigned to all students in that classroom for the variable "recall questions."

As a consequence of the way in which numerical values of "schooling" variables are assigned to individual students, these variables can, in statistical terms, influence only the between-class portion of the variance of tests of student outcomes. More precisely, if students are used as units of investigation and if regression-based techniques are employed to assess the effects of "schooling" variables on students' achievement and attitudes, the maximum amount of variance in these outcomes that can be "explained" by these variables is equal to the between-class variance of the outcome measures. This fact is an immediate consequence of "schooling" variables being assigned constant values within classes.

In the light of the above remarks, a useful preliminary step in multivariate analyses is to examine the proportion of between-class variance in the post-test performance of students across the various studies. This proportion of between-class variance provides an "upper bound" for the relative amount of variance that can be attributed to "schooling" variables, however defined. The proportion of between-class variance in the pretest performance of students is also of interest since it provides an initial assessment of differences among classes in terms of entry-level achievement.

The purpose of this section is to examine the "upper bounds" of the impact of "schooling" variables on two outcome variables, namely cognitive achievement and attitude toward the subject matter. The presentation consists of three parts. In the first part the results of a series of regression analyses which focused on student achievement are described. In the second part the results for student attitudes are discussed. Finally, in the third part a somewhat more elaborate regression model in which student achievement and student attitudes are examined jointly is considered.

Student Achievement

Table 6.2 displays for the pretest and the posttest used in each study the R-square values obtained from three separate analyses of variance (ANOVAs). In addition to the primary analysis with class membership as the independent variable, Table 6.2 displays the R-square values obtained from subsequent analyses including type of school (with a maximum of 5 categories) and location of school (with a maximum of 4 categories) as predictor variables. It will be noted that in some countries these latter two categorical variables were constant (i.e., the type of school in Canada Ontario-French, Hungary, and the Republic of Korea, and the location of school in Australia).

TABLE 6.2   *Pretest and posttest variance explained by class membership, type of school, and location of school (with R-square values multiplied by 1,000)*

Country	Prestest			Posttest		
	Class	Type of School	School Location	Class	Type of School	School Location
Australia	264	022	—	276	036	—
Canada (COE)	250	017	036	263	012	018
Canada (COF)	092	—	014	150	—	024
Canada (CQ)	319	001	011	339	012	069
Hungary	182	—	005	381	—	021
Israel	279	040	007	277	035	002
Korea (ROK)	224	—	137	328	—	125
Netherlands	283	011	025	440	038	032
Thailand	438	196	170	361	171	111

Notes: COE refers to Canada Ontario-English; COF to Canada Ontario-French; CQ to Canada Quebec; and ROK to the Republic of Korea.

As can be seen in Table 6.2, the proportion of total pretest variance that can be attributed to class membership ranges from 9.2 percent in Canada Ontario-French to 43.8 percent in Thailand. The total posttest variance that can be attributed to class membership ranges from 15.0 percent in Canada Ontario-French to 44.0 percent in the Netherlands. When interpreting these values, one must remember that the same test was used for both the pretest and posttest in Australia, Canada Ontario-English, the Republic of Korea, and Thailand. Some degree of overlap between the pretest and the posttest existed in Israel. In all other countries, a different test was used as the pretest and posttest.

The R-square values presented in Table 6.2 should not be compared across countries. At least two reasons can be given for this caveat. First, R-square values constitute standardized coefficients which are generally not directly comparable across different data sets. Second, and more importantly, the achievement tests were developed at each National Center and are, therefore, study- (and, hopefully, curriculum-) specific.

Four comments about the ANOVA results presented in Table 6.2 seem necessary at this point in the discussion. First, in order to examine the impact of "schooling" variables on final achievement, it would be ideal if no substantial between-class differences existed in initial achievement. That is, under ideal circumstances, the proportion of the variance in pretest scores that could be attributed to differences among classes would be zero or fairly close to zero. In this case, all classes would be similar in terms of their average initial achievement and any "schooling" variable would be uncorrelated with initial achievement. If these conditions were met it would be possible to examine, for example, the zero-order correlations between final achievement and "schooling" variables without taking initial achievement differences into account. As evidenced by the results given in Table 6.2 such an examination is not possible since non-zero between-class differences in terms of initial achievement exist in all data sets.

Because the study was designed as a nonexperimental study, this result was to be expected. As a consequence, however, differences among classes in terms of initial achievement must be taken into account when examining effects of "schooling" variables on final achievement. In this regard, the R-square values pertaining to the effect of class membership on final achievement reflect the *maximum* "explained" variance in final achievement of a set of "schooling" predictor variables that *do not include* initial achievement. Thus, these R-square values in fact overestimate the possible impact of "schooling" variables on final achievement because the classes do differ in their initial achievement and, as will be seen later, pretest performance generally constitutes a powerful predictor of posttest performance.

Second, for those countries in which the same (or a very similar) test was used both as pretest and posttest, differences in initial achievement reflect in part differences in the cognitive prerequisites necessary for obtaining high levels of final achievement. Such is the case for Australia, Canada Ontario-English, the Republic of Korea, Thailand, and to a lesser extent, Israel. In the remaining countries an aptitude test was used as the pretest with the assumption that the content to be learned by the students was relatively new to them. Since, as has been mentioned, aptitude and achievement tests were developed at the National Research Centers little information was available as to whether these aptitude tests yielded valid measures of entry-level knowledge and skills. As a consequence, differences among classes in these studies in terms of their entry-level knowledge and skills may be incorrectly estimated by the R-square values displayed in Table 6.2.

The third comment about the ANOVA results in Table 6.2 concerns the R-square values indicating the proportion of between-class variance in final achievement. Although, as mentioned earlier, these R-square values generally tend to overestimate the potential impact of "schooling" variables on final achievement, they are nonetheless informative in the following sense. Suppose one computes zero-order correlations between particular "schooling" variables and final achievement. Then, the maximum possible zero-order correlation in each country is equal to the square root of the corresponding R-square value pertaining to the influence of class membership on posttest performance (see Table 6.2). Consider, for example, the R-square value obtained for the Canadian Ontario-French replication. This value is equal to 0.150. The maximum possible zero-order correlation of any single "schooling" variable with final achievement is, in this data set, equal to 0.387 (or − 0.387 if the "schooling" variable is negatively related to final achievement).

Considering the average amount of between-class variance in final achievement in all studies, the maximum correlation of a single "schooling" variable with final achievement is, on the average, equal to 0.544 in absolute value. In other words, zero-order correlations between "schooling" variables and final achievement are constrained by the relative amount of between-class variance in final achievement. Since similar, though not strictly the same, considerations apply to standardized path coefficients involved in more complex models, this fact must be taken into acount when interpreting effects of "schooling" variables on final achievement.

It should be noted that the above considerations concern correlations computed using students as units of analysis. In many process-product studies, however, it seems to be common practice to examine class-level, correlations, that is, correlations between "schooling" variables and class mean achievement. In this regard, it may be useful to note the analytical relation between such corresponding student-level and class-level correlations.

It can be shown that student-level and class-level correlations between student-based variables such as posttest achievement, and "classroom-based" variables depicted as constants within classes, are proportional to each other. For the present discussion concerning the correlations between final achievement and "schooling" variables, the proportionality constants in the various studies are equal to the square roots of the R-square values in Table 6.2 pertaining to the effect of class membership on final achievement. More precisely, a given student-level correlation may be divided by the appropriate proportionality constant (that is, the square root of the corres-ponding R-square value) to obtain the corresponding class-level correlation. Since R-square values vary between zero and one, class-level correlations must be equal to or *numerically larger than* their student level counterparts.

To give a somewhat extreme example, suppose that in Australia a "schooling" variable could be found with a student-level correlation of 0.525 with final achievement. This coefficient is the maximum possible correlation (namely the square root of the R-square value 0.276 given in Table 6.2). In this case, the corresponding class-level correlation would therefore be equal to unity. At first glance, it may seem strange to say that both correlations provide essentially the same information. However, both correlations do indicate that class mean achievement can be perfectly predicted from the single "schooling" variable. Moreover, the underlying unstandardized regression slopes are the same. The only differences between such student-level and class-level correlations is that the within-class variance in posttest performance is discarded in the class-level analysis. The same is the case for any correlation between "schooling" variables measured as class constants and student-based variables.

The fourth, and final, comment pertaining to the ANOVA results displayed in Table 6.2 concerns the R-square values associated with type of school and location of school. Relatively large effects of type of school, school location, or both exist in the Republic of Korea and Thailand. In all other countries these effects can be regarded as negligible. In the Republic of Korea, the major source of the location of school effect was the difference between rural or suburban schools, on the one hand, and urban and metropolitan schools, on the other. For this reason a dummy variable indicative of school location was generally included in subsequent multivariate analyses performed on the Korean data.

In Thailand, both the type of school and location of school effects are fairly strong. However, certain types of schools were typically found in certain locations. Thirteen of the fourteen private school classes were located in metropolitan or urban areas. In contrast, 51 of the 67 governmental (that is, public) school classes were located in suburban or rural areas. As a consequence, these two categorical variables were confounded. Because of the magnitude of the confounding of these two variables, both could not be included simultaneously in multivariate analyses. While type of school was finally selected for inclusion in the analysis (largely because it provided more potentially useful information), differences attributed to type of school may in Thailand also be attributable to the location of school.

Since, as has been noted, the R-square values for final achievement obtained by means of ANOVAs tend to overestimate the impact of "schooling" variables, a more appropriate assessment of this potential impact can be obtained using Analysis of Covariance (ANCOVA) procedures. Table 6.3 displays the R-square values obtained from regression analyses including both initial achievement or aptitude *and* class membership as predictors of final achievement. In essence, these models constitute simple extensions of the previous analysis of variance models. Table 6.3 also includes the R-square value obtained from a simple regression of final achievement on corresponding initial achievement or aptitude. For convenience, the regression models used to produce the results shown in Table 6.3 will be labeled Model A, Model B, and Model C in the discussion that follows.

TABLE 6.3 *Posttest variance accounted for by three different regression models (with R-square values multiplied by 1,000)*

Country	Classes	Students	Model A	B	C	Difference A-B	B-C
Australia	74	1,739	605	585	497	020	088
Canada (COE)	26	639	690	677	569	013	108
Canada (COF)	17	363	601	577	491	024	086
Canada (CQ)	19	477	540	495	289	045	206
Hungary	36	941	566	539	249	027	290
Israel	21	547	561	533	439	028	094
Korea (ROK)	45	2,307	521	500	298	021	202
Netherlands	47	1,022	537	512	220	025	292
Thailand	81	2,381	541	519	386	022	133

Notes: Model A includes pretest, class membership, and pretest × class membership. Model B includes pretest and class membership only (that is, without the interaction term). Model C includes pretest only (that is, without class membership or the interaction term). The number of classes and students shown in this table are those on which the regression analyses were performed. The discrepancy between these numbers and those in Table 6.1 are because of missing data. Finally, the country abbreviations are the same as those used in Table 6.2.

Models A and B represent standard ANCOVA models which include dummy variables representing class membership as well as initial achievement or aptitude. The only difference between the two models is that Model A includes so-called interaction effects (that is, a class membership × initial achievement or aptitude interaction term) while Model B involves the specification of additive effects of class membership and initial achievement or aptitude. In other words, the interaction term included in Model A was omitted in Model B.

Model A results in the estimation of pretest-posttest relationships by separate regressions for each classroom. That is, within each study Model A involves as many regression coefficients as there are classrooms. Model B, on the other hand, results in a single regression coefficient representing the pretest-posttest relationship for each study. This coefficient is commonly called the pooled within-class regression coefficient. A single regression coefficient relating the pretest and the posttest for each study is also obtained from Model C, which is the simple regression of posttest on pretest. Two differences between R-square values derived from the various regression analyses are displayed in Table 6.3. The first difference is between Models A and B. This difference represents the increase in variation accounted for by the interaction term. The second difference is between Models B and C. This difference represents the increase in variation accounted for by class membership, over and above that accounted for by the pretest alone.

The specification of Models A and B and the examination of the corresponding difference between R-square values served two major purposes. The first was to obtain an initial assessment of the effect of including interaction terms between "schooling" variables and final achievement on the predictive power of regression models involving final achievement as the dependent variable. Stated somewhat differently, the difference between the R-square values obtained from Model A and Model B reflects the loss of predictive power when interaction terms are omitted and when the single pooled within-class regression coefficient is substituted for the individual within-class regression coefficients.

The results shown in Table 6.3 indicate that this loss of predictive power is quite small, ranging from a 1.3 percent decrease of "explained" variance in Canada Ontario-English to a 4.5 percent decrease in Canada Quebec. It should be noted that the core model does not include interaction effects. The same is true for the models presented later in this chapter. Rather, these models specify additive effects of "schooling" variables and initial achievement or aptitude. This choice of model specification is supported by the data in Table 6.3.

The second purpose of comparing Models A and B was related to the choice of an appropriate adjustment for final achievement in subsequent analyses. As will be discussed in Chapter 7, it was deemed necessary to simplify later investigations of effects of "schooling" variables by using posttest scores adjusted for pretest influences. On the basis of the results presented in Table 6.3, the pooled within-class regression coefficient obtained from Model B was selected as the appropriate adjustment factor.

With regard to additive models designed to examine influences of "schooling" variables on final achievement, Models B and C provide some useful information. The R-square value obtained from Model B represents the maximum variance in final achievement that can be "explained" from regression models that include initial achievement or aptitude and any number of "schooling" variables (e.g., type of school, size of class, type of class activities, or frequency of particular types of student-teacher interactions). The difference between the R-square values of Models B and C indicate the loss of explanatory power of such regression models if all "schooling" variables were to be eliminated. Stated somewhat differently, the difference between the R-square values of Models B and C represents the maximum possible unique contribution of "schooling" variables in explaining differences in final achievement when differences in initial achievement or aptitude are taken into account (i.e., if pretest effects are "held constant" or "partialled out"). Quite obviously, if this difference would be zero or very close to zero, then the examination of effects of any type or number of "schooling" variables would make little sense. On the other hand, if this difference is substantial, it becomes useful to try to identify "schooling" variables which likely account for relatively large between-class differences in final achievement.

As can be seen from Table 6.3, the maximum possible *unique* contribution of "school-type" variables to the prediction of final achievement ranges from 8.6 percent "explained" variance in Canada Ontario-French to 29.2 percent "explained" variance in the Netherlands. It should be reiterated at this point that comparisons of these values across countries are inappropriate because study-specific tests are involved and because R-square values constitute standardized coefficients. In general, initial achievement is a powerful predictor of final achievement (as can be seen from the R-square values in Table 6.3 pertaining to Model C). However, pretest is clearly not the only student-based variable that may influence final achievement. For this reason, as stated earlier, the regression results presented in Table 6.3 provide only an initial assessment of the potential impact of "schooling" variables on final achievement.

When examining the results in Table 6.3, the reader may wish to refer back to the analysis of variance results presented earlier in Table 6.2. Consider, for example, the results obtained for Australia. Class membership alone (i.e., any number of "schooling" variables) accounted for 27.6 percent of the variation in final achievement (see Table 6.2). Class membership plus initial achievement accounts for 58.5 percent of the final achievement variance (see Table 6.3, Model B). Hence, the inclusion of initial achievement resulted in an increase of 30.9 percent "explained" variance.

In contrast, the simple regression of the posttest on pretest accounts for 49.7 percent of the posttest variance (see Table 6.3, Model C). If this simple regression model, then, is extended through the inclusion of any number of "schooling" variables, the maximum increase of "explained" variance in final achievement is 8.8 percent, namely the difference between R-square values obtained from Models B and C. Similar, though somewhat less dramatic, differences can be seen in all participating countries.

The results of the regression analyses described in this section yielded two major conclusions. First, the comparison between Models A and B supports the specification of more simple additive models in subsequent analyses. It is recognized that the rather simple approach involved in the comparison of Models A and B does not exclude the possibility that some other, and perhaps more complex, type of interaction effects would be identifiable. Since, however, the multivariate analyses of the data were largely exploratory, the data analytical problems involved in these analyses would likely escalate beyond an acceptable level by including a search for possible interaction effects.

Second, the likelihood of identifying "schooling" variables that strongly influence final achievement is quite small in all studies. The maximum amount of posttest variance than can be "explained" by "schooling" variables, however, defined and measured, would seem to be 44 percent in the Netherlands. And, once pretest differences are taken into consideration, this maximum drops to about 29 percent. As a consequence, one must be satisfied with the identification of "schooling" variables that exert weak, yet noticeable and consistent, influences on final achievement. Subsequent correlations and path coefficients must be interpreted with this point in mind.

Student Attitudes

In the previous section the impact of classroom-based variables on measures of initial and final cognitive achievement was examined. In this section the results of similar analyses concerned with student attitude are described. Two preliminary comments seem necessary in connection with the analyses presented in this section. First, while the cognitive pretests and posttests were study-specific, the questionnaire items intended to measure student attitude were the same across studies. These items were included on the Initial Student Questionnaire (ISQ) and the Final Student Questionnaire (FSQ). With but one exception, data were gathered on all items in all studies. The exception concerns Hungary where the measurement of entry attitude involved a single item that asked students to indicate how well they thought they would learn the subject being studied.

Second, initially a distinction was made between two dimensions of student attitudes: self-related attitudes and subject-related attitudes. Four items were intended to reflect self-related attitudes (e.g., "I am good at math") and six items were likewise intended to reflect subject-related attitudes (e.g., "I think math is fun"). For the purposes of the analyses presented in this section, these items were combined into one mean score. The use of a single composite score simplified the analyses, and was supported by the results of preliminary factor analyses which suggested that the various items could be combined into one scale without substantial loss of information. It should be noted at this point that, for some countries, the factor analyses occasionally revealed quite small loadings associated with particular items. Although these items could have been deleted in order to obtain somewhat more reliable country-unique composites, a decision was made to retain all items to increase the comparability of results across studies. Deletion of specific items was considered in the analyses of the more complex, country-unique models that will be presented later in this chapter.

Table 6.4 presents for initial and final attitudes the R-square values obtained from separate ANOVAs with class, type of school, and school location as independent variables. The results of similar analyses for the student achievement have been presented in Table 6.2.

Two points will be noted in connection with the data displayed in Table 6.4. First, the R-square values associated with the type and location of the school are quite small across all studies for both initial and final attitude. As can be seen in Table 6.4, the largest (and quite exceptional) R-square value indicates that 4.2 percent of the variance in the final attitudes of students in Canada Quebec could be "explained" by the type of school they attended.

Second, compared with the corresponding R-square values for the cognitive

TABLE 6.4 *Variance in initial and outcome attitudes explained by class membership, type of school, and location of school (with R-square values multiplied by 1,000)*

Country	Initial			Outcome		
	Class	Type of school	School location	Class	Type of school	School location
Australia	088	002	—	094	000	—
Canada (COE)	075	001	014	063	003	002
Canada (COF)	093	—	036	113	—	005
Canada (CQ)	088	017	000	161	042	000
Hungary	116	—	016	153	—	017
Israel	073	008	002	147	012	007
Korea (ROK)	118	—	008	087	—	008
Netherlands	128	009	008	112	011	011
Thailand	142	002	007	097	027	013

Note: COE refers to Canada Ontario-English; COF to Canada Ontario-French; CQ to Canada Quebec; and ROK to the Republic of Korea.

tests presented in Table 6.2, the amount of variance attributable to class membership is substantially smaller for both the initial and final student attitude. Consider the results obtained for Australia, for example. In Table 6.2 it can be seen that 27.6 percent of the variation in final achievement in Australia could be attributed to class membership. In contrast, as can be seen in Table 6.4, 9.4 percent of the variation in final attitude can be "explained" by class membership. That is, in Australia class membership accounts for almost three times as much variation in final achievement as in final attitude. The same finding holds true for initial achievement and initial attitude (with the exception of Canada Ontario-French and Hungary). In sum, then, the major conclusion that can be drawn from the comparison between the ANOVA results presented in Tables 6.2 and 6.4 is that between-class differences in initial and final achievement tended to be considerably larger than those pertaining to initial and final attitudes.

As pointed out in the preceding section, to the extent that the classes differ in terms of initial achievement or attitudes, the R-square values obtained from simple ANOVAs generally tend to overestimate the possible impact of "schooling" variables on final achievement or attitudes. A somewhat more appropriate assessment of the possible impact of "schooling" variables is obtained when initial achievement or attitude is taken into account. Table 6.5 presents the R-square values obtained from three different regression analyses which included, in addition to class membership, initial attitude as a predictor of final attitude. Similar to the preceding section, the different models are referred to as Models A, B, and C.

Model C represents the simple regression of final attitude on initial attitude.

TABLE 6.5 *Variance in outcome attitudes accounted for*
by three different regression models
(with R-square values multiplied by 1,000)

Country	Classes	Students	Model			Difference	
			A	B	C	A-B	B-C
Australia	74	1,735	384	342	264	042	078
Canada (COE)	26	632	454	414	368	040	046
Canada (COF)	17	344	514	486	423	028	063
Canada (CQ)	19	509	530	509	447	021	062
Hungary	36	991	434	408	331	026	077
Israel	21	535	412	360	284	052	076
Korea (ROK)	45	2,311	288	242	189	046	053
Netherlands	47	1,011	497	467	391	030	076
Thailand	81	2,197	156	116	021	040	095

Notes: Model A includes pretest, class membership, and pretest × class
membership. Model B includes pretest and class membership only (that is,
without the interaction term). Model C includes pretest only (that is, without
class membership or the interaction term). The number of classes and students
shown in this table are those on which the regression analyses were performed.
The discrepancy between these numbers and those in Tables 6.1 and 6.3 are
the result of missing data. Finally, the country abbreviations are the same as
those used in Table 6.4.

Models A and B represent standard ANCOVA models involved class membership and initial attitude as predictors of final attitude. In Model A, the
relationship between initial and final attitude was estimated by separate
regressions within each class; in Model B, this relationship was estimated by
a so-called pooled within-class regression. Table 6.5 also displays two differences between the R-square values obtained from the various models. As
discussed in the preceding section, the difference between Models A and B
provides an initial assessment of the loss of predictive power when the
influence of initial attitude on final attitude is represented by a single pooled
within-class regression coefficient rather than individual within-class regression
coefficients. The difference between Models B and C provides an initial
assessment of the increase in predictive power when class membership is
added to a model consisting solely of initial and final attitude.

The first point to be noted in connection with the results presented in Table
6.5 (in contrast with Table 6.3) is that the R-square values associated with
Models A and B are generally larger for final achievement than for final
attitude. Consider, for example, the R-square values obtained from Model
B. The median R-square value across studies indicates that 53 percent of the
variation in final achievement can be "explained" by a model including
initial achievement and class membership (see Table 6.3). In contrast, the
corresponding median R-square value in Table 6.5 suggests that 41 percent

of the variation in final attitude can be explained by a model including initial attitude and class membership. Similar differences can be seen for the R-square values pertaining to Model A. These differences in terms of predictive power are primarily due to the differences in terms of the impact of class membership on final achievement and final attitude.

As also can be seen in Tables 6.3 and 6.5, the pattern of differences between the R-square values pertaining to Model C is less consistent across studies than the pattern of R-square differences associated with Models A or B. In some countries, the bivariate relationship between initial and final achievement is somewhat stronger than the corresponding bivariate relationship between initial and final attitude. In other countries the reverse is true. For example, in Australia the R-square values associated with Model C are 0.497 for achievement and 0.264 for attitude. That is, in Australia the bivariate relationship between initial and final achievement is stronger than that between initial and final attitude. In Canada Quebec, on the other hand, the corresponding R-square values are 0.289 for final achievement and 0.447 for final attitude.

One possible explanation for the apparent between-country differences is the use of the same or similar tests as pretests and posttests. As can be seen in Tables 6.3 and 6.5, for all countries in which the same or very similar tests were used as pretests and posttests (Australia, Canada Ontario-English, Israel, the Republic of Korea, and Thailand), the R-square values associated with the regression of posttest on pretest are consistently higher than the R-square values associated with the regression of final attitude on initial attitude. With the exception of Canada Ontario-French, the reverse is true for the remaining countries in which different pretests and posttests were administered.

In retrospect, studies in which the same (or similar) test was used both as pretest and posttest differed from those in which different tests were used in terms of the maximum proportion of variation in final achievement that could be attributed to class membership. With the exception of Canada Ontario-French, in those studies in which different tests were used as pretests and posttests, class membership accounted for between 20.6 and 29.2 percent of the variation in final achievement (beyond that which could be attributed to initial achievement). Similarly, with the exception of the Republic of Korea, in those studies in which the same or similar tests were used as pretests and posttests, class membership accounted for between 8.8 and 13.3 percent of the variation in final achievement (again, beyond that predicted from initial achievement).

While the Canada Ontario-French result is best seen as an anomaly (since this study also was unique in terms of the results pertaining to student attitudes), the results from the Republic of Korea study are explained more easily. The study conducted in the Republic of Korea was of short duration, focused on a single unit of instruction agreed upon by the teachers, included apparently highly valid unit tests, and had observers in the classrooms almost on a daily basis. As a consequence, the study had the potential of identifying "schooling" variables which impact on final achievement. At the same time, however, it must be remembered that, even in the Republic of Korea, these "schooling" variables could only account for about one-fifth of the variation in final achievement, beyond that attributable to initial achievement.

Based on the data presented in Tables 6.3 and 6.5, however, it is clear that initial achievement and attitude are potent predictors of final achievement and attitude. The only exception to this generalization is Thailand in which the R-square value of 0.021 associated with Model C indicates a quite weak bivariate relationship between initial and final attitude.

Finally, the differences between Models A and B were slightly higher for final attitude than for final achievement. For final attitude, the median R-square difference associated with Models A and B is 4.0 percent. In contrast, the median difference for the final achievement was 2.4 percent. This result suggests that the relationship between initial and final attitude was somewhat more class-specific than the relationship between the initial and final achievement. While it may be of some interest at this point to speculate about possible reasons for these differences in terms of the variation of within-class slopes, this issue will not be pursued further. Rather, the major point to be noted in connection with the regression results presented in Table 6.5 is that the decrease in "explained" variance from Model A to Model B is recognizable, but fairly small in all countries. As discussed in the preceding section, this finding supports the specification of more simple path models which do not include interaction effects between "classroom-based" variables and initial attitude.

The differences between the R-square values associated with Models B and C indicate a 7.6 percent decrease of "explained" variance when "schooling" variables are discarded. The corresponding median decrease for final achievement was 13.3 percent. As pointed out in the preceding section, these figures suggest that one cannot expect to obtain very large effects of "classroom-based" predictors on either final attitude and final achievement. Stated somewhat differently, the increase of "explained" variance in student achievement and attitude that may result from the inclusion of any number of "schooling" variables must generally be expected to be comparatively small.

Relationship Between Final Achievement and Final Attitude

The previous sections were concerned with the possible impact of "classroom-based" variables on final achievement and final attitude. As pointed out earlier, the regression analyses presented above can provide only some initial, yet useful, assessment of "schooling" effects because achievement and attitude were examined separately and furthermore because the analysis of covariance models involved only initial achievement or initial attitude as the only "covariate" or "student-based" predictor. While the measures of initial achievement and attitude were generally found to constitute powerful predictors of final achievement and attitude, they are not necessarily the only "student-based" variables that might need to be taken into account when assessing between-classroom differences in student outcomes. Thus, it seems useful to examine one possible extension of the regression models used earlier. This extension concerns the joint, rather than separate, examination of final achievement and attitude. To this end, models that specify the relationships among initial and final measures of student achievement and student attitude must be specified.

Several assumptions have been made in specifying these models. First, initial attitude is believed to effect final achievement. Students who enjoy learning a subject matter and see themselves as capable of learning it will likely learn more about it. Second, initial achievement is hypothesized to effect final attitude. Students who have experienced success in learning a subject matter in the past will come to enjoy the subject matter more and see themselves as successful in learning the subject matter.

In combination, these two assumptions would suggest a model in which initial achievement and initial attitude are predictors of *both* final achievement and final attitude. Such a model can be specified in at least two ways. First, a direct effect of initial attitude on final achievement and a direct effect of initial achievement on final attitude can be specified (see Fig. 6.1).

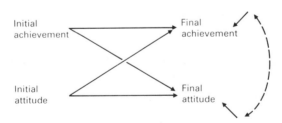

FIG. 6.1   Recursive path model for the relationship between initial and final achievement and attitude.

The diagram in Fig. 6.1 is recognizable as a so-called recursive path model that involves a "cross-lagged" relationship between the respective measures of initial and final achievement and attitude. Following the nomenclature commonly used in the path analytic literature, the double-headed arrow included in Fig. 6.1 represents a non-zero correlation between the residual factors associated with final achievement and attitude. This non-zero correlation is assumed because residual factors (that is, unmeasured or unspecified variables that are uncorrelated with the explanatory variables included in the model) which influence final achievement are likely correlated with residual factors influencing final attitude.

The second alternative, and the one actually adopted in subsequent analyses, is based on the assumption that the relationship between achievement and attitude involves continuous feedback over time. That is, it might be assumed that cognitive achievement at one point in time, say t_1, influences student attitude at a later point in time, say t_2, which, in turn, influences achievement at t_3, which, again in turn, influences attitude at t_4, and so on. This type of cyclic development in cognitive achievement and attitude has been suggested by Bloom (1976) among others. A direct empirical examination of the feedback processes outlined above obviously requires achievement and attitude to be measured at more than two points in time. However, Fisher (1970) has shown that cyclic influence structures as sketched above can be approximated by appropriate nonrecursive path models. Such a model is depicted in Fig. 6.2.

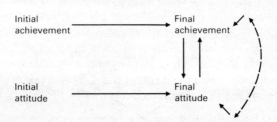

FIG. 6.2 Nonrecursive path model for the relationship
between initial and final achievement and attitude.

The major conceptual difference between the nonrecursive path model shown in Fig. 6.2 and its recursive counterpart displayed in Fig. 6.1 concerns the average time period within which student achievement and student attitude are assumed to influence each other. As specified for the data of the Classroom Environment Study, the model shown in Fig. 6.2 assumes that student achievement and student attitude influence each other in a relatively short time period. Specially, these influences are assumed to operate in a time period *shorter than* that during which the respective initial and final measures were obtained (i.e., the duration of the respective studies). This assumption would seem more appropriate than the one underlying the recursive model shown in Fig. 6.1; namely, that the time period within which influences between student achievement and student attitude takes place corresponds to the duration of the various studies.

At this point one might ask whether it is possible to examine empirically which of the two path models described above yields the "best fit" to the data. In the present case this is not possible because, in statistical parlance, both models are "observationally equivalent." That is, neither the recursive model shown in Fig. 6.1 nor the nonrecursive model displayed in Fig. 6.2 involves overidentifying restrictions that could be used for comparative statistical tests. (See, for example, Duncan (1975) for a discussion of issues surrounding the identification and comparison of path models.) As a consequence, both models fit the data equally well, and the choice between alternative model specifications must be made on conceptual grounds. As a matter of fact, the purpose of the preceding discussion was to spell out the conceptual rationale for preferring the nonrecursive specification over its recursive counterpart.

The nonrecursive model shown in Fig. 6.2 constitutes the basic building block for the formulation of the more complex student variable model that will be presented later in this chapter. In essence, this latter model will add some "student-based" variables as well as some "classroom-based" variables to this rather simple nonrecursive model. As a preliminary step in these analyses it is once again useful to examine the possible class impact on student outcomes. As before, this essentially involves the examination of regression models in which class membership is included in one step and excluded in another. Table 6.6 displays the R-square values obtained from such analyses applied to the path model shown in Fig. 6.2.

TABLE 6.6 *Explained variances from regression models involving class membership and a nonrecursive relationship between final achievement and attitude (with R-square values multiplied by 1,000)*

Study	Class Membership Included		Class Membership Excluded		Differences	
	Ach	Att	Ach	Att	Ach	Att
Australia	590	381	514	308	076	073
Canada (COE)	692	448	587	383	105	065
Canada (COF)	593	503	503	443	090	060
Canada (CQ)	502	521	292	467	210	054
Hungary	561	456	278	350	283	106
Israel	533	362	440	288	093	074
Korea (ROK)	510	249	321	197	189	052
Netherlands	532	480	249	396	283	084
Thailand	528	142	398	062	130	080

Notes: COE refers to Canada Ontario-English, COF refers to Canada Ontario-French, CQ refers to Canada Quebec, and ROK refers to the Republic of Korea.

Before discussing the data presented in Table 6.6, two more technical remarks should be made. First, the R-square values reported were obtained using the Two Stage Least Squares (TSLS) procedure since the more familiar Ordinary Least Squares (OLS) regression procedure is inappropriate for the analysis of nonrecursive path models. The reader is referred to Goldberger (1964, pp. 329-339) for a comprehensive discussion of TSLS estimation of nonrecursive models. The TSLS technique has also been used in the analysis of the aforementioned student variable model.

Second, the data in the major column headed "class membership included" were derived from a pooled within-class analysis of the model shown in Fig. 6.2. That is, the analysis involved additive class effects and corresponds to the regression model denoted in earlier sections as "Model B." Specific within-class analyses (that is, those corresponding to "Model A") were not undertaken because the number of students per class was generally too small. With the exceptions of the Republic of Korea and Thailand, the classes included in the study typically involved between 20 and 30 students. Hence, ignoring regression constants and residual covariances, the analysis of the model in Fig. 6.2 within each class would involve the estimation of four path coefficients on the basis of only 20 to 30 cases. Such an analysis would most likely produce highly unreliable results.

Table 6.6 displays the R-square values obtained from two analyses. As noted above, the first analysis included binary variables representing class membership and corresponds to the pooled within-class regressions denoted previously as "Model B." In the second analysis, class membership was omitted as a predictor of final achievement and final attitude. This analysis corresponds to the regression analyses denoted "Model C" in the preceding subsections. Table 6.6 also displays for both final achievement and final attitude the differences between the R-square values.

The model depicted in Fig. 6.2 basically adds just one "student-based" predictor variable or "covariate" to the regression models described in the preceding sections. This results, of course, in an increase in the amount of "explained" variance. When comparing the R-square values shown in Table 6.6 with the corresponding R-square values for Models B and C given in Tables 6.3 and 6.5 above, however, the increase of R-square is fairly small for both final achievement and final attitude. The results pertaining to the model shown in Fig. 6.2, then, suggest the same conclusions as the regression analyses discussed in the preceding sections.

Although the various regression analyses revealed a high degree of similarity in terms of predictive power and the potential effects of class membership on final achievement and final attitude, it is of interest at this point to examine the direct effects pertaining to the nonrecursive path model shown in Fig. 6.2. Table 6.7 displays the standardized path coefficients estimated from the analysis in which class membership was omitted. Similar estimates were obtained from the analysis which included class effects.

TABLE 6.7 *Standardized two stage least squares estimates of direct effects included in the nonrecursive path model in Fig. 6.2 (with coefficients multiplied by 1,000)*

Variables	Aus	COE	COF	CQ	Hun	Isr	ROK	Net	Tha
Final Achievement									
Initial Ach	667	688	620	517	434	648	479	417	472
Final Att	072	149	133	045	151	054	161	164	177
Final Attitude									
Initial Att	418	496	554	622	434	533	385	593	100
Final Ach	231	188	172	135	158	020	103	061	209

The earlier discussion of the relationship between achievement and attitude would suggest that positive direct effects between the respective measures of initial and final achievement and attitude should be expected. As can be seen in Table 6.7, this expectation holds in all countries. Of particular interest are, of course, the path coefficients associated with the presumed feedback effects between cognitive achievement and attitude. The magnitude of the corresponding effect estimates should be approximately the same if the influences of achievement on attitude are similar to the influences of attitude on achievement. The path coefficients in Table 6.7 associated with the direct effects of final achievement on final attitude, and final attitude on final achievement support this hypothesis for five of the nine data sets included in the analysis. In Australia and Canada Quebec the direct effects of final achievement on final attitude are stronger; the reverse is true for the Netherlands. Finally, in contrast to the other countries, the results for Israel (where the subject was history) suggest that attitude and achievement were unrelated.

In summary, then, the specification of a nonrecursive relationship between final achievement and final attitude would seem to be supported for five studies whereas the empirical evidence would seem to be somewhat limited for the remaining four studies. However, in view of the tentative nature of the preliminary regression analyses presented above, it seems appropriate to undertake further examinations of this relationship in the context of more complex path models.

Opportunity to Learn

Although not explicitly stated to this point in this discussion, an important prerequisite of the analyses included in this chapter is that the final achievement tests used in each study reflect as accurately as possible the knowledge and skills actually taught to the students in the various classes. This basic requirement is all the more important if possible effects of "schooling" variables on achievement or attitude are considered. For example, the previous discussions of the relationship between attitude and achievement obviously require an accurate assessment of "student learning," and an assessment having similar meaning across classrooms. Stated simply, there should be no substantial variation across classes in terms of the content validity of the achievement tests. If, for example, a particular test does not cover, say, 20 percent of the content actually taught, this reduction in content validity should be identical for all classes.

This basic requirement was, of course, recognized in the design of the study. In order to attain maximum possible content validity, the achievement tests were to be developed at the National Research Centers and were to be constructed with regard to the special needs of the study. This section presents data concerning the content validity of the achievement tests used in five countries.

As a national option teachers were asked to indicate the extent to which their students had had the opportunity to learn the content assessed by each item on the final achievement test. Based on the teachers' responses, an opportunity to learn (OTL) index was derived for each class of students. This index represented the percent of items testing content students had had an opportunity to learn either prior to or during the study. For example, an OTL index of 90 indicated that a teacher believed that his or her students had had an opportunity to learn the content associated with 90 percent of the items sometime during their school experience. Because the OTL instrument was a national option, data were not available for all studies. In fact, in only four of the studies were OTL data available: Australia, Canada Ontario-English, the Netherlands, and Thailand.

For those countries in which the same test was used as both pretest and posttest an indirect estimate of OTL using classroom-specific item difficulties was possible. Following a procedure suggested by Mandeville (1984) an attempt was made to empirically estimate OTL in all studies in which the same test was administered as pretest and posttest. These empirical estimates were based on a single assumption. If students in a particular classroom had had an opportunity to learn the content associated with a particular item during the study, then more students in that classroom would be able to answer the item correctly on the posttest than did do on the pretest.

Specifically, two improvement standards were set. The first standard, referred to as the 5 percent rule, was based on an increase of 5 or more percent of the students. That is, if at least five percent more of the students in a given class answered an item correctly on the posttest than did so on the pretest, students in that classroom were said to have had an opportunity to learn the content tested by that item. An empirical OTL estimate of 80 using the 5 percent rule means that for 80 percent of the items at least 5 percent more of the students answered the item correctly on the posttest as compared with the pretest. The second standard, termed the 10 percent rule, was based on an increase of 10 or more percent of the students.

Both judgmental and empirical estimates of OTL have obvious sources of error associated with them. The empirical estimates of OTL are not independent of the posttest scores and are subject to the influence of any factor which might influence student learning relative to specific items (e.g., unusually apt students who are able to deduce the correct answers to questions pertaining to content not actually taught, unusually poorly written or ambiguous questions that confuse students who have received instruction related to the content being tested, or unusually good teachers who help students to learn to apply or generalize the content learned to new and different situations). On the other hand, the judgmental estimates of OTL are not independent of the feelings and beliefs of the teachers as they complete the OTL instrument. If, for example, a teacher feels that his or her pedagogical competence is being evaluated by the instrument, he or she might respond that he or she is, of course, teaching everything to every student. In those situations in which the two estimates are available, then, the empirical estimate may be viewed as an underestimate of actual OTL, while the judgmental estimate may be viewed as an overestimate. As is frequently the case the best estimate is likely to lie somewhere between the two.

Judgmental estimates, empirical estimates, or both were available in five studies: Australia, Canada Ontario-English, the Republic of Korea, the Netherlands, and Thailand. Hungary, Israel, and the remaining two Canadian replications (Ontario-French, Quebec) neither used the OTL instrument nor used the same test for the pretest and posttest. For Australia, Canada Ontario-English, and Thailand, both judgmental and empirical estimates were available. For the Netherlands only the judgmental estimate was available (since different tests were used as pre- and posttest). Finally, for Korea only the empirical estimate was available (since the OTL instrument was not administered).

The data pertaining to OTL are displayed in Table 6.8. Specifically, three columns of data are presented: the judgmental OTL index, the empirical estimate using the 5 percent rule, and the empirical estimate using the 10 percent rule. For each column of data, Table 6.8 displays five descriptive statistics: mean, median, standard deviation, quartile range (that is, the range between the 25 percent and the 75 percent quartile), and range. Finally, the number of classes involved in the judgmental and empirical estimates are given. In all cases the number of classes involved in the judgmental estimate is slightly smaller than the number involved in the empirical estimate. This decrease is due to missing data associated with the judgmental estimates; apparently some teachers refused to complete the OTL instrument.

As can be seen in Table 6.8, the judgmental estimates are, as expected, higher than both empirical estimates. The difference between the judgmental estimates and empirical estimates using the less stringent 5 percent rule range

TABLE 6.8 *Univariate statistics for teachers' ratings and*
empirical estimates of OTL for final achievement tests
(with percentages rounded to the nearest integer)

Study/ Statistic	Teacher rating (OTL)	Estimate (5% rule)	Estimate (10% rule)
Australia			
Mean	67	52	38
Median	75	50	40
Standard Deviation	25	17	17
Quartile Range ($Q_1 - Q_3$)	52-92	40-61	28-48
Range	8-100	20-88	4-80
N	71	74	74
Canada Ontario-English			
Mean	75	65	50
Median	80	65	46
Standard Deviation	17	12	15
Quartile Range ($Q_1 - Q_3$)	66-86	58-73	40-58
Range	28-97	40-93	33-93
N	22	26	26
Korea (ROK)			
Mean	—	85	77
Median	—	84	80
Standard Deviation	—	11	13
Quartile Range ($Q_1 - Q_3$)	—	80-92	70-84
Range	—	48-100	48-100
N		45	45
The Netherlands			
Mean	87	—	—
Median	95	—	—
Standard Deviation	18	—	—
Quartile Range ($Q_1 - Q_3$)	75-100	—	—
Range	30-100	—	—
N	47		
Thailand			
Mean	79	63	52
Median	80	65	46
Standard Deviation	29	14	15
Quartile Range ($Q_1 - Q_3$)	75-100	54-74	43-63
Range	0-100	29-97	17-89
N	80	81	81

Notes: Teachers' ratings of OTL were not used in the Republic of Korea.
Different tests were used as pretests and posttests in the Netherlands.

from 10 percent in Canada Ontario-English to 16 percent in Thailand. The
tendency for teachers to overestimate the extent of their students' learning
can be seen quite clearly in the stem and leaf diagrams shown in Figs. 6.3
and 6.4.

Teacher rating			Estimate (5% criterion)		
Stem	Leaf	Cases	Stem	Leaf	Cases
10	0000000	7	10		0
9	666666	6	9		0
9	22222	5	9		0
8	8888	4	8	8	1
8	00004444	8	8	00044	5
7	566666	6	7	666	3
7	22	2	7	222	3
6	88888	5	6	888	3
6	000024444	9	6	000000444	9
5	6	1	5	66666666	8
5	222	3	5	22222	5
4	8	1	4	88888888	8
4	04	2	4	0000444444444	13
3	6	1	3	6666	4
3	22	2	3	2222	4
2	888	3	2	8888	4
2	0444	4	2	0044	4
1	6	1	1		0
1		0	1		0
0	8	1	0		0

FIG. 6.3   Frequency distributions of Australian teachers' ratings of OTL and empirical estimates of OTL using the 5 percent criterion (with OTL ratings missing for three classes).

Teacher rating			Estimate (5% criterion)		
Stem	Leaf	Cases	Stem	Leaf	Cases
10	0000000000000000000000	22	10		0
9	677777777	9	9	7	1
9	11114444444	11	9	1	1
8	89999	5	8	66669	5
8	0000333333333	13	8	0333	4
7		0	7	77777777	8
7	1144	4	7	11144	5
6	6	1	6	66666666999999	14
6	0	1	6	0000000033333333	16
5	7	1	5	777	3
5	014	3	5	111444444	9
4		0	4	666669999	9
4		0	4	0	1
3		0	3	7	1
3	1	1	3	444	3
2		0	2	9	1
2	8	1	2		0
1	44	2	1		0
1	669	3	1		0
0	000	3	0		0

FIG. 6.4   Frequency distributions of Thailand teachers' ratings of OTL and empirical estimates of OTL using the 5 percent criterion (with OTL rating missing for one class).

The data in Fig. 6.3 pertain to the Australian data; those in Fig. 6.4 to the Thailand data. Thirty-one of the 80 classsrooms in Thailand (or approximately 39 percent) were associated with a judgmental OTL index of 95 or higher. In contrast, only 1 of these 80 classrooms was associated with an empirical OTL index (using the 5 percent criterion) of 95 or higher. With respect to the Australian data the results are almost identical. From Fig. 6.3 it can be seen that 18 of the 71 classrooms (or approximately 25 percent) were associated with a judgmental OTL index of 90 or higher. In contrast, in none of these classrooms was the empirical OTL index (using the 5 percent rule) 90 or higher.

Using the midpoint between the two estimates as our "best" estimate of OTL, students in the participating countries had an opportunity to learn the content related to slightly less than three-fourths of the items included in the posttest. If the OTL index can be viewed as an index of the content validity of a test, the posttest was most valid in the Netherlands (with a median judgmental index of 95) and the Republic of Korea (with a median of OTL index of 82), and least valid in Australia (with a median OTL index of 55).

From the perspective of subsequent analyses the large variation of the OTL indices *within* countries is noteworthy. In all countries the posttest seems inappropriate for at least some small number of classrooms. This fact can be seen in Table 6.8 by comparing the quartile range with the total range. Regardless of the estimate used, the differences between the classrooms in which the students had the most opportunity to learn and those in which they had the least was never less than 50 percent in any country. That is, in certain classrooms in each country students had an opportunity to learn the content associated with two or three times as many test items as did students in other classrooms. The implications of this finding for the study are straightforward. To the extent that the opportunity to learn influences student achievement, students in these different classrooms will perform differently on the posttests independent of the type and quality of instruction they receive. This fact must be taken into account when examining relationships between "schooling" variables and final achievement and attitudes.

The Student Variable Model

As has been discussed earlier in this chapter, because of the wide variation across studies in the number of teachers and classes it was impossible to test the core model reliably in most of the studies. That is, the small number of classrooms in relation to the number of "classroom-based" constructs and manifest variables prohibited a meaningful empirical investigation of the core model as initially specified and described in Chapter 2. As a consequence, a submodel, labelled the student variable model, was constructed. The between-construct relationships of the student variable model are displayed in Fig. 6.5. As suggested by its name, the student variable model focused primarily on variables whose measurement relied on individual student responses (e.g., attitude towards school) or variables for which numerical values could be assigned to individual students (e.g., father's occupation). The student variable model was derived from the core model and could be tested in virtually all countries since the number of students included in the various replications was generally sufficiently large to undertake meaningful statistical analyses (see Table 6.1 for the number of students included in the analysis in each country). The similarities and differences between the core model and the student variable model are noteworthy.

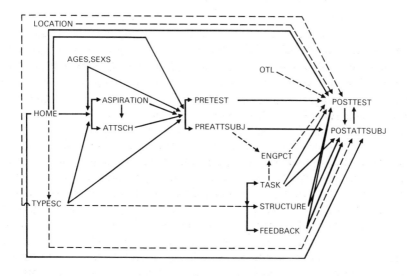

FIG. 6.5   The student variable model.[a]
[a] Broken lines indicate paths not examined in all countries because the subconstructs associated with those paths were not included in all countries.

First, seven of the fifteen constructs included in the core model were eliminated completely. These seven constructs are: teacher perceptions, teacher characteristics, classroom context, orienting students, teaching students, assessing and evaluating students, and managing students. These constructs pertain to teachers and classrooms as observational units. As a consequence, the corresponding numerical values are constant within classes and the number of cases available for an examination of these constructs would be equal to the number of teachers and classes included in the study. In addition to the aforementioned seven "schooling" constructs, the construct "community characteristics" was with but one exception excluded from the student variable model since in the core model no direct effects of this construct on any of the student constructs was hypothesized. The exception concerns the Republic of Korea where the single manifest variable associated with this construct namely "school location" was found to have some impact on the initial and final achievement measures (see Table 6.2). Although in the core model "school location" was not hypothesized to be directly related to any of the student constructs, the inclusion of this variable in the multivariate analysis was judged necessary in order to achieve a somewhat more appropriate examination of the Korean data. The corresponding variable is termed LOCATION in Fig. 6.5 and was coded as "1" for the Korean classes located in metropolitan or urban schools and "0" for the classes located in suburban or rural schools.

Second, the construct "student characteristics" was decomposed into six subconstructs. These subconstructs are student age (AGES), student sex (SEXS, coded as "1" for girls and "0" for boys), aspirations for obtaining further education (ASPIRATION), general attitude towards school (ATTSCH), initial achievement (PRETEST), and initial attitude toward the subject matter being taught (PREATTSUBJ). The hypothesized interrelationships among these subconstructs are shown in Fig. 6.5.

Third, the construct "student perceptions" was decomposed into three subconstructs; namely, the degree to which students perceived their classrooms to be business-like and task-oriented (TASK), the degree to which they saw their teachers as structuring their presentation of the subject matter by highlighting key points, providing clear explanations, and summarizing (STRUCTURE), and the degree to which students believed that they were told about the quality of their work and received extra help as needed (FEEDBACK).

Fourth, the construct "school characteristics" was decomposed into one single manifest variable, namely the type of the school that the students attended (TYPESC, generally coded as "1" for private or parochial schools and "0" for public schools). Similarly, the construct "quantity of instruction" was reduced to a single manifest variable. This construct was defined in terms of the extent to which students were judged by their teachers as having had sufficient opportunity to learn (OTL) the material included on the final achievement test. Since the OTL was a national option in the design of the study, data were only available for a limited number of countries. The variables "opportunity to learn," "type of school," and "school location" were not included in the student variable model in all countries either because the variables were constant (e.g., all students attended the same type of school), or because the results of the preliminary analyses indicated negligible or confounded effects. The fact that the variables OTL, TYPESC, and LOCATION were omitted in some countries is indicated in Fig. 6.5 by broken-line paths.

Fifth, two constructs are simply relabeled in Fig. 6.5. The construct "home characteristics" is abbreviated as HOME while the construct "student participation in learning" is referred to as ENGPCT (for the percent of students in class observed to be engaged in learning or on-task). Because of the way in which the percent of academically engaged students was estimated, the same numerical value was assigned to every student in a particular class. In Fig. 6.5 a broken-line path is associated with ENGPCT. In Hungary valid observer estimates of academic engagement were not available, thus requiring the deletion of ENGPCT in that study.

Finally, two types of student learning outcomes are specified in Fig. 6.5: final achievement (POSTTEST) and final attitude toward the subject matter (POSTATTSUBJ). An interactive or bi-directional relationship between these two outcome variables is specified in the model (that is, the model is specified as nonrecursive). As a consequence of this specification, PRETEST is believed to influence POSTTEST directly, but the influence of PRETEST on POSTATTSUBJ is believed to be indirect only (through its influence on POSTTEST). Similarly, PREATTSUBJ is believed to influence POST-ATTSUBJ directly, but its influence on POSTTEST is hypothesized to be indirect only (through its influence on POSTATTSUBJ).

In summary, then, the student variable model constitutes a reduced but also a somewhat more elaborated or disaggregated submodel of the core model. It is a *reduced* model because the number of "classroom-based" constructs and manifest variables has been reduced drastically. In fact, most of the "classroom-based" constructs involved in the core model have been excluded from the student variable model with just four subconstructs retained (TYPESC, LOCATION, OTL, and ENGPCT). When specifying direct effects of these variables, the number of classes involved in the various data sets was considered. Depending on the number of classes included in a study, no single construct in the student variable model was hypothesized to be directly influenced by more than one, two, or three "classroom-based" subconstructs. This restriction was imposed in order to achieve reasonably high reliability in the estimation of the corresponding path coefficients.

The student variable model constitutes a *disaggregated* version of the core model because a number of "student-based" constructs were decomposed into their components or *subconstructs*. Such a decomposition was necesary because of the somewhat heterogeneous nature of some of the core model constructs. For example, the construct "student characteristics" involves age, sex, aspirations, attitude towards school, attitude towards subject matter and initial achievement as subconstructs. Although useful conceptually, it would be difficult if not impossible to consider this construct as uni-dimensional. As such, it could not be used meaningfully in path analyses. It should also be noted that the disaggregation of core model constructs permitted the examination of relationships between subconstructs that could not be examined in the core model. For example, final achievement and final attitude toward subject matter are in the core model conceived as being

180   *Norbert Sellin and Lorin W. Anderson*

components of one construct, "student outcomes." The student variable model, on the other hand, specified a bi-directional relationship between final achievement and final attitude. That is, in contrast to the core model, the relationship between achievement and attitude is modelled explicitly.

Testing the Student Variable Model

The student variable model was tested using data collected in seven of the studies: Australia, Canada Ontario-English, Canada Ontario-French, Hungary, the Republic of Korea, the Netherlands, and Thailand. Three studies, Canada Quebec, Israel and Nigeria, were excluded from the test of the student variable model either because of the absence or questionable reliability of data pertaining to several of key subconstructs.

Once the structure of the student variable model had been determined, attention turned to the selection of appropriate statistical methods to use in analyzing the data. Since a causal model had been developed, some type of path analytic procedure seemed most appropriate. More precisely, since the student variable model involves several constructs measured indirectly by multiple indicators (i.e., manifest variables), a method was required which could estimate this particular type of path model. Two different approaches to path analysis were considered: LISREL (see, for example, Joreskog 1973) and Partial Least Squares (PLS) (see, for example, Wold 1982). After much deliberation, the PLS approach was selected over the more familiar LISREL approach for at least two reasons.

First, as was the case for the core model, the student variable model was developed *post hoc*; that is, decisions concerning instruments and associated manifest variables were made before the model had been developed. Since the model is not an *a priori* model, the nature of the analysis was seen more as exploratory than confirmatory. The PLS technique has been developed especially for research situations which require a great deal of exploratory analyses. LISREL, on the other hand, is designed primarily for situations which require confirmatory tests of theoretically well-established path models. (See Joreskog and Wold 1982 for a more detailed discussion of this point.)

Second, LISREL employs the maximum likelihood method to obtain parameter estimates and therefore requires quite restrictive distributional assumptions. Specifically, one must assume that the observations are governed by a joint multivariate distribution, usually the multivariate normal distribution. The validity of such assumptions would appear highly questionable for much of the data gathered in this study. As its name implies, PLS uses least squares estimates and, as a consequence, distributional assumptions are not required.

Because of the possible unfamiliarity of the PLS approach to many readers, a brief description of the PLS approach in general and the specific manner in which PLS was applied to the data in this study is included in Appendix B. In the remainder of this chapter the results obtained from the application of the PLS procedure to the data will be discussed and described in a relatively non-technical way.

Remodelling the Student Variable Model

The student variable model depicted in Fig. 6.5 illustrates the relationships between the subconstructs as these relationships were specified initially. The results of a number of preliminary analyses were examined to determine the best "fit" of the model to the data collected in each study. This examination focused on two aspects of the model: (1) the appropriateness of the placement of each manifest variable within a particular subconstruct, and (2) the strength of the paths connecting the subconstructs within one another. As a result of these investigations, subconstructs, manifest variables, and paths were eliminated from the model on a study-by-study basis.

Four subconstructs were excluded prior to the analysis in at least one study. These subconstructs were: LOCATION (school location), TYPESC (type of school), OTL (teachers' ratings of their students' opportunity to learn), and ENGPCT (the percent of students observed to be engaged in the classroom activity). The two most common reasons for eliminating manifest variables were (1) particular questionnaire items were not used in a given study, and (2) large amounts of data pertaining to certain variables were missing (specifically, more than 15 percent of the data). A complete listing of the manifest variables omitted in at least one study will be presented later in this chapter. Because of these deletions and because the achievement tests were developed specifically for each study, somewhat unique "final" versions of the model were specified for each study. Thus, the initial student variable model is best viewed as a starting point for the analysis of the data collected in each study.

Before presenting the final model results for each study, some comments on the criteria and procedures used in evaluating and respecifying the student variable model seem appropriate. In order to aid in the discussion some results pertaining to the initial version of the student variable model will be presented. Table 6.9 presents the PLS loadings for the manifest variables associated with the subconstructs TASK, STRUCTURE, and FEEDBACK. Table 6.10 presents the estimated and total effects of the various subconstructs on POSTTEST and POSTATTSUBJ.

Turning our attention initially to Table 6.9, the PLS loadings will be examined first. PLS loadings are simply the zero-order correlations between manifest variables and the subconstruct (or construct) with which they are associated. When examining PLS results, then, the *magnitude* of these loadings is an important consideration. Specifically, small loadings indicate inappropriate model specification either in terms of the composition or

TABLE 6.9 *Loadings of TASK, STRUCTURE, and FEEDBACK*
in the initial version of the student variable model
(with coefficients multiplied by 1,000)

Manifest variables	Aust	COE	COF	Hung	ROK	Neth	Thai
TASK (Perceived teacher's task orientation)							
Teacher deals with misbehavior quickly	331	495	539	212	481	559	279
Teacher lets class fool around (R)	406	181	− 268	461	409	586	459
Teacher keeps class paying attention	582	604	555	616	707	724	511
Teacher unable to deal with misbehavior (R)	572	557	729	− 382	− 470	599	− 373
Teacher knows what's going on	474	506	604	566	442	544	344
Teacher makes us follow class rules	580	569	487	600	594	607	526
Punish for minor misbehavior (R)	− 045	044	− 260	043	076	104	− 041
Most time spent on lesson	023	443	na	166	266	327	165
People expected to work	349	300	133	406	184	266	275
Talk about other things (R)	386	286	409	454	271	647	448
Getting work done very important	343	377	266	165	185	181	187
Most people don't work (R)	462	538	369	422	333	682	347
Usually do what set out to do	364	404	216	230	381	625	317
Absentees trouble to catch up	− 064	250	− 068	− 070	298	046	370
Teacher talks about other things (R)	242	169	476	285	151	049	394
More time fun than learn (R)	377	362	197	545	230	673	476
Teacher sticks to work	197	299	009	264	182	203	163
STRUCTURE (Perceived structuring of lessons)							
Teacher explains things	678	822	851	833	746	918	481
Teacher gets us to think of solutions	705	649	478	441	709	673	728
Teacher tells what is important	613	258	680	523	555	377	660
Teacher reviews important things at end	376	372	369	552	628	257	452
FEEDBACK (Perceived feedback)							
Teacher gives me more help	380	618	827	549	456	057	610
Teacher checks work	598	313	466	804	705	680	719
Teacher tells why answer wrong	868	848	624	672	796	740	623

Notes: Entries marked "na" indicate data on the manifest variable were not available. (R) indicates a reversal in scoring. That is, a negative response to the item is scored positively. Finally, study abbreviations are similar to those in previous tables.

structure of the subconstruct or the hypothesized between-subconstruct relationships.

Another important aspect is the *sign* (that is, positive or negative) of the estimated loadings. When formulating PLS models, one should generally specify the expected signs of the loadings associated with each latent variable (Wold 1982). The model results can then be evaluated in terms of discrepancies between expected signs and actually obtained signs. For the student variable model all loadings were expected to be positive. From Table 6.2 it can be seen, however, that several loadings in terms of TASK, STRUCTURE, and seen, however, that several loadings in terms of TASK, STRUCTURE, and FEEDBACK were negative. While no manifest variable has consistently negative loadings across all data sets, some manifest variables have, in fact, fairly large negative loadings within certain studies. For example, consider the fourth manifest variable belonging to the subconstruct TASK. (This item asserted that the "teacher was unable to deal with misbehavior." The coding of the responses to this item was reflected so that a high numerical value indicates that teachers were able to deal with misbehavior.) This variable has rather large positive loadings in Australia, Canada Ontario-English, Canada Ontario-French, and the Netherlands, but negative loadings in Hungary, the Republic of Korea, and Thailand. An examination of the corresponding frequency distributions in the latter three countries revealed that the student responses to this particular item were heavily skewed in that almost all of the students agreed that their teachers were able to deal with misbehavior. Leaving aside the question of whether this response reflects reality or an unwillingness on the part of students to endorse a statement critical of their teacher, this particular manifest variable did not "fit" within the construct TASK in these three countries. As a consequence this manifest variable was eliminated from further analysis in these countries.

While unexpected negative loadings can generally be interpreted as providing a clear indication that a given manifest variable should be eliminated, a more difficult aspect is to determine when loadings are sufficiently large to retain the corresponding manifest variable. That is, some criteria must be specified to evaluate the estimated within-construct relationships (that is, the relationships between manifest variables and constructs). Three options were considered.

One option would be to apply standard statistical tests. As noted earlier, PLS loadings are defined as zero-order correlations between manifest variables and their associated constructs (or subconstructs). The key feature of PLS is the explicit estimation of constructs as weighted linear composites of their manifest variables. These loadings are formally obtained by Ordinary Least Squares (OLS) regression of each manifest variable on the estimate of the construct with which it is associated. Standard test statistics, such as the familiar t-test, could thus be computed for each loading. This approach has, for example, been used by Noonan and Wold (1983). It is well known, however, that standard statistical tests require quite restrictive distributional assumptions, notably normality and independence of residuals. The response options for several of the manifest variables belonging to the subconstruct TASK were simply "Yes" and "No." In this case, such distributional assumptions would be untenable. Furthermore, intact classes were included in the study. As a consequence, assumptions concerning the independence of residuals would most likely be violated. The most important point, however, was that the data sets were not random samples. With the possible exception of Australia, all data sets were convenience samples. Under these circumstances, it makes little sense to employ standard statistical tests since essential sampling requirements were not fulfilled.

A second option would have been to employ less demanding statistical techniques, such as the Stone-Geisser test of predictive relevance proposed by Wold (1982). As described in Appendix B, the Stone-Geisser test is based on Tukey's jackknife procedure and produces jackknife estimates of residual variances which can be used for testing purposes. Jackknife standard deviations of point estimates can be obtained as a by-product. The Stone-Geisser test is distribution-free in the sense that normality and independence of residuals are not required. To compute jackknife test statistics, however, raw data rather than crossproduct data (that is, correlations or covariances) must be fed into computer. Moreover, the PLS programs available for data analyses required raw input data sets which were free from missing data.

Because of the latter requirement, it was not possible to use jackknifing to evaluate the results of the student variable model. Missing data occurred for virtually all variables involved in the analysis and, except for some special cases, it was judged inappropriate to replace all missing data by some numerical estimates. Within the limited available time, it was also not possible to develop a PLS program that could handle missing data properly. As a consequence, the PLS analyses described in this chapter were based on correlation matrices prepared using standard computer software packages. With but few exceptions in which imputation techniques (e.g., the insertion of class means for missing data) were judged appropriate, routine procedures such as "pairwise deletion" were used when missing values were encountered.

A third option for evaluating the strength of relationships between manifest variables and constructs is to apply some prespecified *ad hoc* criteria. This option has been chosen for the PLS analyses reported in this chapter. In general, modifications of within-construct relationships were considered when estimated loadings were found to be smaller than 0.2, an obviously rather weak criterion. In view of the somewhat heterogeneous nature of the TASK, STRUCTURE and FEEDBACK subconstructs, however, the acceptance of a fairly broad range of estimated loadings seemed appropriate. In the Netherlands, for example, this criterion would result in the deletion of three additional manifest variables associated with the subconstruct TASK (with two manifest variables having been deleted because of negative loadings) and no additional manifest variables associated with the other two subconstructs.

Manifest variables were not eliminated solely on the basis of an examination of initial model results since such a practice would be inappropriate. When using PLS, it is important to remember that the estimation of constructs and hence the estimation of loadings depends not only on the specification of within-construct relationships, but also on the specification of between-construct relationships. In fact, the respecification of between-construct relationships, such as the deletion of particular paths, generally influences *all* estimates involved in a given model, including the loadings. For example, the initial between-construct effects displayed in Table 6.10 would suggest the elimination of the hypothesized direct effect of STRUCTURE on POSTTEST since the coefficient representing this effect is near zero in all countries, with a small, uninterpretable negative effect obtained for Australia, Canada Ontario-English, the Republic of Korea, the Netherlands, and Thailand. The deletion of the path from STRUCTURE to POSTTEST will generally effect not only the loadings obtained for STRUCTURE, but also the loadings obtained for TASK and FEEDBACK. This modification will, in fact, influence the loadings obtained for all subconstructs involved in the student variable model, except for subconstructs comprising just one manifest variable (when the loading is necessarily equal to unity).

Similarly, the elimination of particular manifest variables will usually effect estimated between-construct relationships. For example, as indicated above, the loadings displayed in Table 6.9 would suggest the elimination of several manifest variables from the construct TASK in all studies. Deleting these variables will usually influence all direct effects involving TASK, and also direct effects involving STRUCTURE and FEEDBACK. The elimination of these manifest variables will also influence the magnitude of descriptive indices reflecting the predictive power of within-construct and between-construct relationships. The extent to which changes in the actual estimates and predictive power indices occur must, of course, be examined empirically. Indeed, the systematic exploration of alternative model specifications is imperative in PLS modelling.

The general strategy for examining the student variable model, then, was to examine the outcomes of a number of competitive versions of the model in terms of both loadings and direct effects. Changes in the predictive power indices (e.g., the R-square value of POSTTEST) that occurred from one version to the next also were considered. Several results were quite common across countries. First, deleting paths had no recognizable impact on the estimated loadings. Second, eliminating manifest variables with small or negative loadings resulted in either no loss of predictive power and, in most cases, an increase in predictive power. As a consequence, several manifest variables were eliminated from the model in various countries.

As a general rule, the possibility of deleting paths was considered when the magnitude of the path coefficients was lower than 0.1 in absolute value. Once again, a rather weak criterion was established; one that corresponds to an increase of one percent "explained" variance in final achievement or attitude, given that specific subconstructs are uncorrelated with all other subconstructs in a specified model. In general, however, the subconstructs included in the student variable model were usually correlated. Hence, what may be termed the "unique" contribution of a subconstruct to the "explained" variation in final achievement or attitude (that is, the increase in R-square when the subconstruct is entered last in a given equation) is generally smaller

TABLE 6.10 Estimated direct (D) and total (T) effects on POSTTEST and POSTATTSUBJ in the initial version of the student variable model (with coefficients multiplied by 1,000)

POSTTEST	Aust D	Aust T	COE D	COE T	COF D	COF T	Hung D	Hung T	ROK D	ROK T	Neth D	Neth T	Thai D	Thai T
LOCATION									081	153				
HOME	058	193	-012	106	084	211	062	182	135	230	065	113	023	244
AGE	-	021	-	-123	-	-068	-	020	-	-004	-	-063	-	-038
SEX	-	-030	-	078	-	045	-	049	-	043	-	080	-	006
TYPESC	-068	-150	074	095	-	123	-	-	-	-	022	022	-089	-276
ASPIRATION	-	124	-	144	-	098	-	102	-	097	-	077	-	057
ATTSCH	-	-003	-	023	-	-	-	024	-	078	-	054	-	080
PRETEST	641	649	641	662	526	548	408	417	352	360	335	343	426	450
PREATTSUBJ	-	030	-	095	-	116	-	053	-	078	-	130	-	042
TASK	085	098	058	087	041	080	105	112	054	080	103	147	027	100
FEEDBACK	000	004	014	021	-032	-029	034	036	002	005	033	045	-032	-030
STRUCTURE	-028	-020	-031	-008	024	072	024	046	-031	-004	-064	-004	-049	-011
OTL	078	079	079	081	-	-	-	-	-	-	272	279	040	041
ENGPCT	033	033	046	048	106	110	-	-	016	017	055	056	047	049
POSTATTSUBJ	068	069	176	182	222	231	112	114	191	196	241	246	302	319

Table 6.10 *(continued)*

	Aust D	Aust T	COE D	COE T	COF D	COF T	Hung D	Hung T	ROK D	ROK T	Neth D	Neth T	Thai D	Thai T
POSTATTSUBJ														
LOCATION									-	020				
HOME	-	043	-	-033	-	093	-	159	-	105	-	062	-	110
AGE	-	011	-	-056	-	-076	-	020	-	-009	-	-047	-	-014
SEX	-	-017	-	077	-	056	-	017	-	032	-	160	-	-006
TYPESC	034	-003	-083	-079							054	126	005	-143
ASPIRATION	-	138	-	146	-	161	-	188	-	091	-	110	-	031
ATTSCH	-	212	-	187	-	263	-	087	-	213	-	185	-	059
PRETEST	-	124	-	120	-	102	-	081	-	054	-	032	-	079
PREATTSUBJ	449	455	497	514	542	564	467	477	397	407	540	543	110	118
TASK	060	078	137	153	037	052	040	061	126	137	-046	-035	216	233
FEEDBACK	051	051	035	038	018	013	009	016	018	018	045	049	097	097
STRUCTURE	117	113	129	128	201	214	186	195	143	143	249	249	125	123
OTL	-	015	-	015							-	026	-	007
ENGPCT	-	006	-	009	-	021			-	002	-	005	-	009
POSTTEST	191	194	182	188	187	195	194	199	130	133	093	095	175	185

Notes: Entries marked "-" indicate direct effects or paths eliminated from the model. Blank entries indicate constructs deleted from the model.

than one percent when the path coefficient is equal to 0.1. The "unique" contribution of subconstructs with path coefficients smaller than 0.1 is generally negligible, if not zero; that is, the subconstruct generally contributes nothing to the predictive power of the model.

There were some exceptions to the application of this general criterion concerning the magnitude of path coefficients. These exceptions concerned the direct effects of TASK and ENGPCT on POSTTEST. These paths were not eliminated although, as will be seen later, the corresponding coefficients were generally smaller than 0.1. This decision to override the criterion was made on the theoretical grounds. For example, ENGPCT was regarded as an important mediating factor between student entry characteristics and final achievement. Furthermore, since ENGPCT was estimated for entire classes of students rather than individual students, numerically large direct effects of ENGPCT on final achievement were not expected. Possible reasons for the apparent lack of predictive power of the constructs TASK and ENGPCT will be discussed below.

In summary, a number of PLS analyses of the student variable model were undertaken in order to remove manifest variables providing irrelevant information, to improve the model in terms of predictive power, and to obtain a more parsimonious model in terms of between-construct relations. We now turn to the presentation of the results of these analyses.

The Deletion of Manifest Variables

The manifest variables associated with each subconstruct included in the student variable model are displayed in the left hand column of Table 6.11. Table 6.11 also presents a study-by-study summary of the loadings of the manifest variables retained in the analysis. Hyphens (-) are used to denote manifest variables deleted from existing subconstructs. Asterisks (*) are used to indicate manifest variables deleted because the associated subconstruct was eliminated. "Na" indicates manifest variables for which data were not collected. "Om" denotes manifest variables omitted from the initial model based on the preliminary analyses. Constructs with single manifest variables (LOCATION, TYPESC, AGES, and SEXS) or with predefined aggregation rules (ASPIRATION, OTL, PRETEST, and POSTTEST) are not included in Table 6.11 because the loadings of subconstructs consisting of just one manifest variable are necessarily equal to unity. In the ensuing discussion, the data will be discussed subconstruct-by-subconstruct rather than study-by-study.

Across all countries HOME ("home background") is defined at least in part by the occupation of the student's father. In Hungary, this manifest variable alone defines the subconstruct. In all other countries additional manifest variables are included. In Canada Ontario-French, the Republic of Korea, and the Netherlands, the manifest variables "father's education" and "mother's

TABLE 6.11 *Loadings of manifest variables in the final version of the student variable model (with coefficients multiplied by 1,000)*

Manifest variable	Aust	COE	COF	Hung	ROK	Neth	Thai
HOME (Home Background)							
Father's Occupation	901	656	752	1,000	890	721	779
Father's Education	na	om	834	na	846	870	827
Mother's Education	na	om	793	na	769	727	749
Language in Home	618	911	-	-	-	-	431
ATTSCH (Attitude Toward School)							
School most enjoyable	756	688	635	409	638	533	375
Dislike school work (R)	770	669	635	605	708	572	450
Enjoy everything in school	768	697	665	393	657	474	421
Want as much education as possible	472	600	581	764	604	669	695
Find school challenging	773	410	568	-	659	333	480
School not very enjoyable (R)	806	726	721	-	682	668	490
Only like to meet friends (R)	-	502	547	645	-	544	-
School days happiest days	755	681	669	476	664	529	548
PREATTSUBJ (Entry Attitude Toward Subject)							
Want to do well	562	443	528	na	649	-	685
Usually understand in class	613	701	749	na	667	752	518
Not good at subject (R)	665	721	682	na	644	863	-
Look forward to more	780	686	572	na	639	-	595
Not do subject on own time (R)	583	501	-	na	525	-	375
Think subject is fun	791	738	673	na	761	589	476
Subject hard for me (R)	623	639	685	na	-	699	-
Don't do well in subject (R)	-	706	717	1,000	-	795	-
Subject important for good job	-	-	-	na	-	-	475
Can get along without subject (R)	-	-	-	na	-	-	420
TASK (Perceived Teacher's Task Orientation)							
Teacher deals with misbehavior quickly	337	488	565	241	487	577	303
Teacher lets class fool around (R)	407	-	-	462	359	598	464
Teacher keeps class paying attention	587	627	573	654	711	724	534
Teacher unable to deal with misbehavior (R)	579	576	764	-	-	602	-
Teacher knows what's going on	469	547	620	593	473	533	377
Teacher makes us follow class rules	595	583	530	653	615	624	556
Punish for minor misbehavior (R)	-	-	-	-	-	-	-
Most time spent on lesson	-	391	na	-	269	330	-
People expected to work	350	302	-	431	202	263	301
Talk about other things (R)	382	273	405	468	266	644	434
Getting work done very important	344	408	266	-	-	-	-
Most people don't work (R)	467	536	409	408	334	669	351
Usually do what set out to do	365	425	226	246	399	618	316
Absentees trouble to catch up	-	-	-	-	311	-	372
Teacher talks about other things (R)	242	-	464	293	-	-	395
More time fun than learn (R)	367	359	-	579	230	668	477
Teacher sticks to work	-	267	-	290	-	-	-

Continued...

TABLE 6.11   *(Contd.)*

Manifest variable	Aust	COE	COF	Hung	ROK	Neth	Thai
STRUCTURE (Perceived structuring of lessons)							
Teacher explains things	641	814	852	837	742	960	489
Teacher gets us to think of solutions	731	614	485	440	704	591	730
Teacher tells what is important	609	341	676	519	554	307	653
Teacher reviews important things at end	407	425	369	546	638	-	451
FEEDBACK (Perceived feedback)							
Teacher gives me more help	*	*	*	*	*	*	629
Teacher checks work	*	*	*	*	*	*	708
Teacher tells why answer wrong	*	*	*	*	*	*	616
ENGPCT (Percent Engaged Rating)							
Snapshot rating	-	-	847	om	785	1,000	871
IAR rating	1,000	1,000	916	om	904	na	908
POSTATTSUBJ (Outcome attitude toward subject)							
Really want to do well	522	552	548	578	634	-	576
Usually understand discussion	656	718	741	605	703	754	450
Not so good in subject (R)	746	725	716	757	640	833	-
Look forward to more	690	737	600	466	616	-	477
Subject not on own time (R)	477	392	-	503	503	-	450
Think subject is fun	412	676	607	633	676	629	400
Subject hard for me (R)	691	610	745	730	-	721	-
Have to work hard (R)	-	-	-	704	400	747	-
Subject important for good job	-	431	-	-	-	-	538
Can get along without subject (R)	-	444	458	-	-	-	513

Notes: Entries marked "-" indicate deleted manifest variables. Entries marked "na" indicate manifest variables not included in a particular study. Entries marked "om" indicate manifest variables omitted from the initial model. Entries marked "*" indicate manifest variables dropped because the associated subconstruct was deleted. (R) indicates a reversal in scoring. That is, a negative response is scored positively.

education" also are included within HOME. In Australia and Canada Ontario-English the compatibility of the language of instruction with that spoken in the home, labeled "language in home," is included in HOME, while father's education and mother's education are not. Finally, in Thailand all four prespecified manifest variables combine to form HOME. In summary, then, the common denominator in defining HOME across all countries is the occupation of the student's father.

ATTSCH ("attitude toward school") was originally defined in terms of an eight-item scale. With few exceptions, ATTSCH was ultimately defined by students' responses to these eight items. The exceptions are in Hungary (where two of the items were eliminated because of low PLS loadings) and Australia, the Republic of Korea, and Thailand (where the same single item was eliminated). In the remaining countries (Canada Ontario-English, Canada Ontario-French, and the Netherlands) no items were eliminated.

PREATTSUBJ ("initial attitude toward subject matter") was originally defined by a ten-item scale. As can be seen in Table 6.11, several different items were eliminated across countries. In Hungary, in fact, only a single item was administered to the students. Excluding Hungary, eight of the ten items were eliminated in at least one country. If only the two common items are considered, then students with higher scores on PREATTSUBJ tended to report that they (1) usually understood the subject being presented, and (2) thought studying the subject was enjoyable.

TASK ("perceived task orientation") was initially defined by 17 items. Seven were concerned with the extent to which teachers were able to control student behavior (that is, keep the students paying attention or on-task), and ten of the items pertained to the overall climate of the classroom (that is, the extent to which the class was perceived to be task-oriented). As can be seen in Table 6.11, seven of these items had sufficiently high PLS loadings to be included in TASK in all countries. Several of the remaining ten items were included in some countries and excluded in others. Based on the common items, students receiving higher TASK scores tended to report that their teachers (1) were able to deal with misbehavior quickly and effectively, (2) kept them paying attention and following class rules, and (3) knew what was going on in the classroom at all times. In addition, these students saw the classroom as a place where working hard and completing assignments was the rule, not the exception.

STRUCTURE ("perceived structuring") and FEEDBACK ("perceived feedback") were initially defined in terms of responses to four and three items, respectively. With only one exception, the initial items were retained after the preliminary analysis. The exception occurred in the Netherlands where one item was eliminated from STRUCTURE and one from FEEDBACK. In general, higher scores on STRUCTURE meant that students perceived their teachers as clarifying for them what was important to learn, explaining and summarizing key ideas and major points, and helping students to think for themselves. Higher FEEDBACK scores meant that teachers held students accountable for the completion of their work, told students why answers were incorrect, and provided students with extra help as needed.

Data pertaining to the ENGPCT ("percent academically engaged students") came from two sources; the Classroom Snapshot (SNAP) and the Individual Activity Record (IAR). To code academic engagement using the SNAP, the observers identified the various groupings of students in the classroom (which would be one group during whole-class instruction) and counted the number of students in each grouping that were observed to be on-task or otherwise engaged in learning. These counts were used to derive the SNAP estimate of the mean percent of students engaged in learning. Using the IAR the observers watched eight randomly selected students and recorded for each student whether she or he was observedly engaged in learning. The corresponding records were used to derive the IAR estimate of the mean percent of academically engaged students in a given class. This was based on the assumption that the behavior of the eight preselected was representative of the behavior of the whole class. As reported by Mandeville (1984) the two estimates of academic engagement were quite different (see also Chapter 5). In general the SNAP estimate was higher than the IAR estimate. Furthermore, the correlation between the two estimates in many countries was moderate, rather than high.

As can be seen in Table 6.11 the ENGPCT is defined by both the SNAP and IAR estimates in three studies: Canada Ontario-French, the Republic of Korea, and Thailand. In Australia and Canada Ontario-English ENGPCT was ultimately defined by the IAR estimate only because the PLS loadings associated with the SNAP estimates were close to zero in both countries. In the Netherlands ENGPCT was defined by the SNAP estimate alone because the IAR was not used. Finally, as has been mentioned earlier, neither estimate was judged appropriate in Hungary. As a consequence, ENGPCT was eliminated from the Hungarian student variable model.

Finally, with minor exceptions (e.g., the Hungarian model) the items defining POSTATTSUBJ ("final attitude toward subject") were identical to those defining the PREATTSUBJ. As was true for PREATTSUBJ, several manifest variables were eliminated from POSTATTSUBJ in the various countries. In fact, only two of the ten items initially common to PREATTSUBJ and POSTATTSUBJ were retained in both instruments in all studies following the preliminary analyses. These two items concerned the extent to which students reported understanding the subject and the extent to which they said they enjoyed learning it. Three of the items were excluded from POST-ATTSUBJ in one-half or more of the studies. These items pertained to student beliefs about the difficulty of the subject matter and the importance of the subject matter for job- and life-success. In general, however, the items included in PREATTSUBJ also were included in POSTATTSUBJ. Thus, the meaning of higher score is quite similar for both.

The Deletion of Paths and Constructs

Tables 6.12 and 6.13 present summaries of deleted paths and subconstructs. Table 6.12 shows the direct effects which were initially specified but eliminated during the final analysis in at least one study. Each asterisk represents a study in which the path was deleted; the studies are identified in the right hand column of the table. Table 6.13 summarizes the subconstructs that were deleted in one or more studies and indicates the reasons for elimination. A subconstruct was deleted when either (1) all manifest variables associated

with that construct were eliminated, (2) all hypothesized paths between that
subconstruct and others were deleted, or (3) for those subconstructs defined
in terms of a single manifest variable, the distribution of the data was
severely skewed or had no variance.

TABLE 6.12   *A summary of paths deleted in the*
final versions of the student model

Predicted construct	Predictor construct	Deleted paths	Studies
ASPIRATION	TYPESC	**	COE, Neth
	HOME	*	COE
	AGES	****	Aust, Hung, ROK, Neth
	SEXS	***	COF, Neth, Thai
ATTSCH	TYPESC	**	Neth, Thai
	HOME	**	COF, Hung
	AGES	******	Aust, COE, COF, Hung, Neth, Thai
	SEXS	***	ROK, Neth, Thai
PRETEST	TYPESC	*	Neth
	HOME	*	Neth
	AGES	***	Aust, Hung, ROK
	SEXS	****	Aust, COF, ROK, Thai
	ATTSCH	****	Aust, COE, Hung, Neth
PREATTSUBJ	TYPESC	**	Aust, COE
	HOME	*	COE
	AGES	*****	Aust, COE, Hung, ROK, Neth
	SEXS	****	COF, Hung, ROK, Thai
TASK	TYPESC	***	Aust, COE, Neth
STRUCTURE	TYPESC	***	Aust, COE, Neth
FEEDBACK	TYPESC	***	Aust, COE, Neth
ENGPCT	PREATTSUBJ	******	Aust, COE, COF, ROK, Neth, Thai
POSTTEST	TYPESC	***	Aust, COE, Neth
	HOME	******	Aust, COE, COF, Hung, Neth, Thai
	OTL	**	COE, Thai
	STRUCTURE	*******	Aust, COE, COF, Hung, ROK, Neth, Thai
	FEEDBACK	*******	Aust, COE, COF, Hung, ROK, Neth, Thai
	TASK	*	COE
POSTATTSUBJ	TYPESC	***	Aust, COE, Neth
	TASK	*	Neth
	FEEDBACK	******	Aust, COE, COF, Hung, ROK, Neth

Notes: TYPESC was omitted from the initial model in Canada Ontario-French, Hungary, and the
Republic of Korea. ENGPCT was omitted from the initial model in Hungary. Finally, OTL was omitted
from the initial model in Canada Ontario-French, Hungary, and the Republic of Korea.

TABLE 6.13   *A summary of subconstructs deleted from
the final versions of the student variable model*

Subconstructs	Aust	COE	COF	Studies Hung	ROK	Neth	Thai
TYPESC			nv	nv	sk		
AGES	np			np			
SEXS					np		np
OTL		np	nd	nd	nd		np
FEEDBACK	np	np	np	np	np	np	
ENGPCT				nm			

Notes: Five reasons for deletion are given in the table. These are: no
variance (nv), skewness (sk), no data collected (nd), no manifest
variables (nm), and no associated paths in the final model (np).

In Australia a number of paths were eliminated. All paths leading from
AGES were deleted. As a consequence, AGES was also deleted. Most paths
leading to PRETEST and PREATTSUBJ were deleted. After deleting paths,
only TYPESC, HOME, and ASPIRATION were found to influence PRE-
ATTSUBJ. Furthermore, most paths leading from TYPESC were deleted.
The results of the preliminary analyses suggest that in Australia TYPESC
had no substantial direct effects on PREATTSUBJ, TASK, STRUCTURE,
and POSTATTSUBJ. Other deleted paths and constructs can be noted in
Tables 6.12 and 6.13.

In Canada Ontario-English nineteen of the paths initially included in the
student variable model were eliminated. Most paths leading from TYPESC
were deleted so that only the paths from TYPESC to ATTSCH and from
TYPESC to PRETEST remained. Three of the paths leading to PREATTSUBJ
were deleted, namely the paths from HOME, TYPESC and AGES. Interestingly, the paths from TYPESC and HOME to POSTTEST also were
eliminated because the associated path coefficients were found to be close to
zero. More will be said about the direct effect of HOME on POSTTEST later
in this chapter. Finally, the variable OTL was removed from the model
because the final PLS analysis yielded a small direct effect for this variable
that contributed nothing to the prediction of POSTTEST. Once again, other
deleted paths and constructs can be seen in Tables 6.12 and 6.13.

In contrast to Canada Ontario-English, only six paths were deleted from
the student variable model in Canada Ontario-French. The only particularly
noteworthy deletions are the paths from HOME to ATTSCH and from
HOME to POSTTEST. TYPESC was eliminated from the model because all
students attended the same type of school. OTL was removed because data
were not collected during the Canadian Ontario-French study.

In Hungary all paths leading from AGES were eliminated. These deletions resulted in the elimination of AGES. TYPESC and ENGPCT also were eliminated; TYPESC because, like their counterparts in Canada Ontario-French, all students attended the same type of school, and ENGPCT because of the absence of valid manifest variables. Finally, the OTL was removed from the model since no data were collected. Other deleted paths can be noted in Table 6.12.

In the Republic of Korea all paths leading from AGES were once again deleted, resulting in the elimination of AGES. TYPESC was eliminated because of severe skewness in the frequency distribution (with most students attending one type of school). Finally, OTL was removed from the model since no data were collected.

In the Netherlands, virtually all paths leading from TYPESC were deleted. Only the path from TYPESC to PREATTSUBJ remained. The paths leading to and from FEEDBACK were eliminated. Thus, FEEDBACK was deleted from the student variable model in the Netherlands. Although not mentioned previously, this path was also deleted in all other countries with the exception of Thailand.

Finally, in Thailand all paths from SEXS were deleted, resulting in the deletion of SEXS from the model. In addition, the single path leading from OTL to POSTTEST was deleted because, similarly to Canada Ontario-English, the associated direct effect was nil. This deletion resulted in the elimination of OTL from the student variable model. Other deletions of paths can be seen in Table 6.12.

The deletions of manifest variables, paths, and subconstructs resulted in revised versions of the student variable model for each country. These "study-unique" models as specified were entered into the PLS program and a final PLS analysis was performed on the data from each study. The results of these final analyses are presented in the next section of the chapter.

The Results for the Student Variable Model

Summaries of the direct and total effects of the subconstructs in the model on POSTTEST and POSTATTSUBJ are displayed in Tables 6.14 and 6.15, respectively. The data included in these tables will be discussed study-by-study. Before discussing the results, however, a brief explanation of the nature of the data included in these tables is in order.

The entries in Table 6.14 represent the direct (D) and total (T) effects of the various subconstructs on POSTTEST in each study. "Direct effect" is defined as the magnitude of the coefficients corresponding with a path connecting a subconstruct *directly* with POSTTEST. "Total effect," on the other hand, is the combined magnitude of the coefficients of *all* paths leading from a given subconstruct to POSTTEST either directly or indirectly (that is, via paths to other subconstructs, which in turn are connected with POST-TEST). The computation of total effects involves, first, the multiplication

TABLE 6.14 Estimated direct (D) and total (T) effects on POSTTEST in the final versions of the student variable model (with coefficients multiplied by 1,000)

	Aust		COE		COF		Hung		Neth		ROK		Thai	
	D	T	D	T	D	T	D	T	D	T	D	T	D	T
LOCATION											087	160		
HOME	-	126	-	085	-	127	-	126	-	024	138	257	-	254
AGE	-	-015	-	-117	-	-070			-	-056			-	-033
SEX	-	-080	-	076	-	015	-	045	-	074	-	034		
TYPESC	-	-006	-	-006					-	012			-116	-334
ASPIRATION	-	129	-	140	-	132	-	112	-	072	-	087	-	058
ATTSCH	-	008	-	029	-	061	-	013	-	033	-	078	-	080
PRETEST	674	679	646	660	543	567	412	425	313	320	369	379	478	489
PREATTSUBJ	-	017	-	082	-	041	-	077	-	133	-	071	-	029
TASK	088	099	050	076	009	042	102	106	095	121	054	080	103	135
FEEDBACK													-	016
STRUCTURE	-	006	-	019	-	053	-	032	-	060	-	031	-	025
OTL	100	102							275	281				
ENGPCT	040	041	064	065	118	123			058	059	020	021	080	081
POSTATTSUBJ	037	038	152	156	245	255	159	164	246	251	187	192	150	154

Notes: Entries marked "-" indicate omitted direct effects or paths. Blank entries indicate constructs omitted from the model.

TABLE 6.15: *Estimated direct (D) and total (T) effects on POSTATTSUBJ in the final versions of the student variable model (with coefficients multiplied by 1,000)*

	Aust		COE		COF		Hung		Neth		ROK		Thai	
	D	T	D	T	D	T	D	T	D	T	D	T	D	T
LOCATION	-								-	035		023		
HOME	-	009	-	-011	-	056	-	167	-	-004	-	076	-	100
AGE	-		-	-030	-	-079							-	-012
SEX	-	-015	-	073	-	061	-	045	-	140	-	006		
TYPESC	-	-080	-	-042					-	050			-	-142
ASPIRATION	-	140	-	140	-	170	-	188	-	084	-	087	-	029
ATTSCH	-	226	-	188	-	249	-	083	-	132	-	208	-	061
PRETEST	-	134	-	097	-	098	-	087	-	025	-	062	-	070
PREATTSUBJ	454	457	527	539	552	576	470	484	531	541	368	377	113	117
TASK	-	020	162	173	062	070	-	022	-	009	118	131	191	210
FEEDBACK													105	108
STRUCTURE	153	154	125	128	207	217	194	200	239	244	159	162	161	165
OTL	-	020								022				
ENGPCT	-	008	-	009	-	021			-	005	-	002	-	012
POSTTEST	197	199	146	149	172	180	209	215	077	079	148	152	142	146

Notes: Entries marked "-" indicate omitted direct effects or paths. Blank entries indicate constructs omitted from the model.

of the coefficients associated with indirect effects on POSTTEST via other constructs. Second, the resultant multiplicative terms are summed. Third, the coefficient of the direct path, if specified, is added to the sum.

Although not displayed in Table 6.14, the corresponding indirect effects can easily be computed by subtracting the direct effect from the total effect. Quite obviously, when no direct effect is specified in the model or when the estimated direct effect is zero, the total effect and the indirect effect are identical. Consider, as an example, the subconstruct HOME in the Republic of Korea in Table 6.14. The direct effect (D) of HOME on POST-TEST is 0.138. The total effect (T) of HOME on POSTTEST is 0.257. Hence, using subtraction, the indirect effect of HOME or POSTTEST (via ASPIRATION, PREATTSUBJ, and PRETEST) is in the Korean student variable model equal to 0.119. Note that in Table 6.14 no direct effect of HOME on POSTTEST was included in the final analysis in any other study. In these studies, therefore, the ensuing total effects are identical to the indirect effects.

Australia

In Australia only PRETEST and OTL had comparatively large direct effects on POSTTEST (using a minimum path coefficient of 0.1 criterion). The direct effects of TASK, ENGPCT and POSTATTSUBJ were quite small (ranging from 0.037 to 0.088). When total effects are considered, the coefficients of several subconstructs approach or exceed the 0.1 criterion: HOME (with a total effect or, in this case, indirect effect of 0.126), ASPIRATION (with an indirect effect of 0.129), and TASK (with a total effect of 0.099). In addition, PRETEST and OTL which have direct effects larger than 0.1 have, of course, also total effects larger than 0.1. Not surprisingly, PRETEST, with its direct effect of 0.674 and its total effect of 0.679, is by far the most powerful predictor of POSTTEST.

With respect to POSTATTSUBJ the picture is somewhat different and slightly more complex. As can be seen in Table 6.15, three subconstructs have fairly substantial direct effects on POSTATTSUBJ; namely, PREATTSUBJ (as expected), STRUCTURE, and POSTTEST. In combination these results suggest that the extent to which students develop positive attitudes toward the subject being taught was directly effected by their initial attitude toward the subject, the extent to which they perceived that teachers presented the subject in a structured manner (by emphasizing what is important to learn, giving clear explanations, getting students to think for themselves, and summarizing major points), and the extent to which they learned the subject being taught.

Three additional subconstructs had indirect effects on POSTATTSUBJ; namely, ATTSCH (0.226), ASPIRATION (0.140) and PRETEST (0.134).

That is, the students' final attitude toward the subject was influenced indirectly by their general attitude toward school, their desire for further education, and the amount of knowledge of the subject they possessed prior to the study.

Canada Ontario-English

As in Australia, PRETEST had a major influence on POSTTEST. In addition, however, POSTATTSUBJ had a fairly substantial influence on POSTTEST. The extent students enjoyed learning the subject matter influenced the extent to which they learned it. Two subconstructs were found to have moderate indirect effects on POSTTEST. Again similar to Australia, a positive effect of ASPIRATION (0.140) was obtained. In contrast with Australia, however, AGES had an indirect effect on POSTTEST (-0.117). The negative direction of this effect indicates that older students achieved less well than did younger students. Since in Canada Ontario-English older students were likely to be those who had repeated a course or grade level because of poor achievement in the past, this finding is not surprising.

Four subconstructs directly influenced POSTATTSUBJ. As expected, the major influence on POSTATTSUBJ was PREATTSUBJ. The final attitudes of students toward the subject were influenced primarily by their initial attitudes toward the subject. In addition, however, TASK, STRUCTURE, and POSTTEST also directly influenced POSTATTSUBJ. Students who developed more positive final attitudes toward the subject also tended to (1) perceive the classroom as work-oriented and led by a teacher able to maintain control over student attention and behavior, (2) perceive that the teacher provided structure necessary to learn the subject (as was the case in Australia), and (3) learned more of the subject being taught.

Finally, two subconstructs were found to have indirect effects on POST-ATTSUBJ: ASPIRATION (0.140) and ATTSCH (0.188). In combination, then, students who indicated a desire for further education and who in general liked school tended to develop more positive attitudes toward the subject.

Canada Ontario-French

The results for Canada Ontario-French are slightly different from those for Australia and Canada Ontario-English. Like the results for both of these previously mentioned studies, the major direct influence on POSTTEST was PRETEST. Also, like the results for Canada Ontario-English, POST-ATTSUBJ had a direct effect on POSTTEST. In contrast to the results for both Australia and Canada Ontario-English, however, ENGPCT (0.118) had a direct effect on POSTTEST. In fact, as can be seen in Table 6.14, only in Canada Ontario-French did ENGPCT have a direct effect on POSTTEST.

This result suggests that the extent to which students spent more of their time actively engaged in learning directly influenced the extent of their learning.

It should be reiterated at this point that the manifest variables associated with ENGPCT constituted highly aggregated estimates of overt academic engagement, with numerical values that were constant within classes. That is, the respective manifest variables derived from the SNAP and the IAR are "classroom-based," not "student-based" variables. Thus, ENGPCT provides a rather rough estimate for the time that individual students were engaged in learning, a fact that may explain the weak effects of ENGPCT on POSTTEST obtained for most of the studies.

Like both Australia and Canada Ontario-English ASPIRATION had an indirect effect on POSTTEST (0.132). Furthermore, like Australia, HOME had a fairly substantial indirect effect on POSTTEST (0.127). Thus, students from homes in which parents had more education and fathers worked at higher status jobs, and students who expressed a desire for further education tended to learn more of the subject being taught.

The results pertaining to the direct and indirect effects of the various constructs on POSTATTSUBJ in Canada Ontario-French were virtually identical to the results obtained in Australia and quite similar to those found in Canada Ontario-English. PREATTSUBJ, STRUCTURE, and POSTTEST had direct effects on POSTATTSUBJ. In addition, POSTATTSUBJ was indirectly influenced by ASPIRATION (0.170) and ATTSCH (0.249).

Hungary

In Hungary three subconstructs were found to have direct effects on POSTTEST. Once again, PRETEST had the largest effect. As was true in both Canadian replications mentioned above, POSTATTSUBJ had a direct effect on POSTTEST. In addition, TASK had a small positive direct effect (0.102). That is, students who perceived their teachers as more able to appropriately control the behavior of their students and manage their classrooms as a place where academic work was expected tended to achieve somewhat more.

Two subconstructs were found to indirectly influence POSTTEST, both of which had similar influences in other countries. As was true in both Australia and Canada Ontario-French, HOME exerted an indirect effect on POSTTEST (0.126). And, as was true in all previous countries, ASPIRATION indirectly effected POSTTEST (0.112).

The results pertaining to the direct effects on POSTATTSUBJ were quite similar to those in Australia and Canada Ontario-French. PREATTSUBJ, STRUCTURE, and POSTTEST all were found to have substantial direct effects on POSTATTSUBJ. The indirect effects on POSTATTSUBJ were slightly different from those found in the previously described countries. A common result was that ASPIRATION had an indirect effect on POST-ATTSUBJ (0.188). Unlike previous results, however, HOME also had an indirect effect on POSTATTSUBJ (0.167). That is, students whose fathers were employed in higher status jobs tended to develop more positive attitudes toward the subject.

Korea (ROK)

As noted earlier, preliminary analyses of the Korean data suggested that a binary variable indicating the school location be included in the analysis because classes located in metropolitan or urban schools tended to have higher pretest and posttest scores than classes located in suburban or rural schools. As was to be expected from these preliminary analyses, LOCATION (coded as "1" for metropolitan/urban schools and "0" for suburban/rural schools) was found to have positive direct and total effects on POSTTEST. The direct effect of LOCATION on POSTTEST (0.087) was fairly small, but the corresponding path was retained in order to achieve somewhat more appropriate estimates for the effects of the remaining sub-constructs included in the model. That is, in the analysis of the Korean student variable model, school location constituted a "control factor" that was included in order to accommodate existing between-school differences. The total effect of LOCATION on POSTTEST (0.160) was considerably larger than the direct effect primarily because LOCATION had a fairly substantial direct effect on PRETEST.

Apart from the effects pertaining to the variable LOCATION (which was included only in the Korean model), a direct effect of HOME on POSTTEST was unique to this study. In fact, both the direct and indirect effects of HOME on POSTTEST were quite large (0.138 and 0.257, respectively). In addition to HOME, PRETEST directly influenced POSTTEST (0.369) as did POSTATTSUBJ (0.186).

Four subconstructs—PREATTSUBJ, TASK, STRUCTURE, and POST-TEST—had a direct effect on POSTATTSUBJ. All have been found to exert a direct influence on POSTATTSUBJ in at least one of the studies whose results have been described previously. Furthermore, ATTSCH was found to indirectly affect POSTATTSUBJ (0.208). Finally, in contrast with all other previously described studies, ASPIRATION was found to exert only a small indirect effect on POSTATTSUBJ (0.087). As can be seen in Table 6.15, this lack of an indirect effect of ASPIRATION on POSTATTSUBJ was replicated in the Netherlands and in Thailand.

Netherlands

The results for the Netherlands in general were quite different from those of the previously discussed studies. PRETEST, OTL, and POSTATTSUBJ all had direct effects on POSTTEST of similar magnitudes (0.313, 0.275, and 0.246, respectively). Thus, of all of the studies, the direct effect of

PRETEST on POSTTEST is the smallest in the Netherlands (possibly because different tests were administered as PRETEST and POSTTEST). Furthermore, only in the Netherlands was the direct effect of OTL on POSTTEST quite clear.

The reader should keep in mind, however, that the OTL was a national option; in addition to the Netherlands, OTL data were collected only in Australia (where a positive OTL effect of 0.100 was obtained), and Canada Ontario-English and Thailand (where the respective paths from OTL to POST-TEST were removed in the final analysis because the ensuing direct effects were found to be close to zero). Finally, the influence of POSTATTSUBJ on POSTTEST was far stronger than that of POSTTEST on POSTATTSUBJ. This result is in contrast to the other countries previously described in which the magnitudes of the two effects were virtually identical. These results suggest that how well students learned to like a subject influenced how much they learned about it. The reverse, however, was not true. That is, how much they learned about a subject had no great influence on how much they came to enjoy learning it.

PREATTSUBJ and STRUCTURE both directly affected POSTATTSUBJ. These results replicate those in each of the previously discussed countries. ATTSCH and SEXS indirectly influenced POSTATTSUBJ. While the effect of ATTSCH on POSTATTSUBJ was replicated in every country except Hungary, the indirect effect of SEXS on POSTATTSUBJ is unique to the Netherlands. Boys tended to develop a greater liking of the subject, mathematics, by the end of the study than did girls.

Thailand

Thailand is the only country in which TYPESC (coded as "1" for governmental or public schools and "0" for private schools) exerted a direct effect on POSTTEST. In addition, the indirect effects of TYPESC on POSTTEST (via PRETEST) were quite strong. The magnitude of the total effect of TYPESC on POSTTEST (-0.334) is in absolute value second only to the effect of PRETEST on POSTTEST. The negative direction of this effect indicates that students in public school classes had, on the average, lower pretest and posttest scores than students located in private schools.

In addition to TYPESC, HOME had a quite strong indirect effect on POSTTEST (0.254) which primarily operated via a positive direct effect of HOME on PRETEST and a negative direct effect of HOME on TYPESC. That is, students attending private schools generally came from homes in which parents had higher education levels and fathers worked at higher status jobs. (The reader will note that the *negative* effect of HOME on TYPESC multiplied by the *negative* effect of TYPESC on POSTTEST results in the *positive* indirect effect of HOME on TYPESC.) Apart from TYPESC and HOME, PRETEST had, as expected, a strong direct effect on POSTTEST, while POSTATTSUBJ and TASK had weaker direct influences.

Of all the countries in which the student variable model was tested, the direct effect of PREATTSUBJ on POSTATTSUBJ (0.113) was the weakest in Thailand, possibly because the duration of the study in Thailand was the longest of all the studies (9 months). The relationship between initial and final attitude may be somewhat less stable over longer time periods. TASK, STRUCTURE, and POSTTEST had slightly stronger direct effects on POSTATTSUBJ than did PREATTSUBJ. FEEDBACK also had a small direct effect on POSTATTSUBJ, a result which was unique to Thailand. In all other countries, the direct effect of FEEDBACK on POSTATTSUBJ was virtually zero, and FEEDBACK was thus generally eliminated from the model. Finally, both HOME and TYPESC had small indirect effects on POSTATTSUBJ (0.100 and −0.142, respectively).

In Thailand, then, the home background of the students and the type of school they attended (i.e., governmental vs. private) exerted strong influences on both what they learned and how well they liked what they learned. Furthermore, students' perceptions of the classroom and their teachers also directly influenced their attitude toward the subject and, to a somewhat lesser extent, their achievement.

Toward a Composite Student Variable Model

In the previous sections of this chapter the results pertaining to the student variable model were presented and discussed on a study-by-study basis. The purpose of this section is to compare the major results across studies and to derive, to the extent possible, a composite student variable model. While the results unique to particular countries have been noted in the previous sections, the following discussion concentrates on the major paths of the student variable model that were, to some extent, common across countries. The reader should note that in the discussion that follows, Canada will be considered as a single country with two replications. Thus, references to six countries will be made throughout.

A summary of the major paths in the student variable model for each country is displayed in Table 6.16. Only paths with coefficients greater or equal to 0.1 in at least *three* of the *six* countries are shown in the table. The discussion in this section will be centered around constructs that tended to be major causal influences in the model.

HOME

In the student variable model HOME was initially hypothesized to be directly related to seven constructs: TYPESC, ASPIRATION, ATTSCH, PRETEST, PREATTSUBJ, POSTATTSUBJ and POSTTEST. The data across the six countries suggest that HOME does directly affect three of these constructs: TYPESC, ASPIRATION, and PRETEST. Interestingly, HOME

TABLE 6.16 *Major paths of the student variable model*
(with coefficients multiplied by 1,000)

Path	Aust	COE	COF	Hung	ROK	Neth	Thai	Median
HOME to								
TYPESC	18	58					35	35
PRETEST	13	10	17	20	22			17
ASPIRATION	13		23	26	36	29	36	28
ASPIRATION to								
ATTSCH	26	29	31		21	24	27	27
PRETEST	18	18	15	20	17	18		18
PREATTSUBJ	13	13	12	30				13
ATTSCH to								
PREATTSUBJ	49	35	43		54		44	44
PRETEST to								
POSTTEST	67	65	54	41	37	31	48	48
PREATTSUBJ to								
POSTATTSUBJ	45	53	55	47	37	53	11	47
TASK to								
ENGPCT	19		21		14	40		20
POSTTEST				10		10	10	10
POSTATTSUBJ		16			12		19	16
STRUCTURE to								
POSTATTSUBJ	15	13	21	19	16	24	16	16
POSTATTSUBJ to								
POSTTEST		15	25	16	19	25	15	18
POSTTEST to								
POSTATTSUBJ	20	15	17	21	14		14	16

Notes: The entries in the column labeled "median" are the medians of the paths included in the table. Thus, for example, the median for HOME to TYPESC is 35, based on the values of 18 (in Australia), 35 (in Thailand), and 58 (in Canada Ontario-English).

does not directly affect either POSTTEST or POSTATTSUBJ, nor does it directly influence PREATTSUBJ or ATTSCH.

In three of the four countries in which TYPESC was included in the student variable model, HOME was found to be negatively related to TYPESC. Stated simply, in these countries, students from upper and middle class home backgrounds tended to enroll in private schools; students from working class or lower class home backgrounds tended to attend public schools.

The effect of HOME on PRETEST was supported in four of the six countries. Again, students from upper and middle class homes tended to enter school with greater knowledge of the subject being taught than those from lower or working class homes.

The most consistent influence of the students' home background, however, was on their educational aspirations. In all six countries students from middle or upper class homes (in contrast to those from lower or working class homes) indicated they intended to continue their schooling beyond their compulsory attendance age and on into institutions of higher learning.

ASPIRATION

In the initial student variable model ASPIRATION was hypothesized to directly influence three constructs: ATTSCH, PRETEST, and PREATTSUBJ. All three of these hypothesized direct effects were supported by the data. The direct effect of ASPIRATION on PRETEST and on ATTSCH was supported in all countries except Thailand and Hungary, respectively. The direct effect of ASPIRATION on PREATTSUBJ tended to be somewhat weaker both in terms of the number of countries (three) and the magnitude of the effect (a median effect of 0.13, in contrast to a median effect of 0.27 for ATTSCH and 0.18 for PRETEST). The results indicate that students with a greater desire for further education tended to begin their study of the subject with more knowledge of that subject and more favorable attitudes toward the subject and school.

ATTSCH

As hypothesized, ATTSCH was found to directly affect PREATTSUBJ in four of the six countries. Exceptions to this generalization were Hungary and the Netherlands. In general, then, students with more positive attitudes toward school also tended to have more positive attitudes toward the subject being taught. ATTSCH did not directly affect PRETEST.

PRETEST

Quite obviously, the least surprising finding across all countries was the substantial effect of PRETEST on POSTTEST. In all countries except the Netherlands (where different tests were administered as pre- and posttests) the magnitude of the direct effect of PRETEST on POSTTEST far surpassed the combined direct and indirect effect of any of the other subconstructs included in the model.

PREATTSUBJ

Interestingly, the direct effect of PREATTSUBJ on POSTATTSUBJ was very similar to the direct effect of PRETEST on POSTTEST. The median path coefficient of PREATTSUBJ on POSTATTSUBJ across the seven replications was 0.47 in comparison with the median path coefficient of PRETEST on POSTTEST of 0.48. Furthermore, the effect of PREATTSUBJ on POSTATTSUBJ was quite substantial in all countries except Thailand (where the path coefficient was only 0.11). The attitudes with which students complete their study of a subject are influenced by those attitudes they held when they began their study.

TASK

In the original student variable model TASK was hypothesized to exert a direct effect on ENGPCT, POSTTEST, and POSTATTSUBJ. The results support all hypothesized direct effects. In four of the six countries, TASK was found to directly affect ENGPCT. Students who perceived their classes as more work-oriented and their teachers as effective managers of student attention and behavior did spend more of their time engaged in "business" or "work." This finding, while not surprising conceptually, is somewhat unexpected since the estimate of ENGPCT was the percent of students in the entire class who were observed to be "on-task." Hence, as has been mentioned, all students in each class were assigned the same numerical value for ENGPCT. In contrast, each student in every class was assigned a unique score based on his or her responses to the items that made up the self report student perception instruments. One possible reason for this finding is the similarity of the perceptions of students in a given classroom concerning the task-orientation of that classroom. Task-oriented classrooms may be so obvious to all students and so different from classrooms that are not task-oriented that students know that work is expected and, as consequence, spend their time working.

The direct effect of TASK on POSTTEST is quite weak and was present in only three countries (Hungary, the Netherlands, and Thailand). In general, students who perceived their teachers as emphasizing academic work, and their classroom as "workplaces" tended to achieve slightly more than those who did not.

The direct effect of TASK on POSTATTSUBJ is also quite weak and was also present in only three countries, although a somewhat different set of countries than those previously mentioned. The effect of TASK on POST-ATTSUBJ was noted in Canada Ontario-English, the Republic of Korea, and Thailand.

STRUCTURE

In the original student variable model STRUCTURE was hypothesized to influence POSTTEST and POSTATTSUBJ. While STRUCTURE did not directly affect POSTTEST, the consistency of the effect of structure on POSTATTSUBJ was perhaps one of the most surprising results of the study. In all six countries (including *both* Canadian replications), the magnitude of the path coefficient exceeded 0.10, with a range from 0.11 to 0.24 and median value of 0.16. This finding suggests that across all participating countries students who perceived teachers as providing structure for their learning tended to enjoy the subject being taught. A slightly different interpretation of this finding is that students gain a greater appreciation and enjoyment of a subject when the important ideas are emphasized, clearly explained, and summarized periodically.

POSTTEST and POSTATTSUBJ

The effect of POSTATTSUBJ on POSTTEST and the effect of POSTTEST on POSTATTSUBJ were, as hypothesized, positive and virtually identical in all countries except Australia and the Netherlands. In Australia the direct effect is quite clearly from POSTTEST to POSTATTSUBJ. In the Netherlands the reverse is true; namely POSTATTSUBJ directly influenced POSTTEST. In all other countries direct effects were in both directions and fluctuated between 0.13 and 0.20, centering around 0.16. In general, then, the hypothesized bidirectional nature of the relationship between POST-TEST and POSTATTSUBJ was supported by the results of the student variable model.

Summary

On the basis of the common results discussed above, several generalizations can be made. Four major generalizations will be offered in this final section of this chapter.

The History of the Learner

Once again we see the impact of the history of the learners on their current level of knowing and feeling. The primary influence on final achievement is initial achievement. Likewise, the primary influence on final attitude toward the subject is the initial attitude toward the subject. In general, this influence is so great that few if any variables can compensate for it.

The history of the learner is far more complex than the specific knowledge and attitudes which he or she brings to the study of a particular subject. The type of home in which the child is raised exerts a substantial effect on his or her initial achievement which is consistent across countries, and a weaker effect on his or her subject-related attitude, which is less consistent across countries. The aspirations students have for the future, particularly the extent to which those aspirations involve the acquisition of additional education, also influence students' achievement and attitudes in many countries. Finally, the attitudes students have toward school in general, which quite likely develop over a fairly extensive period of time, also influence the extent to which students develop positive attitudes toward particular subjects within school.

In general, it seems that both learning and failing to learn are cumulative. Although the strength of the influence of prior history on present knowledge and feelings may be diminished somewhat by using different measures at the beginnning and end of a course, a term, or a year (as was true in the Netherlands, for example), the influence of years of learning well or not learning at all is not likely to be overcome during a relatively short period of time regardless of how intensive or powerful the experiences during that short time period may be.

The Influence of the Home

In contrast with the beliefs of some educators, the home environment had no direct effect on final achievement. Rather, the influence of the home on final achievement was quite consistently found to be indirect, via its direct effect on initial achievement and educational aspirations. Quite naturally, students who enter school with greater knowledge and/or greater need to achieve (in light of their future aspirations) do better in school. Thus, the home environment would seem to serve generally a preparatory function but only sometimes an actualization function. As a consequence, the effects of the home on final achievement could potentially be minimized if ways could be found to intervene between the beginning and the end of some course or study. Unfortunately, as we shall see in Chapter 7, it is very difficult to establish the nature of the needed interventions.

Student Perceptions

Student perceptions of the task-orientation of their classrooms, the ways in which their teachers control student attention and behavior in those classrooms, and the ways in which those teachers structure the presentation of the subject exert weak, but consistent, influences on achievement and attitude. One conclusion, supported by the results in all six countries, is that the students enjoy subjects more when their teachers provide structure for learning them. Providing structure means that teachers emphasize the important ideas and main points, give clear explanations (thereby helping the students to differentiate the relevant from the irrelevant), make students think about solutions to problems, and summarize the relevant material periodically. Students also enjoy subjects more when they are taught in a classroom where time spent on academic work is the norm.

What do these results suggest about teachers and classrooms that contribute to less positive attitudes toward the subject being taught? Less positive attitudes would tend to be held by students who are expected to provide their own structure for the subject, or students whose teachers engage in lectures or conversations about the subject with little clear direction or purpose, that is, teachers who are "talking a lot" but saying little of perceived relevance or importance. Furthermore, less positive attitudes would tend to be held by students in classrooms in which the emphasis is on having fun, playing games, and socializing, rather than on academic work.

In approximately one-half of the countries the extent to which students perceived the classrooms as business-like and task-oriented also influenced somewhat the students' final achievement. Thus, not only do students develop greater enjoyment of the subject in such classes, they also tend to learn more. As a consequence, the creation of classrooms in which expectations for work and learning are clear and functional seems a sensible beginning in the search for effective teaching strategies and practices.

Student Aspirations

In many ways student aspirations emerged as the lynchpin in the student variable model. The level of student aspiration, defined in terms of the desire for further education, was influenced by the home background of the student. Students whose fathers are gainfully employed at the upper levels of the occupational "ladder" tended to have higher aspirations. Although this finding is not particularly surprising, the fact that the home exerts a stronger influence on the students' aspirations than on the students' knowledge (either prior to, or following, the completion of the course of study) may be somewhat surprising. Also somewhat surprising is the power of the student aspirations in the light of the fact that the questions asked students about their desire to attend colleges and universities and the students themselves were several years away from college (10 to 13 years old). One possible interpretation of this finding is that the home background of children tends to influence their basic values concerning the need for and the role of education in their lives. These values in turn influence a host of other factors. Within the student variable model some of these factors are the students' attitudes toward school, their attitudes toward the specific subject under study, and the level of knowledge about the subject they bring to school. As a consequence, student aspirations contribute a weak, but consistent, influence on both final achievement and final attitude toward the subject.

The generalizations gleaned from the results presented in this chapter may be thought of as those seen through the students' eyes. Are there similar generalizations that follow from constructs and variables external to the student? It is to this question that we turn in Chapter 7.

7

The Core Model

In the previous chapter the results pertaining to the student variable model were presented and discussed. In this chapter the results pertaining to the core model, that is, the general conceptual model underlying the study, will similarly be described. In essence, the core model adds a set of "schooling" variables (that is, classroom, teacher, and teaching variables) to the student variable model. The purpose of this chapter, then, is to investigate the extent to which "schooling" variables contribute to our understanding of the ways in which students acquire knowledge, skills, and attitudes in classrooms throughout the world.

To gain a better understanding of the conceptual background of the statistical analyses presented in this chapter, consider the path diagram depicted in Fig. 7.1.

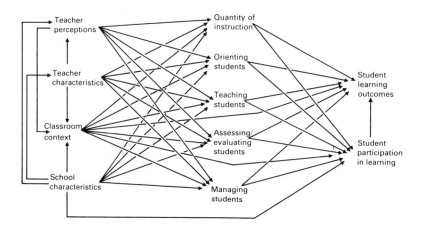

FIG. 7.1 Core model relationships among the "schooling" constructs.

This chapter was written by Norbert Sellin and Lorin W. Anderson.

Figure 7.1 includes the constructs of the core model associated with manifest "schooling" variables. The only construct in Fig. 7.1 consisting of "student-based" measures is the construct termed "Student Learning Outcomes." All paths (that is, direct effects) linking the various constructs in Fig. 7.1 are shown as they were hypothesized in the core model (see Chapter 2).

The model shown in Fig. 7.1 is, on the surface, quite simple. As explained in Chapter 2, the left-hand portion of the model consists of constructs associated with contextual variables such as the characteristics of schools, classrooms and teachers, which are believed to influence the ways in which teachers behave in their classrooms. The middle part of the model consists primarily of constructs which comprise the teaching process as defined in the study. Finally, the right-hand portion consists of constructs reflecting student participation (specifically, student engagement in learning) and student outcomes (that is, achievement and attitudes). As can be seen in Fig. 7.1, student engagement in learning is hypothesized to have a direct effect on student outcomes.

The general assumption underlying the model, then, is that elements of the context within which "schooling" takes place influence the teaching that occurs which, in turn, influences the learning processes and student outcomes. With but a few exceptions, all possible direct effects among these three general domains of "schooling"—context, teaching, and outcomes—were specified. The portion of the core model shown in Fig. 7.1, then, involves 11 constructs (ten of which are associated with "schooling" variables), 72 manifest variables associated with these 11 constructs, and 38 paths representing direct effects of these constructs on constructs containing outcome variables.

The initial plans for the multivariate analyses of the data included the exploration of the within-construct and between-construct relationships explicated in the above model in much the same way as described in Chapter 6 for the student variable model. Three basic steps were to be involved in this procedure. First, manifest variables with little if any variation were to have been eliminated. Second, an initial PLS analysis of the specified model was to have been undertaken. Third, based on the initial results and the results of a series of further analyses, manifest variables within constructs as well as paths between constructs were to have been eliminated. Thus, a "final," unique model was to be developed for each study. In short, using the conceptual framework set out in the core model as a point of departure, it was intended to derive a "final" model for each study on the basis of exploratory statistical analyses.

At first blush, the data analytical approach sketched above may seem feasible; all the more so since the student variable model presented in the previous chapter was derived in essentially the same way. Unfortunately, this approach was not appropriate for the data sets available for a number of reasons. The most important and most obvious reason was the small number of classes included in most of the studies. In investigating the relationships among constructs the number of "cases" available is equal to the number of classes included in the study. As has been pointed out in Chapter 6, the number of classes included in multivariate analyses varied considerably across participating countries, from 17 in Canada Ontario-French to 81 in Thailand.

Consider, for example, only the path coefficients (that is, the direct effects) in Fig. 7.1 that would have to be estimated simultaneously by means of multiple regression techniques. If a class-to-coefficient ratio of 10 to 1 is regarded as a minimum criterion for the conduct of meaningful regression analyses, the data analytical approach sketched above would not produce interpretable results for the majority of the participating countries. In fact, if the above criterion was employed, only two countries, Australia and Thailand, would remain for testing the core model empirically.

The small number of classes, however, was not the only problem encountered in applying the analyses described in this chapter. A second problem stemmed from the severe multicollinearity among the "schooling" constructs and their associated manifest variables. Primarily because of this problem, preliminary tests of the core model performed on the Australian and Thai data sets produced virtually uninterpretable results.

In sum, then, the initial plans for investigating the effects of the "schooling" constructs on student outcomes had to be modified. After much discussion and deliberation as to the formal requirements for meaningful multivariate analyses which included "schooling" variables, two major decisions were made.

First, for studies with fewer than 40 classes, only the zero-order correlations between "schooling" variables and student outcomes would be considered. This decision applied to the three Canadian studies (Ontario-English, Ontario-French, and Quebec), Hungary and Israel. The reader should note that the examination of zero-order correlations seems to constitute the predominant data analytical approach in much of the process-product research, presumably because these researchers also must confront the analytic problem caused by the small number of classes. At the same time, however, the reader should be aware that even zero-order correlations must be examined and interpreted with great caution when computed on the basis of such a small number of cases.

Second, for studies with more than 40 classes it was deemed feasible to formulate and test more complex path models. These studies were Australia, the Republic of Korea, the Netherlands, and Thailand. To facilitate meaningful analyses, however, the number of "schooling" constructs and/or manifest variables had to be reduced drastically. A decision was also made to concentrate on models predicting achievement, not attitude, since this restriction greatly reduced the number of paths to be estimated and, hence, the complexity of the models.

In view of this discussion, this chapter is organized around two major themes. The first concerns the bivariate relationships between "schooling" variables and student processes and outcomes. The discussion of this theme is organized into four sections. In the first section several technical issues pertaining to the data are described. These issues include the adjustment of posttest scores, units of analysis, and statistical testing. In the second section examples are used to highlight the major points made in the previous section. In the third section the zero-order correlations between the "schooling" variables and student achievement are presented. And, in the fourth section the zero-order correlations between the "schooling" variables and student engagement in learning are displayed.

The second theme concerns the multivariate relationships among the "schooling" variables themselves, and between the "schooling" variables and student outcomes. This theme is addressed in two sections. In the first section the general model structure and the steps involved in the PLS analysis are described. In the second section, the results from the PLS analysis applied to four studies (Australia, the Republic of Korea, the Netherlands, and Thailand) are presented. A brief summary section concludes the chapter.

Technical Issues in Multivariate Analyses

Before any correlations could be computed, several technical issues had to be resolved. These issues and their resolution are the topic of this section.

Data Sets and Missing Data

The data sets used in the analysis of the student variable model (Chapter 6) also were used in the analyses reported in this chapter. As was pointed out in previous chapters, the data preparation for the multivariate analyses resulted in the exclusion of a number of classes in several studies. As a consequence, small differences will be observed in the univariate statistics reported in this chapter and those reported earlier in Chapter 4. However, the univariate statistics reported in this chapter are those on which the correlations were actually computed. Furthermore, in order to perform the analyses on as complete data sets as possible, missing data on most variables were replaced by the overall means on those variables. In general, such replacement was needed only on those variables derived from teachers' questionnaires, not from observers' records.

Adjustment of Posttest Scores

While zero-order correlations between the "schooling" variables and final achievement as measured by the posttests in the various studies could have been computed, a decision was made to consider differences in initial achievement in the analysis. As a consequence, adjusted or "residualized" posttest scores were derived prior to computing the correlations. "Residualized" posttest scores were defined as the class mean posttest scores adjusted for differences in class mean pretest scores. This "adjustment" was made by means of a so-called "pooled within-class regression" of the posttest scores on the pretest scores. (See Keesling and Wiley 1974, and Wiley 1976 for additional details.) This particular adjustment was deemed appropriate based on the results of the analysis of covariance presented in the previous chapter.

This adjustment procedure is based on two general assumptions. The first is that the influences of pretest performance on posttest performance operate at the within-class (or between-student) level. The second assumption is that between-class differences in posttest performance can be regarded as caused by "classroom-based" variables only. If these assumptions are valid, then a two-step procedure can be used to assess effects of "classroom-based" variables on student achievement. The first step involves the estimation of pretest influences on posttest partialling out all possible effects of "classroom-based" variables. This step is performed using the results of the pooled within-class regression mentioned earlier. The second step involves the examination of the effects of "classroom-based" variables on student achievement partialling out the within-class pretest effects determined in the first step.

Unit of Analysis

In research on teaching, a variety of units of analysis are available: students, classrooms (or teachers), methods or programs, even schools. In the analysis to be described, classrooms were selected as the unit of analysis. The correlations and R-square values to be reported should be interpreted as being strictly "classroom-based" statistics. As has been mentioned in Chapter 6, class-level correlations and R-square values are necessarily numerically larger than their student-level counterparts. However, using the adjustment procedure outlined above, the underlying *unstandardized* regression coefficients can be shown to be numerically the same irrespective of whether students or classes are used as units of investigation. In other words, there is no essential difference between the corresponding student-level and class-level relationships. Numerical differences between standardized coefficients (i.e., correlations, path coefficients, and R-square values) are simply due to differences of standardization factors, namely the corresponding student-level and class-level posttest variances. Such differences should be considered, for example, when the class-level coefficients displayed in this chapter are compared with the corresponding path coefficients reported in Chapter 6 for the student variable model. Apart from the fact that the student variable model is more complex than the simple regression model employed in this section, the primary source of differences in terms of the magnitude of effect estimates is simply the differences in terms of standardization factors.

Statistical Testing

As has been mentioned earlier, the examination of zero-order correlations seems to be the most common data analytical approach in related process-product research (see, for example, Brophy and Good 1986). Furthermore, a common approach to evaluating the magnitude of these correlations between "schooling" variables and outcome measures seems to be the use of standard significance tests. Such tests were not used in this study for several reasons, all of which have been mentioned previously (see Chapter 6). The most important reason was that virtually all samples were "samples of convenience." That is, the schools and classrooms were generally not selected from well-defined populations using probability sampling procedures. Given this situation it makes no sense to test, for example, whether a particular correlation is significantly different from zero in the population. Moreover, it is well known that classical significance tests require restrictive distributional assumptions, notably normality and independence of residuals. These assumptions would appear quite unrealistic for most of the data considered in this section.

So-called jackknife procedures provide a general alternative to classical significance testing in situations where distributional assumptions would seem untenable (see, for example, Tukey 1977). Jackknife statistics are distribution-free in that normality and independence of residuals are not required. For the present analyses, however, the most important point is that jackknifing constitutes a useful and simple device to evaluate statistical relationships in terms of their sensitivity to minor modifications in the data set. Two jackknife statistics are the jackknife standard deviation, and the Q-square statistic proposed by Stone (1974) and Geisser (1974). Wold (1982) refers to the Q-square statistic as the Stone-Geisser test of predictive relevance and has suggested the general use of this test in PLS analyses.

The general idea of the Stone-Geisser test is to omit from a given data set one case (e.g., classroom) at a time and to re-estimate statistical relationships (that is, correlations, regression coefficients, or path coefficients) on the basis of the remaining cases. The outcome variable for the omitted case is to be predicted from the re-estimated relationships. Jackknife standard deviations of coefficient estimates (see Miller 1974) can be obtained as a by-product of this re-estimation and prediction process.

The Stone-Geisser test can be seen as a specific case of more general cross-validation procedures. Rather than using one sample to estimate particular model parameters and another sample to assess the validity of the estimates, the data set at hand is repeatedly split into an "estimation set" comprising n-1 cases and a "confirmation set" involving just one case. As noted by Lohmoeller (1984), the Stone-Geisser test can be seen as a generalization approach since an attempt is made to generalize from n-1 cases to the nth case. The Q-square statistic represents the extent to which this generalization was successful. A particularly useful interpretation can be made by regarding the Q-square statistic as a jackknife analogue of the familiar R-square statistic. As pointed out by Wold (1982), since the predicted case is omitted from the model estimation, the Q-square is nothing else than a measure of "explained" variance computed without loss of degrees of freedom.

A negative Q-square value indicates that the inclusion of a variable in the regression model actually *decreases* the predictive power beyond that expected with the so-called "trivial prediction." "Trivial prediction" is based solely on the sample mean of the outcome variable. Thus, in terms of the relationships examined in this section, a negative Q-square value indicates that the overall sample mean of the adjusted posttest provides a more accurate prediction of class mean posttest performance than the prediction derived from the regression of the residualized posttest on a particular predictor variable.

Consider the following example. Suppose five classrooms, each containing the same number of students, were included in a study. The mean adjusted posttest scores for these five classrooms are 8, 10, 12, 14, and 16, respectively. Suppose, further, that we believe that the number of questions asked by teachers in these classrooms is predictive of the adjusted posttest scores. We compute the correlation between "number of questions asked" and "mean adjusted posttest scores." Based on this correlation we formulate a regression equation of the form $y = b_0 + b_1 x + e$ (where y is the "mean adjusted posttest scores," x is the "number of questions asked," b_0 is the constant equating x with y, b_1 is the rate at which y changes for each unit of x, and e is the random error). Based on this equation we predict for each classroom an *estimated* mean adjusted posttest score which we then compare with the *actual* adjusted posttest score.

Now, suppose that we compare the differences between these estimates and the actual adjusted posttest scores with the differences between the overall mean and the actual adjusted posttest scores for the five classrooms. The results may be something like those shown in Table 7.1. If we compare the sums of these differences (independent of their direction), we see that the combined differences between the actual classroom means and the predicted means ($|A-B|$) are *greater than* the differences between the actual classroom means and the overall mean ($|A-C|$). In such a case, the Q-square value would be *negative*.

TABLE 7.1   *Example of data producing a negative Q-square value*

Class	Actual adj. scores (A)	Scores predicted from equation (B)	Mean of all class scores (C)	$|A-B|$	$|A-C|$
A	8	5	12	3	4
B	10	7	12	3	2
C	12	10	12	2	0
D	14	15	12	1	2
E	16	20	12	4	4
Total difference				13	12

Such negative Q-square values are often due to considerable variation or instability in the parameter estimation when single cases are deleted. This instability of coefficients is also reflected by relatively large jackknife standard deviations. As a general rule, the higher the Q-square (in a positive direction), the more predictive relevance the tested model has. Negative Q-squares indicate the irrelevance of including additional constructs or variables in the model. And, finally, Q-square values near zero constitute borderline cases where the decision concerning the validity of the model is uncertain (Wold 1982).

Statistical Concepts and Issues

The purpose of this section is to provide further discussion and, when necessary, concrete illustrations of a number of statistical concepts and issues that bear on the analysis and interpretation of the data to be presented later in this chapter. Issues including the interpretation of the Q-square values as well as use of the information obtained from the Q-square and the "case diagnostics" will be addressed.

Q-square Values

To further clarify the meaning and interpretation of the Q-square values it is useful to examine some examples. Figure 7.2 displays, for the Canada Ontario-French study, the plot corresponding to the regression of residualized posttest scores on the FMI variable "teacher to student probes." Both variables are expressed in a percentage metric. The solid line represents the unstandardized regression line.

The correlation corresponding with the data in Fig. 7.2 is 0.265, the jackknife standard deviation is 0.252, and the Q-square is − 1.606. This Q-square value is the lowest obtained for the "schooling" variables included in the Canadian Ontario-French data set. The Q-square value of − 1.606 indicates that the prediction of adjusted posttest scores made from the overall sample mean is about 160 percent better than the prediction derived from the regression of the adjusted posttest scores on the variable "teacher to student probes." In Wold's (1982) terminology, the underlying bivariate regression model has no predictive relevance and is to be regarded as misleading because it generates inadequate and unreliable predictions of adjusted posttest scores.

In Fig. 7.2 it can readily be seen that the lack of predictive relevance is due to the fact that the regression line is essentially fitted to just one case (i.e., classroom) which has an exceptional or "outlying" value for the predictor variable "teacher to student probes." Further insight into the nature of this problem can be gained by examining the statistics presented in Table 7.2.

Table 7.2 displays for each of the 17 cases involved in the regression, the residual posttest scores, the jackknife residual (that is, the residual obtained

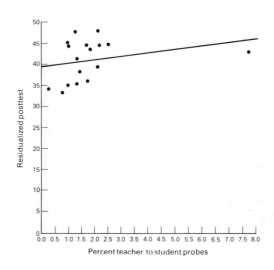

FIG. 7.2   Plot for the regression of residualized posttest scores
on the percent of teacher to student probes.[a]
[a] Canada Ontario-French, $N = 17$ classes.

by deleting the ith case and re-estimating the regression), the diagonal element of the least squares projection matrix (termed Diag Hat), the Andrews-Pregibon statistic, and the Cook's Distance statistic. In addition, Table 7.2 reports the correlation (Corr(i)) and the Q-square (Q-square(i)) obtained when the ith case is deleted from the data set. The reader is referred to Cook and Weisberg (1982) for a comprehensive discussion of the Diag Hat and Cook's distance statistics. For details about the Andrews-Pregibon statistic see Andrews and Pregibon (1978) and Draper and John (1981). It should be noted that Table 7.2 reports the Andrews-Pregibon statistic as one minus the square root of the statistic originally proposed in the article by Andrews and Pregibon. With this transformation, high values of the statistic correspond to "remote" observations in the factor space associated with the dependent and independent variables involved in a given regression model (Andrews and Pregibon 1978, p. 88).

TABLE 7.2 *Case diagnostics for the regression of residualized posttest scores on the percent of teacher to student probes*

Case no.	Residual	Jackknife residual	Diag. hat	Andrews/ Pregibon	Cook's dist.	Corr (i)	Q-square (i)
1	− 5.705	− 6.462	0.117	0.110	0.102	0.192	− 1.421
2	− 1.873	− 1.993	0.061	0.036	0.005	0.269	− 2.176
3	− 5.450	− 5.902	0.077	0.083	0.056	0.235	− 1.518
4	− 5.017	− 5.332	0.059	0.067	0.035	0.270	− 2.081
5	3.082	3.313	0.070	0.049	0.016	0.250	− 1.843
6	0.586	0.627	0.065	0.033	0.001	0.266	− 1.628
7	2.501	2.663	0.059	0.039	0.009	0.267	− 1.571
8	4.735	5.127	0.076	0.072	0.042	0.303	− 2.169
9	− 2.931	− 24.433	0.880	0.690	10.996	0.499	0.066
10	− 5.310	− 5.679	0.065	0.075	0.044	0.252	− 1.707
11	− 2.489	− 2.655	0.063	0.041	0.009	0.258	− 1.668
12	− 6.989	− 7.643	0.086	0.118	0.105	0.217	− 1.384
13	3.205	3.415	0.062	0.046	0.015	0.259	− 1.595
14	7.137	7.648	0.067	0.111	0.082	0.318	− 2.016
15	4.167	4.508	0.076	0.064	0.032	0.297	− 2.074
16	6.746	7.181	0.061	0.099	0.065	0.267	− 1.313
17	3.599	3.826	0.059	0.049	0.018	0.273	− 1.548

Note: The data are from the Canada Ontario-French study with 17 classes.

Cases with comparatively high values on any of the aforementioned case statistics are said to constitute "outlying" or "influential" cases. That is, these statistics can be used to assess the relative influence a given case exerts on the estimation of the regression model considered. Each case statistic reflects somewhat different aspects of the regression model considered. High values of the Diag Hat statistic (which has a maximum value of 1.0) are associated with cases having outlying values for the predictor variable. Comparatively large values of the Andrews-Pregibon statistic indicate outlying cases with regard to both the predictor variable and the predicted variable. Cook's Distance measures the relative effect a given case exerts on the estimation of regression coefficients.

As can be seen in Table 7.2, case 9 is by far the most influential case. In Fig. 7.2 case 9 has the most extreme value in the variable "teacher to student probes" (7.7 percent). The correlation between "teacher to student probes" and adjusted posttest scores changes from 0.265 to 0.499 if case 9 is deleted (see Table 7.2). Corresponding Q-square changes from − 1.606 to 0.060. This analysis suggests that the lack of predictive relevance of the regression shown in Fig. 7.2 is, indeed, primarily due to just one case.

As can be seen in Fig. 7.2, negative Q-square values are not necessarily associated with data structures in which the data points are, more or less, randomly or unsystematically scattered around the regression line. If this were the situation, the correlation would be near zero and the Q-square would normally be negative. Rather, jackknifing and the examination of jackknife statistics become most useful techniques in situations where statistical relationships are strongly influenced, either positively or negatively, by just a few outlying data points and cases. That is, jackknife statistics such as Q-square values can be used as a safeguard against drawing conclusions from statistical relationships primarily fitted to a small subset of the analyzed data.

What to do with Outliers?

Situations such as that described above were quite common for the data collected during the study, particularly for variables derived from classroom observations. Although the above example constitutes a somewhat extreme case, similar data structures were found in data sets for all studies. An important question, then, became how best to deal with such situations. Specifically three options were considered: *ad hoc* rescaling, nonlinear scale transformation, and deletion of outlying cases.

Ad hoc rescaling. The first option considered was to introduce some *ad hoc* rescaling of the observational variables. For example, a given observational variable could be rescaled such that a zero would be assigned to classrooms in which the variable accounted for fewer than one percent of all behaviors, while a one would be assigned to classrooms in which the variable accounted for more than one percent of all behaviors. As a second example, an observational variable could be rescaled so that a zero would indicate that a teacher never exhibited a particular behavior while a one would indicate that a teacher exhibited that behavior at least once during the observations. Such rescaling may help to eliminate data analytical problems associated with outlying data points because exceptional data points might be absorbed into broader categories represented by zeros and ones, for example.

At least two problems were associated with this approach. First, it was often difficult and in some cases impossible to introduce a reasonable and defensible rescaling procedure. For example, in the regression shown in Fig. 7.2 it is impossible to rescale the variable "teacher to student probes" in such a way that the rescaling would be defensible and would at the same time eliminate the problem associated with the single outlying case. Second, and more importantly, the rescaling of observational variables in such a way that the rescaling would be consistent across countries turned out to be impossible. That is, a particular type of rescaling judged appropriate in one study was generally found to be inappropriate in other studies. As a consequence, the *ad hoc* rescaling of observational variables would have had to be study-specific. Apart from the fact that the pretests and posttests were different across studies, the *ad hoc* rescaling would have introduced an additional threat to the comparability of variables and results across studies. Primarily because of the latter reason, *ad hoc* re ʳaling procedures were rejected as inappropriate.

Nonlinear scale transformation. In order to reduce the relative distance of seemingly outlying data points, the use of nonlinear scale transformations, specifically the use of power transformations (see, for example, Emerson and Stoto 1982), was considered. For the regression presented in Fig. 7.2, for example, the cubic root of the percent of "teacher to student probes" rather than raw percentages can be used. Figure 7.3 shows the corresponding regression plot. The correlation between the adjusted posttest scores and the cubic root of the percent of "teacher to student probes" is equal to 0.401, with a Q-square equal to −0.243. Table 7.3 displays the case diagnostics for the regression shown in Fig. 7.3.

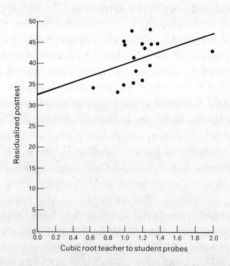

FIG. 7.3 Plot for the regression of residualized posttest scores
on the cubic root of the percent of teacher to student probes.[a]
[a] Canada Ontario-French, *N* = 17 classes.

TABLE 7.3   *Case diagnostics for the regression of residualized posttest scores
on the cubic root of the percent of teacher to student probes*

Case no.	Residual	Jackknife residual	Diag. hat	Andrews/ Pregibon	Cook's dist.	Corr (i)	Q-square (i)
1	− 3.169	− 4.469	0.291	0.177	0.134	0.271	− 0.434
2	− 2.528	− 2.722	0.071	0.047	0.012	0.415	− 0.328
3	− 4.900	− 5.348	0.084	0.082	0.055	0.372	− 0.292
4	− 5.384	− 5.728	0.060	0.078	0.046	0.426	− 0.335
5	2.196	2.418	0.092	0.055	0.012	0.379	− 0.286
6	0.616	0.657	0.062	0.032	0.001	0.402	− 0.249
7	2.072	2.208	0.062	0.038	0.007	0.398	− 0.246
8	5.279	5.760	0.083	0.088	0.064	0.451	− 0.253
9	− 4.086	− 10.571	0.613	0.421	1.590	0.516	0.114
10	− 5.261	− 5.610	0.062	0.077	0.045	0.402	− 0.301
11	− 2.570	− 2.734	0.060	0.041	0.010	0.401	− 0.276
12	− 6.073	− 6.817	0.109	0.119	0.117	0.344	− 0.301
13	2.509	2.709	0.074	0.048	0.012	0.387	− 0.258
14	7.268	7.770	0.065	0.121	0.090	0.458	− 0.222
15	4.680	5.096	0.081	0.077	0.049	0.442	− 0.252
16	6.090	6.558	0.071	0.098	0.071	0.388	− 0.214
17	3.261	3.468	0.060	0.047	0.017	0.402	− 0.234

Note: The data are from the Canada Ontario-French study with 17 classes.

As can be seen from the data presented in Fig. 7.3 and Table 7.3, the cubic root transformation strengthened the linear relationship between "teacher to student probes" and the adjusted posttest. This increase is primarily due to the fact that the cubic root transformation reduces the relative distance between case 9 and the rest of the cases. As noted above, the correlation increases from 0.265 to 0.401 when the raw percentages are transformed by calculating cubic roots. Changes of this magnitude also have been reported by Mandeville (1984) who used the arcsine function for transforming the scales of observational variables. Despite this increase in the correlation, however, Q-square remains negative (although much less negative than reported earlier). Indeed, as can be seen in Table 7.3, case 9 still dominates the regression in much the same way as it did in the case diagnostics presented in Table 7.2.

Since these results could be caused by the somewhat extreme nature of the above example, the effects of nonlinear scale transformations were examined for all observational variables in all studies. A computer program, written for this purpose, tested the change of Q-square values when several potentially useful scale transformations were applied (namely, the arcsine transformation, and power transformations with powers between 0.1 and 0.9). By far the most common result was that no substantial changes in terms of correlation coefficients and Q-square values were observed. Specifically negative Q-square values almost never became positive. More precisely, in a few cases small negative Q-square values changed to small positive Q-square values.

Apart from the small payoff in terms of changes in the magnitude of correlations and Q-square values, another critical point associated with nonlinear scale transformations was difficulties in interpreting the ensuing correlations. It is by no means a straightforward matter to interpret correlations or path coefficients for cubic roots of observational variables. Neither is it a straightforward matter to interpret differences between the estimated effect of, say, the square root of the percent of "disciplinary activities" and the estimated effect of the percent of "procedural interactions" raised, for instance, to a power of 0.1. (It should be noted in passing that the tenth root rather than the cubic root actually produced the smallest negative Q-square value (-0.054) for the regression of adjusted posttest scores on "teacher to student probes" discussed above. The cubic root transformation was used in Fig. 7.3 for illustrative purposes because this transformation seemed to be more readily comprehensible than the tenth root.)

Finally, the use of power transformations can hardly be justified on theoretical terms. Given the state of theoretical knowledge about teaching effects there seems to be little, if any, theoretical basis for introducing power transformations. Rather, the major justification for nonlinear scale transformations would be to modify the shape of the distribution of the data for the specific regression problem encountered in a specific study.

Deletion of outlying cases. The third option that might be considered is the deletion of outlying and influential cases. As noted earlier, for the regression shown in Fig. 7.2 the deletion of just one case would increase the correlation between adjusted posttest scores and the percent of "teacher to student probes" from 0.265 to 0.499; the Q-square would increase from -1.606 to 0.060. Unless, however, there is strong evidence that particular cases have either invalid data (due to incorrect recording, for example) or are, indeed, unusual or exceptional cases in some specifiable non-statistical sense, the deletion of cases is inappropriate. Fitting data to a prespecified statistical relationship, although always possible with the aid of the case diagnostics, is inappropriate. (See Hocking 1983 for a discussion of this issue.)

Another critical point associated with the deletion of influential cases is that cases being "outliers" with regard to one statistical relationship may not be outlying cases in others. This point can be illustrated by Fig. 7.4 which displays, again for the Canadian Ontario-French data set, the plot of the regression of adjusted posttest scores on the variable "teacher to group probes." The correlation for this regression is equal to -0.204 with a jack-knife standard deviation of 0.288 and a Q-square of -0.339. Table 7.4 presents the corresponding case diagnostics.

In Table 7.4 it can be seen that case 5 is the most influential for the regression of adjusted posttest scores on the percent of "teacher to group probes." Case 5 is located in the upper righthand corner of the plot shown in Fig. 7.4. Case 9, which was the most influential case for the regression of

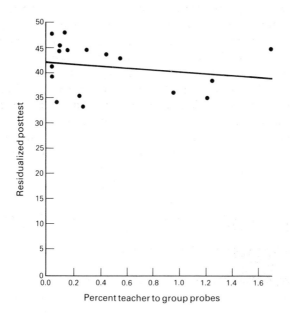

FIG. 7.4   Plot of the regression of residualized posttest scores
on the percent of teacher to group probes.[a]
[a] Canada Ontario-French, $N = 17$ classes.

TABLE 7.4   *Case diagnostics for the regression of residualized posttest*
scores on the percent of teacher to group probes

Case no.	Residual	Jackknife residual	Diag. hat	Andrews/ Pregibon	Cook's dist.	Corr (i)	Q-square (i)
1	−7.675	−8.452	0.091	0.135	0.133	−0.295	−0.352
2	−2.436	−2.701	0.098	0.059	0.014	−0.224	−0.356
3	−4.677	−5.822	0.197	0.137	0.135	−0.089	−0.382
4	−4.126	−4.688	0.120	0.086	0.054	−0.142	−0.379
5	6.014	10.498	0.427	0.311	0.954	−0.417	−0.005
6	−0.059	−0.663	0.099	0.051	0.001	−0.203	−0.359
7	2.577	2.740	0.059	0.039	0.009	−0.206	−0.363
8	3.367	3.694	0.088	0.061	0.024	−0.170	−0.367
9	1.964	2.092	0.061	0.036	0.005	−0.208	−0.363
10	−6.118	−6.571	0.069	0.089	0.060	−0.245	−0.352
11	−1.277	−1.615	0.209	0.113	0.011	−0.157	−0.487
12	−8.178	−8.759	0.066	0.132	0.103	−0.262	−0.364
13	3.177	3.397	0.065	0.047	0.015	−0.190	−0.263
14	5.887	6.533	0.099	0.101	0.086	−0.140	−0.380
15	2.932	3.184	0.079	0.052	0.016	−0.179	−0.363
16	6.360	6.931	0.082	0.101	0.080	−0.156	−0.387
17	2.805	3.079	0.089	0.057	0.017	−0.174	−0.365

Notes: The data are from the Canada Ontario-French study with 17 classes.

adjusted posttest scores on "teacher to student probes," is an "inlying" case in the regression shown in Fig. 7.4.

This shift from "outlying" to "inlying" was expected because the variables "teacher to group probes" and "teacher to student probes" are obviously related to one another. In fact, when "teacher probes," "teacher to group probes," and "teacher to student probes" are included in the same analysis, an analytical relationship exists between "teacher to group probes" and "teacher to student probes" since they must sum to the total of "teacher probes." Hence a teacher having a relatively high value for the variable "teacher to student probes" must have a correspondingly small value for the variable "teacher to group probes." Similar considerations apply to the variables "probes for recall questions" and "probes for higher level questions" as well as "teacher to group questions" and "teacher to student questions."

For the Canada Ontario-French study, the data analytical problems discussed above extend to all variables which involve probes as a component. Either case 9, case 5, or both cases will usually constitute "outlying" observations. Moreover, this result will most likely hold true irrespective of the dependent variable considered (e.g., adjusted posttest scores, percent of students engaged in learning, student attitudes).

In summary, then, all three options for dealing with outlying cases—*ad hoc* rescaling, nonlinear transformations, and deletion—were judged to be inappropriate. As a consequence, the analyses presented in this chapter were, as initially planned, undertaken on the basis of raw percentages of observational variables.

Additional Examples

Since the examples presented above constitute somewhat extreme cases encountered in just one study, however, the discussion of the meaning and interpretation of the Q-square statistic will conclude with a brief examination of three additional examples.

The Netherlands. Figure 7.5 presents for the Netherlands study the plot corresponding with the regression of adjusted posttest scores on the *total* number of probes (that is, the sum of "teacher to group probes" and "teacher to student probes"). The corresponding correlation is equal to 0.106, with a jackknife standard deviation of 0.158, and a Q-square value of -0.080.

The regression shown in Fig. 7.5 involves 47 cases and represents an example where the data points are essentially randomly scattered around the regression line. This randomness is reflected by the small correlation, the large jackknife standard deviation (relative to the magnitude of the correlation coefficient), and the negative Q-square value. The shape of the regression shown in Fig. 7.5 is quite different from the shape of the regression displayed

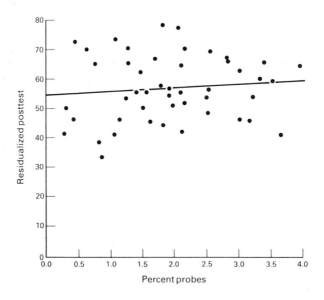

FIG. 7.5   Plot for the regression of residualized posttest scores
on the percent of probes.[a]
[a] The Netherlands, $N = 47$ classes.

in Fig. 7.2, for example. As discussed earlier, the regression shown in Fig. 7.2 is dominated by one outlying case and the Q-square value is negative because the regression line is primarily fitted to this case. In Fig. 7.5, on the other hand, no particular outlying or influential subset of cases seems to exist. Rather, the variable "total number of probes" is simply unrelated to the adjusted posttest scores.

Thailand. The second example is taken from the Thailand study which involves 81 cases. Figure 7.6 displays for Thailand the plot of the regression of adjusted posttest scores on the percent of "student questions." The corresponding correlation is equal to 0.238, the associated jackknife standard deviation is equal to 0.106, and the Q-square value is 0.021.

The regression shown in Fig. 7.6 is a particularly interesting example for two reasons. First, it represents an example where the Q-square value is close to zero. That is, the regression constitutes an example for what Wold (1982) calls a "borderline case" where the decision regarding the predictive relevance

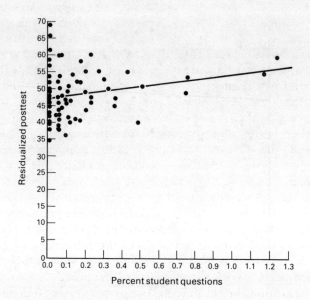

FIG. 7.6   Plot of the regression of residualized posttest scores
on the percent of student questions.[a]
[a] Thailand, N = 81 classes.
[b]Multiple classes are represented by a single point on the vertical axis of the graph.

of the tested model is uncertain. Second, jackknifing based on the deletion of just one case at a time provides, for this particular regression, somewhat less than optimal accuracy in the assessment of predictive relevance. As can be seen in Fig. 7.6, the regression is obviously influenced by the two right-most *pairs* of cases which have the highest values for the variable "student questions." Specifically the two most extreme cases (which are the only cases in which "student questions" account for more than one percent of all coded behaviors) exert a great deal of influence on the estimation of the correlation coefficient. If these two cases are deleted, the correlation drops from 0.238 to 0.123, and the Q-square drops from 0.021 to −0.026. Hence, in order to assess the sensitivity of the regression shown in Fig. 7.6 with regard to the deletion of particular cases, jackknifing based on the deletion of *pairs* of cases would seem somewhat more appropriate than jackknifing based on the deletion of single cases.

The question of whether sensitivity tests and influence analyses should be based on groups of cases (that is, deleting all possible pairs, triples, quadruples, and the like) rather than single cases has received considerable attention in the statistical literature. (See Hocking 1983 for a review.) It is well known that jackknifing based on the deletion of single cases may occasionally fail to unravel strong influences exerted by small subsets of the data set. Because of the potential importance of this issue, a computer program was written which produced jackknife statistics based on the deletion of all possible subsets of up to five cases. The ensuing results were compared with the jackknife statistics obtained by the deletion of single cases.

Two major results emerged from this examination. First, as was to be expected, the larger the number of omitted cases, the smaller the Q-square values. For example, Q-square values obtained on the basis of the deletion of all possible pairs of cases were always numerically smaller than the corresponding Q-square values based on the deletion of single cases. Second, the magnitude of the differences in terms of jackknife standard deviations and Q-square values were generally quite small and in most of the cases negligible. These results suggested that the computationally simpler approach of deleting just one case at a time provided a sufficiently accurate assessment of predictive relevance for the data sets included in the study. The results of the aforementioned examination of jackknife procedures suggested as a general rule of thumb that Q-square values smaller than 0.05 be considered "borderline cases." With Q-square values this small, the corresponding Q-square values obtained by omitting two or more cases often turned out to be negative.

Canada Ontario-French. The third, and final, example is once again taken from the Canadian Ontario-French study. Figure 7.7 shows the plot of the regression of adjusted posttest scores on the percent of "recall questions." The corresponding correlation is equal to 0.793, the jackknife standard deviation is equal to 0.091, and the Q-square value is equal to 0.523.

In any subset of the data displayed in Fig. 7.7 obtained by deleting just one case a fairly strong and stable linear relationship between the adjusted posttest scores and the percent of "recall questions" can be observed. The jackknife standard deviations are generally small and the Q-square values are generally large.

The above detailed discussion of the use of jackknife techniques was to serve three purposes. First, since jackknifing does not appear to constitute a standard approach in related research on classroom teaching and school learning, the presentation was to foster a better understanding of the meaning and the data analytical background of jackknife standard deviations and the Q-square values. Second, the presentation was to illustrate data typical of those obtained in the studies. Figures 7.2 and 7.4 represent examples of relationships strongly influenced by "outlying" cases. Figure 7.5 is an example in which the data points are essentially randomly scattered around the regression line. Figure 7.6 is an example of a so-called "borderline case"

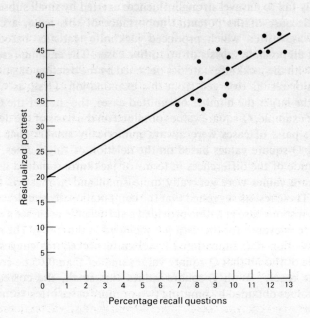

FIG. 7.7   Plot for the regression of residualized posttest scores
on the percent of recall questions.[a]
[a] Canada Ontario-French, $N = 17$ classes.

where the decision regarding the predictive relevance of the tested regression model is uncertain. Finally, Fig. 7.7 represents an example of a fairly strong linear relationship that is insensitive to the deletion of single cases. Third, the presentation was to give a brief account of some procedures, such as the rescaling of variables by means of power transformations and jackknifing based on the deletion of multiple cases, which have been examined for use in analyzing the data to be presented in this section. As stated earlier, the results of these examinations led to the decision to use, as initially planned, the raw percentage scales for observational variables and to employ jackknife techniques based on the deletion of single cases.

Correlation of "Schooling" Variables with Final Achievement

Tables 7.5a through 7.5i display the zero-order correlations between 56 "schooling" variables and student achievement. The correlations represent the relationships between the "schooling" variables and final achievement after within-class differences in initial achievement have been taken into account. In the previous discussion this measure of final achievement has been referred to as "residualized posttest scores."

To assist in the interpretation of the correlation coefficients, five columns of descriptive statistics are included in the tables. These descriptive statistics are the mean, median, standard deviation, minimum value, and maximum value. In addition, columns representing the jackknife standard deviation (denoted as JStd(R)), the squared correlation (denoted as R-square), and the Q-square value are included.

The "schooling" variables included in these tables have been arranged into six sets or clusters. The first cluster includes classroom activities from the SNAP. The second cluster contains three "teacher roles" also from the SNAP. The third cluster includes teacher and student behaviors from the FMI. The fourth cluster contains "composite" variables from the FMI. Such variables were formed by considering the relationship between pairs of behavior codes included on the FMI. For example, by examining the "who to whom" codes and the "question" codes, at least three composite variables could be formed: teacher questions the group, teacher questions an individual student, or student questions the teacher. The fifth cluster of variables included in Tables 7.5a through 7.5i are the percents of students engaged in learning as estimated from the SNAP and from the IAR. Finally, the sixth cluster of variables contains those obtained from various teacher questionnaires and self-report instruments. The variables in this cluster were selected on the basis of preliminary investigations of the correlations between them and "residualized posttest scores" in the various studies.

Finally, several cells in the tables do not contain any data. When an entire row is blank, data on the variable associated with that row either were not collected in the particular study or had to be excluded because of large amounts of missing data. If only the correlation coefficient is missing, either the corresponding variable had virtually no variance or the frequency distribution of the variable was so highly skewed that further consideration of the coefficient would be meaningless. With respect to the deletion of correlation coefficients, it should be emphasized that extremely liberal criteria were used.

Even a cursory examination of the data presented in the Q-square column in Tables 7.5a through 7.5i will result in an awareness that few of the correlations have positive Q-square values associated with them. Because of the large amounts of data included in these tables, Table 7.6 was prepared. Table 7.6 displays for all studies the correlations for which the Q-square value was greater than zero. So-called "borderline cases" are included in this table. The Q-square value associated with each correlation can be determined by referring back to Tables 7.5a through 7.5i.

Concentrating first on the correlations for the variables derived from classroom observations, none of these variables are associated with positive Q-square values in three of the studies: Canada Ontario-English, Israel, and

TABLE 7.5a   *Zero-order correlations with residualized posttest scores in Australia*

Variable	Mean	Median	Std	Min	Max	R	JStd(R)	R-square	Q-square
Lecture/Explain/Demonstrate	20.415	20.183	10.420	0.000	48.145	0.127	0.105	0.016	-0.036
Review Previous Content	7.840	6.810	6.222	0.000	22.980	0.152	0.101	0.023	-0.022
Discourse/Discussion	5.609	4.507	5.609	0.000	22.093	-0.105	0.080	0.011	-0.028
Oral Practice/Drill	4.800	2.000	6.429	0.000	24.071	-0.101	0.114	0.010	-0.045
Seatwork-Test	5.352	3.214	6.877	0.000	30.554	0.195	0.184	0.038	-0.053
Seatwork-Reading	0.122	0.000	0.689	0.000	5.332	.	.	.	.
Seatwork-Written	32.983	31.507	13.353	3.571	79.494	-0.104	0.103	0.011	-0.036
Seatwork-Laboratory	8.648	6.035	8.935	0.000	40.137	-0.242	0.070	0.059	0.014
Composite Management	13.159	13.215	7.233	0.000	34.372	0.180	0.093	0.032	-0.017
Other Activity	1.056	0.000	2.269	0.000	10.948	.	.	.	.
Teacher Interacting	52.277	54.820	14.331	16.844	82.503	0.033	0.135	0.001	-0.062
Teacher Monitoring	43.357	40.839	14.319	17.494	73.628	-0.005	0.138	0.000	-0.065
Uninvolved Teacher	4.361	2.873	7.773	0.000	64.184	-0.051	0.071	0.003	-0.064
Explanation	5.462	4.967	2.926	0.466	13.649	0.092	0.087	0.008	-0.034
Explanation with Materials	11.123	10.491	5.698	2.763	33.232	-0.050	0.095	0.002	-0.042
Demonstration	0.811	0.553	0.837	0.000	3.361	-0.196	0.109	0.039	-0.013
Use of Examples	0.090	0.000	0.257	0.000	1.386	.	.	.	.
Structuring Cues	1.204	0.828	0.988	0.036	4.198	-0.034	0.135	0.001	-0.064
Directives	7.392	6.901	3.573	1.202	18.576	0.004	0.112	0.000	-0.052
Probes (total number)	1.413	1.309	0.956	0.000	4.675	-0.010	0.173	0.000	-0.088
Higher Order Question	0.185	0.111	0.201	0.000	1.065	0.154	0.156	0.024	-0.068
Recall Question	10.820	10.389	3.082	4.907	22.719	-0.068	0.138	0.009	-0.060
Opinion Question	0.011	0.000	0.034	0.000	0.239	.	.	.	.
Redirect Question	1.146	1.032	0.755	0.028	3.521	-0.063	0.119	0.004	-0.055
Teacher or Student Response	19.426	19.570	4.269	9.586	32.728	0.080	0.175	0.006	-0.081
Extended Student Response	1.432	1.049	1.305	0.000	5.699	-0.009	0.092	0.000	-0.044
Student Task Related Statement	1.810	1.421	1.498	0.000	6.915	0.031	0.080	0.001	-0.040
Acknowledge Correct Answer	3.990	3.341	2.852	0.762	19.317	-0.116	0.094	0.013	-0.031

Table 7.5a (continued)

Teacher Says Student Answer Wrong	0.562	0.447	0.361	0.000	1.540	−0.208	0.112	0.043	−0.013
Effectiveness Question	0.692	0.627	0.530	0.000	3.016	0.025	0.109	0.001	−0.050
Silence	12.048	12.002	6.197	1.694	25.418	0.286	0.121	0.082	0.020
Discipline	4.321	3.481	3.037	0.545	18.527	−0.285	0.077	0.081	0.039
Procedural Interaction	12.192	10.995	6.291	1.931	40.296	−0.032	0.134	0.001	−0.060
Social Interaction	0.899	0.639	0.971	0.000	7.035	0.011	0.092	0.000	−0.046
Teacher Question to Group	4.459	4.438	2.497	0.000	11.805	0.116	0.106	0.014	−0.039
Teacher Question to Student	4.992	4.872	2.001	1.171	11.594	−0.122	0.127	0.015	−0.047
Probes for Higher Level Question	0.053	0.029	0.080	0.000	0.391	0.040	0.112	0.002	−0.051
Probes for Recall Question	0.883	0.763	0.711	0.000	3.565	−0.035	0.183	0.001	−0.096
Probes Teacher to Group	0.260	0.168	0.351	0.000	2.316	0.087	0.086	0.007	−0.034
Probes Teacher to Student	1.156	0.998	0.801	0.000	4.066	−0.046	0.177	0.002	−0.089
Student Questions	2.553	2.276	1.468	0.145	7.932	−0.192	0.088	0.037	−0.005
Student Contribution	3.325	3.080	2.177	0.082	11.287	0.009	0.084	0.000	−0.041
Teacher Waits for Student Answer	0.599	0.589	0.401	0.079	2.108	−0.085	0.174	0.007	−0.079
Objectives with Stress	0.006	0.000	0.033	0.000	0.242	.	.	.	.
Lecture with Stress	0.016	0.000	0.052	0.000	0.392	.	.	.	.
Student Unable to Answer	0.007	0.000	0.026	0.000	0.205	.	.	.	.
Rating of Academic Engagement (SNAP)	81.891	83.165	9.339	57.951	98.767	−0.026	0.123	0.001	−0.057
Rating of Academic Engagement (IAR)	83.018	84.832	8.656	55.384	97.421	0.185	0.103	0.034	−0.009
Years of Teaching Experience	9.892	7.000	7.789	1.000	31.000	0.297	0.147	0.083	0.018
Size of Class	27.878	28.000	4.999	13.000	38.000	0.023	0.157	0.001	−0.076
Number of Homework Assignments	1.486	1.000	1.698	0.000	11.000	0.288	0.153	0.083	−0.078
Prop. Obs with Emphasis Expand	0.025	0.000	0.079	0.000	0.500	.	.	.	.
Prop. Obs with Emphasis Intro	0.066	0.000	0.149	0.000	0.800	.	.	.	.
Prop. Obs with Emphasis Review	0.910	1.000	0.171	0.200	1.000	−0.218	0.138	0.048	−0.028
Opportunity to Learn Rating	68.751	72.000	24.608	8.000	100.000	0.352	0.109	0.124	0.068
Time Allocated to Instruction	49.342	49.850	6.016	31.000	66.300	0.006	0.132	0.000	−0.062

Note: N = 74 classes

Norbert Sellin and Lorin W. Anderson

TABLE 7.5b Zero-order correlations with residualized posttest scores in Canada Ontario-English

Variable	Mean	Median	Std	Min	Max	R	JStd(R)	R-square	Q-square
Lecture/Explain/Demonstrate	25.011	21.247	14.450	2.500	53.955	0.039	0.218	0.002	-0.169
Review Previous Content	13.666	4.999	17.189	0.000	47.021	-0.315	0.110	0.099	-0.032
Discourse/Discussion	10.310	6.249	12.051	0.000	43.747	0.101	0.108	0.010	-0.092
Oral Practice/Drill	0.857	0.000	2.461	0.000	11.999	.	.	.	.
Seatwork-Test	3.128	0.000	6.674	0.000	24.998	.	.	.	.
Seatwork-Reading	0.865	0.000	3.159	0.000	15.937	.	.	.	.
Seatwork-Written	29.512	26.039	18.066	0.000	74.372	0.297	0.122	0.088	-0.036
Seatwork-Laboratory	0.865	0.000	2.544	0.000	9.999	.	.	.	.
Composite Management	15.776	15.786	6.880	5.312	29.997	-0.030	0.213	0.001	-0.170
Other Activity	0.000	0.000	0.000	0.000	0.000	.	.	.	.
Teacher Interacting	52.986	52.496	14.929	14.998	84.998	-0.287	0.093	0.083	-0.018
Teacher Monitoring	38.828	37.497	17.302	4.999	82.498	0.242	0.132	0.059	-0.070
Uninvolved Teacher	8.179	6.041	8.284	0.000	27.497	0.012	0.269	0.000	-0.214
Explanation	8.578	7.057	5.068	1.289	18.531	-0.205	0.215	0.042	-0.077
Explanation with Materials	10.615	11.682	5.713	1.312	29.278	0.371	0.207	0.137	-0.013
Demonstration	1.610	1.339	1.359	0.072	5.944	-0.051	0.200	0.003	-0.192
Use of Examples	0.327	0.074	0.548	0.000	2.196	-0.243	0.102	0.059	-0.100
Structuring Cues	3.925	3.390	2.649	0.738	10.526	-0.013	0.169	0.000	-0.127
Directives	3.205	3.008	1.472	1.156	7.747	0.091	0.295	0.008	-0.249
Probes (total number)	1.616	1.414	0.928	0.000	3.526	-0.240	0.132	0.058	-0.076
Higher Order Question	1.737	1.213	1.738	0.000	6.221	0.148	0.206	0.022	-0.172
Recall Question	9.489	9.749	3.400	4.088	19.712	-0.138	0.156	0.019	-0.093
Opinion Question	0.037	0.000	0.109	0.000	0.540	.	.	.	.
Redirect Question	0.799	0.752	0.581	0.000	2.865	-0.382	0.065	0.146	-0.030
Teacher or Student Response	13.778	13.882	3.343	4.669	21.363	-0.097	0.154	0.009	-0.127
Extended Student Response	0.538	0.471	0.417	0.000	1.776	0.060	0.163	0.004	-0.134
Student Task Related Statement	0.995	0.895	0.764	0.000	2.633	0.034	0.349	0.001	-0.250
Acknowledge Correct Answer	2.552	2.562	1.723	0.000	6.351	0.121	0.211	0.015	-0.155

Table 7.5b *(continued)*

Teacher Says Student Answer Wrong	0.647	0.635	0.450	0.056	1.576	0.143	0.236	0.020	-0.185
Effectiveness Question	0.647	0.545	0.434	0.076	1.537	-0.156	0.120	0.024	-0.099
Silence	16.812	14.308	11.549	5.457	62.141	-0.009	0.161	0.000	-0.171
Discipline	1.132	0.959	0.873	0.000	3.103	-0.182	0.158	0.033	-0.113
Procedural Interaction	12.671	10.391	10.596	0.125	41.938	0.094	0.255	0.009	-0.146
Social Interaction	0.738	0.315	1.285	0.000	5.680	0.142	0.084	0.020	-0.075
Teacher Question to Group	5.537	4.874	2.541	0.586	10.647	0.041	0.251	0.002	-0.176
Teacher Question to Student	4.543	4.333	2.067	1.674	9.077	-0.287	0.094	0.082	-0.026
Probes for Higher Level Question	0.181	0.094	0.204	0.000	0.653	0.091	0.180	0.008	-0.149
Probes for Recall Question	0.802	0.797	0.505	0.000	2.155	-0.229	0.125	0.053	-0.082
Probes Teacher to Group	0.553	0.432	0.449	0.000	1.610	-0.270	0.147	0.073	-0.031
Probes Teacher to Student	1.049	1.044	0.610	0.000	2.286	-0.153	0.169	0.023	-0.132
Student Questions	1.943	1.830	1.278	0.083	4.960	0.048	0.182	0.002	-0.143
Student Contribution	.	.	.	.	.	.	.	.	.
Teacher Waits for Student Answer	0.025	0.000	0.054	0.000	0.183	.	.	.	.
Objectives with Stress	0.000	0.000	0.000	0.000	0.000	.	.	.	.
Lecture with Stress	0.105	0.039	0.138	0.000	0.567	0.030	0.223	0.001	-0.208
Student Unable to Answer									
Rating of Academic Engagement (SNAP)	76.592	76.733	8.202	63.829	92.083	0.101	0.193	0.010	-0.159
Rating of Academic Engagement (IAR)	78.943	78.943	5.869	63.988	89.734	0.159	0.270	0.025	-0.167
Years of Teaching Experience	14.344	13.500	7.297	4.000	36.000	0.419	0.469	0.176	-0.295
Size of Class	27.846	27.500	4.478	15.000	35.000	0.080	0.156	0.006	-0.114
Number of Homework Assignments	4.221	4.188	1.294	1.000	8.000	-0.063	0.183	0.004	-0.109
Prop. Obs with Emphasis Expand	0.283	0.290	0.141	0.000	0.500	0.121	0.313	0.015	-0.217
Prop. Obs with Emphasis Intro	0.362	0.380	0.223	0.000	0.750	0.131	0.171	0.017	-0.126
Prop. Obs with Emphasis Review	0.357	0.360	0.219	0.000	0.880	-0.226	0.221	0.051	-0.173
Opportunity to Learn Rating	75.427	78.750	15.174	27.500	97.400	0.081	0.214	0.007	-0.164
Time Allocated to Instruction	45.377	41.000	11.531	32.100	74.300	-0.235	0.180	0.055	-0.115

Note: N = 26 classes

TABLE 7.5c *Zero-order correlations with residualized posttest scores in Canada Ontario-French*

Variable	Mean	Median	Std	Min	Max	R	JStd(R)	R-square	Q-square
Lecture/Explain/Demonstrate	26.112	23.451	13.289	2.857	54.996	−0.142	0.294	0.020	−0.209
Review Previous Content	20.738	19.997	14.333	2.500	52.855	0.156	0.194	0.024	−0.179
Discourse/Discussion	0.735	0.000	1.929	0.000	7.500	.	.	.	.
Oral Practice/Drill	6.260	5.000	5.583	0.000	17.498	−0.014	0.283	0.000	−0.311
Seatwork-Test	1.197	0.000	2.647	0.000	7.500	.	.	.	.
Seatwork-Reading	0.147	0.000	0.606	0.000	2.500	.	.	.	.
Seatwork-Written	26.151	26.665	8.517	10.832	44.402	0.027	0.301	0.001	−0.333
Seatwork-Laboratory	0.441	0.000	1.819	0.000	7.499	.	.	.	.
Composite Management	15.488	15.950	6.859	2.500	27.736	−0.020	0.308	0.000	−0.337
Other Activity	2.521	0.000	3.355	0.000	8.035	.	.	.	.
Teacher Interacting	62.347	64.997	14.961	30.951	80.712	0.205	0.290	0.042	−0.263
Teacher Monitoring	21.398	19.998	11.845	5.000	47.497	0.192	0.212	0.037	−0.179
Uninvolved Teacher	16.349	17.497	11.219	0.000	42.022	−0.476	0.196	0.227	0.071
Explanation	7.263	7.263	4.142	1.083	15.415	0.418	0.296	0.175	−0.190
Explanation with Materials	11.693	11.000	3.372	7.463	19.893	−0.254	0.259	0.065	−0.189
Demonstration	0.459	0.329	0.578	0.000	2.038	−0.212	0.289	0.045	−0.244
Use of Examples	0.745	0.671	0.648	0.104	2.620	0.186	0.241	0.034	−0.193
Structuring Cues	4.847	4.506	2.438	1.511	9.288	−0.100	0.225	0.010	−0.230
Directives	2.960	2.960	1.198	1.207	6.259	0.106	0.399	0.011	−0.496
Probes (total number)	2.265	2.126	1.781	0.316	8.250	0.184	0.154	0.034	−0.209
Higher Order Question	0.153	0.082	0.168	0.000	0.598	0.460	0.144	0.211	0.025
Recall Question	9.738	9.633	1.775	6.884	12.732	0.784	0.091	0.615	0.523
Opinion Question	0.100	0.000	0.209	0.000	0.712	.	.	.	.
Redirect Question	0.587	0.607	0.353	0.196	1.424	0.023	0.220	0.001	−0.235
Teacher or Student Response	13.876	13.954	3.486	9.361	21.341	0.430	0.217	0.185	−0.064
Extended Student Response	0.397	0.350	1.427	0.000	4.672	0.347	0.121	0.120	−0.031
Student Task Related Statement	0.794	0.569	0.831	0.000	2.535	0.095	0.269	0.009	−0.283
Acknowledge Correct Answer	3.456	3.350	1.425	1.694	6.911	0.207	0.246	0.043	−0.027

Table 7.5c *(continued)*

Teacher Says Student Answer Wrong	0.694	0.568	0.476	0.159	2.149	0.394	0.234	0.155	-0.017
Effectiveness Question	1.302	1.302	0.691	0.293	2.587	-0.253	0.312	0.064	-0.258
Silence	8.773	8.530	6.819	0.228	20.678	0.435	0.184	0.189	0.003
Discipline	1.026	0.805	0.752	0.094	2.603	-0.149	0.280	0.022	-0.274
Procedural Interaction	19.660	18.391	10.139	3.306	37.754	-0.447	0.231	0.200	-0.075
Social Interaction	1.471	1.218	1.344	0.026	5.319	-0.285	0.327	0.081	-0.223
Teacher Question to Group	3.521	3.521	1.566	0.604	6.171	-0.409	0.238	0.168	-0.047
Teacher Question to Student	5.627	4.752	2.460	1.681	11.653	0.479	0.151	0.229	0.057
Probes for Higher Level Question	0.329	0.029	0.043	0.000	0.160	0.417	0.098	0.174	-0.083
Probes for Recall Question	0.819	0.753	0.552	0.137	2.058	0.184	0.229	0.034	-0.198
Probes Teacher to Group	0.442	0.236	0.515	0.033	1.696	-0.204	0.288	0.042	-0.339
Probes Teacher to Student	1.816	1.417	1.625	0.246	7.703	0.265	0.252	0.070	-1.606
Student Questions	1.522	1.084	1.693	0.000	7.097	0.580	0.109	0.337	-0.040
Student Contribution	.	.	.	.	.	.	.	.	.
Teacher Waits for Student Answer	.	.	.	.	.	.	.	.	.
Objectives with Stress	0.064	0.000	0.133	0.000	0.391	.	.	.	.
Lecture with Stress	0.000	0.000	0.000	0.000	0.000	.	.	.	.
Student Unable to Answer	0.002	0.000	0.008	0.000	0.033	.	.	.	.
Rating of Academic Engagement (SNAP)	87.994	94.088	12.011	67.865	100.000	0.322	0.286	0.104	-0.169
Rating of Academic Engagement (IAR)	80.809	86.562	10.969	59.687	94.375	0.436	0.273	0.190	-0.061
Years of Teaching Experience	18.824	19.000	6.267	8.000	29.000	0.022	0.265	0.000	-0.279
Size of Class	24.118	23.000	4.121	17.000	32.000	-0.226	0.153	0.051	-0.118
Number of Homework Assignments	3.176	4.000	1.334	1.000	5.000	0.522	0.163	0.273	0.116
Prop. Obs with Emphasis Expand	.	.	.	.	.	.	.	.	.
Prop. Obs with Emphasis Intro	.	.	.	.	.	.	.	.	.
Prop. Obs with Emphasis Review	.	.	.	.	.	.	.	.	.
Opportunity to Learn Rating	.	.	.	.	.	.	.	.	.
Time Allocated to Instruction	35.038	35.000	9.679	24.700	68.000	0.326	0.320	0.106	-0.156

Note: N = 17 classes

TABLE 7.5d *Zero-order correlations with residualized posttest scores in Canada Quebec*

Variable	Mean	Median	Std	Min	Max	R	JStd(R)	R-square	Q-square
Lecture/Explain/Demonstrate	29.481	29.825	9.943	10.856	52.319	-0.057	0.260	0.003	-0.251
Review Previous Content	16.176	15.041	8.805	5.668	34.331	-0.013	0.192	0.000	-0.194
Discourse/Discussion	0.862	0.000	1.341	0.000	4.286	.	.	.	.
Oral Practice/Drill	8.144	2.000	12.327	0.000	41.998	0.277	0.270	0.077	-0.187
Seatwork-Test	1.207	0.000	2.048	0.000	6.500	.	.	.	.
Seatwork-Reading	0.000	0.000	0.000	0.000	0.000	.	.	.	.
Seatwork-Written	25.604	28.980	13.860	2.000	44.065	-0.276	0.242	0.076	-0.158
Seatwork-Laboratory	0.626	0.000	1.161	0.000	4.000	.	.	.	.
Composite Management	15.377	12.332	8.612	0.000	37.173	0.212	0.166	0.045	-0.130
Other Activity	2.515	1.000	3.239	0.000	10.396	.	.	.	.
Teacher Interacting	72.544	69.398	12.476	50.353	94.332	0.247	0.272	0.061	-0.208
Teacher Monitoring	4.856	3.999	4.800	0.000	20.665	-0.132	0.200	0.017	-0.169
Uninvolved Teacher	22.595	23.236	11.992	0.000	41.116	-0.204	0.279	0.042	-0.243
Explanation	14.106	12.726	4.927	6.205	22.563	-0.195	0.277	0.038	-0.232
Explanation with Materials	15.867	15.568	6.017	3.759	23.711	-0.192	0.241	0.037	-0.190
Demonstration	0.868	0.371	1.096	0.000	4.149	-0.246	0.287	0.060	-0.209
Use of Examples	0.547	0.178	0.757	0.028	2.711	0.055	0.301	0.003	-0.351
Structuring Cues	6.143	6.088	1.957	3.578	9.693	-0.436	0.192	0.191	-0.021
Directives	3.308	3.374	1.463	1.349	5.848	-0.062	0.283	0.004	-0.281
Probes (total number)	3.656	2.593	2.600	0.593	9.101	-0.253	0.198	0.064	-0.159
Higher Order Question	0.375	0.090	0.667	0.000	2.219	0.366	0.203	0.134	-0.048
Recall Question	9.520	9.608	3.660	3.674	16.062	0.295	0.257	0.087	-0.152
Opinion Question	0.094	0.000	0.154	0.000	0.544	.	.	.	.
Redirect Question	0.428	0.279	0.466	0.027	1.612	-0.006	0.256	0.000	-0.258
Teacher or Student Response	12.262	12.159	3.787	5.225	19.278	0.387	0.239	0.150	-0.072
Extended Student Response	0.153	0.136	0.157	0.000	0.624	-0.034	0.462	0.001	-0.688
Student Task Related Statement	1.103	0.984	0.701	0.286	2.333	0.379	0.241	0.143	-0.067
Acknowledge Correct Answer	1.581	1.237	1.107	0.268	4.582	0.467	0.262	0.218	0.027

Table 7.5d *(continued)*

Teacher Says Student Answer Wrong	0.818	0.655	0.587	0.211	2.128	0.508	0.211	0.258	0.100
Effectiveness Question	0.796	0.501	0.677	0.027	2.368	0.315	0.260	0.099	−0.217
Silence	7.495	6.846	4.570	1.920	16.779	−0.072	0.253	0.005	−0.240
Discipline	1.638	1.487	1.338	0.284	5.934	−0.004	0.169	0.000	−0.184
Procedural Interaction	6.599	6.121	4.114	0.981	20.853	0.069	0.189	0.005	−0.190
Social Interaction	3.442	3.269	1.573	1.260	7.592	0.347	0.160	0.120	−0.105
Teacher Question to Group									
Teacher Question to Student									
Probes for Higher Level Question									
Probes for Recall Question									
Probes Teacher to Group									
Probes Teacher to Student									
Student Questions									
Student Contribution									
Teacher Waits for Student Answer									
Objectives with Stress									
Lecture with Stress									
Student Unable to Answer									
Rating of Academic Engagement (SNAP)	79.799	83.020	10.721	53.339	97.580	−0.028	0.185	0.001	−0.181
Rating of Academic Engagement (IAR)									
Years of Teaching Experience	17.632	17.000	6.825	9.000	33.000	−0.523	0.182	0.274	0.135
Size of Class	28.737	29.000	2.642	24.000	33.000	0.065	0.248	0.004	−0.234
Number of Homework Assignments	3.368	4.000	1.165	1.000	5.000	−0.057	0.302	0.003	−0.309
Prop. Obs with Emphasis Expand									
Prop. Obs with Emphasis Intro									
Prop. Obs with Emphasis Review									
Opportunity to Learn Rating									
Time Allocated to Instruction	51.289	50.400	4.195	45.000	59.800	−0.076	0.258	0.006	−0.239

Note: N = 19 classes

TABLE 7.5e   *Zero-order correlations with residualized posttest scores in Hungary*

Variable	Mean	Median	Std	Min	Max	R	JStd(R)	R-square	Q-square
Lecture/Explain/Demonstrate	13.057	10.110	12.145	0.000	47.996	0.092	0.223	0.008	-0.165
Review Previous Content	8.876	3.999	10.482	0.000	46.569	-0.069	0.142	0.005	-0.092
Discourse/Discussion	50.219	49.663	19.768	11.998	91.999	-0.065	0.176	0.004	-0.119
Oral Practice/Drill	0.222	0.000	0.929	0.000	3.999	.	.	.	.
Seatwork-Test	0.303	0.000	1.289	0.000	6.221	.	.	.	.
Seatwork-Reading	0.811	0.000	1.820	0.000	7.999	.	.	.	.
Seatwork-Written	11.314	11.998	7.111	0.000	27.426	0.425	0.169	0.180	0.063
Seatwork-Laboratory	10.821	11.111	8.895	0.000	33.888	-0.112	0.158	0.012	-0.095
Composite Management	2.675	0.000	3.950	0.000	15.999	.	.	.	.
Other Activity	1.512	0.000	3.449	0.000	12.570	.	.	.	.
Teacher Interacting	79.011	79.504	14.993	39.498	100.000	-0.168	0.204	0.028	-0.127
Teacher Monitoring	16.423	15.998	11.716	0.000	56.498	0.184	0.221	0.034	-0.172
Uninvolved Teacher	4.565	1.111	7.074	0.000	27.998	0.050	0.240	0.003	-0.183
Explanation	11.603	11.416	4.796	4.884	24.391	-0.048	0.152	0.002	-0.105
Explanation with Materials	5.744	5.030	2.912	0.792	14.395	-0.329	0.161	0.108	0.007
Demonstration	1.323	0.656	1.683	0.000	6.005	-0.086	0.183	0.007	-0.124
Use of Examples	0.782	0.490	0.794	0.000	3.375	0.082	0.190	0.007	-0.136
Structuring Cues	2.215	2.286	1.304	0.331	5.888	-0.152	0.164	0.023	-0.086
Directives	4.129	3.617	2.656	0.825	11.905	0.072	0.200	0.005	-0.134
Probes (total number)	5.203	5.414	1.515	2.638	8.227	-0.009	0.155	0.000	-0.107
Higher Order Question	6.805	6.612	2.169	2.202	11.596	-0.339	0.161	0.115	-0.006
Recall Question	3.469	3.121	2.497	0.333	14.257	0.218	0.160	0.047	-0.040
Opinion Question	0.573	0.137	1.013	0.000	4.221	0.116	0.163	0.014	-0.104
Redirect Question	1.511	1.316	1.016	0.220	3.788	-0.085	0.146	0.007	-0.094
Teacher or Student Response	17.683	17.122	4.745	10.459	27.834	-0.167	0.166	0.026	-0.092
Extended Student Response	1.191	0.845	1.016	0.000	3.522	0.399	0.150	0.159	0.044
Student Task-Related Statement	0.769	0.587	0.795	0.000	3.243	-0.023	0.169	0.001	-0.124
Acknowledge Correct Answer	3.251	2.966	1.698	0.661	7.953	-0.012	0.149	0.000	-0.104

Table 7.5e *(continued)*

Teacher Says Student Answer Wrong	0.745	0.630	0.495	0.067	2.348	-0.105	0.240	0.011	-0.196
Effectiveness Question	0.489	0.318	0.492	0.000	1.941	0.020	0.219	0.000	-0.161
Silence	14.003	12.578	6.319	3.851	31.292	0.381	0.136	0.145	0.061
Discipline	1.452	1.437	0.776	0.221	3.003	-0.168	0.175	0.028	-0.091
Procedural Interaction	9.084	8.209	6.720	0.129	24.547	-0.077	0.203	0.006	-0.136
Social Interaction	0.411	0.098	0.683	0.000	2.879	-0.183	0.184	0.033	-0.090
Teacher Question to Group	7.475	6.581	2.561	3.980	13.662	-0.363	0.146	0.132	0.026
Teacher Question to Student	4.725	4.195	3.217	1.446	19.833	0.228	0.154	0.052	-0.023
Probes for Higher Level Question	2.575	2.536	1.333	0.282	5.096	-0.322	0.136	0.104	0.015
Probes for Recall Question	0.864	0.508	0.796	0.000	3.474	0.137	0.182	0.019	-0.105
Probes Teacher to Group	1.154	1.019	0.835	0.000	3.712	-0.302	0.126	0.091	-0.010
Probes Teacher to Student	4.163	4.047	1.657	1.550	8.440	0.154	0.139	0.024	-0.073
Student Questions	0.131	0.000	0.311	0.000	1.760	.	.	.	.
Student Contribution	3.601	3.468	2.594	0.058	10.014	0.113	0.165	0.013	-0.105
Teacher Waits for Student Answer	2.838	1.970	2.614	0.591	12.829	0.213	0.176	0.045	-0.073
Objectives with Stress	0.313	0.131	0.408	0.000	1.456	-0.169	0.152	0.029	-0.069
Lecture with Stress	0.551	0.179	1.056	0.000	5.712	0.061	0.203	0.004	-0.262
Student Unable to Answer	0.409	0.289	0.429	0.000	1.942	-0.048	0.262	0.002	-0.231
Rating of Academic Engagement (SNAP)	.	.	.	.	.	.	.	.	.
Rating of Academic Engagement (IAR)	.	.	.	.	.	.	.	.	.
Years of Teaching Experience	14.741	14.844	8.949	1.000	36.000	0.152	0.154	0.023	-0.091
Size of Class	29.139	29.000	4.776	18.000	40.000	0.106	0.167	0.011	-0.103
Number of Homework Assignments	1.001	0.500	1.242	0.000	5.000	-0.004	0.225	0.000	-0.172
Prop. Obs with Emphasis Expand	.	.	.	.	.	.	.	.	.
Prop. Obs with Emphasis Intro	.	.	.	.	.	.	.	.	.
Prop. Obs with Emphasis Review	.	.	.	.	.	.	.	.	.
Opportunity to Learn Rating	.	.	.	.	.	.	.	.	.
Time Allocated to Instruction	35.097	36.200	5.973	21.200	45.000	0.150	0.196	0.022	-0.116

Note: N = 36 classes

TABLE 7.5f *Zero-order correlations with residualized posttest scores in Israel*

Variable	Mean	Median	Std	Min	Max	R	JStd(R)	R-square	Q-square
Lecture/Explain/Demonstrate	41.366	41.366	15.260	7.999	74.998	−0.266	0.155	0.071	−0.103
Review Previous Content	4.938	3.999	4.731	0.000	14.997	0.179	0.459	0.032	−0.310
Discourse/Discussion	16.963	16.963	13.907	0.000	46.884	0.430	0.200	0.185	−0.032
Oral Practice/Drill	3.491	3.491	4.787	0.000	19.999	0.161	0.172	0.026	−0.201
Seatwork-Test	1.895	0.000	5.421	0.000	19.999	.	.	.	.
Seatwork-Reading	6.911	4.999	7.708	0.000	22.664	0.119	0.256	0.014	−0.232
Seatwork-Written	7.508	3.999	11.289	0.000	39.996	0.042	0.156	0.002	−0.147
Seatwork-Laboratory	0.263	0.000	1.088	0.000	4.999	.	.	.	.
Composite Management	7.929	6.665	8.920	0.000	28.999	−0.322	0.242	0.104	−0.185
Other Activity	8.727	7.999	9.282	0.000	33.333	.	.	.	.
Teacher Interacting	79.033	83.333	14.135	47.996	100.000	−0.062	0.184	0.004	−0.161
Teacher Monitoring	15.349	11.998	12.450	0.000	39.997	0.006	0.162	0.000	−0.152
Uninvolved Teacher	5.613	4.999	5.395	0.000	19.997	0.150	0.250	0.023	−0.228
Explanation	11.446	10.207	7.975	1.543	38.163	−0.301	0.210	0.090	−0.256
Explanation with Materials	1.772	1.141	2.411	0.000	9.993	0.097	0.148	0.009	−0.151
Demonstration	0.672	0.404	1.281	0.000	5.898	−0.084	0.210	0.007	−0.293
Use of Examples	3.277	2.411	3.410	0.120	14.581	0.035	0.078	0.001	−0.115
Structuring Cues	1.742	1.742	1.216	0.000	4.336	0.069	0.154	0.005	−0.149
Directives	4.953	4.712	3.272	0.000	11.875	0.249	0.168	0.062	−0.085
Probes (total number)	2.710	2.075	2.858	0.000	10.680	0.189	0.203	0.036	−0.160
Higher Order Question	3.198	2.636	2.521	0.000	7.805	−0.013	0.160	0.000	−0.160
Recall Question	3.340	2.567	2.641	0.000	10.444	−0.030	0.128	0.001	−0.138
Opinion Question	3.229	3.229	2.109	0.000	7.570	−0.012	0.190	0.000	−0.184
Redirect Question	3.690	3.421	2.682	0.368	9.280	0.125	0.166	0.016	−0.140
Teacher or Student Response	12.525	11.116	6.208	0.000	23.469	−0.013	0.206	0.000	−0.193
Extended Student Response	5.990	5.203	4.740	1.780	19.099	−0.244	0.156	0.060	−0.114
Student Task Related Statement	3.937	3.398	3.677	0.250	12.466	0.195	0.164	0.038	−0.108
Acknowledge Correct Answer	4.825	3.629	3.311	0.575	12.725	0.284	0.185	0.080	−0.062

Table 7.5f *(continued)*

Teacher Says Student Answer Wrong	1.216	1.066	1.229	0.000	4.514	0.130	0.212	0.017	−0.169
Effectiveness Question	2.454	0.956	3.577	0.000	13.348	0.170	0.180	0.029	−0.161
Silence	1.547	0.755	2.873	0.000	13.390	0.064	0.163	0.004	−0.472
Discipline	8.311	6.492	9.596	0.000	41.504	−0.034	0.117	0.001	−0.159
Procedural Interaction	4.891	3.452	3.992	0.096	16.584	0.235	0.184	0.055	−0.090
Social Interaction	1.786	0.841	2.938	0.000	12.619	−0.024	0.179	0.001	−0.182
Teacher Question to Group									
Teacher Question to Student									
Probes for Higher Level Question									
Probes for Recall Question									
Probes Teacher to Group									
Probes Teacher to Student									
Student Questions									
Student Contribution									
Teacher Waits for Student Answer									
Objectives with Stress									
Lecture with Stress									
Student Unable to Answer									
Rating of Academic Engagement (SNAP)	59.932	59.932	20.008	10.889	88.557	0.317	0.193	0.101	−0.088
Rating of Academic Engagement (IAR)									
Years of Teaching Experience	14.893	13.000	6.899	5.000	30.000	−0.136	0.406	0.019	−0.287
Size of Class	31.190	31.000	4.611	21.000	39.000	0.312	0.253	0.097	−0.152
Number of Homework Assignments	1.639	2.000	0.356	1.000	2.000	0.058	0.155	0.003	−0.134
Prop. Obs with Emphasis Expand									
Prop. Obs with Emphasis Intro									
Prop. Obs with Emphasis Review									
Opportunity to Learn Rating									
Time Allocated to Instruction									

Note: N = 21 classes

TABLE 7.5g *Zero-order correlations with residualized posttest scores in the Republic of Korea*

Variable	Mean	Median	Std	Min	Max	R	JStd(R)	R-square	Q-square
Lecture/Explain/Demonstrate	30.105	27.497	13.154	9.998	62.497	-0.010	0.170	0.000	-0.102
Review Previous Content	2.880	2.500	3.228	0.000	13.123	-0.116	0.105	0.014	-0.058
Discourse/Discussion	22.995	21.248	10.607	5.000	49.996	-0.051	0.170	0.003	-0.100
Oral Practice/Drill	0.111	0.000	0.521	0.000	2.500	.	.	.	.
Seatwork-Test	0.333	0.000	1.011	0.000	5.000	.	.	.	.
Seatwork-Reading	0.333	0.000	0.859	0.000	2.500	.	.	.	.
Seatwork-Written	6.891	4.999	6.222	0.000	22.497	0.252	0.124	0.064	-0.008
Seatwork-Laboratory	26.504	24.998	10.099	9.998	48.956	-0.155	0.103	0.024	-0.043
Composite Management	9.724	9.998	6.927	0.000	24.996	0.139	0.149	0.019	-0.066
Other Activity	0.111	0.000	0.521	0.000	2.500	.	.	.	.
Teacher Interacting	61.363	59.996	11.819	24.374	84.998	-0.158	0.129	0.025	-0.052
Teacher Monitoring	29.557	29.997	10.419	9.999	58.956	0.165	0.129	0.027	-0.052
Uninvolved Teacher	9.072	9.998	6.225	0.000	24.996	0.023	0.159	0.001	-0.097
Explanation	6.969	6.941	3.188	1.520	15.712	-0.069	0.133	0.005	-0.074
Explanation with Materials	8.093	7.130	4.332	2.080	17.559	0.074	0.166	0.006	-0.093
Demonstration	5.027	4.086	4.024	0.370	18.786	-0.306	0.112	0.094	0.027
Use of Examples	0.509	0.323	0.712	0.000	3.341	-0.150	0.134	0.023	-0.059
Structuring Cues	5.888	5.573	2.424	2.074	11.931	0.044	0.157	0.002	-0.094
Directives	7.316	7.076	1.967	3.130	11.095	0.268	0.140	0.072	-0.014
Probes (total number)	1.174	1.056	0.626	0.394	3.014	-0.129	0.115	0.017	-0.058
Higher Order Question	1.426	1.390	0.686	0.301	2.960	0.014	0.157	0.000	-0.096
Recall Question	5.181	5.033	1.829	2.283	9.902	-0.102	0.154	0.010	-0.086
Opinion Question	0.265	0.167	0.291	0.000	1.053	0.007	0.141	0.000	-0.087
Redirect Question	0.261	0.252	0.169	0.000	0.593	0.051	0.159	0.003	-0.091
Teacher or Student Response	14.909	15.055	3.542	7.100	22.435	0.256	0.154	0.065	-0.021
Extended Student Response	1.600	0.640	1.908	0.000	8.413	0.006	0.143	0.000	-0.090
Student Task Related Statement	0.351	0.249	0.368	0.000	1.695	-0.093	0.128	0.009	-0.069
Acknowledge Correct Answer	0.799	0.684	0.559	0.199	3.143	0.177	0.179	0.031	-0.134

Table 7.5g *(continued)*

Teacher Says Student Answer Wrong	0.107	0.079	0.112	0.478	0.000	0.159	0.143	0.020	-0.066
Effectiveness Question	0.872	0.864	0.597	2.522	0.032	0.131	0.044	0.002	-0.077
Silence	24.299	25.443	7.950	41.974	6.361	0.186	0.054	0.003	-0.112
Discipline	1.493	1.496	1.045	5.651	0.077	0.138	-0.050	0.003	-0.084
Procedural Interaction	6.922	6.210	2.703	13.927	2.007	0.119	-0.181	0.033	-0.049
Social Interaction	1.086	0.695	1.087	4.280	0.035	0.107	0.079	0.006	-0.061
Teacher Question to Group	6.160	5.967	2.093	11.522	2.806	0.149	-0.123	0.015	-0.078
Teacher Question to Student	0.957	0.821	0.563	2.677	0.000	0.148	0.168	0.028	-0.056
Probes for Higher Level Question	.	.	.	.	.	.	.	.	.
Probes for Recall Question	1.011	0.930	0.609	-2.919	0.219	0.113	-0.112	0.013	-0.061
Probes Teacher to Group	0.162	0.105	0.147	0.655	0.000	0.139	-0.091	0.008	-0.074
Probes Teacher to Student	0.000	0.000	0.000	0.000	0.000	.	.	.	.
Student Questions	.	.	.	.	.	.	.	.	.
Student Contribution	.	.	.	.	.	.	.	.	.
Teacher Waits for Student Answer	.	.	.	.	.	.	.	.	.
Objectives with Stress	.	.	.	.	.	.	.	.	.
Lecture with Stress	.	.	.	.	.	.	.	.	.
Student Unable to Answer	.	.	.	.	.	.	.	.	.
Rating of Academic Engagement (SNAP)	83.375	85.270	6.808	94.826	66.644	0.174	-0.018	0.000	-0.108
Rating of Academic Engagement (IAR)	78.540	79.375	8.985	94.375	59.375	0.166	0.109	0.012	-0.091
Years of Teaching Experience	12.356	10.000	7.793	30.000	1.000	0.144	-0.123	0.015	-0.076
Size of Class	54.422	56.000	7.387	68.000	41.000	0.140	0.155	0.024	-0.056
Number of Homework Assignments	2.828	3.000	1.042	4.000	1.000	0.147	0.200	0.040	-0.056
Prop. Obs with Emphasis Expand	0.315	0.250	0.287	1.000	0.000	0.146	0.183	0.033	-0.058
Prop. Obs with Emphasis Intro	0.655	0.750	0.285	1.000	0.000	0.147	-0.194	0.038	-0.054
Prop. Obs with Emphasis Review	0.032	0.000	0.067	0.250	0.000	.	.	.	.
Opportunity to Learn Rating	.	.	.	.	.	.	.	.	.
Time Allocated to Instruction	36.642	37.700	3.103	40.000	26.700	0.206	-0.330	0.109	-0.015

Note: N = 45 classes

TABLE 7.5h　*Zero-order correlations with residualized posttest scores in The Netherlands*

Variable	Mean	Median	Std	Min	Max	R	JStd(R)	R-square	Q-square
Lecture/Explain/Demonstrate	24.142	22.497	12.661	5.952	78.748	0.012	0.126	0.000	-0.078
Review Previous Content	27.824	26.865	12.157	4.082	51.724	0.271	0.137	0.073	-0.003
Discourse/Discussion	11.719	9.100	12.704	0.000	60.831	-0.115	0.160	0.013	-0.077
Oral Practice/Drill	0.106	0.000	0.729	0.000	5.000	.	.	.	.
Seatwork-Test	0.850	0.000	2.183	0.000	8.571	.	.	.	.
Seatwork-Reading	0.053	0.000	0.365	0.000	2.500	.	.	.	.
Seatwork-Written	19.951	19.581	11.852	0.000	61.108	-0.131	0.159	0.017	-0.071
Seatwork-Laboratory	0.076	0.000	0.521	0.000	3.571	.	.	.	.
Composite Management	14.963	14.997	6.153	2.500	27.496	0.001	0.160	0.000	-0.096
Other Activity	0.306	0.000	0.752	0.000	2.500	.	.	.	.
Teacher Interacting	80.070	79.998	10.281	56.249	97.500	0.140	0.135	0.020	-0.061
Teacher Monitoring	17.059	17.497	9.015	2.500	38.540	-0.124	0.144	0.015	-0.071
Uninvolved Teacher	2.867	2.500	3.441	0.000	18.227	-0.093	0.108	0.009	-0.067
Explanation	6.218	6.019	3.122	1.403	13.426	-0.029	0.135	0.001	-0.080
Explanation with Materials	4.922	13.436	6.342	5.746	38.215	0.036	0.155	0.001	-0.091
Demonstration	2.356	1.956	2.019	0.288	11.762	-0.076	0.109	0.006	-0.062
Use of Examples	0.130	0.036	0.238	0.000	1.233	-0.225	0.149	0.051	-0.073
Structuring Cues	13.293	12.910	3.866	4.787	21.260	0.057	0.137	0.003	-0.080
Directives	0.462	0.336	0.404	0.038	1.586	-0.232	0.157	0.054	-0.033
Probes (total number)	1.921	1.913	0.958	0.268	3.932	0.106	0.158	0.011	-0.083
Higher Order Question	3.387	2.675	2.451	0.150	12.387	0.160	0.145	0.025	-0.056
Recall Question	11.156	10.880	2.930	4.328	17.274	-0.062	0.142	0.004	-0.081
Opinion Question	0.062	0.035	0.093	0.000	0.475	-0.161	0.135	0.026	-0.045
Redirect Question	0.483	0.432	0.332	0.039	1.441	0.128	0.122	0.016	-0.061
Teacher or Student Response	16.818	16.362	3.497	10.707	23.825	0.098	0.160	0.010	-0.088
Extended Student Response	0.817	0.421	1.121	0.000	6.116	-0.094	0.184	0.009	-0.105
Student Task Related Statement	2.016	1.704	1.226	0.073	5.328	-0.083	0.159	0.007	-0.089
Acknowledge Correct Answer	1.271	1.254	0.643	0.349	3.220	0.189	0.133	0.036	-0.045

Table 7.5h *(continued)*

Teacher Says Student Answer Wrong	0.474	0.388	0.327	0.076	1.698	0.114	0.119	0.013	-0.058
Effectiveness Question	1.090	0.924	0.713	0.111	3.611	0.226	0.140	0.051	-0.021
Silence	7.984	7.829	3.207	2.681	17.746	0.005	0.131	0.000	-0.080
Discipline	2.344	1.390	2.626	0.110	12.613	-0.227	0.149	0.052	-0.025
Procedural Interaction	6.657	6.593	2.714	1.876	13.228	-0.130	0.124	0.017	-0.063
Social Interaction	1.112	0.971	0.862	0.039	3.373	-0.251	0.107	0.062	-0.001
Teacher Question to Group	2.474	1.926	1.730	0.414	7.292	0.079	0.120	0.006	-0.068
Teacher Question to Student	8.003	7.826	3.040	3.439	16.649	0.129	0.129	0.017	-0.061
Probes for Higher Level Question	0.469	0.345	0.385	0.000	1.970	0.069	0.147	0.005	-0.083
Probes for Recall Question	0.572	0.513	0.301	0.115	1.360	0.008	0.137	0.000	-0.082
Probes Teacher to Group	0.134	0.074	0.147	0.000	0.625	0.089	0.117	0.008	-0.069
Probes Teacher to Student	1.785	1.783	0.929	0.256	3.858	0.096	0.156	0.009	-0.084
Student Questions	2.504	2.357	1.061	0.559	5.258	-0.147	0.179	0.021	-0.092
Student Contribution	2.520	2.115	1.488	0.454	7.258	-0.235	0.147	0.055	-0.020
Teacher Waits for Student Answer	1.456	1.368	0.797	0.186	3.277	0.181	0.133	0.033	-0.048
Objectives with Stress	0.009	0.000	0.028	0.000	0.164	.	.	.	.
Lecture with Stress	0.000	0.000	0.000	0.000	0.000	.	.	.	.
Student Unable to Answer	0.074	0.045	0.074	0.000	0.299	-0.038	0.113	0.001	-0.068
Rating of Academic Engagement (SNAP)	74.517	73.993	9.601	45.617	96.458	0.232	0.146	0.054	-0.046
Rating of Academic Engagement (IAR)	.	.	.	.	.	.	.	.	.
Years of Teaching Experience	10.915	8.426	10.000	0.000	36.000	0.030	0.193	0.001	-0.120
Size of Class	25.128	4.402	26.000	13.000	33.000	-0.196	0.132	0.038	-0.036
Number of Homework Assignments	2.894	0.938	3.000	0.000	5.000	-0.198	0.147	0.039	-0.049
Prop. Obs with Emphasis Expand	0.523	0.240	0.500	0.000	0.880	-0.088	0.169	0.008	-0.095
Prop. Obs with Emphasis Intro	0.000	0.000	0.000	0.000	0.000	.	.	.	.
Prop. Obs with Emphasis Review	0.477	0.237	0.500	0.130	1.010	0.085	0.172	0.007	-0.097
Opportunity to Learn Rating	85.638	17.681	95.000	30.000	100.000	0.463	0.104	0.214	0.152
Time Allocated to Instruction	44.511	3.392	44.900	30.000	49.500	0.240	0.117	0.057	-0.008

Note: $N = 47$ classes

TABLE 7.5i *Zero-order correlations with residualized posttest scores in Thailand*

Variable	Mean	Median	Std	Min	Max	R	JStd(R)	R-square	Q-square
Lecture/Explain/Demonstrate	54.555	56.663	16.995	9.998	100.000	−0.022	0.129	0.000	−0.058
Review Previous Content	10.452	6.666	10.577	0.000	49.997	−0.054	0.108	0.003	−0.044
Discourse/Discussion	1.070	0.000	3.449	0.000	19.998	.	.	.	.
Oral Practice/Drill	2.428	0.000	4.801	0.000	29.997	.	.	.	.
Seatwork-Test	0.494	0.000	1.980	0.000	13.333	.	.	.	.
Seatwork-Reading	0.082	0.000	0.520	0.000	3.333	.	.	.	.
Seatwork-Written	29.514	26.664	16.179	0.000	73.331	0.106	0.113	0.011	−0.040
Seatwork-Laboratory	0.123	0.000	1.111	0.000	9.999	.	.	.	.
Composite Management	0.987	0.000	1.932	0.000	6.666	.	.	.	.
Other Activity	0.288	0.000	1.201	0.000	6.665	.	.	.	.
Teacher Interacting	75.883	76.664	14.116	39.997	100.000	−0.028	0.116	0.001	−0.051
Teacher Monitoring	19.875	19.997	12.115	0.000	53.331	0.077	0.112	0.006	−0.044
Uninvolved Teacher	4.236	0.000	7.168	0.000	39.999	−0.080	0.101	0.006	−0.039
Explanation	12.141	11.163	5.723	1.491	25.268	−0.185	0.121	0.034	−0.021
Explanation with Materials	16.067	15.260	6.164	4.843	30.294	−0.152	0.107	0.023	−0.026
Demonstration	3.389	3.084	2.262	0.000	9.767	−0.083	0.121	0.007	−0.049
Use of Examples	0.298	0.132	0.440	0.000	2.804	−0.027	0.075	0.001	−0.036
Structuring Cues	0.821	0.773	0.504	0.067	2.106	0.134	0.110	0.018	−0.034
Directives	1.951	1.880	0.867	0.299	4.557	−0.004	0.106	0.000	−0.048
Probes (total number)	2.207	1.950	1.673	0.139	9.767	0.072	0.107	0.005	−0.042
Higher Order Question	0.263	0.102	0.456	0.000	3.433	0.124	0.069	0.015	−0.019
Recall Question	10.312	10.393	3.212	3.718	17.503	0.129	0.114	0.017	−0.035
Opinion Question	0.042	0.000	0.103	0.000	0.835	.	.	.	.
Redirect Question	0.522	0.300	0.603	0.000	3.575	0.054	0.100	0.003	−0.046
Teacher or Student Response	12.993	12.874	4.187	5.073	26.605	0.105	0.102	0.011	−0.035
Extended Student Response	2.712	1.822	2.799	0.000	17.131	−0.133	0.103	0.018	−0.027
Student Task Related Statement	1.921	1.711	1.556	0.000	8.458	0.042	0.086	0.002	−0.039
Acknowledge Correct Answer	0.939	0.740	0.794	0.000	4.297	0.032	0.112	0.001	−0.051

Table 7.5i *(continued)*

Teacher Says Student Answer Wrong	0.232	0.212	0.198	0.000	0.955	-0.180	0.110	0.032	-0.020
Effectiveness Question	0.692	0.664	0.413	0.051	1.860	0.156	0.112	0.024	-0.026
Silence	20.182	18.665	9.988	4.056	47.602	0.116	0.103	0.014	-0.035
Discipline	0.688	0.582	0.620	0.000	2.585	0.111	0.115	0.012	-0.039
Procedural Interaction	5.530	4.169	4.997	0.472	30.500	-0.043	0.099	0.002	-0.045
Social Interaction	0.734	0.423	1.269	0.000	9.873	-0.014	0.078	0.000	-0.039
Teacher Question to Group	7.122	6.911	2.604	1.349	13.958	0.054	0.123	0.003	-0.053
Teacher Question to Student	3.608	3.272	2.399	0.154	14.950	0.110	0.085	0.012	-0.027
Probes for Higher Level Question	0.063	0.000	0.116	0.000	0.587				
Probes for Recall Question	1.267	1.055	0.981	0.056	6.067	0.108	0.097	0.012	-0.031
Probes Teacher to Group	1.055	0.805	0.880	0.000	3.501	0.089	0.139	0.008	-0.057
Probes Teacher to Student	1.085	0.767	1.146	0.000	8.645	0.056	0.078	0.003	-0.032
Student Questions	0.132	0.053	0.231	0.000	1.228	0.238	0.106	0.057	0.021
Student Contribution	14.457	14.554	5.395	3.901	32.263	-0.013	0.105	0.000	-0.047
Teacher Waits for Student Answer	0.996	0.832	0.585	0.118	2.687	-0.091	0.122	0.008	-0.046
Objectives with Stress	0.001	0.000	0.005	0.000	0.041	·	·	·	·
Lecture with Stress	0.062	0.000	0.216	0.000	1.248	·	·	·	·
Student Unable to Answer	0.012	0.000	0.067	0.000	0.593	·	·	·	·
Rating of Academic Engagement (SNAP)	96.104	96.789	2.852	87.635	100.000	0.351	0.088	0.123	0.080
Rating of Academic Engagement (IAR)	94.013	95.298	4.670	79.301	100.000	0.312	0.092	0.098	0.053
Years of Teaching Experience	12.721	11.000	6.540	2.000	28.000	0.003	0.106	0.000	-0.048
Size of Class	32.864	31.000	8.779	17.000	57.000	0.141	0.113	0.020	-0.031
Number of Homework Assignments	3.320	3.000	1.078	1.000	5.000	0.084	0.110	0.007	-0.041
Prop. Obs with Emphasis Expand	0.456	0.330	0.318	0.000	1.000	0.042	0.127	0.002	-0.055
Prop. Obs with Emphasis Intro	0.292	0.330	0.305	0.000	1.000	-0.087	0.113	0.008	-0.044
Prop. Obs with Emphasis Review	0.250	0.330	0.237	0.000	1.000	0.055	0.125	0.003	-0.053
Opportunity to Learn Rating	79.181	91.400	29.039	0.000	100.000	0.064	0.111	0.004	-0.047
Time Allocated to Instruction	51.783	53.300	5.212	36.800	60.000	-0.146	0.111	0.021	-0.030

Note: N = 81 classes

Norbert Sellin and Lorin W. Anderson

TABLE 7.6 *Correlations with residualized posttest scores associated with Q-square values greater than zero*

Variable	Aust	Can-E	Can-F	Can-Q	Hung	Israel	ROK	Neth	Thai
Lecture/Explain/Demonstrate	.	.	.	.	.	.	.	.	.
Review Previous Content	.	.	.	.	.	.	.	.	.
Discourse/Discussion	.	.	.	.	.	.	.	.	.
Oral Practice/Drill	.	.	.	.	.	.	.	.	.
Seatwork-Test	.	.	.	.	.	.	.	.	.
Seatwork-Reading	.	.	.	.	.	.	.	.	.
Seatwork-Written	.	.	.	.	0.425	.	.	.	.
Seatwork-Laboratory	−0.242	.	.	.	.	.	.	.	.
Composite Management	.	.	.	.	.	.	.	.	.
Other Activity	.	.	.	.	.	.	.	.	.
Teacher Interacting	.	.	.	.	.	.	.	.	.
Teacher Monitoring	.	.	.	.	.	.	.	.	.
Uninvolved Teacher	.	.	−0.476	.	.	.	.	.	.
Explanation	.	.	.	.	.	.	.	.	.
Explanation with Materials	.	.	.	.	−0.329	.	.	.	.
Demonstration	.	.	.	.	.	.	−0.306	.	.
Use of Examples	.	.	.	.	.	.	.	.	.
Structuring Cues	.	.	.	.	.	.	.	.	.
Directives	.	.	.	.	.	.	.	.	.
Probes (total number)	.	.	.	.	.	.	.	.	.
Higher Order Question	.	.	0.460	.	.	.	.	.	.
Recall Question	.	.	0.784	.	.	.	.	.	.
Opinion Question	.	.	.	.	.	.	.	.	.
Redirect Question	.	.	.	.	.	.	.	.	.
Teacher or Student Response	.	.	.	.	.	.	.	.	.
Extended Student Response	.	.	.	.	0.399	.	.	.	.
Student Task Related Statement	.	.	.	.	.	.	.	.	.
Acknowledge Correct Answer	.	.	.	0.467	.	.	.	.	.

Variable	Aust	Can-E	Can-F	Can-Q	Hung	Israel	ROK	Neth	Thai
Teacher Says Student Answer Wrong	.	.	.	0.508	.	.	.	.	.
Effectiveness Question	.	.	.	.	.	.	.	.	.
Silence	0.286	.	0.435	.	0.381	.	.	.	.
Discipline	−0.285	.	.	.	.	.	.	.	.
Procedural Interaction	.	.	.	.	.	.	.	.	.
Social Interaction	.	.	.	.	.	.	.	.	.
Teacher Question to Group	.	.	.	.	−0.363	.	.	.	.
Teacher Question to Student	.	.	0.479	.	.	.	.	.	.
Probes for Higher Level Question	.	.	.	.	−0.322	.	.	.	.
Probes for Recall Question	.	.	.	.	.	.	.	.	.
Probes Teacher to Group	.	.	.	.	.	.	.	.	.
Probes Teacher to Student	.	.	.	.	.	.	.	.	.
Student Questions	.	.	.	.	.	.	.	.	0.238
Student Contribution	.	.	.	.	.	.	.	.	.
Teacher Waits for Student Answer	.	.	.	.	.	.	.	.	.
Objectives with Stress	.	.	.	.	.	.	.	.	.
Lecture with Stress	.	.	.	.	.	.	.	.	.
Student Unable to Answer	.	.	.	.	.	.	.	.	.
Rating of Academic Engagement (SNAP)	.	.	.	.	.	.	.	.	0.351
Rating of Academic Engagement (IAR)	.	.	.	.	.	.	.	.	0.312
Years of Teaching Experience	0.297	.	.	.	.	.	.	.	.
Size of Class	.	.	.	−0.523	.	.	.	.	.
Number of Homework Assignments	.	.	0.522	.	.	.	.	.	.
Prop. Obs with Emphasis Expand	.	.	.	.	.	.	.	.	.
Prop. Obs with Emphasis Intro	.	.	.	.	.	.	.	.	.
Prop. Obs with Emphasis Review	.	.	.	.	.	.	.	0.463	.
Opportunity to Learn Rating	0.352	.	.	.	.	.	.	.	.
Time Allocated to Instruction	.	.	.	.	.	.	.	.	.

Note: The exact Q-square values are shown in Tables 7.5a through 7.5i.

the Netherlands. In the Republic of Korea, only one FMI variable, "demonstration," has a corresponding Q-square value greater than 0. The negative correlation of -0.306 corresponds with Q-square value of 0.027 (see Table 7.5g). This relationship, then, constitutes a borderline case.

In Canada Quebec two observational variables, "acknowledges correct answer" and "teacher says student answer wrong," are positively related to the residualized posttest scores. In Australia and Thailand, three observational variables are related to the residualized posttest scores. In Australia these variables are the amount of laboratory seatwork ($r = -0.242$), silence ($r = 0.286$), and discipline ($r = -0.285$). The Q-squares associated with these correlations range from 0.14 to 0.39. In Thailand the observational variables related to "residualized posttest scores" are student questions (see Fig. 7.6 and earlier discussion) and both estimates of student engagement in learning.

In Canada Ontario-French the correlations for five of the observational variables are associated with positive Q-square values. The variable "recall questions" has the highest positive correlation and Q-square value. (See Fig. 7.7 for the corresponding regression plot.) Other observational variables with positive Q-square values are uninvolved teacher ($r = -0.476$), higher order questions ($r = 0.460$), silence ($r = 0.435$), and teacher questions individual students ($r = 0.479$). In Hungary, six observational variables are related to the adjusted posttest. These variables are written seatwork ($r = 0.425$), explain with materials ($r = -0.329$), extended student response ($r = 0.399$), silence ($r = 0.381$), teacher questions the group ($r = -0.363$), and probes following higher level question ($r = -0.322$). However, with the exception of the variables "written seatwork" and "silence," all correlations have borderline Q-square values.

Like the observational variables, few of the teacher questionnaire and self-report variables were related to final achievement. In Canada Ontario-English, Hungary, Israel, the Republic of Korea, and Thailand, none of these variables were associated with "residualized posttest scores" (using the minimum Q-square criterion). "Years of teaching experience" was positively associated with final achievement in Australia and negatively associated with final achievement in Canada Quebec. "Number of homework assignments per week" was positively related to final achievement in Canada Ontario-French. Finally, teachers' ratings of "opportunity to learn" were positively related to final achievement in both Australia and the Netherlands.

The major conclusion that follows from the data presented in Table 7.6 is straightforward. Most of the variables derived from classroom observations are unrelated to final achievement across all studies. Those few observational variables which are related to final achievement (in terms of positive Q-square values) typically have correlations of less than 0.45 with "residualized posttest scores." As mentioned in Chapter 6, however, correlations of this magnitude are the largest that can be expected given in between-class differences in pretest scores.

Across studies, only "silence" and "opportunity to learn" (OTL) were found to be associated with final achievement in more than one study. The first finding is somewhat surprising in view of the fact that the FMI was primarily concerned with verbal interactions between teachers and students. In Australia, Canada Ontario-French, and Hungary, silence was positively correlated with "residualized posttest scores." As has been shown in Chapters 4 and 5, "silence" is coded most frequently when students are working at their seats, desks, or tables. Thus, in these countries, permitting students to work quietly on their assignments was positively related to final achievement. The relationship of OTL and final achievement, on the other hand, was to be expected given the history of previous IEA studies (see, for example, Husen 1967).

Correlations of "Schooling" Variables with Student Engagement in Learning

In the core model student engagement in learning (or simply, "academic engagement") was conceived as being a key mediating factor between teaching and learning. That is, teaching behaviors were presumed to influence academic engagement, which in turn was expected to influence final achievement. Jackson (1968), among others, has rather convincingly argued that the teacher's daily behavior focuses primarily on academic engagement (that is, on keeping the class paying attention and on-task) rather than on long-term cognitive achievement as measured by summative tests. Hence, academic engagement constitutes an important outcome variable with regard to the relationship between teaching and learning. In this section the zero-order correlations between the 56 "schooling" variables considered in the previous section and the percent of students engaged in learning estimated either from the SNAP or IAR are presented and discussed. These correlations are displayed in Tables 7.7a through 7.7h.

Three preliminary comments seem necessary in connection with the data presented in these tables. First, Hungary had to be excluded from the analysis because valid data were not available for academic engagement. As a consequence, the data for eight rather than nine studies are displayed.

Second, with but one exception, the same variables and statistics included in Tables 7.5a through 7.5i are also included in Tables 7.7a through 7.7h. The exception concerns the variables termed "composite management" which was derived from the SNAP. The correlations between this variable and academic engagement were excluded in *all* studies because the observers were instructed to code "non-engagement" whenever they coded "composite management." Hence, the correlation between "academic engagement" and "composite management" will be highly negative by definition.

Third, with the exception of Canada Quebec, Israel, and the Netherlands, two measures of academic engagement were available in each country. One

TABLE 7.7a: *Zero-order correlations with academic engagement in Australia*

Variable	Mean	Median	Std	Min	Max	R	JStd(R)	R-square	Q-square
Lecture/Explain/Demonstrate	20.415	20.183	10.420	0.000	48.145	0.196	0.116	0.039	−0.018
Review Previous Content	7.848	6.810	6.222	0.000	22.980	0.041	0.134	0.002	−0.060
Discourse/Discussion	5.609	4.507	5.609	0.000	22.093	0.223	0.087	0.050	0.006
Oral Practice/Drill	4.800	2.000	6.429	0.000	24.071	0.298	0.117	0.089	0.033
Seatwork-Test	5.532	3.214	6.877	0.000	30.554	0.005	0.091	0.000	−0.044
Seatwork-Reading	0.122	0.000	0.689	0.000	5.332	.	.	.	.
Seatwork-Written	32.983	31.507	13.353	3.571	79.494	−0.093	0.144	0.009	−0.060
Seatwork-Laboratory	8.648	6.035	8.935	0.000	40.137	−0.291	0.123	0.085	0.012
Composite Management	13.159	13.215	7.233	0.000	34.372	.	.	.	.
Other Activity	1.056	0.000	2.269	0.000	10.948	.	.	.	.
Teacher Interacting	52.277	54.820	14.331	16.844	82.503	0.246	0.119	0.061	0.001
Teacher Monitoring	43.357	40.839	14.319	17.494	73.628	−0.175	0.128	0.031	−0.034
Uninvolved Teacher	4.361	2.873	7.773	0.000	64.184	−0.131	0.192	0.017	−0.092
Explanation	5.462	4.967	2.926	0.466	13.649	0.051	0.114	0.003	−0.052
Explanation with Materials	11.123	10.491	5.698	2.763	33.232	−0.035	0.128	0.001	−0.058
Demonstration	0.811	0.553	0.837	0.000	3.361	0.117	0.099	0.014	−0.035
Use of Examples	0.090	0.000	0.257	0.000	1.386	.	.	.	.
Structuring Cues	1.204	0.828	0.988	0.036	4.198	0.197	0.106	0.039	−0.014
Directives	7.392	6.901	3.573	1.202	18.576	0.239	0.109	0.057	0.002
Probes (total number)	1.413	1.309	0.956	0.000	4.675	0.111	0.098	0.012	−0.031
Higher Order Question	0.185	0.111	0.201	0.000	1.065	−0.004	0.143	0.000	−0.071
Recall Question	10.820	10.389	3.082	4.907	22.719	0.136	0.102	0.019	−0.029
Opinion Question	0.011	0.000	0.034	0.000	0.238	.	.	.	.
Redirect Question	1.148	1.032	0.755	0.028	3.521	0.232	0.107	0.054	−0.003
Teacher or Student Response	19.426	19.570	4.269	9.586	32.728	0.279	0.135	0.078	0.009
Extended Student Response	1.432	1.049	1.305	0.000	5.699	0.187	0.112	0.035	−0.026
Student Task Related Statement	1.810	1.421	1.498	0.000	6.915	−0.033	0.096	0.001	−0.045
Acknowledge Correct Answer	3.990	3.341	2.852	0.762	19.317	−0.133	0.284	0.023	−0.159

Table 7.7a *(continued)*

Teacher Says Student Answer Wrong	0.562	0.447	0.381	0.000	1.540	0.272	0.087	0.074	0.033
Effectiveness Question	0.692	0.627	0.530	0.000	3.016	0.050	0.136	0.003	−0.063
Silence	12.048	12.0C2	6.197	1.694	25.418	0.165	0.137	0.027	−0.034
Discipline	4.321	3.481	3.037	0.545	18.527	−0.492	0.105	0.242	0.187
Procedural Interaction	12.192	10.995	6.291	1.931	40.296	−0.312	0.117	0.104	0.053
Social Interaction	0.899	0.639	0.971	0.000	7.035	−0.099	0.096	0.010	−0.031
Teacher Question to Group	4.459	4.438	2.497	0.000	11.805	0.312	0.109	0.104	0.048
Teacher Question to Student	4.992	4.872	2.001	1.171	11.594	0.030	0.118	0.001	−0.054
Probes for Higher Level Question	0.053	0.029	0.080	0.000	0.391	−0.011	0.109	0.000	−0.053
Probes for Recall Question	0.883	0.763	0.711	0.000	3.565	0.015	0.119	0.000	−0.056
Probes Teacher to Group	0.260	0.168	0.351	0.000	2.316	0.112	0.128	0.013	−0.080
Probes Teacher to Student	1.156	0.998	0.801	0.000	4.066	0.063	0.110	0.004	−0.045
Student Questions	2.553	2.276	1.468	0.145	7.932	−0.212	0.090	0.041	−0.004
Student Contribution	3.325	3.080	2.177	0.082	11.287	0.000	0.109	0.006	−0.049
Teacher Waits for Student Answer	0.599	0.589	0.401	0.079	2.108	0.000	0.157	0.000	−0.076
Objectives with Stress	0.006	0.000	0.033	0.000	0.242	·	·	·	·
Lecture with Stress	0.016	0.000	0.052	0.000	0.392	·	·	·	·
Student Unable to Answer	0.007	0.000	0.026	0.000	0.205	·	·	·	·
Rating of Academic Engagement (SNAP)	81.891	83.165	9.339	57.951	98.787	0.661	0.067	0.437	0.400
Rating of Academic Engagement (IAR)	83.018	84.832	8.656	55.384	97.421	1.010	0.000	1.000	1.000
Years of Teaching Experience	9.892	7.000	7.789	1.000	31.000	0.183	0.090	0.035	−0.009
Size of Class	27.878	28.000	4.999	13.000	38.000	−0.216	0.100	0.047	0.002
Number of Homework Assignments	1.486	1.000	1.698	0.000	11.000	0.146	0.100	0.028	−0.013
Prop. Obs with Emphasis Expand	0.025	0.000	0.079	0.000	0.500	·	·	·	·
Prop. Obs with Emphasis Intro	0.066	0.000	0.149	0.000	0.800	·	·	·	·
Prop. Obs with Emphasis Review	0.910	1.000	0.171	0.200	1.000	0.014	0.136	0.000	−0.069
Opportunity to Learn Rating	68.751	72.000	24.608	8.000	100.000	−0.055	0.107	0.003	−0.047
Time Allocated to Instruction	49.342	49.850	6.016	31.000	66.300	−0.103	0.120	0.012	−0.043

Note: N = 74 classes

TABLE 7.7b   *Zero-order correlations with academic engagement in Canada Ontario-English*

Variable	Mean	Median	Std	Min	Max	R	JStd(R)	R-square	Q-square
Lecture/Explain/Demonstrate	25.011	21.247	14.450	2.500	53.955	-0.137	0.216	0.019	-0.146
Review Previous Content	13.666	4.999	17.189	0.000	47.221	-0.042	0.261	0.002	-0.215
Discourse/Discussion	10.310	6.249	12.051	0.000	43.747	0.218	0.210	0.047	-0.106
Oral Practice/Drill	0.857	0.000	2.461	0.000	11.999	.	.	.	.
Seatwork-Test	3.128	0.000	6.674	0.000	24.998	.	.	.	.
Seatwork-Reading	0.865	0.000	3.159	0.000	15.937	.	.	.	.
Seatwork-Written	29.512	26.039	18.066	0.000	74.372	0.174	0.215	0.030	-0.148
Seatwork-Laboratory	0.865	0.000	2.544	0.000	9.999	.	.	.	.
Composite Management	15.776	15.786	6.880	5.312	29.997	.	.	.	.
Other Activity	0.000	0.000	0.000	0.000	0.000	.	.	.	.
Teacher Interacting	52.986	52.496	14.929	14.998	84.998	-0.009	0.193	0.000	-0.158
Teacher Monitoring	38.828	37.497	17.302	4.999	82.498	0.169	0.230	0.029	-0.157
Uninvolved Teacher	8.179	6.041	8.284	0.000	27.497	-0.338	0.244	0.114	-0.099
Explanation	8.578	7.057	5.068	1.289	18.531	-0.058	0.234	0.003	-0.193
Explanation with Materials	10.615	11.682	5.713	1.312	29.278	0.143	0.325	0.021	-0.288
Demonstration	1.610	1.339	1.359	0.072	5.944	-0.399	0.176	0.159	0.023
Use of Examples	-0.327	0.074	0.548	0.000	2.196	-0.098	0.280	0.010	-0.249
Structuring Cues	3.925	3.390	2.649	0.738	10.526	0.175	0.225	0.031	-0.144
Directives	3.205	3.008	1.472	1.156	7.474	-0.073	0.160	0.005	-0.126
Probes (total number)	1.616	1.414	0.928	0.000	3.526	-0.052	0.223	0.003	-0.187
Higher Order Question	1.737	1.213	1.738	0.000	6.221	0.054	0.211	0.003	-0.184
Recall Question	9.489	9.749	3.400	4.088	19.712	0.157	0.132	0.025	-0.103
Opinion Question	0.037	0.000	0.109	0.000	0.540	.	.	.	.
Redirect Question	0.799	0.752	0.581	0.000	2.865	0.188	0.266	0.035	-0.171
Teacher or Student Response	13.778	13.882	3.343	4.669	21.363	0.197	0.106	0.039	-0.082
Extended Student Response	0.538	0.471	0.417	0.000	1.776	-0.160	0.130	0.026	-0.098
Student Task Related Statement	0.995	0.895	0.764	0.000	2.633	-0.406	0.182	0.165	-0.005
Acknowledge Correct Answer	2.552	2.562	1.723	0.000	6.351	0.035	0.245	0.001	-0.203

Table 7.7b *(continued)*

	1	2	3	4	5	6	7	8	9
Teacher Says Student Answer Wrong	0.647	0.635	0.450	0.056	1.576	−0.132	0.209	0.017	−0.143
Effectiveness Question	0.647	0.545	0.434	0.076	1.537	−0.162	0.172	0.026	−0.124
Silence	16.812	14.308	11.549	5.457	62.141	0.060	0.155	0.004	−0.166
Discipline	1.132	0.959	0.873	0.000	3.113	−0.303	0.144	0.092	−0.031
Procedural Interaction	12.671	10.391	10.596	0.125	41.938	−0.302	0.135	0.091	−0.060
Social Interaction	0.738	0.315	1.285	0.000	5.690	−0.043	0.138	0.002	−0.152
Teacher Question to Group	5.537	4.874	2.541	0.586	10.647	0.331	0.151	0.110	−0.031
Teacher Question to Student	4.543	4.333	2.067	1.874	9.277	−0.013	0.188	0.000	−0.157
Probes for Higher Level Question	0.181	0.094	0.204	0.000	0.653	0.040	0.227	0.002	−0.189
Probes for Recall Question	0.802	0.797	0.505	0.000	2.155	0.088	0.230	0.008	−0.179
Probes Teacher to Group	0.553	0.432	0.449	0.000	1.610	−0.032	0.217	0.001	−0.178
Probes Teacher to Student	1.049	1.044	0.610	0.000	2.286	−0.046	0.225	0.002	−0.190
Student Questions	1.943	1.830	1.278	0.083	4.960	−0.048	0.188	0.002	−0.152
Student Contribution	.	.	.	.	.	.	.	.	.
Teacher Waits for Student Answer	.	.	.	.	.	.	.	.	.
Objectives with Stress	0.025	0.000	0.054	0.000	0.133	.	.	.	.
Lecture with Stress	0.000	0.000	0.000	0.000	0.000	.	.	.	.
Student Unable to Answer	0.105	0.039	0.138	0.000	0.567	−0.058	0.276	0.003	−0.244
Rating of Academic Engagement (SNAP)	76.592	76.733	8.202	63.829	92.033	0.467	0.180	0.218	0.043
Rating of Academic Engagement (IAR)	78.943	78.943	5.869	63.988	89.734	1.000	0.000	1.000	1.000
Years of Teaching Experience	14.344	13.500	7.297	4.000	36.000	0.074	0.229	0.006	−0.192
Size of Class	27.846	27.500	4.478	15.000	35.000	0.224	0.138	0.050	−0.072
Number of Homework Assignments	4.221	4.188	1.294	1.000	8.000	−0.136	0.203	0.019	−0.147
Prop. Obs with Emphasis Expand	0.283	0.290	0.141	0.000	0.510	−0.119	0.161	0.014	−0.129
Prop. Obs with Emphasis Intro	0.362	0.380	0.223	0.000	0.730	0.224	0.208	0.050	−0.114
Prop. Obs with Emphasis Review	0.357	0.360	0.219	0.000	0.890	−0.121	0.214	0.015	−0.161
Opportunity to Learn Rating	75.427	78.750	15.174	27.500	97.490	−0.022	0.228	0.000	−0.193
Time Allocated to Instruction	45.377	41.000	11.531	32.100	74.300	−0.050	0.147	0.003	−0.124

Note: N = 16 classes

TABLE 7.7c   *Zero-order correlations with academic engagement in Canada Ontario-French*

Variable	Mean	Median	Std	Min	Max	R	JStd(R)	R-square	Q-square
Lecture/Explain/Demonstrate	26.112	23.451	13.269	2.857	54.996	-0.167	0.376	0.028	-0.407
Review Previous Content	20.738	19.997	14.333	2.500	52.855	0.049	0.372	0.002	-0.456
Discourse/Discussion	0.735	0.000	1.929	0.000	7.500	.	.	.	.
Oral Practice/Drill	6.260	5.000	5.583	0.000	17.498	0.051	0.249	0.003	-0.263
Seatwork-Test	1.397	0.000	2.047	0.000	7.500	.	.	.	.
Seatwork-Reading	0.147	0.000	0.606	0.000	2.500	.	.	.	.
Seatwork-Written	26.151	26.665	8.517	10.832	44.402	0.407	0.204	0.166	-0.035
Seatwork-Laboratory	0.441	0.000	1.819	0.000	7.499	.	.	.	.
Composite Management	15.488	15.950	6.659	2.500	27.736	.	.	.	.
Other Activity	2.521	0.000	3.355	0.000	8.035	.	.	.	.
Teacher Interacting	62.047	64.997	14.961	30.951	80.712	0.468	0.174	0.219	0.054
Teacher Monitoring	21.089	19.998	11.845	5.000	47.497	-0.217	0.232	0.047	-0.232
Uninvolved Teacher	16.849	17.497	11.219	0.000	42.022	-0.395	0.190	0.156	-0.039
Explanation	7.263	7.263	4.142	1.083	15.415	-0.115	0.271	0.013	-0.277
Explanation with Materials	11.693	11.000	3.372	7.463	19.893	0.010	0.365	0.000	-0.408
Demonstration	0.459	0.329	0.578	0.000	2.038	0.160	0.227	0.026	-0.286
Use of Examples	0.745	0.671	0.648	0.104	2.620	0.450	0.157	0.202	-0.107
Structuring Cues	4.847	4.506	2.438	1.511	9.288	-0.111	0.237	0.012	-0.255
Directives	2.960	2.960	1.198	1.207	6.259	-0.147	0.365	0.022	-0.580
Probes (total number)	2.265	2.126	1.781	0.316	8.250	0.082	0.360	0.007	-0.636
Higher Order Question	0.153	0.082	0.168	0.000	0.598	0.050	0.211	0.003	-0.256
Recall Question	9.738	9.633	1.775	6.884	12.732	0.339	0.194	0.115	-0.080
Opinion Question	0.010	0.000	0.209	0.000	0.712	.	.	.	.
Redirect Question	0.687	0.607	0.353	0.196	0.424	-0.041	0.227	0.002	-0.251
Teacher or Student Response	13.876	13.954	3.486	9.361	21.341	0.037	0.274	0.001	-0.295
Extended Student Response	0.997	0.350	1.427	0.000	4.672	0.156	0.156	0.024	-0.142
Student Task Related Statement	0.794	0.569	0.831	0.000	2.535	-0.179	0.316	0.032	-0.356
Acknowledge Correct Answer	3.456	3.350	1.425	1.694	6.911	0.423	0.186	0.179	-0.012

Table 7.7c *(continued)*

Teacher Says Student Answer Wrong	0.694	0.568	0.478	0.159	2.149	0.348	0.154	0.121	-0.025
Effectiveness Question	1.302	1.302	0.691	0.293	2.587	-0.399	0.256	0.160	-0.101
Silence	8.773	8.530	6.819	0.228	20.878	0.083	0.222	0.007	-0.229
Discipline	1.026	0.805	0.752	0.094	2.603	-0.623	0.165	0.388	0.221
Procedural Interaction	19.660	18.391	10.139	3.306	37.754	-0.208	0.252	0.043	-0.225
Social Interaction	1.471	1.218	1.344	0.028	5.319	-0.243	0.163	0.059	-0.119
Teacher Question to Group	3.521	3.521	1.566	0.604	6.171	-0.056	0.272	0.003	-0.295
Teacher Question to Student	5.627	4.752	2.460	1.681	11.653	-0.061	0.238	0.004	-0.279
Probes for Higher Level Question	0.029	0.029	0.043	0.000	0.160	0.119	0.291	0.014	-0.489
Probes for Recall Question	0.819	0.753	0.552	0.137	2.058	-0.216	0.276	0.047	-0.310
Probes Teacher to Group	0.442	0.236	0.515	0.033	1.696	-0.354	0.225	0.125	-0.137
Probes Teacher to Student	1.816	1.417	1.625	0.246	7.703	0.203	0.290	0.041	-0.305
Student Questions	1.522	1.084	1.693	0.000	7.097	0.503	0.104	0.253	-0.167
Student Contribution									
Teacher Waits for Student Answer									
Objectives with Stress	0.064	0.000	0.133	0.000	0.391				
Lecture with Stress	0.000	0.000	0.000	0.000	0.000				
Student Unable to Answer	0.002	0.000	0.008	0.000	0.033				
Rating of Academic Engagement (SNAP)	87.994	94.088	12.011	67.865	100.000	0.570	0.192	0.325	0.150
Rating of Academic Engagement (IAR)	80.809	86.562	10.969	59.587	94.375	1.000	0.000	1.000	1.000
Years of Teaching Experience	18.824	19.000	6.267	8.000	29.000	0.107	0.223	0.012	-0.223
Size of Class	24.118	23.000	4.121	17.000	32.000	-0.364	0.188	0.132	-0.050
Number of Homework Assignments	3.176	4.000	1.334	1.000	5.000	0.366	0.225	0.134	-0.096
Prop. Obs with Emphasis Expand									
Prop. Obs with Emphasis Intro									
Prop. Obs with Emphasis Review									
Opportunity to Learn Rating									
Time Allocated to Instruction	35.038	35.000	9.679	24.700	68.000	0.411	0.122	0.169	-0.217

Note: N = 17 classes

TABLE 7.7d *Zero-order correlations with academic engagement in Canada Quebec*

Variable	Mean	Median	Std	Min	Max	R	JStd(R)	R-square	Q-square
Lecture/Explain/Demonstrate	29.481	29.825	9.943	10.856	52.319	0.152	0.185	0.023	-0.163
Review Previous Content	16.176	15.041	8.805	5.666	34.331	0.296	0.218	0.088	-0.147
Discourse/Discussion	0.862	0.000	1.341	0.000	4.286	.	.	.	.
Oral Practice/Drill	8.144	2.000	12.327	0.000	41.998	0.317	0.137	0.100	-0.096
Seatwork-Test	1.207	0.000	2.046	0.000	6.500	.	.	.	.
Seatwork-Reading	0.000	0.000	0.000	0.000	0.000	.	.	.	.
Seatwork-Written	25.604	28.980	13.860	2.000	44.065	0.107	0.220	0.012	-0.211
Seatwork-Laboratory	0.626	0.000	1.161	0.000	4.000	.	.	.	.
Composite Management	15.377	12.332	8.612	0.000	37.173	.	.	.	.
Other Activity	2.515	1.000	3.239	0.000	10.396	.	.	.	.
Teacher Interacting	72.544	69.398	12.476	50.353	94.332	0.377	0.261	0.142	-0.112
Teacher Monitoring	4.856	3.999	4.800	0.000	20.665	0.123	0.519	0.015	-0.813
Uninvolved Teacher	22.595	23.236	11.992	0.000	41.116	-0.442	0.202	0.195	-0.052
Explanation	14.106	12.726	4.927	6.205	22.563	-0.135	0.204	0.018	-0.178
Explanation with Materials	15.667	15.586	6.017	3.759	23.711	0.356	0.270	0.127	-0.123
Demonstration	0.868	0.371	1.096	0.028	4.149	-0.454	0.361	0.206	-0.681
Use of Examples	0.547	0.178	0.757	0.028	2.711	0.204	0.165	0.042	-0.165
Structuring Cues	6.143	6.088	1.957	3.578	9.963	0.008	0.271	0.000	-0.259
Directives	3.308	3.374	1.463	1.349	5.848	-0.072	0.240	0.005	-0.223
Probes (total number)	3.656	2.593	2.600	0.593	9.101	-0.537	0.243	0.288	0.062
Higher Order Question	0.375	0.090	0.667	0.000	2.219	0.282	0.139	0.080	-0.100
Recall Question	9.520	9.608	3.660	3.674	16.062	0.201	0.348	0.041	-0.303
Opinion Question	0.094	0.000	0.154	0.000	0.544	.	.	.	.
Redirect Question	0.428	0.279	0.466	0.027	1.612	0.176	0.178	0.031	-0.190
Teacher or Student Response	12.262	12.159	3.878	5.225	19.788	0.199	0.255	0.039	-0.211
Extended Student Response	0.153	0.138	0.157	0.000	0.624	0.057	0.203	0.003	-0.193
Student Task Related Statement	1.103	0.984	0.701	0.288	2.333	-0.153	0.213	0.023	-0.163
Acknowledge Correct Answer	1.581	1.237	1.107	0.268	4.582	0.238	0.150	0.057	-0.099

Table 7.7d *(continued)*

Teacher Says Student Answer Wrong	0.818	0.655	0.587	0.211	2.128	0.570	0.100	0.325	0.164
Effectiveness Question	0.796	0.501	0.677	0.027	2.368	0.055	0.201	0.003	-0.193
Silence	7.495	6.846	4.570	1.920	16.779	-0.025	0.328	0.001	-0.335
Discipline	1.638	1.487	1.338	0.284	5.934	-0.322	0.345	0.104	-0.734
Procedural Interaction	6.559	6.121	4.114	0.981	20.853	-0.592	0.391	0.351	0.142
Social Interaction	3.442	3.269	1.573	1.260	7.592	-0.292	0.464	0.086	-0.407
Teacher Question to Group	.	.	.	.	.	.	.	.	.
Teacher Question to Student	.	.	.	.	.	.	.	.	.
Probes for Higher Level Question	.	.	.	.	.	.	.	.	.
Probes for Recall Question	.	.	.	.	.	.	.	.	.
Probes Teacher to Group	.	.	.	.	.	.	.	.	.
Probes Teacher to Student	.	.	.	.	.	.	.	.	.
Student Questions	.	.	.	.	.	.	.	.	.
Student Contribution	.	.	.	.	.	.	.	.	.
Teacher Waits for Student Answer	.	.	.	.	.	.	.	.	.
Objectives with Stress	.	.	.	.	.	.	.	.	.
Lecture with Stress	.	.	.	.	.	.	.	.	.
Student Unable to Answer	.	.	.	.	.	.	.	.	.
Rating of Academic Engagement (SNAP)	79.799	83.020	10.721	53.339	97.580	1.000	0.000	1.000	1.000
Rating of Academic Engagement (IAR)	.	.	.	.	.	.	1.000	.	.
Years of Teaching Experience	17.632	17.000	6.825	9.000	33.000	0.223	0.189	0.050	-0.140
Size of Class	28.737	29.000	2.642	24.000	33.000	0.418	0.305	0.175	-0.179
Number of Homework Assignments	3.368	4.000	1.165	1.000	5.000	-0.126	0.200	0.016	-0.193
Prop. Obs with Emphasis Expand	.	.	.	.	.	.	.	.	.
Prop. Obs with Emphasis Intro	.	.	.	.	.	.	.	.	.
Prop. Obs with Emphasis Review	.	.	.	.	.	.	.	.	.
Opportunity to Learn Rating	.	.	.	.	.	.	.	.	.
Time Allocated to Instruction	51.289	50.400	4.195	45.000	59.800	0.404	0.208	0.163	-0.049

Note: N = 19 classes

TABLE 7.7e   Zero-order correlations with academic engagement in Israel

Variable	Mean	Median	Std	Min	Max	R	JStd(R)	R-square	Q-square
Lecture/Explain/Demonstrate	41.366	41.366	15.260	7.999	74.998	0.173	0.235	0.030	-0.196
Review Previous Content	4.938	3.999	4.731	0.000	14.997	-0.101	0.261	0.010	-0.207
Discourse/Discussion	16.963	16.963	13.907	0.000	46.664	-0.045	0.224	0.002	-0.213
Oral Practice/Drill	3.491	3.491	4.787	0.000	19.999	0.354	0.132	0.125	-0.048
Seatwork-Test	1.895	0.000	5.421	0.000	19.999	.	.	.	.
Seatwork-Reading	6.911	4.999	7.708	0.000	22.664	0.367	0.181	0.135	-0.027
Seatwork-Written	7.508	3.999	11.289	0.000	39.996	0.286	0.148	0.082	-0.061
Seatwork-Laboratory	0.263	0.000	1.088	0.000	4.999	.	.	.	.
Composite Management	7.929	6.665	8.920	0.000	28.999	-0.371	0.269	0.138	-0.022
Other Activity	8.727	7.999	9.282	0.000	33.333	.	.	.	.
Teacher Interacting	79.033	83.333	14.135	47.996	100.000	0.188	0.191	0.035	-0.141
Teacher Monitoring	15.349	11.998	12.450	0.000	39.997	-0.114	0.279	0.013	-0.213
Uninvolved Teacher	5.613	4.999	5.395	0.000	19.997	-0.230	0.323	0.053	-0.295
Explanation	11.446	10.207	7.975	1.543	38.163	-0.367	0.180	0.135	-0.116
Explanation with Materials	1.772	1.141	2.411	0.000	9.993	0.293	0.155	0.086	-0.060
Demonstration	0.672	0.404	1.281	0.000	5.898	0.291	0.120	0.085	0.110
Use of Examples	3.277	2.411	3.410	0.120	14.581	0.457	0.151	0.209	-0.090
Structuring Cues	1.742	1.742	1.216	0.000	4.336	0.277	0.179	0.077	-0.089
Directives	4.953	4.712	3.272	0.000	11.875	0.284	0.218	0.081	-0.133
Probes (total number)	2.710	2.075	2.858	0.000	10.680	0.194	0.223	0.038	-0.213
Higher Order Question	3.198	2.636	2.521	0.000	7.805	-0.037	0.200	0.001	-0.186
Recall Question	3.340	2.567	2.641	0.000	10.444	-0.136	0.223	0.019	-0.180
Opinion Question	3.229	3.229	2.109	0.368	7.570	0.127	0.291	0.016	-0.222
Redirect Question	3.690	3.421	2.682	0.000	9.280	-0.108	0.173	0.012	-0.155
Teacher or Student Response	12.525	11.116	6.208	1.780	23.469	0.097	0.235	0.009	-0.211
Extended Student Response	5.990	5.203	4.740	0.250	19.099	-0.034	0.223	0.001	-0.198
Student Task Related Statement	3.937	3.398	3.677	0.000	12.466	0.123	0.235	0.015	-0.197
Acknowledge Correct Answer	4.825	3.629	3.311	0.575	12.725	0.266	0.204	0.071	-0.149

Table 7.7e *(continued)*

Teacher Says Student Answer Wrong	1.218	1.066	1.229	0.000	4.514	−0.049	0.249	0.002	−0.247
Effectiveness Question	2.454	0.956	3.577	0.000	13.348	−0.130	0.157	0.017	−0.120
Silence	1.547	0.755	2.873	0.000	13.390	−0.079	0.141	0.006	−0.123
Discipline	8.311	6.492	9.596	0.000	41.504	−0.108	0.197	0.012	−0.241
Procedural Interaction	4.891	3.452	3.992	0.096	16.584	0.253	0.224	0.064	−0.120
Social Interaction	1.766	0.841	2.938	0.000	12.619	−0.177	0.265	0.031	−0.207
Teacher Question to Group	.	.	.	.	.	.	.	.	.
Teacher Question to Student	.	.	.	.	.	.	.	.	.
Probes for Higher Level Question	.	.	.	.	.	.	.	.	.
Probes for Recall Question	.	.	.	.	.	.	.	.	.
Probes Teacher to Group	.	.	.	.	.	.	.	.	.
Probes Teacher to Student	.	.	.	.	.	.	.	.	.
Student Questions	.	.	.	.	.	.	.	.	.
Student Contribution	.	.	.	.	.	.	.	.	.
Teacher Waits for Student Answer	.	.	.	.	.	.	.	.	.
Objectives with Stress	.	.	.	.	.	.	.	.	.
Lecture with Stress	.	.	.	.	.	.	.	.	.
Student Unable to Answer	.	.	.	.	.	.	.	.	.
Rating of Academic Engagement (SNAP)	59.932	59.932	20.008	10.889	88.557	1.000	0.000	1.000	1.000
Rating of Academic Engagement (IAR)	.	.	.	.	.	.	.	.	.
Years of Teaching Experience	14.893	13.000	6.899	5.000	30.000	−0.105	0.337	0.011	−0.320
Size of Class	31.190	31.000	4.611	21.000	39.000	0.517	0.233	0.268	0.077
Number of Homework Assignments	1.839	2.000	0.356	1.000	2.000	−0.056	0.185	0.003	−0.179
Prop. Obs with Emphasis Expand	.	.	.	.	.	.	.	.	.
Prop. Obs with Emphasis Intro	.	.	.	.	.	.	.	.	.
Prop. Obs with Emphasis Review	.	.	.	.	.	.	.	.	.
Opportunity to Learn Rating	.	.	.	.	.	.	.	.	.
Time Allocated to Instruction	.	.	.	.	.	.	.	.	.

Note: N = 21 classes

TABLE 7.7f   *Zero-order correlations with academic engagement in the Republic of Korea*

Variable	Mean	Median	Std	Min	Max	R	JStd(R)	R-square	Q-square
Lecture/Explain/Demonstrate	30.105	27.497	13.154	9.998	62.497	-0.077	0.175	0.006	-0.104
Review Previous Content	2.880	2.500	3.228	0.000	13.123	0.039	0.183	0.002	-0.118
Discourse/Discussion	22.995	21.248	10.607	5.000	49.996	0.445	0.117	0.198	0.135
Oral Practice/Drill	0.111	0.000	0.521	0.000	2.500	.	.	.	.
Seatwork-Test	0.333	0.000	1.011	0.000	5.000	.	.	.	.
Seatwork-Reading	0.333	0.000	0.859	0.000	2.500	.	.	.	.
Seatwork-Written	6.891	4.999	6.222	0.000	22.497	-0.187	0.132	0.035	-0.043
Seatwork-Laboratory	26.504	24.998	10.099	9.998	48.956	-0.129	0.153	0.017	-0.079
Composite Management	9.724	9.998	6.927	0.000	24.996	.	.	.	.
Other Activity	0.111	0.000	0.521	0.000	2.500	.	.	.	.
Teacher Interacting	61.363	59.996	11.819	24.374	84.998	0.402	0.116	0.162	0.089
Teacher Monitoring	29.557	29.997	10.419	9.999	58.956	-0.372	0.110	0.138	0.069
Uninvolved Teacher	9.072	9.998	6.225	0.000	24.996	-0.141	0.144	0.020	-0.072
Explanation	6.969	6.941	3.188	1.520	15.712	0.042	0.147	0.002	-0.088
Explanation with Materials	8.093	7.130	4.332	2.180	17.559	-0.171	0.151	0.029	-0.059
Demonstration	5.027	4.086	4.024	0.370	18.786	-0.073	0.146	0.005	-0.090
Use of Examples	0.509	0.323	0.712	0.000	3.341	0.100	0.101	0.010	-0.059
Structuring Cues	5.888	5.573	2.424	2.374	11.931	0.024	0.169	0.001	-0.104
Directives	7.316	7.076	1.987	3.130	11.095	0.280	0.170	0.078	-0.030
Probes (total number)	1.174	1.056	0.626	0.394	3.014	0.297	0.116	0.088	0.009
Higher Order Question	1.426	1.390	0.686	0.301	2.960	0.060	0.159	0.004	-0.093
Recall Question	5.181	5.033	1.829	2.283	9.902	-0.040	0.134	0.002	-0.081
Opinion Question	0.265	0.167	0.291	0.000	1.053	0.176	0.114	0.031	-0.042
Redirect Question	0.261	0.252	0.169	0.000	0.593	0.004	0.151	0.000	-0.093
Teacher or Student Response	14.909	15.055	3.542	7.100	22.435	0.357	0.143	0.127	0.035
Extended Student Response	1.600	0.640	1.908	0.000	8.413	0.352	0.144	0.124	0.042
Student Task Related Statement	0.351	0.249	0.368	0.000	1.695	0.073	0.137	0.005	-0.078
Acknowledge Correct Answer	0.799	0.684	0.559	0.199	3.143	0.406	0.108	0.165	0.100

Table 7.7f *(continued)*

Teacher Says Student Answer Wrong	0.107	0.079	0.112	0.000	0.478	0.002	0.120	0.000	−0.075
Effectiveness Question	0.872	0.864	0.597	0.032	2.522	0.037	0.197	0.001	−0.126
Silence	24.299	25.443	7.950	6.361	41.974	0.036	0.148	0.001	−0.090
Discipline	1.493	1.496	1.045	0.077	5.651	−0.559	0.099	0.313	0.261
Procedural Interaction	6.922	6.210	2.703	2.007	13.927	−0.631	0.095	0.399	0.353
Social Interaction	1.086	0.695	1.087	0.035	4.280	−0.020	0.092	0.000	−0.063
Teacher Question to Group	6.160	5.967	2.093	2.306	11.522	0.040	0.134	0.002	−0.081
Teacher Question to Student	0.957	0.821	0.563	0.000	2.677	−0.108	0.137	0.012	−0.073
Probes for Higher Level Question	.	.	.	.	.	.	.	.	.
Probes for Recall Question	.	.	.	0.219	.	.	.	.	.
Probes Teacher to Group	1.011	0.930	0.609	0.000	2.919	0.277	0.120	0.077	−0.004
Probes Teacher to Student	0.162	0.105	0.147	0.000	0.655	0.110	0.121	0.012	−0.063
Student Questions	0.000	0.000	0.000	0.000	0.000				
Student Contribution	.	.	.	.	.	.	.	.	.
Teacher Waits for Student Answer	.	.	.	.	.	.	.	.	.
Objectives with Stress	.	.	.	.	.	.	.	.	.
Lecture with Stress	.	.	.	.	.	.	.	.	.
Student Unable to Answer	.	.	.	.	.	.	.	.	.
Rating of Academic Engagement (SNAP)	83.375	85.270	6.808	66.644	94.826	0.440	0.122	0.194	0.125
Rating of Academic Engagement (IAR)	78.540	79.375	8.985	59.375	94.375	1.000	0.000	1.000	1.000
Years of Teaching Experience	12.356	10.000	7.793	1.000	30.000	0.169	0.132	0.028	−0.055
Size of Class	54.422	56.000	7.387	41.000	68.000	−0.245	0.163	0.060	−0.037
Number of Homework Assignments	2.828	3.000	1.042	1.000	4.000	0.129	0.158	0.017	−0.080
Prop. Obs with Emphasis Expand	0.315	0.250	0.287	0.000	1.000	0.151	0.216	0.023	−0.120
Prop. Obs with Emphasis Intro	0.655	0.750	0.285	0.000	1.000	−0.201	0.211	0.040	−0.096
Prop. Obs with Emphasis Review	0.032	0.000	0.067	0.000	0.250				
Opportunity to Learn Rating	.	.	.	.	.	.	.	.	.
Time Allocated to Instruction	36.642	37.700	3.103	26.700	40.000	−0.086	0.160	0.007	−0.091

Note: $N = 45$ classes

TABLE 7.7g: *Zero-order correlations with academic engagement in The Netherlands*

Variable	Mean	Median	Std	Min	Max	R	JStd(R)	R-square	Q-square
Lecture/Explain/Demonstrate	24.142	22.497	12.661	5.952	78.748	0.392	0.182	0.154	0.082
Review Previous Content	27.824	26.665	12.157	4.062	51.724	0.226	0.166	0.051	−0.044
Discourse/Discussion	11.719	9.166	12.704	0.000	60.831	0.254	0.101	0.065	−0.003
Oral Practice/Drill	0.106	0.000	0.729	0.000	5.000	.	.	.	.
Seatwork-Test	0.850	0.000	2.183	0.000	8.571	.	.	.	.
Seatwork-Reading	0.053	0.000	0.365	0.000	2.500	.	.	.	.
Seatwork-Written	19.951	19.581	11.852	0.000	61.108	−0.495	0.101	0.245	0.176
Seatwork-Laboratory	0.076	0.000	0.521	0.000	3.571	.	.	.	.
Composite Management	14.963	14.997	6.153	2.500	27.496	.	.	.	.
Other Activity	0.306	0.000	0.752	0.000	2.500	.	.	.	.
Teacher Interacting	80.070	79.998	10.281	56.249	97.500	0.432	0.130	0.187	0.103
Teacher Monitoring	17.059	17.497	9.015	2.500	38.540	−0.491	0.131	0.241	0.155
Uninvolved Teacher	2.867	2.500	3.441	0.000	18.277	−0.004	0.116	0.000	−0.072
Explanation	6.218	6.019	3.122	1.403	13.426	−0.336	0.156	0.113	0.015
Explanation with Materials	14.922	13.436	6.342	5.746	38.215	0.317	0.187	0.100	0.010
Demonstration	2.356	1.956	2.019	0.288	11.762	0.093	0.135	0.009	−0.070
Use of Examples	0.130	0.036	0.238	0.000	1.223	0.118	0.113	0.014	−0.053
Structuring Cues	13.293	12.910	3.866	4.787	21.260	0.261	0.179	0.068	−0.039
Directives	0.462	0.336	0.404	0.038	1.586	−0.095	0.140	0.009	−0.071
Probes (total number)	1.921	1.913	0.958	0.268	3.932	0.245	0.118	0.060	−0.016
Higher Order Question	3.387	2.675	2.451	0.150	12.387	0.333	0.105	0.111	0.053
Recall Question	11.156	10.880	2.930	4.328	17.274	−0.207	0.182	0.043	−0.070
Opinion Question	0.062	0.035	0.093	0.039	0.475	0.032	0.153	0.001	−0.107
Redirect Question	0.483	0.432	0.332	0.039	1.441	0.328	0.123	0.108	0.028
Teacher or Student Response	16.818	16.362	3.497	10.707	23.825	0.213	0.165	0.046	−0.050
Extended Student Response	0.817	0.421	0.121	0.000	6.116	0.038	0.216	0.001	−0.186
Student Task Related Statement	2.016	1.704	1.226	0.073	5.328	−0.536	0.103	0.287	0.218
Acknowledge Correct Answer	1.271	1.254	0.643	0.349	3.220	0.394	0.108	0.156	0.094

Table 7.7g *(continued)*

Teacher Says Student Answer Wrong	0.474	0.388	0.327	0.076	1.698	0.105	0.187	0.011	-0.123
Effectiveness Question	1.090	0.924	0.713	0.111	3.611	0.269	0.141	0.072	-0.013
Silence	7.984	7.829	3.207	2.681	17.746	0.151	0.124	0.023	-0.054
Discipline	2.344	1.390	2.626	0.110	12.613	-0.673	0.062	0.453	0.346
Procedural Interaction	6.657	6.593	2.714	1.876	13.228	-0.515	0.127	0.265	0.183
Social Interaction	1.112	0.971	0.862	0.039	3.373	-0.275	0.172	0.075	-0.016
Teacher Question to Group	2.474	1.926	1.730	0.414	7.282	0.212	0.139	0.045	-0.045
Teacher Question to Student	8.003	7.826	3.040	3.439	16.649	0.444	0.120	0.197	0.122
Probes for Higher Level Question	0.469	0.345	0.385	0.000	1.970	0.189	0.121	0.036	-0.040
Probes for Recall Question	0.572	0.513	0.301	0.115	1.360	0.106	0.125	0.011	-0.067
Probes Teacher to Group	0.134	0.074	0.147	0.000	0.625	0.005	0.116	0.000	-0.071
Probes Teacher to Student	1.785	1.783	0.929	0.256	3.858	0.252	0.120	0.063	-0.014
Student Questions	2.504	2.357	1.061	0.559	5.258	-0.331	0.141	0.109	0.032
Student Contribution	2.520	2.115	1.488	0.454	7.258	-0.239	0.113	0.057	-0.013
Teacher Waits for Student Answer	1.456	1.368	0.797	0.186	3.277	0.439	0.093	0.193	0.128
Objectives with Stress	0.009	0.000	0.028	0.000	0.164	.	.	.	.
Lecture with Stress	0.000	0.000	0.000	0.000	0.000	.	.	.	.
Student Unable to Answer	0.074	0.045	0.074	0.000	0.299	0.299	0.131	0.090	0.011
Rating of Academic Engagement (SNAP)	74.517	73.993	9.601	45.617	96.458	1.000	0.000	0.000	1.000
Rating of Academic Engagement (IAR)	.	.	.	.	.	.	.	.	.
Years of Teaching Experience	10.915	10.000	8.426	0.000	36.000	0.387	0.115	0.150	0.080
Size of Class	25.128	26.000	4.402	13.000	33.000	-0.216	0.185	0.046	-0.051
Number of Homework Assignments	2.894	3.000	0.938	0.000	5.000	0.009	0.156	0.000	-0.093
Prop. Obs with Emphasis Expand	0.523	0.500	0.240	0.000	0.880	0.093	0.118	0.009	-0.065
Prop. Obs with Emphasis Intro	0.000	0.000	0.000	0.000	0.000	.	.	.	.
Prop. Obs with Emphasis Review	0.477	0.500	0.237	0.130	1.010	-0.100	0.118	0.010	-0.063
Opportunity to Learn Rating	85.638	95.000	17.681	30.000	100.000	0.082	0.118	0.007	-0.065
Time Allocated to Instruction	44.511	44.900	3.392	30.000	49.500	0.049	0.128	0.002	-0.075

Note: $N = 47$ classes

TABLE 7.7h   Zero-order correlations with academic engagement in Thailand

Variable	Mean	Median	Std	Min	Max	R	JStd(R)	R-square	Q-square
Lecture/Explain/Demonstrate	54.555	56.663	16.995	9.998	100.000	0.260	0.100	0.067	0.018
Review Previous Content	10.452	6.666	10.577	0.000	49.997	-0.135	0.133	0.018	-0.040
Discourse/Discussion	1.070	0.000	3.449	0.000	19.998	.	.	.	.
Oral Practice/Drill	2.428	0.000	4.801	0.000	29.997	.	.	.	.
Seatwork-Test	0.494	0.000	1.980	0.000	13.333	.	.	.	.
Seatwork-Reading	0.082	0.000	0.520	0.000	3.333	.	.	.	.
Seatwork-Written	29.514	26.664	16.179	0.000	73.331	-0.115	0.095	0.013	-0.031
Seatwork-Laboratory	0.123	0.000	1.111	0.000	9.999	.	.	.	.
Composite Management	0.987	0.000	1.932	0.000	6.666	.	.	.	.
Other Activity	0.286	0.000	1.201	0.000	6.665	.	.	.	.
Teacher Interacting	75.883	76.664	14.116	39.997	100.000	0.194	0.109	0.038	-0.010
Teacher Monitoring	19.875	19.997	12.115	0.000	53.331	-0.073	0.103	0.005	-0.041
Uninvolved Teacher	4.238	0.000	7.168	0.000	39.999	-0.260	0.111	0.067	0.006
Explanation	12.141	11.163	5.723	1.491	25.268	-0.132	0.120	0.018	-0.038
Explanation with Materials	16.067	15.260	6.164	4.843	30.294	-0.145	0.105	0.021	-0.028
Demonstration	3.389	3.084	2.262	0.000	9.767	0.122	0.101	0.015	-0.029
Use of Examples	0.298	0.132	0.440	0.000	2.804	0.104	0.131	0.011	-0.046
Structuring Cues	0.821	0.773	0.504	0.067	2.106	0.096	0.100	0.009	-0.037
Directives	1.951	1.880	0.867	0.299	4.557	-0.083	0.116	0.007	-0.045
Probes (total number)	2.207	1.950	1.673	0.139	9.767	0.145	0.097	0.021	-0.023
Higher Order Question	0.263	0.102	0.456	0.000	3.433	0.060	0.086	0.004	-0.034
Recall Question	10.312	10.393	3.212	3.718	17.503	0.287	0.081	0.083	0.040
Opinion Question	0.042	0.000	0.103	0.000	0.835	.	.	.	.
Redirect Question	0.522	0.300	0.603	0.000	3.575	-0.163	0.121	0.027	-0.018
Teacher or Student Response	12.993	12.874	4.187	5.073	26.605	0.173	0.074	0.030	-0.008
Extended Student Response	2.712	1.822	2.799	0.000	17.131	-0.096	0.111	0.009	-0.037
Student Task Related Statement	1.921	1.711	1.556	0.000	8.458	0.036	0.109	0.001	-0.048
Acknowledge Correct Answer	0.939	0.740	0.794	0.000	4.287	0.115	0.100	0.013	-0.038

Table 7.7h (continued)

Teacher Says Student Answer Wrong	0.232	0.212	0.198	0.000	0.955	−0.145	0.182	0.021	−0.068
Effectiveness Question	0.692	0.664	0.413	0.051	1.860	0.230	0.110	0.053	0.000
Silence	20.182	18.665	9.988	4.056	47.602	0.082	0.091	0.007	−0.036
Discipline	0.688	0.582	0.620	0.000	2.585	0.000	0.118	0.000	−0.053
Procedural Interaction	5.530	4.169	4.997	0.472	30.500	−0.283	0.102	0.080	0.032
Social Interaction	0.734	0.423	1.269	0.000	9.873	0.047	0.148	0.002	−0.079
Teacher Question to Group	7.122	6.911	2.604	1.349	13.958	0.237	0.099	0.056	0.010
Teacher Question to Student	3.608	3.272	2.399	0.154	14.950	0.077	0.098	0.006	0.038
Probes for Higher Level Question	0.063	0.000	0.116	0.000	0.587	.	.	.	.
Probes for Recall Question	1.267	1.055	0.981	0.056	6.067	0.163	0.082	0.027	−0.011
Probes Teacher to Group	1.055	0.805	0.880	0.000	3.501	0.152	0.094	0.023	−0.022
Probes Teacher to Student	1.085	0.767	1.146	0.000	8.645	0.102	0.100	0.010	−0.030
Student Questions	0.132	0.053	0.231	0.000	1.228	−0.047	0.150	0.002	−0.075
Student Contribution	14.457	14.554	5.395	3.901	32.263	0.046	0.101	0.002	−0.045
Teacher Waits for Student Answer	0.996	0.832	0.585	0.118	2.687	0.147	0.091	0.022	−0.022
Objectives with Stress	0.001	0.000	0.005	0.000	0.041	.	.	.	.
Lecture with Stress	0.062	0.000	0.216	0.000	1.248	.	.	.	.
Student Unable to Answer	0.012	0.000	0.067	0.000	0.593	.	.	.	.
Rating of Academic Engagement (SNAP)	96.104	96.789	2.852	87.635	100.000	0.598	0.099	0.358	0.314
Rating of Academic Engagement (IAR)	94.013	95.298	4.670	79.301	100.000	1.000	0.000	1.000	1.000
Years of Teaching Experience	12.721	11.000	6.540	2.000	28.000	0.183	0.096	0.033	−0.011
Size of Class	32.864	31.000	8.779	17.000	57.000	−0.015	0.108	0.000	−0.049
Number of Homework Assignments	3.320	3.000	1.078	1.000	5.000	−0.024	0.107	0.001	−0.047
Prop. Obs with Emphasis Expand	0.456	0.330	0.318	0.000	1.000	0.036	0.120	0.001	−0.053
Prop. Obs with Emphasis Intro	0.292	0.330	0.305	0.000	1.000	−0.078	0.139	0.006	−0.057
Prop. Obs with Emphasis Review	0.250	0.330	0.237	0.000	1.000	0.050	0.131	0.003	−0.055
Opportunity to Learn Rating	79.181	81.400	29.039	0.000	100.000	0.025	0.154	0.001	−0.071
Time Allocated to Instruction	51.783	53.300	5.212	36.800	60.000	0.084	0.136	0.007	−0.056

Note: N = 81 classes

was derived from the SNAP, the other from the IAR. A choice had to be made as to which estimate was to be used. For reasons given in earlier chapters, the estimate of academic engagement derived from the IAR was preferred over the corresponding SNAP estimate in those countries where both instruments were used. In Canada Quebec and the Netherlands, only the SNAP were used. In Israel, the IAR was coded only during a few lessons so that the corresponding data were incomplete. As a consequence, the SNAP estimate of academic engagement was used in these three studies. In the remaining studies the IAR estimate was used. As can be seen in these tables the correlations between these two estimates ranged from 0.440 in the Republic of Korea to 0.661 in Australia.

In general, the "schooling" variables were more strongly related to academic engagement than they were to the "adjusted posttest scores." Consider the data for the Netherlands, for example. Seventeen of the 56 "schooling" variables are associated with the SNAP estimate of academic engagement (see Table 7.5h). In contrast, *none* of these variables were associated with "residualized posttest scores" in the Netherlands (see Table 7.7g). With one exception (namely, Canada Ontario-French) similar, although somewhat less dramatic, differences can be seen in all studies.

Once again, a separate table has been prepared to summarize the relationships of the "schooling" variables and academic engagement across studies (see Table 7.8).

In all three Canadian replications and in Israel, very few "schooling" variables were related to academic engagement (three or fewer across studies). In the remaining countries from 6 to 17 "schooling" variables were related to academic engagement.

Several of the "schooling" variables were found to be related to academic engagement in two or more of the studies. First, the use of lecture was positively related to academic engagement in both the Netherlands and Thailand. In the Netherlands, however, using materials during the lecture was positively associated with academic engagement, while lecturing without materials was negatively associated with academic engagement.

Second, the use of discourse or discussion was positively related to academic engagement in Australia and the Republic of Korea. In both Australia and the Netherlands, teacher-led activities were positively related to academic engagement while seatwork activities were negatively related to academic engagement.

Third, and in support of the previous findings, the more that teachers interacted with their students (rather than monitoring or not being involved with them), the more their students were academically engaged (in Australia, Canada Ontario-French, the Republic of Korea, and the Netherlands). And, the more teachers monitored their students, the less the students were academically engaged (in the Republic of Korea and the Netherlands). Finally, the less that teachers were involved with their students (either interacting or monitoring), the less they were academically engaged (in Thailand).

TABLE 7.8 Correlations with academic engagement associated with Q-square values greater than zero

Variable	Aust	Can-E	Can-F	Can-Q	Israel	Korea	Neth	Thai
Lecture/Explain/Demonstrate							0.392	0.260
Review Previous Content								
Discourse/Discussion	0.223					0.445		
Oral Practice/Drill	0.298							
Seatwork-Test								
Seatwork-Reading								
Seatwork-Written								
Seatwork-Laboratory	−0.291						−0.495	
Composite Management								
Other Activity								
Teacher Interacting	0.246		0.468			0.402	0.432	
Teacher Monitoring						−0.372	−0.491	
Uninvolved Teacher								−0.260
Explanation							−0.336	
Explanation with Materials							0.317	
Demonstration		−0.399						
Use of Examples					0.457			
Structuring Cues								
Directives	0.239							
Probes (total number)				−0.537				
Higher Order Question						0.297	0.333	
Recall Question								0.287
Opinion Question								
Redirect Question							0.328	
Teacher or Student Response	0.279					0.357		
Extended Student Response						0.352		
Student Task-Related Statement							−0.536	
Acknowledge Correct Answer						0.406	0.394	

Table 7.8 *(continued)*

Variable	Aust	Can-E	Can-F	Can-Q	Israel	Korea	Neth	Thai
Teacher Says Student Answer Wrong	0.272							
Effectiveness Question				0.570				0.230
Silence								
Discipline	−0.492					−0.559	−0.673	
Procedural Interaction	−0.322		−0.623			−0.631	−0.515	−0.283
Social Interaction				−0.592				
Teacher Question to Group	0.322							0.237
Teacher Question to Student							0.444	
Probes for Higher Level Question								
Probes for Recall Question								
Probes Teacher to Group								
Probes Teacher to Student								
Student Questions							−0.331	
Student Contribution								
Teacher Waits for Student Answer							0.439	
Objectives with Stress								
Lecture with Stress								
Student Unable to Answer							0.299	
Rating of Academic Engagement (SNAP)	0.661	0.467	0.570	1.000	1.000	0.440	1.000	0.598
Rating of Academic Engagement (IAR)	1.000	1.000	1.000			1.000	1.000	1.000
Years of Teaching Experience								
Size of Class	−0.216				0.517		0.387	
Number of Homework Assignments								
Prop. Obs with Emphasis Expand								
Prop. Obs with Emphasis Intro								
Prop. Obs with Emphasis Review								
Opportunity to Learn Rating								
Time Allocated to Instruction								

Note: The exact Q-square values are shown in Tables 7.7a through 7.7h.

Fourth, the number of responses made to questions either by students or teachers was positively related to academic engagement in Australia and the Republic of Korea. Fifth, some type of teacher reaction to student responses to questions (either positive in the Republic of Korea or the Netherlands, or negative in Australia or Canada Quebec) was positively related to academic engagement.

Sixth, directing questions to groups of students (rather than individual students) was associated with academic engagement. The use of probes was positively related to academic engagement in the Republic of Korea, but negatively related to academic engagement in Canada Quebec. And, the size of class (a teacher-report variable) was positively related to academic engagement in Israel, but negatively related to academic engagement in Australia.

A strong negative correlation was expected between composite management discipline and academic engagement. Likewise, a strong negative correlation could be expected between time spent in procedural interactions (that is, such housekeeping activities as taking attendance, and distributing or collecting papers) and academic engagement. These negative correlations were evident in the majority of the studies. In fact, in all studies except Canada Ontario-English and Israel these correlations were negative for either composite management discipline, procedural interactions, or both. The positive relationship between procedural interactions and academic engagement is unique to Israel.

Despite the exceptions noted in the discussion, the major conclusion that can be drawn from a comparison of the results presented in Tables 7.6 and 7.8 is that "schooling" variables are more highly related to the extent to which students are engaged in learning than what they actually learn. This generalization is especially valid in Australia, the Republic of Korea, the Netherlands, and Thailand. Stated somewhat simply, these findings suggest that what teachers *do* in their classrooms is more highly related to what their students *do*, than what their students *learn*.

Quite interestingly, the results in terms of final achievement and academic engagement are somewhat contradictory. For example, while the absence of verbal interaction (presumably during seatwork) is positively related with final achievement, the presence of verbal interaction (via lecture, discourse, and discussion) is positively related with academic engagement. A number of factors can be associated with these discrepant results.

First, estimates of academic engagement regardless of the instrument used may be inaccurate. Second, estimates of final achievement may be inaccurate because the tests were not equally valid across classes. Third, perhaps what teachers do to "keep students busy" is different from what they do to "get them to learn." If this latter supposition is valid, then both behaviors linked with "gaining involvement" (e.g., providing incentives for participation) and those linked with "increased achievement" (e.g., providing opportunity to learn) may be important in the understanding and improvement of student learning. Fourth, academic engagement may indeed be the focal point of teachers' efforts in their classrooms. That is, teachers may engage in behaviors intended to gain and maintain student engagement in learning, with the assumption that such engagement will ultimately lead to the desired learning. (In essence, their hypothesis is identical to the one underlying the Classroom Environment Study).

The Class Level Reduced Core Model

In this section, the PLS analyses performed on the data from four countries will be described briefly and the results of these analyses will be presented. As mentioned earlier, the four countries were Australia, the Republic of Korea, the Netherlands, and Thailand. The remaining countries were excluded from these analyses by virtue of the small number of classrooms included in their studies.

The PLS analyses reported in this section were undertaken on a country-by-country basis and were guided by the general conceptual framework of the core model (see Chapter 2). Because of the small number of classrooms relative to the large number of "schooling" variables included in the studies, the core model could not be tested as initially specified. In addition, preliminary multivariate analyses revealed severe multicollinearity problems among the "schooling" variables both within-constructs and between-constructs. In essence, then, while the core model was quite useful for organizing the large number of student-based, classroom-based, and school-based variables included in the study, a direct empirical test of the model was impossible.

General Model Structure

Figure 7.8 illustrates the general structure of the path model examined in this section. Specifically, the figure displays those between-construct relationships, or paths, that were common across studies (as indicated by solid lines) and those between-construct relationships that were omitted in at least one study (as indicated by broken lines). Constructs included in all studies and constructs omitted in at least one study are displayed in a similar way.

Table 7.9 presents, for the four countries included in the analysis, information concerning the constructs and their associated manifest variables. The manifest variables included in the model in each country define what may be termed the structure of the constructs.

Several points must be made in connection with the between-construct relationships shown in Fig. 7.8 and the within-construct relationships presented in Table 7.9. First, in contrast with the core model, the model depicted in Fig. 7.8 includes, with one exception, constructs consisting of

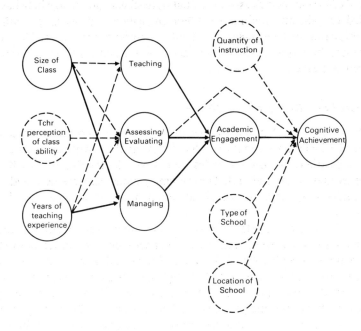

FIG. 7.8   Between-construct relationships in the class level reduced model.[a]
[a]Broken-line paths and constructs were omitted in at least one study.

schooling variables only. The exception is the variable termed "cognitive achievement." As indicated in Table 7.9, this variable was, for the purposes of the analyses described in this section, defined as the class mean posttest score adjusted for pretest effects by means of a pooled within-class regression. This "adjusted" or "residualized" posttest score was also used in the computation of the zero-order correlations presented in an earlier section. The path model considered here is referred to as a "reduced" model because the analysis omitted all non-schooling constructs included in the original core model and because the analysis focused on cognitive achievement as the only measure of student outcomes. The path model is referred to as a "class level" model because all variables were defined at the class level and because the analyses were undertaken using classes as units of investigation.

Second, it must be emphasized at this time that the between-construct relationship shown in Fig. 7.8 and the within-construct relationships described in Table 7.9 reflect the ultimate models as specified after extensive exploratory data analyses and model testing. As a matter of fact, a set of country specific

TABLE 7.9 *Summary of constructs and associated manifest variables included in the class level reduced model (by study)*

Construct	Manifest variable(s)	Aus	Kor	Net	Tha
Class Size	Class Size	*	*	*	*
Teacher Perception of Class Ability	High Ability? (1 = yes)	-	-	*	-
	Low Ability? (1 = yes)	*	-	-	*
	Need Remedial Work?	*	-	*	*
Years of Teaching Experience	Years of Teaching Experience	*	*	*	*
School Location	School Location (1 = urban/metropolitan; 0 = rural/suburban)	-	*	-	-
Type of School	Type of School (1 = governmental; 0 = non-governmental)	-	-	-	*
Teaching	Lecture/explain/demonstrate (SNAP)	*	-	-	*
	Discourse/discussion (SNAP)	-	*	-	-
	Oral practice/drill (SNAP)	*	-	-	-
	Teacher interacting (SNAP)	*	*	-	-
	Directives (FMI)	*	*	-	*
	Structuring Cues (FMI)	*	-	*	*
	Explanation (FMI)	-	-	*	-
	Explanation with materials (FMI)	-	-	*	-
	Demonstration (FMI)	-	*	-	-
	Use of examples (FMI)	-	-	-	*
	Effectiveness questions (FMI)	-	-	*	-
Assess/Evaluate	Probes:total number (FMI)	*	-	-	-
	Probes:tch to student (FMI)	-	-	*	-
	Probes:tch to group (FMI)	-	*	-	*
	Redirect questions (FMI)	*	-	*	*
	Acknowledge correct answer (FMI)	-	*	*	-
	Tch says answer wrong (FMI)	*	-	*	-
	Question:tch to group (FMI)	*	*	-	*
	Question:tch to stud. (FMI)	-	-	*	*
	Effectiveness questions (FMI)	-	-	*	*
Managing	Procedural interaction (FMI)	*	*	*	*
	Disciplinary activities (FMI)	*	*	*	-
	Teacher uninvolved (SNAP)	-	-	-	*
Quantity of Instruction	Opportunity to learn (Teacher rating)	*	na	*	-
	Number of homework assignments (week)	*	*	-	-
	Percent of time allocated to instruction	-	-	*	-
Academic Engagement	SNAP estimate of percent engaged students	-	-	*	-
	IAR estimate of percent engaged students	*	*	na	*
Cognitive Achievement	Class mean posttest score adjusted by pooled within-class regression	*	*	*	*

Notes: Table entries marked "*" indicate variables included in the final model in each study. Entries marked "na" indicate that information was not available for that particular study. Entries marked "-" indicate that the corresponding manifest variable was not included in the final model in that study.

models, rather than a single model, is depicted in Fig. 7.8 since the broken-line paths and constructs were included in the model for some countries but excluded for others.

As can be seen in Table 7.9, the structure of several of the constructs was quite different across countries in the final version of the model. Consider the construct "teaching," for example. In the Republic of Korea, the construct is defined by four manifest variables, namely the variables "discourse/discussion" and "teacher interacting" derived from the SNAP, and the variables "directives" and "demonstration" derived from the FMI. In the Netherlands, on the other hand, the construct is defined by five manifest variables, all of them derived from the FMI: structuring cues, explanation, explanation with materials, use of examples and effectiveness questions. As can be seen, these two sets of manifest variables are mutually exclusive. In fact, not one of the eleven manifest variables initially associated with the construct "teaching" is ultimately associated with the construct in all four countries. Decisions to include and exclude manifest variables were made based on the results of exploratory analyses undertaken on a country-by-country basis. Since it is not possible to give a detailed account of the exploratory analyses undertaken in each country, it must suffice to sketch the major steps involved in the development of the ultimate model versions referred to above. A more detailed description of PLS is contained in Appendix B, and an application of PLS analyses to the data collected in the Netherlands is included as Appendix C.

Remodeling the Models

The first step was generally the examination of descriptive statistics for all "schooling" variables initially involved in the core model. This step usually resulted in the elimination of several variables which had little if any variation, or variables which were so highly skewed that they could not be used in correlational analyses. Other variables were excluded on the basis of theoretical considerations. For example, the manifest variable "size of school" was in the core model associated with the construct "school characteristics." The construct "school characteristics" was hypothesized to have direct effects on all constructs reflecting teaching as well as on the constructs "quantity of instuction" and "student participation in learning" (see Chapter 2). Hence, "size of school," being a component of the construct "school characteristics," was believed to be connected to all these constructs. While there may exist some complex indirect relationship between the size of the school and the aforementioned constructs, it was deemed unreasonable to assume any direct connection. As a consequence, the variable "size of school" was eliminated from the construct "school characteristics."

Another consideration that led to the elimination of particular variables was linear dependency among manifest variables. An example is the set of three variables derived from the SNAP that reflected the role of the teacher. These variables were "teacher interacting," "teacher monitoring," and "teacher uninvolved." Since the SNAP required the classification of the teacher's role into one of these categories, the associated class mean percentages must add up to 100 percent. If, for example, "teacher interacting" plus "teacher monitoring" equals 80 percent, the value of the variable "teacher uninvolved" must be 20 percent. Hence, one of these variables provides redundant information and must be eliminated from any multivariate analysis. Similar considerations apply to the ten SNAP categories that reflected class activities, and to the set of FMI categories which reflected the nature of interactions occurring in the classroom. The number of linearly dependent manifest variables was usually smaller than the total number of variables derived from the SNAP and the FMI since some behaviors included on these instruments were rarely observed and coded. As a consequence, and as has been seen in Chapter 4, a subset of SNAP class activities and a subset of FMI categories was typically found to add up to 100 percent, or nearly 100 percent.

A somewhat more complex example of analytical dependency among observational variables is the relationship between the SNAP category "management activity" and the SNAP rating of the percent of academically engaged students. Observers were instructed to record the code for "non-engagement" for students whenever they coded "management" for teachers. Obviously, one of these variables must be eliminated since the ensuing bivariate relationship between the SNAP variable "management" and the observer rating of academic engagement must by definition be negative. Since academic engagement was hypothesized in the core model as being a key mediating factor between teaching behaviors and student achievement, the SNAP variable "management activity" was generally dropped prior to PLS analyses.

The next step of the PLS analyses usually involved the testing of an initial version of the model. On the basis of these initial results, the elimination of additional manifest variables was considered and, most importantly, the restructuring of "schooling" constructs was considered. This restructuring was important for two reasons.

First, in order to facilitate meaningful between-construct path analyses the reduction of "schooling" constructs based on the initial results and theoretical considerations was necessary. Second, since the initial modeling results generally revealed severe collinearity among the "schooling" constructs (which, of course, emanated from collinearity among manifest variables), the constructs needed to be restructured in such a way that multicollinearity problems would be reduced to a minimum.

Results for Class Level Reduced Models

The results of the PLS analysis for Australia, the Republic of Korea, the

Netherlands, and Thailand are presented in Tables 7.10, 7.11, and 7.12. Table 7.10 displays the loadings of the manifest variables for each construct. In essence, the data in Table 7.10 simply replace the asterisks in Table 7.9 with numerical values.

For each manifest variable associated with a construct in a specific country two numerical estimates (designated A and B) are reported. The first set of estimates (A) is based on the analysis of class mean percentages of the observation variables. That is, the data were aggregated across lessons to the classroom level, and class mean percentages were computed. This procedure corresponds to the general plans for data analysis made during the inception of the study as well as the approach commonly used in related process-product research. The second set of estimates (B) is based on the analysis of lesson-level observational data. That is, the data pertaining to the observational variables were aggregated to the lesson level (see Chapter 5), and these lesson-level percentages were used in the PLS analyses. The key difference between versions A and B is that version A employs predefined composites of observational data with the *same weights* assigned to each lesson level percentage, while in version B the calculation of the equivalent of a "grand mean" across lessons is a result of the PLS iteration process which assigned *differential weights* to the lesson-level percentages. Version B was expected to improve the stability and the predictive power of estimated relationships among the observational variables. Additional information pertaining to the distinction between versions A and B is included in Appendix C.

The number of observed lessons and, hence, the number of lesson-level indicators of the observational variables varied from country to country. In Thailand, each class was observed six times while in the Republic of Korea and in the Netherlands each class was observed on eight occasions. In Australia, the majority of the classes were also observed on eight occasions, but a few classes were observed more frequently, namely nine or ten times. Since the PLS analysis of version B required an equal number of lesson-level indicators for each observational category, the data pertaining to the eighth, ninth and tenth observed lessons were averaged for those Australian classes observed on more than eight occasions. As a result, each observational variable in version B for Australia was represented by eight lesson-level indicators.

Table 7.10 reports for version B the mean loadings calculated across eight lesson-level indicators for Australia, the Republic of Korea, and the Netherlands and the mean loadings for the six lesson-level indicators available in Thailand. In order to enable an assessment of the variability of the loadings of lesson-level indicators, Table 7.11 presents additional data pertaining to the loadings of version B, namely the median loading, minimum loading, and maximum loading for each observational variable included in the final model for each country.

As can be seen in Table 7.10, loadings based on the lesson-level data

TABLE 7.10   *PLS loadings for models using class mean percentages*
(Version A) and models using lesson level percentages (Version B)

Construct/ Variable	Australia A	B	Korea (ROK) A	B	Netherlands A	B	Thailand A	B
Teacher Perception								
High Ability?	-	-	-	-	855	998	-	-
Low Ability?	-876	-858	-	-	-	-	-953	-957
Remediation?	-938	-949	-	-	-655	-114	-807	-800
Teaching								
Lecture/Explain/Demo	429	208	-	-	-	-	878	426
Discourse/Discussion	-	-	544	262	-	-	-	-
Oral practice	651	272	-	-	-	-	-	-
Teacher interacting	538	348	944	399	-	-	-	-
Directives	521	461	191	150	-	-	-199	-027
Structuring cues	430	339	-	-	475	262	545	236
Explanation	-	-	-	-	-429	-347	-	-
Explanation w. material	-	-	-	-	618	430	-	-
Demonstration	-	-	315	208	-	-	-	-
Use examples	-	-	-	-	-	-	573	323
Effectiveness quest.	-	-	-	-	705	432	-	-
Assessing/Evaluating								
Probes (total)	427	254	-	-	-	-	-	-
Probes: Tchr to stud	-	-	-	-	677	437	-	-
Probes: Tchr to group	-	-	660	216	-	-	445	216
Redirect question	582	372	-	-	763	371	438	228
Acknowledges answer	-	-	706	408	722	412	-	-
Says answer wrong	810	421	-	-	593	278	-	-
Quest: Tchr to stud	-	-	-	-	857	657	420	291
Quest: Tchr to group	752	431	248	208	-	-	630	339
Effectiveness quest.	-	-	-	-	-	-	594	233
Managing								
Procedural	601	183	952	395	403	175	835	393
Discipline	682	691	583	456	989	855	-	-
Teacher uninvolved	-	-	-	-	-	-	867	522
Academic Engagement								
SNAP estimate	-	-	-	-	1000	674	-	-
IAR estimate	1000	582	1000	602	na	na	1000	527
Quantity								
Opp. to Learn	799	799	na	na	910	910	-	-
Homework assignments	653	653	1000	1000	-	-	-	-
Pct instructional time	-	-	-	-	472	472	-	-

Notes: All coefficients are multiplied by 1,000. For version B, mean loadings over lesson level indicators are reported. Entries marked "na" indicate that information was not available for that particular study. Entries marked "-" indicate that the corresponding manifest variable was eliminated from the tested model. Constructs associated with a single manifest variable are not included in the table.

(version B) are almost always smaller than those based on the class mean percentages (version A). Furthermore, as can be seen in Table 7.11, the differences between the minimum and maximum loadings for the lesson-level data are quite large in all countries, sometimes associated with different signs (e.g., "demonstration" in the Republic of Korea; "directives" in Thailand).

The impact of the class-level and lesson-level analyses on the between-construct relationships (that is, direct effects) can be seen in Table 7.12. With minor exceptions, the size of the direct between-construct effects is larger for the lesson-level data than for the class-level data. Also with these few exceptions, both the R-square and Q-square values associated with models based on the lesson-level data are larger. Thus, as hypothesized, the use of lesson-level data did improve the stability and predictive power of the models. (See also Appendix C.)

Let us consider now the results presented in Table 7.12. The results will be examined construct-by-construct with similarities and differences across countries pointed out as they arise.

In both the Republic of Korea and the Netherlands, a negative direct effect of class size on teaching was found. That is, the larger the class size, the fewer the number of observed teaching behaviors (e.g, teacher interacting or demonstrating in the Republic of Korea, and teacher use of effectiveness questions or explaining using materials in the Netherlands). Also, in the Netherlands, years of teaching experience had a positive direct effect on teaching. That is, teachers with more years of teaching experience spent more time explaining with materials, providing structuring cues, and asking effectiveness questions. In the Republic of Korea, class size accounted for almost 18 percent of the variation in teaching (version B), while in the Netherlands, class size and years of teaching experience in combination accounted for almost 24 percent of the variation in teaching (version B).

In Australia, the Netherlands, and Thailand, teachers' perceptions of the ability of their students had a negative direct effect on assessing and evaluating students. That is, the lower the ability of the class as perceived by the teacher and the larger the number of students perceived to be in need of remediation, the more time teachers spent assessing and evaluating their students (e.g., asking questions, probing the students, and reacting to their answers). In Thailand, class size also had a negative direct effect on assessing and evaluating students, indicating that teachers in larger classes spent less time asking, probing, and reacting. In the Netherlands, years of teaching experience had a positive direct effect on assessing and evaluating students. That is, teachers with more years of teaching experience tended to spend more time asking, probing, and reacting.

In Australia, teachers' perceptions only accounted for about 7 percent of the variation in assessing and evaluating students. In the Netherlands, teachers' perceptions and years of experience combined to account for about

TABLE 7.11 *Median, minimum, and maximum loadings for lesson level indicators for observational variables (Version B)*

Construct/Variable	Australia Med	Australia Min	Australia Max	Korea (ROK) Med	Korea (ROK) Min	Korea (ROK) Max	Netherlands Med	Netherlands Min	Netherlands Max	Thailand Med	Thailand Min	Thailand Max
Teaching												
Lecture/Explain/Demo	247	036	390	-	-	-	-	-	-	429	290	648
Discourse/Discussion	-	-	-	370	019	490	-	-	-	-	-	-
Oral practice	316	076	395	-	-	-	-	-	-	-	-	-
Teacher interacting	359	260	380	558	-112	587	-	-	-	-	-	-
Directives	491	345	586	179	-059	330	-	-	-	-030	-316	263
Structuring cues	384	200	400	-	-	-	298	026	516	199	039	492
Explanation	-	-	-	-	-	-	-208	-490	-018	-	-	-
Explanation w. material	-	-	-	-	-	-	483	255	559	-	-	-
Demonstration	-	-	-	381	-215	609	-	-	-	-	-	-
Use examples	-	-	-	-	-	-	-	-	-	365	111	432
Effectiveness questions	-	-	-	-	-	-	497	250	694	-	-	-
Assessing/Evaluating												
Probes (total)	303	188	377	-	-	-	-	-	-	-	-	-
Probes: Tchr to stud	-	-	-	-	-	-	450	141	649	-	-	-
Probes: Tchr to group	-	-	-	246	082	407	-	-	-	228	-060	472
Redirect question	419	232	566	-	-	-	432	230	564	164	-108	508
Acknowledges answer	-	-	-	596	175	651	462	264	527	387	142	540
Says answer wrong	-	-	-	-	-	-	298	193	376	-	-	-
Quest: Tchr to stud	427	185	705	-	-	-	680	530	690	304	111	479
Quest: Tchr to group	463	342	491	328	-118	549	-	-	-	335	157	474
Effectiveness questions	-	-	-	-	-	-	-	-	-	239	086	462
Managing												
Procedural	236	-030	357	508	153	568	206	-138	636	416	113	681
Discipline	743	534	757	510	300	637	867	803	934	543	205	715
Teacher uninvolved	-	-	-	-	-	-	-	-	-	-	-	-
Academic Engagement												
SNAP estimate	-	-	-	-	-	-	739	484	754	-	-	-
IAR estimate	597	409	733	623	475	746	-	-	-	529	265	719

Note: All coefficients are multiplied by 1,000.

TABLE 7.12 *Direct between-construct effects, R-square and Q-square values for model versions A and B*

Predicted/Predictor	Country/Model							
	Australia		Korea (ROK)		Netherlands		Thailand	
	A	B	A	B	A	B	A	B
Teaching								
Class Size	-	-	−178	−419	−213	−350	-	-
Teacher Experience	-	-	-	-	231	300	-	-
R-square			032	175	110	237		
Q-square			008	081	042	107		
Assessing/Evaluating								
Class Size	-	-	-	-	-	-	−215	−266
Teacher Perception	−246	−271	-	-	−197	−260	−193	−268
Teacher Experience	-	-	-	-	244	290	-	-
R-square	061	073			094	140	099	169
Q-square	008	002			018	030	034	108
Managing								
Class Size	127	094	047	123	114	132	058	042
Teacher Experience	−112	−173	−372	−428	−428	−434	−184	−246
R-square	029	040	141	198	196	205	034	062
Q-square	−043	−033	005	093	109	124	−028	003
Academic Engagement								
Teaching	290	384	195	277	325	404	121	275
Assessing/Evaluating	033	049	137	390	189	303	155	194
Managing	−541	−495	−527	−267	−483	−366	−227	−207
R-square	490	554	537	568	597	667	147	262
Q-square	432	506	454	387	466	571	044	165
Cognitive Achievement								
School Location	-	-	258	256	-	-	-	-
School Type	-	-	-	-	-	-	−424	−447
Assessing/Evaluating	-	-	-	-	-	-	133	227
Academic Engagement	160	165	109	080	186	186	245	210
Quantity of Instruction	431	428	188	188	491	492	-	-
R-square	220	221	112	107	293	293	280	313
Q-square	148	148	−073	−075	176	173	215	243

Note: All coefficients are multiplied by 1,000.

14 percent of the variation in assessing and evaluating students (version B). Finally, in Thailand, class size and teachers' perceptions combined to account for about 17 percent of the variation in assessing and evaluating students (version B).

In all four countries, class size had a small direct positive effect on classroom management, while years of teaching experience had a moderate to large direct negative effect on classroom management. That is, teachers in larger classes spent more time on classroom management, while more experienced teachers spent less time on class management. In combination, class size and years of teaching experience accounted for 4 percent of the variation in classroom management in Australia, 19.8 percent in the Republic of Korea, 20.5 percent in the Netherlands, and 6.2 percent in Thailand (version B).

In all four countries, teaching and assessing/evaluating had a positive direct effect on academic engagement while managing had a negative direct effect on academic engagement. In combination, these three constructs accounted for 55.4 percent of the variance in Australia, 56.8 percent in the Republic of Korea, 66.7 percent in the Netherlands, and 26.2 percent in Thailand.

Finally, academic engagement had a direct positive effect on cognitive achievement in all four countries. In Australia, the Republic of Korea, and the Netherlands, quantity of instruction had a small positive direct effect on cognitive achievement. The construct "quantity of instruction" was defined differently in all three countries. In Australia, "quantity of instruction" was defined in terms of "opportunity to learn" and "homework assignments." In the Republic of Korea, "quantity of instruction" was defined solely in terms of "homework assignments." And, in the Netherlands, "quantity of instruction" was defined in terms of "opportunity to learn" and "the percent of class time spent on instruction." As was mentioned in Chapter 6, school location had a direct effect on cognitive achievement in the Republic of Korea, while school type had a direct effect on cognitive achievement in Thailand.

Finally, only in Thailand did a construct composed of observational variables have a direct effect on cognitive achievement. The construct was "assessing and evaluating students" and the observational variables pertained to questioning, probing, and reacting. Overall, the various country-unique models accounted for about 22 percent of the variance in achievement in Australia, about 11 percent in the Republic of Korea, about 29 percent in the Netherlands, and about 30 percent in Thailand.

Summary

The data presented in this chapter provide little support for the general hypothesis that observed classroom activities and teaching behaviors are associated with, let alone influence, student achievement. Of the more than 300 correlations between the observational variables and student achievement presented in the chapter, only 18 were associated with positive Q-square values.[1]

[1] As a historical note, Jayne (1945) computed a total of 336 correlations between 84 activities and behaviors and 4 indicators of student achievement. In his words, "only 55 coefficients, or slightly over 16% of the total, (were) more than twice their standard error. ... To be statistically significant, that is to be relatively certain that the relationship indicated by the coefficient is not due to chance, a coefficient should be at least three times as large as its standard error. ... Only 20, or about 8% of the total, had correlations large enough to be statistically significant" (p. 113).

Since the use of classical significance tests and the identification of statistically significant correlations appears to constitute one cornerstone of process-product research, it may be noted in passing that the Q-square statistic is closely related to standard test statistics *provided* that classical sampling requirements and distributional assumptions have been met. As shown by Dijkstra (1981) on the basis of conventional statistical theory, the expectation of the Q-square statistics is, in fact, *positive* if the "true" effect of a given variable is *zero* in the population. That is, the Q-square statistic provides a liberal, rather than conservative, measure of statistical significance. Jackknife standard deviations, on the other hand, tend to be conservative estimates. Thus, the "true" sampling variance of point estimates is generally smaller than the corresponding jackknife estimate of sampling variance. The most important point to be made, however, is that jackknife techniques can be used in situations in which conventional statistical tests cannot be used.

While further discussion of so few significant correlations may be viewed as futile, three points of interest seem worth noting. First, silence was significantly related to student achievement in three studies (Australia, Canada Ontario-French, and Hungary). In fact, of all observational variables, only silence was associated with student achievement in more than one study. Second, the amount of feedback given to students when they responded to questions (in Canada Quebec) and the number of questions asked by the students (in Thailand) were the only observational variables associated with student achievement in these two studies. In the remaining four studies, either no observational variables were related to student achievement (Canada Ontario-English, Israel, and the Netherlands) or a single observational variable (namely, demonstration) was *negatively* related to student achievement (the Republic of Korea).

Although these rather sketchy findings can be interpreted in a number of ways, one possible interpretation is that observational variables focusing on the students, rather than the teachers, are more likely to be associated with student achievement. Such an interpretation would be consistent with the results concerning students' perceptions presented in Chapter 6. Unfortunately, the vast majority of the variables included on the observation instruments were focused on the teachers. Thus, this interpretation should be viewed as tentative, but potentially intriguing.

In general, the observational variables were more strongly and more consistently related to academic engagement than to student achievement, particularly in Australia, the Republic of Korea, the Netherlands, and Thailand. In the three Canadian replications and in Israel, a total of 7 significant correlations of the observational variables with academic engagement were noted using the positive Q-square criterion. Thus, in these four studies the observational variables were associated neither with academic engagement nor student achievement. It is worth noting that these were the four studies with the smallest sample sizes (ranging from 16 in Canada Ontario-English to 21 in Israel). Thus, as might be expected, studies with such small samples are more susceptible to the influence of extreme classes on the magnitude of the correlation coefficients.

In Australia, the Republic of Korea, the Netherlands, and Thailand, on the other hand, the results pertaining to academic engagement are quite consistent. The more teachers interacted with their students, the greater the students' academic engagement (Australia, the Republic of Korea, and the Netherlands). The more teachers monitored and supervised their students (the Republic of Korea and the Netherlands) or were not involved with their students in any way (Thailand), the less the students' academic engagement. In the Netherlands and Thailand the use of lectures was positively correlated with academic engagement, while in Australia and the Republic of Korea the use of discourse was positively correlated with academic engagement.

As might be expected, time spent in discipline or in various procedural matters was negatively related to academic engagement. These correlations were the largest of all the correlations involving observational variables in five of the studies (including Canada Ontario-French and Canada Quebec, but excluding Thailand).

Across all studies only three observational variables were correlated with *both* academic engagement and student achievement. In Australia, time spent in laboratory work and the number of disciplinary actions were both negatively related with academic engagement and student achievement. In Canada Quebec, the frequency with which teachers stated their students' answers were incorrect was positively related to both academic engagement and student achievement.

In the class-level reduced model, several constructs were found to influence those constructs which included the observational variables. Specifically, class size influenced either the extent to which teachers engaged in teaching (the Republic of Korea and the Netherlands) or assessing/evaluating (Thailand). Class size also influenced the extent to which teachers engaged in classroom management (all studies except Thailand). The direction of these influences were opposite, with a positive effect of class size on teaching and assessing/ evaluating, and a negative effect of class size on classroom management. Finally, in all four studies, years of teaching experience had a negative direct effect on classroom management. That is, the more years of experience, the less time spent on classroom management.

As has been suggested earlier, teaching, assessing/evaluating, or both had a positive direct effect on academic engagement in all four studies. Classroom management had a substantial negative effect on academic engagement in all four studies.

Finally, none of the constructs including the observational variables had a direct effect on cognitive achievement in any of the studies except Thailand. And, quantity of instruction, although defined differently in the various studies, had a positive direct effect on cognitive achievement in the three studies in which the constuct remained in the final model (that is, Australia, the Republic of Korea, and the Netherlands).

8

Summary, Conclusions, and Implications

The Classroom Environment Study is the largest cross-national observational study of schools and classrooms to date. A set of interesting, potentially useful, findings has emerged from the study. Based on these findings, a set of conclusions can be drawn and recommendations offered. The purpose of this chapter is to summarize the findings, draw reasonable conclusions, and offer appropriate recommendations.

This final chapter is organized into two major sections. The first summarizes the primary findings of the study. The second presents interpretations and conclusions that can be drawn from the findings. Recommendations are offered in this latter section as deemed necessary and appropriate. A related set of generalizations derived from the study has been presented by Anderson (1987a).

Summary of Major Findings

Two types of findings can be derived from the study. The first describes a set of conditions, perceptions, behaviors, and outcomes that characterized most, and in some cases all, of the studies. The second describes associations among these conditions, perceptions, behaviors, and outcomes. These two types of findings are included in the two subsections that follow. Each subsection contains a listing of primary results of the study.

Descriptive Findings

1. Participating countries differed widely in the size and location of schools, the experience and training of their teachers, the educational and occupational levels of the students' parents, and the educational aspirations of the students themselves. Within-country differences on most of these variables, including differences in initial student achievement across classrooms, were also evident.

2. The majority of teachers in most countries reported that few of their students needed remedial instruction prior to their entry into the classrooms.

This chapter was written by Lorin W. Anderson.

289

At the same time, however, teachers differed in their perceptions of the ability levels of their students. These differences were prevalent both within-countries (that is, from classroom to classroom) and across-countries. One possible interpretation of this apparent discrepancy is that teachers adapt the content to be taught to the ability levels of their students. More will be said about this interpretation later.

3. Teachers reported more autonomy related to activities within their classrooms than outside them. Specifically, teachers reported more autonomy in their assignment of homework, organization of classrooms, and use of tests, than in the curriculum they were expected to follow and the meetings they were expected to hold with the parents. At the same time, however, the amount of autonomy reported by teachers in general varied from country to country.

4. Countries differed widely in the number of students in the classes. Within-country differences in class size were also found to exist. Across countries, attendance rates were quite high and only one adult inhabited each classroom (namely, the teacher). Published textbooks were a staple in the educational diet of students. Furthermore, the vast majority of students had access to the textbooks outside of class. Teachers reported infrequent use of audio-visual materials and programmed texts.

5. Across countries, teachers relied heavily on whole class instruction. Little time was spent in small group instruction or work. The vast majority of classroom time was spent on instruction, with some time spent on "house-keeping" matters or social interactions.

6. Across countries, teachers tended to use homework assignments to identify learning deficiencies and to use more formal tests to assign grades. Projects or written reports were used less frequently for either purpose.

7. Across countries, students reported that their teachers provided the necessary structure and feedback to aid in their learning, their teachers were able to manage student behavior in an appropriate manner, and their class-rooms were task-oriented and business-like learning environments.

8. While most teachers reported they provided extra help to at least some of the students in their classrooms, differences among the teachers in the various countries were evident in terms of when that help was provided (e.g., during or after class), and whether the help was provided to individual students or groups.

9. With the exception of the Republic of Korea, teachers reported that a fairly large number of the observed lessons were devoted to the review of previously taught content and material.

10. The opportunity students had to learn the content included on the final test differed greatly within countries. Students in some classrooms were taught two to three times more of the content than were students in other classrooms.

11. Across countries, teachers assumed a very active role in their classrooms.

They spent the majority of their time interacting with their students (rather than monitoring them or not being involved with them at all). Most of the communication that occurred in the classrooms was directed from the teacher to the students (rather than vice versa). When students did communicate, they tended to respond to questions asked by teachers and give fairly brief answers. Interestingly, students almost always gave answers to the questions they were asked (whether they were "right" or "wrong").

12. Three of the ten classroom activities included on the Snapshot accounted for from one-half to more than four-fifths of all the activities observed in all countries except Hungary. These activities were lecture, seatwork (either written or laboratory, depending primarily on the subject being taught), and management. In seven of the studies, these activities accounted for two-thirds or more of all observed activities. In Hungary, lecture was replaced by discourse (which occurred over 50 percent of the time).

13. Six of the more than 20 behavioral categories included on the Five-Minute Interaction instrument accounted for from one-half to more than three-fourths of all behaviors observed in all countries except Israel. These behaviors were (a) explanation, (b) explanation with materials, (c) asking recall questions, (d) responding to questions, (e) attending to procedural matters, and (f) silence. In Israel, all but one of the categories included on the FMI (namely, demonstration) accounted for a minimum of one percent of all behaviors and interactions coded.

14. Several of the behavioral categories included on the Five-Minute Interaction instrument were observed infrequently. Specifically, each accounted for less than 1 percent of the total number of behaviors coded. These behaviors were (1) using examples (in 9 studies), (2) asking opinion questions (in 9 studies), (3) saying the answer given was incorrect (in 9 studies), (4) redirecting questions to other students (in 7 studies), (5) asking effectiveness questions (that is, "do you understand?") (in 7 studies), (6) asking higher-order questions (in 5 studies), and (7) the presence of extended responses on the part of the students (5 studies). In general, teachers reacted to students' responses to questions by indicating the answer was correct, repeating the answer, or probing for additional information.

15. Most lessons contained multiple activity segments, each lasting an average of 10 to 15 minutes. During lecture, review, and discourse segments, teachers were engaged in explaining, questioning, and reacting. During seatwork segments, more time was spent in silence, quiet talk, and attending to procedural matters. Within countries, however, teachers differed in the role they assumed during the seatwork segments (with some being very active and others withdrawing).

Associations and Influences

1. Students' home backgrounds impact primarily on initial achievement

and aspirations, not on final achievement. In virtually all countries, home background did not have a direct effect on student achievement.

2. Students' educational aspirations influenced their initial attitude toward school more than their initial achievement or their initial attitude toward the subject being taught.

3. Students' initial achievement influenced their final achievement; their initial attitudes influenced their final attitudes. Aspirations, initial attitudes, and entering achievement can be thought of composing what Bloom (1976) refers to as the "history of the learner," a "history" which exerts a great deal of influence on final achievement and final attitude.

4. Students' perceptions of the task-orientation of their classrooms influenced their academic engagement and final achievement; their perceptions of the structure provided by their teachers influenced their final attitude toward the subject being taught.

5. There appears to be a bi-directional relationship between final achievement and final attitude. That is, rather than achievement affecting attitude or attitude affecting achievement, the influence appears to be mutual in most countries.

6. In general, specific observable teacher behaviors were unrelated to final achievement. Interestingly, behavioral categories such as "silence" and "student initiation" were related to final achievement in one or more countries.

7. Teacher behaviors were more consistently associated with academic engagement than with final achievement. Thus, what teachers do in their classrooms appears more highly related to what students do, than what they learn.

8. Teachers confronted with larger class sizes spent less time in teaching (that is, explaining, structuring, and directing). Similarly, these teachers spent more time in classroom management.

9. Teachers who perceived the students in their classes to be of lower ability spent more time assessing and evaluating them by asking questions and probing.

10. Teachers who spent more time teaching and assessing/evaluating students had students who spent more time engaged in learning. Conversely, teachers who spent more time in classroom management had students who spent less time engaged in learning.

11. Teachers with more years of teaching experience spent less time on classroom management.

12. Students who spent more time engaged in learning tended to achieve higher posttest scores (adjusted for pretest scores).

13. The quantity of instruction students received (defined in terms of opportunity to learn, homework assignments, or both) directly influenced the amount students learned. This relationship was particularly strong in Australia and the Netherlands.

Interpretations and Conclusions

As is the case for most research studies, this study raised more questions than it answered. Five general areas of questions follow from the results of the Classroom Environment Study. These areas are: (1) the nature of class-room teaching, (2) the nature of the paradigms we use to study teaching, (3) concerns for proper design and instrumentation, (4) the impact of the subject matter on teachers and teaching, and (5) the way in which prospective teachers are "trained." Each of these areas will be addressed in one of the following subsections.

The Nature of Classroom Teaching

One clear finding of this study is that differences in teacher behaviors are not related to differences in student achievement. Why is this so? One potential reason is strongly supported by the results of the study, namely, teachers operate within a variety of constraints in their classrooms (both real and imagined) and their behavior conforms to these constraints. Thus, variation in many teacher behaviors was quite small. In many of the studies, teacher behaviors were influenced by a number of contextual factors including class size, the perceived ability levels of the students, and the teachers' experiential backgrounds. The apparent impact of similar variables (as well as additional variables such as subject matter and time of year) on teacher behavior has been found by Barr and Dreeben (1983), Evertson and her colleagues (e.g., Evertson, Anderson, Anderson, and Brophy 1980; Brophy and Evertson 1978; Evertson and Veldman 1981), and Stodolsky (1988).

Partly because of such constraints teachers routinely make use of a small number of the classroom activities and engage in a limited number of the behaviors available to them. As schoolteachers they must attend to procedural matters such as calling roll, collecting lunch money, and at the upper grade levels, moving students in and out of the classroom. Confronted with fairly large classes they talk to or with the students and assign work for them to do at their seats, desks, or laboratory tables. Within these general formats, they provide explanations, ask questions, react to answers to those questions, and permit or expect silence.

Some of the external factors which influence teachers change from hour to hour, day to day, or season to season. As a consequence, their behavior is quite likely to be inconsistent over time. This inconsistency was quite evident in the Classroom Environment Study. As was seen in Chapter 5, teachers in a few countries used a novel lesson structure almost every time (or every other time) they were observed. Furthermore, additional analyses of the data summarized in Chapters 4 and 7 also supported the inconsistency of teacher behavior.

Using the lesson-level data, the consistency of behavior across lessons within each study was examined. Specifically, eta square coefficients were computed within a linear model that included "teacher behavior," "teachers," and "lessons." These coefficients represent the proportion of variance in a particular teacher behavior that can be attributed to differences in teachers, as opposed to differences in lessons.

For the behaviors included on the FMI instrument, the eta square coefficients ranged from 0 to about 0.61 across all studies. If the behavior "directives" was omitted, the range of the coefficients was from 0 to about 0.34. In both cases, the median eta square coefficient was slightly less than 0.10. That is, slightly less than 10 percent of the variation in the observed teacher behaviors could be attributed to between-teacher differences. The remainder of the variance could be attributed to differences in the lessons or the occasions on which the teachers were observed. In a word, observed teacher behaviors did not *reliably* differentiate among the teachers.

Rather than suggest this unreliability is random error, however, the contention here is that such inconsistency reflects teachers' ways of adapting to different setting or situational constraints. Teaching behavior, thus, is hypothesized to be purposeful, not random. Regardless of the interpretation of the "error," however, substantial or statistically significant correlations between teacher behavior and student achievement are highly unlikely because of its magnitude.

One way of enhancing the reliability of teacher behavior is to form composites of teacher behaviors. This practice seems to have been begun by Jayne (1945) who composited seven behaviors (e.g., percent of thought questions, number of participations growing out of spontaneous pupil discussion) to form an "index of meaningful discussion." As expected, the reliability of the composite index was considerably higher as was its correlation with achievement in two separate studies. Unfortunately, the sign of the correlation was *opposite* in the two studies, being positive in the longer study (which lasted about one academic year and used a final achievement measure which included higher-level questions) and negative in the shorter study (which lasted less than one week and used a final achievement measure which included primarily factual recall questions).

In the Classroom Environment Study, the constructs served the same compositing function. However, although the reliability of the behavioral measures quite obviously increased, the correlations of the teaching, assessing/evaluating, and managing constructs with student achievement were neither substantial nor significant.

In view of the results of the Jayne Study and the Classroom Environment Study, alternative ways of dealing with the nature of classroom teaching must be considered if both the reliability of the measures and the magnitude of their correlations with student outcomes are to be increased. Several such ways currently exist. All center around the development of larger "units" of classroom teaching than the behavioral "unit."

The classroom activities included on the Snapshot instrument provide one example of larger "units." In fact, the eta square coefficients for the activity "lecture" ranged from 0.59 to 0.82 across studies, with a median eta square of 0.70. Similarly, for "review," "discourse," and "written seatwork" the median eta squares were 0.66, 0.67, and 0.57, respectively. The median eta squares for laboratory seatwork was quite low primarily because of its infrequent use in the mathematics and history classrooms. Thus, the time-worn concept of "teaching method" (Gage, 1969) apparently provides larger and more reliable units than does the "teaching behavior." Gump (1967) has included the classroom activity in a complex construct referred to an activity structure and has developed a theoretical framework within which to view the importance of activity structures.

Different "units" have been suggested by Rosenshine (Rosenshine 1983; Rosenshine and Stevens 1986) and Brophy (1981). They suggest a functional analysis of teacher behaviors. In a functional analysis, the organizing principle would be the intended or actual purpose or meaning of the behavior. All behaviors having the same intended or actual purpose or meaning would be termed "functionally equivalent" (Smith and Geoffrey 1968). Thus, all such behaviors would be placed in the same functional "unit." While an interesting concept, the determination of functionally equivalent behaviors remains problematic. At the same time, however, teaching functions as meaningful "units" would seem to have great promise if the methodological problems can be solved.

Finally, Good and Grouws (1979) suggest that the lesson can also be a meaningful "unit." Furthermore, they contend that lessons can be structured in such a way as to enhance student achievement. Quite likely, if a particular lesson structure is taught to teachers, as recommended by Good and Grouws, the lesson structure will remain fairly stable over time (or at least during the observations of those lessons). Recent data from Thailand, in fact, support the effect of a lesson structure quite similar to that recommended by Good and Grouws on student achievement (Nitsaisook 1987). Furthermore, the use of lesson-level data in the Classroom Environment Study increased the stability and predictive power of the conceptual models beyond that possible using class-level data.

The Nature of Paradigms on Teaching

The ways in which we view teaching and conceive studies of teaching are influenced largely by paradigms (Doyle, 1978) or ideologies (Popkewitz 1984). The paradigm within which Classroom Environment Study was conceived was the process-product paradigm (Doyle 1987). Thus, as has been mentioned in Chapters 3, 6, and 7, the constructs associated with teacher behaviors were the focal point of the conceptual model and resultant analyses.

Preliminary data analyses, however, suggested that data collected did not support the process-product paradigm (Ryan and Anderson 1984).

Part of the problem inherent in the process-product paradigm lies in the use of correlational and regression methods to analyze the data. One problem in examining the adequacy of the process-product paradigm (or any paradigm hypothesizing a direct relationship between teacher behavior and student learning) is the limit imposed by the maximum potential impact of "schooling" variables on gains in achievement and increases in attitudes.

Using "dummy variables" for classrooms, the results clearly indicated that no more than 38 percent of the achievement variation in any study could be attributed to "schooling" variables, no matter how they were defined or measured. In some studies, this maximum potential impact of "schooling" variables was about 15 percent. If final achievement were adjusted for differences in initial achievement, the maximum potential impact of "schooling" variables on student achievement decreased to a median of 13 percent. Thus, correlations between teacher behaviors and "residualized" student achievement greater than 0.35 could not be expected to occur with any reasonable frequency. When this result is combined with the inconsistency of teacher behavior mentioned in the previous section, correlations of 0.20 could be considered to be "large." Furthermore, when small sample sizes are used in studies of the process-product paradigm, the magnitude of the correlations can be effected greatly by a single classroom or teacher. Hence, the negative Q-square values in all countries.

If, either for conceptual or methodological reasons, the process-product paradigm is discarded, with what should it be replaced? The results of the Classroom Environment Study support an alternative paradigm, one which conforms most closely with what Doyle (1978) refers to as the "mediating process paradigm." In essence, this paradigm implies that the focus of classroom research should be on students rather than teachers. Several findings of the Classroom Environment Study support this paradigm.

First, the knowledge and aspirations students bring to the classroom are highly predictive of what they will ultimately learn and how they will feel about what they are being taught. To the extent that this knowledge and these aspirations are the result of early schooling experiences, schooling can be said to have a cumulative effect on student achievement and attitudes. Second, students' perceptions of their classrooms (in terms of task-orientation) are more predictive of their academic engagement as well as their final achievement, than are observers' records. Third, students' perceptions of their teachers (in terms of the structure these teachers provide for them) are somewhat predictive of their enjoyment of the subject matter being taught. Fourth, the behavioral categories of "silence" (during which students are supposedly engaged in work at their seats, desks, or tables) and "student initiation" (during which students are raising questions or contributing substantive comments to the classroom discussion) were positively related to student achievement in one or more of the studies. These findings emerged despite the fact that the observation instruments focused almost exclusively on teacher behaviors. Fifth, and finally, within the reduced class-level model, the more students engaged in class activities, or were "on-task," the greater the "residualized" student achievement.

While any one of these findings can be disputed with evidence from other studies, the composite points to the important role of students in their own learning. This role is hardly a novel concept. Almost forty years ago Tyler (1950) asserted that learning was dependent on the activities of the student, not those of the teacher. More recently Stayrook, Corno, and Winne (1978) concluded, based on the results of their study, that "student perceptions of teacher behavior can influence causal relationships in the classroom. It is recommended that future models of research on teaching include student mediating process variables" (p. 56).

That students' perceptions may differ from teachers' perceptions as well as observers' perceptions underlies the anthropological concept of triangulation as applied to the study of classrooms (Morine-Dershimer 1985). Differences between the perceptions of teachers and observers have been noted throughout this study (particularly in Chapter 4). Differences between the perceptions of observers and students also are evident. The results suggest that the perceptions of students (as well as their behavior in the classroom) are more predictive of their achievement than are the perceptions of observers, regardless of how "objective" they might be.

Interestingly, Doyle (1987) suggests that "the study of mediating processes would seem at its present stage, at least, to have limited utility for classroom teachers or teacher educators, although it probably will make important contributions to instructional design and methods" (p.119). Perhaps, instruction designed with students in mind and generic methods of instruction which are concerned with the "academic engagement" of the students will pay great dividends both in terms of our understanding and improvement of the teaching-learning process, far greater than our continued search for the "right" or "best" behaviors or practices.

One final note about paradigms and ideologies should be mentioned. Often when theorists and researchers speak of paradigms and ideologies they focus exclusively on those that define a research community. At the same time, however, individual teachers adhere to the premises of their own paradigms and ideologies. For example, teachers who believe in using whole class instruction because they are responsible for covering a certain amount of material per year are quite likely to use whole class instruction and cover as much material as possible. Similarly, teachers who believe that "slow" students should be taught at a slow pace are likely to cover fewer pages per school year and, as a consequence, provide less opportunity for their students to learn what is to be included on the "final" tests. The role of the "practical paradigm" or "practical ideology" in the nature of teaching is important if we are to understand and ultimately improve both teaching and learning.

The Design of Studies of Teaching

The results of the Classroom Environment Study shed much light on the ideal design of studies of classroms and classroom teaching. Several components of the ideal design can be described.

First, classrooms should be similar in terms of the initial ability or achievement of the students. Stated simply, the greater the differences in initial achievement or ability, the smaller the potential impact of "schooling" variables on final achievement.

Second, variables must be both conceptually sound and capable of being measured reliably before they are included in the design. Conceptual frameworks should be developed as part of the design of every study of classroom teaching. Conceptual frameworks serve a variety of useful functions, not the least of which is enhancing the meaning of the results of the study (Anderson and Burns, 1989).

Third, experimental studies may pay far greater dividends in terms of understanding and improving teaching and learning than correlational studies conducted in naturally-occurring classrooms. The results of the experimental study in Thailand (Nitsaisook, 1987) were far more positive than were the results of the Thai correlational study. Gage and Needels (1989) have summarized the results of several experimental studies with equally positive results.

Fourth, concerns for proper instrumentation must be addressed. In terms of measures of final achievement, differential validity can not be permitted. In the Classroom Environment Study, differential validity was estimated using judgmental or empirical estimates of opportunity to learn. The result was large differences among classrooms in the extent to which students in those classrooms had an opportunity to learn the knowledge and skills included on the final achievement test. Furthermore, in several of the countries included in final analysis, opportunity to learn was quite highly associated with student achievement.

Thus, at the very least, differences in validity or opportunity to learn constitute a serious threat to our ability to identify instructional or teaching variables associated with student achievement. As Anderson (1987b) has suggested, "if differences in curricula, instructional programs, or teaching are to be examined validly, differences in opportunity to learn must be controlled or estimated. In this context opportunity to learn is best considered (a potent) extraneous variable" (p. 371).

Fifth, several issues can be raised concerning the nature of classroom observation. One such issue is the appropriateness of structured observational instruments such as the FMI, SNAP, and IAR for use in classroom research.

Arguments can be and have been made for less structured instruments which attempt to capture the data in as "raw" form as possible. Examples are audiotape and videotape recordings and written narratives. To the extent that data are maintained in "raw" form they can be subjected to multiple analyses.

In many respects, then, the argument can be reduced to a distinction between categories used for *data recording* and those used for *data analysis*. Structured observations require *a priori* data recording categories; unstructured observations do not. With unstructured observations, on the other hand, data analytic categories can either be established *a priori* or *post hoc*. Whether such categories should guide observers' codings or guide the analysts' examination of the "raw" data would seem to depend on the experience and expertise of the observers or analysts. Whether these categories should be formed *a priori* or *post hoc* would seem to depend primarily on the knowledge one possesses when entering a given field of study. Simply stated, the more knowledge, the greater the likelihood of predetermined categories.

Another issue in classroom observation concerns the nature of the observational data. This question asks whether simply counting the number of behaviors observed results in the same understanding as considering the nature of those behaviors or the context in which the behaviors were exhibited. In general, the answer is "No." Frequency counts of behaviors are typically less informative than the "quality" of those behaviors or the "appropriateness" of the behaviors given the context in which they were exhibited.

At the same time, however, one must recognize that even those researchers who engage in "simple" counting of behaviors tended to count them within *qualitatively-distinct* categories. Consider the frequency of questions asked by teachers, for example. We know quite certainly that large numbers of questions are asked by large numbers of teachers in a variety of countries. This finding transcends the methodology used to study questioning. Differences among studies appear to exist in the categories of questions that are formed (whether *a priori* or *post hoc*). Furthermore, and both as expected and as appropriate, the categories formed seemed to depend on the purpose or purposes of the study. In the Classroom Environment Study, for example, the questioning categories included "recall" questions, "higher-order" questions, "opinion" questions, and "effectiveness" questions. In the Morine-Dershimer (1985) study, on the other hand, the questioning categories included "informative," "instructional," "routine interactive," or "no codable function."

The choice of observational instrument, whether a structured observational schedule or a television camera and video cassette recorder, is not trivial. It impacts quite clearly on the nature of the data gathered. In the Classroom Environment Study, for example, quite different estimates of academic engagement resulted from instruments that focused on groups as opposed to individual students. In general, group-focused instruments tended to over-estimate the extent to which students were engaged in the classroom activities. Furthermore, the median correlation between the two estimates was 0.570 in those five studies in which both were available.

A final issue concerning classroom observation concerns the different perspectives or points of view taken by those conducting the observations or analyzing the observational data. Quite typically, in structured observations the impact of differing perspectives or points of view are minimized by training all observers to "view" the classroom in a particular manner. The counter-argument is that people operating from multiple perspectives are needed to understand the complexities of the classroom. As has been mentioned earlier, people viewing the same phenomenon from different perspectives are likely to perceive it differently. Whether these different perspectives are confusing or enlightening is an issue that will likely be debated for some time.

The Subject Matter and Teaching

Stodolsky (1988) has written a book entitled *The Subject Matters*. Aside from being a clever play on words, there is a profound truth in the title that has been disregarded in classroom research in recent years. That fundamental truth is that the structure of the subject matter determines the nature of appropriate pedagogy. Recently, both Jackson (1986) and Shulman (1986) have argued in favor of this apparent truism.

Several aspects of the Classroom Environment Study support the impact of the subject matter on classroom teaching. First, more time was reportedly spent on mathematics than on science or history. One must remember that the studies were conducted primarily in self-contained elementary classrooms in which teachers had at least some control over what subjects were and were not taught, and for how long.

Second, across all studies approximately two-fifths of the teachers held a specialist's degree in the subject taught. In the Republic of Korea, however, over 80 percent of the teachers held a specialist's degree. Conversely, only one-fourth of the teachers in Israel had achieved that degree level. Science was taught in the Republic of Korea while ancient history was taught in Israel.

Third, a smaller proportion of recall questions (and, consequently, a larger proportion of higher-order and opinion questions) occurred in those countries in which science and history were taught. The vast majority of the questions asked in mathematics classrooms across all studies required students to recall what they had been taught.

Fourth, and quite obviously, the nature of seatwork differed according to the subject matter being taught. In mathematics, written seatwork predominated. In science, laboratory seatwork was quite apparent. Finally, only in history was reading seatwork evident at all.

Finally, lessons were more complex (in terms of the number of lesson segments) in the science lessons as compared with the mathematics lessons. Furthermore, lessons were more likely to end with a lecture or discourse segment in science, but with a seatwork segment in mathematics.

One may attribute some of these differences to country or cultural differences. It must be remembered, however, that many similarities in the teaching of science were noted between Hungary and the Republic of Korea. Furthermore, similarities in the teaching of mathematics were noted between Canada Ontario-English and Thailand.

Classroom Research and Teacher Training

Based on the results of the Classroom Environment Study one could speculate that teacher training which emphasizes teacher behaviors and teaching practices without also emphasizing the need to make decisions concerning why, when, and for how long to engage in those behaviors and practices is unlikely to produce effective teachers (Clark and Peterson 1986).

As a consequence, results of correlational research cannot and should not be translated directly into teacher education programs. It seems ludicrous to base programmatic decisions on variations in behaviors that account for, at best, 4 or 5 percent of the variation in student achievement (assuming a correlation near 0.20). Some theoretical basis or conceptual framework for such programs must be formed. At that point in time, an examination of all classroom research (including correlational studies) may help to clarify issues and decide among alternative paths available to the program developer.

In addition, with a particular framework, an examination of the frequencies with which behaviors occur may be at least as informative as an examination of the correlations themselves. If, for example, it is imperative that teachers help their students make the abstract concrete, the infrequent use of examples is indeed a weakness. Similarly, if teachers are to help students develop a set of thinking and reasoning strategies and skills, the infrequent use of opinion and higher-order questions becomes problematic. Finally, if teachers are to continually monitor the clarity and communication value of their explanations, then the limited use of effectiveness questions is a deficiency. Note, however, that frequent or infrequent uses of behaviors may be strengths or weaknesses depending on the conceptual framework.

Concerns for "proper" teacher education have been voiced at least since the Commonwealth Teacher Training Study (Charters and Waples 1929). In their introduction, Charters and Waples state that a "radical reorganization of the curricula of teaching-training institutions is demanded by a variety of conditions. Teacher-training curricula, like others, have been developed without clear definition of objectives and with no logical plan of procedure" (p. v). Despite the care taken to develop a "master-list of traits and illustrative trait actions found to be important for teachers of all types" and a "master-list of teachers' activities" which teachers did perform and ought to perform, few teacher-training curricula were affected permanently by the study.

The potential impact of the Classroom Environment Study on teacher-training curricula is likely to suffer the same fate as the Commonwealth Teacher Training Study. Nonetheless, the data reported in this study have much to say to those responsible for designing and implementing both pre-service and inservice teacher education.

A Final Comment

In most respects, the results of the Classroom Environment Study are neither novel nor earthshaking. Descriptively the results are similar to those presented by Goodlad (1984) in the United States. Some comparability with the results of Galton, Simon, and Croll (1980) in Great Britain also exists (see particularly Chapters 4 and 5). Classroom teaching would appear to be classroom teaching around the world.

Correlationally, the results were pre-ordained by Jayne (1945) and echoed by Dunkin and Biddle (1974). "Perhaps the greatest single flaw in much of the research we have reviewed is the persistent assumption that appears to underlie much of it—that teaching can somehow be reduced to a scalar value that can be indicated by a frequency of occurrence for some teaching behavior. We suspect ... that this simply is not true" (p. 353).

Undoubtedly, many people will be disappointed that the Classroom Environment Study did not result in the identification of a series of classroom activities and teacher behaviors that would virtually guarantee that teachers would teach better and students would learn more. Although we, like most educators, wish for simple, straightforward solutions to complex problems, such solutions are not readily available. Rather, both wise educators and increased knowledge are necessary. Our hope is that this volume has contributed to our knowledge; wisdom is beyond its scope.

References

Aitken M, Bennett S N, Hesketch J 1981 Teaching styles and pupil progress: A reanalysis. *Br. J. Educ. Psychol.* 51: 170-186.

Anderson L M, Evertson C, Brophy J 1979 An experimental study of effective teaching in first-grade reading groups. *Elem. Sch. J.* 79: 193-223.

Anderson L W 1982 *Models for Classroom Research.* Unpublished manuscript, University of South Carolina, Columbia.

Anderson L W 1984 Concerns for appropriate instrumentation in research on classroom teaching. *Eval. Educ.: Int. Rev. Series.* 8: 133-152.

Anderson L W 1987a The Classroom Environment Study: Teaching for learning. *Comp. Educ. Rev.* 31: 69-87.

Anderson L W 1987b Opportunity to learn. In: Dunkin M J (ed.) *International Encyclopedia of Teaching and Teacher Education.* Pergamon Press, Oxford.

Anderson L W, Burns R B 1989 *Research in Classrooms: The Study of Teachers, Teaching, and Instruction.* Pergamon Press, Oxford.

Andrews D F, Pregibon D 1978 Finding outliers that matter. *J. Roy. Stat. Soc.* 40: 85-93.

Areskoug, B 1982 The first canonical correlation: Theoretical PLS and simulation experiments. In: Joreskog K G, Wold H (eds.) *Systems Under Indirect Observation, Part II.* North-Holland Press, Amsterdam.

Avalos B 1983 *Preliminary Report on the Investigative Situation of the Participant Countries in the IEA Classroom Environment Study: Teaching for learning.* Ontario Institute for Studies in Education, Toronto.

Ball R J 1963 The significance of simultaneous methods of parameter estimation in econometric models. *Appl. Stat.* 12: 14-25.

Barr A S 1945 Some introductory comments. *J. Exp. Educ.* 14: 1-5.

Barr R, Dreeben R 1983 *How Schools Work.* University of Chicago Press, Chicago.

Bennett S N, Jordon J, Long G, Wade B 1976 *Teaching Styles and Pupil Progress.* Harvard University Press, Cambridge.

Block J H, Burns R B 1976 Mastery learning. In: Shulman L S (ed.) *Review of Research on Teaching, Volume 4.* F. E. Peacock, Itasca, Illinois.

Bloom B S 1976 *Human Characteristics and School Learning.* McGraw-Hill, New York.

Borg W, Ascione F 1979 Changing on-task, off-task, and disruptive pupil behavior in elementary mainstreaming classrooms. *J. Educ. Res.* 72: 243-252.

Borg W, Ascione F 1982 Classroom management in elementary mainstreaming classrooms. *J. Educ. Psychol.* 74: 85-95.

Brophy J 1981 Teacher praise: A functional analysis. *Rev. Educ. Res.* 51: 5-32.

Brophy J, Evertson C 1976 *Learning from Teaching: A Developmental Perspective.* Allyn and Bacon, Boston.

Brophy J, Evertson C 1978 Context variables in teaching. *Educ. Psych.* 12: 310-316.

Brophy J, Good T 1986 Teacher behavior and student achievement. In: Wittrock M C (ed.) *Handbook of research on teaching, 3rd edition.* Macmillan, New York.

Carroll J B 1975 *French as a Foreign Language in Seven Countries: An Empirical Study.* Almqvist and Wiksell, Stockholm.

Charters W W, Waples D 1929 *The Commonwealth Teacher-Training Study.* University of Chicago Press, Chicago.

Clark C, Gage N L, Marx R. Peterson P, Stayrook N. Winne P 1979 A factorial experiment on teacher structuring, soliciting, and reacting. *J. Educ. Psychol.* 71: 534-552.

Clark C, Peterson P L 1986 Teachers' thought processes. In: Wittrock M C (ed.) *Handbook of research on teaching, 3rd edition.* Macmillan, New York.

Cook R D, Weisberg S 1982 Criticism and influence analysis in regression. In: Leinhardt S (ed.) *Sociological Methodology.* Jossey-Bass, San Francisco.

Comber L C, Keeves J P 1973 *Science Education in Nineteen Countries: An Empirical Study.* John Wiley, New York.

Crawford J, Gage N L 1977 Developing a research-based teacher education program. *Cal. J. Teach. Educ.* 4: 105-123.

Crawford J, Gage N L, Corno L, Stayrook N, Mitman A, Schunk D, Stallings J 1978 *An Experiment on Teacher Effectiveness and Parent-Assisted Instruction in the Third Grade.* Center for Educational Research at Stanford (CERAS), Stanford, California.

Delamont S, Galton M 1986 *Inside the Secondary Classroom.* Routledge and Kegan Paul, London.

Dijkstra, T. K. 1981 Latent Variables in Linear Stochastic Models: Reflections on 'Maximum Likelihood' and 'Partial Least Squares' Methods. Doctoral thesis, University of Groningen, Groningen.

Doyle W 1978 Paradigms for research on teacher effectiveness. In: Shulman L S (ed.) *Review of Research in Education, Volume 5.* F. E. Peacock, Itasca, Illinois.

Doyle W 1987 Paradigms for research. In: Dunkin M J (ed.) *International Encyclopedia of Teaching and Teacher Education.* Pergamon Press, Oxford.

Draper N, John J A 1981 Influential observations and outliers in regression. *Technometrics,* 23: 21-26.

Duncan O D 1975 *Introduction to Structural Equation Models.* John Wiley, New York.

Dunkin M J, Biddle B J 1974 *The Study of Teaching.* Holt, Rinehart, and Winston, New York.

Emerson J D, Stoto M A 1982 Exploratory methods for choosing power transformations. *J. Am. Stat. Assoc.* 77: 102-108.

Emmer E, Evertson C, Anderson L M 1980 Effective classroom management at the beginning of the school year. *Elem. Sch. J.* 80: 219-231.

Evertson C, Anderson C, Anderson L M, Brophy J 1980 Relationships between classroom behaviors and student outcomes in junior high mathematics and English classes. *Am. Educ. Res. J.* 17: 43-60.

Evertson C, Veldman D 1981 Changes over time in process measures of classroom behavior. *J. Educ. Psych.* 73: 156-163.

Evertson C, Emmer E 1982 Effective management at the beginning of the school year in junior high classes. *J. Educ. Psychol.* 74: 485-498.

Farnen R F, Marklund S, Oppenheim A N, Torney J V 1976 *Civic Education in Ten Countries: An Empirical Study.* Almqvist and Wiksell, Stockholm.

Fisher C, Filby N, Marliave R, Cahen L, Dishaw M, Moore J, Berliner D 1978 *Teaching Behaviors, Academic Learning Time, and Student Achievement: Final Report of Phase III-B, Beginning Teacher Evaluation Study.* Far West Laboratory for Educational Research and Development, San Francisco.

Fisher F M 1970 A correspondence principle for simultaneous equation models. *Econometrica, 38,* 73-92.

Gage N L 1972 *Teacher Effectiveness and Teacher Education.* Pacific Books, Palo Alto.

Gage N L 1978 *The Scientific Basis for the Art of Teaching.* Teachers College Press, New York.

Gage N L, Needels M C 1989 Process-product research on teaching: A review of the criticisms. *Elem. Sch. J. 89:* 253-300.

Gage N L 1969 Teaching methods. In: Ebel R L (ed.) *Encyclopedia of Educational Research, Fourth Edition.* Macmillan, New York.

Galton M, Simon B, Croll P 1980 *Inside the Primary Classroom.* Routledge and Kegan Paul, London.

Geisser S 1974 A predictive approach to the random effects model. *Biometrika, 61,* 101-107.

Goldberger A S 1964 *Econometric theory.* John Wiley, New York.

Goldstein J, Weber W 1979 *Managerial Behaviors of Elementary School Teachers and On-task Behavior.* Paper presented at the annual meeting of the American Educational Research Association, San Francisco.

Good T, Grouws D 1977 Teaching effects: A process-product study in fourth-grade mathematics classrooms. *J. Teach. Educ.* 28: 49-54.

Good T, Grouws D 1979 The Missouri Mathematics Effectiveness Project: An experimental study in fourth-grade classrooms. *J. Educ. Psychol.* 71: 355-362.

Goodlad, J I 1984 *A Place Called School.* McGraw-Hill, New York.

Gump P V 1967 *The Classroom Behavior Setting: Its Nature and Relation to Student Behavior.* Midwest Psychological Field Station, University of Kansas, Lawrence.

Hausser, R M 1973 Disaggregating a social-psychological model of educational attainment. In: Goldberger A S, Duncan, O D (eds.) *Structural Equation Models in the Social Sciences.* Seminar Press, New York.

Helmke A, Schneider W, Weinert F W 1986 Quality of instruction and classroom learning outcomes—Results of the German contribution to the Classroom Environment Study of the IEA. *Teaching and Teach. Educ.* 2: 1-18.

Hocking. R. R. 1983 Developments in Linear Regression Methodology: 1959-1982 (with discussion). *Technometrics, 25*(3), 219-230.

Hui B S, Wold H 1982 Consistency and consistency at large of partial least squares estimates. In: Joreskog K G, Wold H (eds.) *Systems under Indirect Observation, Part II.* North-Holland Press, Amsterdam.

Husen T (ed.) 1967 *International Study of Achievement in Mathematics: A Comparison of Twelve Countries.* John Wiley, New York.

Jackson P W 1968 *Life in Classrooms.* Holt, Rinehart, and Winston, New York.

Jackson P W 1986 *The Practice of Teaching.* Teachers College Press, New York.

Jayne C D 1945 A study of the relationship between teaching procedures and educational outcomes. *J. Exp. Educ.* 14: 101-134.

Joreskog K G 1973 A general method for estimating a linear structural equation system. In: Goldberger A S, Duncan O D (eds.) *Structural Equation Models in the Social Sciences.* John Wiley, New York.

Joreskog K G 1979 Basic Ideas of Factor and Component Analysis. In: Joreskog K G and Sorbom D (eds.) *Advances in Factor Analysis and Structural Equation Models.* Abt Books, Cambridge, Mass., pp. 5-20.

Joreskog K G, Wold H 1982 The ML and PLS techniques for modeling with latent variables: Historical and comparative aspects. In: Joreskog K G , Wold H (eds.) *Systems under Indirect Observation, Part I.* North-Holland Press, Amsterdam.

Keesling J W, Wiley D E 1974 Regression Models for Hierarchial Data. Paper presented at the annual meeting of the Psychometric Society, Stanford, California.

Kounin J 1970 *Discipline and Group Management in Classrooms.* Holt, Rinehart, and Winston, New York.

Levin T, Gasner A, Libman Z, Maharshak R 1977 *Trends and Findings in Classroom Environment Research, Research Report No. 1.* School of Education, Tel Aviv.

Levin T 1981 *Effective Instruction.* Association for Supervision and Curriculum Development, Alexandria, Virginia.

Lewis E G 1975 *English as a Foreign Language in Ten Countries: An Empirical Study.* Almqvist and Wiksell, Stockholm.

Lohmoeller J B 1981 *LVPLS 1.6 Program Manual.* Hochschule der Bundeswehr, Research Report No. 81.04, Munich.

Lohmoeller J B 1984 *The Basic Principles of Model Building.* Paper presented at the Thirteenth International Conference on the Unity of the Sciences, Washington, D.C.

Mandeville G K 1984 Reanalyzing teaching research data: Problems and promises. *Eval. in Educ.: Int. Rev. Series.* 8: 153-166.

McDonald F, Elias P, Stone M, Wheeler P, Lambert N, Calfee R, Sandoval J, Ekstrom R, Lockheed M 1975 *Final Report of Phase II, Beginning Teacher Evaluation Study.* Educational Testing Service, Princeton.

Miller R G 1974 The jackknife—a review. *Biometrika.* 61: 1-15.

Morine-Dershimer G 1985 *Talking, Listening, and Learning in Elementary Classrooms.* Longman, New York.

Nitsaisook M 1987 *The Classroom Environment Study, Phase 2: The Experimental Study.* Department of Teacher Education, Ministry of Education, Bangkok.

Noonan R, Wold H 1983 Evaluating school systems using Partial Least Squares. *Eval. in Educ.: Int. Rev. Series.* 7: entire.

Peacock E, Weber W 1980 *Training in Classroom Management and the Managerial Behaviors of Teachers.* Paper presented at the annual meeting of the American Educational Research Association, Boston.

Popkewitz T S 1984 *Paradigm and Ideology in Educational Research.* The Falmer Press, London.

Purves A C 1973 *Literature Education in Ten Countries: An Empirical Study.* John Wiley, New York.

Rosenshine B 1976 Classroom instruction. In: Gage N L (ed.) *The Psychology of Teaching Methods.* University of Chicago Press, Chicago.

Rosenshine B 1978 Academic engaged time, content covered, and direct instruction. *J. Educ.* 160: 38-66.

Rosenshine B 1979 Content, time, and direct instruction. In: Peterson P L, Walberg H J (eds.) *Research on Teaching: Concepts, Findings, and Implications.* McCutchan, Berkeley.

Rosenshine B 1983 Teaching functions in instructional programs. *Elem. Sch. J.* 83: 335-351.

Rosenshine B, Stevens R 1986 Teaching functions. In: Wittrock M C (ed.) *Handbook of Research on Teaching, 3rd edition.* Macmillan, New York.

Ryan D W 1981 *An Organizing Framework for the IEA Classroom Environment Study.* Unpublished manuscript, O.I.S.E., Toronto.

Ryan D W, Anderson L W 1984 Rethinking research on teaching: Lessons learned from an international study. *Eval. Educ.: Int. Rev. Series.* 8:83-178.

Sanford J, Evertson C 1981 Classroom management in low SES junior high schools: Three case studies. *J. Teach. Educ.* 32: 34-38.

Schieber N 1983 *PLSPATH Version A: Program Manual.* University of Hamburg, Department of Education, Hamburg.

Sellin N 1985a *Model building in research on classroom instruction: An application of Partial Least Squares to data from the IEA Classroom Environment Study.* Paper presented at the Annual Meeting of the American Educational Research Association, Chicago.

Sellin N 1985b *PLSPATH Version B.1—Subprogram PLSRAW: A modified and extended version of Lohmoeller's LVPLSX.* University of Hamburg, Department of Education, Hamburg.

Shulman L S 1986 Those who understand: Knowledge growth in teaching. *Educ. Res.* 15(2): 4-14.

Smith L, Geoffrey W 1968 *The Complexities of an Urban Classroom.* Holt, Rinehart, and Winston, New York.

Soar R, Soar R 1976 An attempt to identify measures of teacher effectiveness from four studies. *J. Teach. Educ.* 27: 261-267.

Stallings J 1976 *Learning to Look.* Wadworth Publishing Company, Belmont, California.

Stallings J, Kaskowitz D 1974 *Follow-Through Classroom Observation Evaluation, 1972-1973.* Stanford Research Institute, Stanford.

Stallings J, Needels M, Stayrook N 1979 *How to Change the Process of Teaching Basic Reading Skills in Secondary Schools: Phase II and Phase III.* SRI International, Menlo Park.

Stayrook N G, Corno L, Winne P H 1978 Path analyses relating student perceptions of teacher behavior to student achievement. *J. Teach. Educ.* 29: 51-56.

Stodolsky S S 1988 *The Subject Matters.* University of Chicago Press, Chicago.

Stone M 1984 Cross-validatory choice and assessment of statistical predictions. *J. Roy. Stat. Soc.* 36: 111-147.

Thorndike R L 1973 *Reading Comprehension Eduation in Fifteen Countries: An Empirical Study.* John Wiley, New York.

Travers R M W (ed.) 1973 *Second Handbook of Research on Teaching.* Rand McNally, Chicago.

Tukey J 1977 *Exploratory Data Analysis.* Addison-Wesley, Reading, Massachusetts.

Tyler R W 1950 *Basic Principles of Curriculum.* University of Chicago, Chicago.

Van den Wollenberg A L 1977 Redundancy Analysis: An Alternative for Canonical Correlation Analysis. *Psychometrika, 42*(2), 207-219.

Wiley D E 1975 Another Hour Another Day. In: Hauser R M, Sewell W H, and Alwin D (eds.) *Schooling and Achievement in American Society.* Stanford University. Stanford, California.

Wold H 1975 Path models with latent variables: The NIPALS approach. In: Blalock H M (ed.) *Quantitative Sociology.* Seminar Press, New York.

Wold H 1979 *Model Construction and Evaluation when Theoretical Knowledge is Scarce, Cahier 79.06.* University of Geneva, Department of Econometrics, Geneva.

Wold H 1982 Soft modelling: The basic design and some extensions. In: Joreskog K G, Wold H (eds.) *Systems under Indirect Observation, Part II.* North-Holland Press, Amsterdam.

Appendix A

National Reports and Related Publications

Australia
Fordham, A. M. *The context of teaching and learning.* Hawthorn, Victoria: ACER, 1983.
Bourke, S. F. *The teaching and learning of mathematics.* Hawthorn, Victoria: ACER, 1984.
Bourke, S. F. The study of classroom contexts and practices. *Teaching and Teacher Education*, 1985, *1*, 33-50.

Canada Ontario-English
Ryan, D. W., Hildyard, A., Jantzi, D., Pike, R., and Hanna, G. *The Ontario IEA Classroom Environment Study.* Toronto: OISE, 1985.

Canada Ontario-French
Churchill, S., Frenette, N., and Hanna, G. *La classe et son environment dans les écoles franco-ontariennes.* Toronto: Ministère de l'education, microfiche ONO 3519, 1986.

Canada Quebec
Leclerc, M., Bertrand, R., Maunsell, E., and Theaume, D. *Classroom Environment Study: Correlational Phase (IEA).* Document R-159. Ste-Foy, Quebec: INRS-Education, 1983.
Bertrand, R. and Leclerc, M. Reliability of observational data on teaching practices in secondary school mathematics. *Teaching and Teacher Education*, 1985, *1*, 187-198.
Leclerc, M., Bertrand, R., and Dufour, N. Correlations between teaching practices and class achievement in introductory algebra. *Teaching and Teacher Education*, 1986, *2*, 355-365.

Federal Republic of Germany
Helmke, A., Schneider, W., and Weinert, F. E. Quality of instruction and classroom learning outcomes. Results of the German contribution to the Classroom Environment Study of the IEA. *Teaching and Teacher Education*, 1986, *2*, 1-18.
Helmke, A. and Schrader, F.W. Interactional effects of instructional quality and teacher judgment accuracy and achievement. *Teaching and Teacher Education*, 1987, *3*, 91-98.

Hungary
Joo, A. *The IEA Classroom Environment Study.* Budapest: Center for Evaluation, National Institute of Education, 1985.

Korea
Huh, Un-na. *IEA Classroom Environment Study—Interim Report I.* Seoul: KEDI, 1982.
Hun, Un-na. *IEA Classroom Environment Study—Interim Report II.* Seoul: KEDI, 1983.

The Netherlands
Tomic, W. *Docentgedrag en leerresultaten (Teacher behavior and learning outcomes).* Enskede: W. Tomic en Grafoplan, 1985.

Thailand
Nitsaisook, M. *Classroom Environment Study, Phase I: The correlational study.* Bangkok: Department of Teacher Education, Ministry of Education, 1985.

Appendix B

An Overview of Partial Least Squares (PLS) Analysis

The Partial Least Squares (PLS) algorithm developed by H. Wold (see Wold 1975, 1979, 1982) is a general technique for estimating path models involving latent constructs indirectly observed by multiple indicators. The key feature of PLS is the explicit estimation of latent variable scores by means of Least Squares methods. This has considerable advantages. Three points should be noted. (1) Based on Least Squares, PLS is technically simple, speedy on the computer and, most important, does not require stringent distributional assumptions. (2) No identification problems arise if the specified model is recursive. For nonrecursive models, the well-known classical conditions of identifiability (i.e., rank and order condition) can be applied so that identification is rarely a problem. (3) The PLS algorithm provides estimated case values of latent variables which can be used for testing purposes and case oriented analyses. It is, for example, possible to employ distribution-free statistical methods, such as jackknifing (Tukey 1977), in order to evaluate PLS modeling results.

It is beyond the scope of this appendix to present the PLS algorithm in great detail. Reference is made to Wold (1982) for a comprehensive and thorough exposition of PLS. Simulation experiments focusing on statistical properties of PLS parameter estimates have been reported by Hui and Wold (1982) and Areskoug (1982), among others. For the purposes of this paper it will suffice to review briefly three aspects of PLS modeling, namely the formal specification, the estimation, and the evaluation of PLS models. For the sake of simplicity, the presentation will be restricted to what Wold (1982) calls the basic PLS design.

Formal Specification

A PLS model is formally defined by two sets of linear equations, called the *inner model* and the *outer model*. The inner model specifies the hypothesized relationships among latent variables (LVs), and the outer model specifies the relationships between LVs and observed or manifest variables (MVs). Without loss of generality, it can be assumed that LVs and MVs are scaled to zero

This appendix was written by Norbert Sellin.

means so that location parameters can be discarded in the equations that follow. The inner model equation can be written as:

$$\eta = B\eta + \Gamma\xi + \zeta \qquad (1)$$

where η symbolizes a $(g \times n)$ matrix of endogenous LVs and ξ a $(h \times n)$ matrix of exogenous LVs, with n denoting the number of cases. B and Γ denote $(g \times g)$ and $(g \times h)$ coefficient matrices, respectively, and ζ represents the $(g \times n)$ matrix of inner model residuals. The basic PLS design assumes a recursive inner structure. The endogenous LVs can then be arranged in such a way that B is lower triangular with zero diagonal elements. The inner model equation (1) is subject to *predictor specification:*

$$E(\eta|\eta\xi) = B\eta + \Gamma\xi \qquad (2)$$

which implies $E(\xi\zeta') = 0$ and $E(\eta\zeta') = \zeta\zeta'$, with $\zeta\zeta'$ being a $(g \times g)$ diagonal matrix. That is, the inner model is assumed to constitute a causal chain system with uncorrelated residuals.

The outer model equations are given by:

$$x = \Pi_x\xi + \epsilon_x \qquad (3a)$$
$$y = \Pi_y\eta + \epsilon_y \qquad (3b)$$

where x and y denote $(k \times n)$ and $(m \times n)$ matrices of MVs. Π_x and Π_y represent $(k \times h)$ and $(m \times g)$ coefficient matrices, while ϵ_x and ϵ_y symbolize the matrices containing outer model residuals. In the basic PLS design, the MVs are assumed to be grouped into *disjoint blocks*, with each block representing one LV. That is, each MV is assumed to belong to just one LV and, hence, each row of Π_y and Π_x is assumed to contain just one non-zero entry. The non-zero elements of Π_x and Π_y are called *loadings*. Since both the loadings and the LVs are unknown, some standardization is necessary to avoid scale ambiguity. As a general rule, all LVs are assumed to be standardized to unit variance; i.e., $\text{VAR}(\xi_h) = \text{VAR}(\eta_g) = 1.0$. Similar to the inner model, predictor specification is adopted for the outer model equations. For example, predictor specification applied to equation (3b) gives:

$$E(y|\eta) = \Pi_y\eta \qquad (4)$$

with $E(\eta\epsilon'_y) = E(\xi\epsilon'_y) = E(\zeta\epsilon'_y) = 0$. In words, the outer model residuals are assumed to be uncorrelated with the LVs and with the inner model residuals.

In addition to predictor specification applied to inner model and outer model equations, a fundamental principle of PLS modeling is the assumption that all information between observables is exclusively conveyed by latent constructs. This has two implications, namely (a) that PLS models do not involve any direct relationships among MVs, and (b) that the outer residuals of one block are assumed to be uncorrelated with the outer residuals of all other blocks.

The formal specification of PLS models also includes relations for substitutive prediction of endogenous MVs. The corresponding relations are obtained when the inner model equation (1) is used to substitute the endogenous LVs involved in the outer model equation (3b). This gives:

$$y = \Pi_y(B\eta + \Gamma\xi) + \nu \tag{5}$$

with $\nu = \Pi_y\zeta + \epsilon_y$. Wold (1982) calls this *substitutive elimination of latent variables* or briefly SELV. As can be seen from equation (5), the SELV relation connects endogenous MVs with LVs that are *indirectly* connected (via the inner model) with the respective sets of MVs. The ensuing residuals are, in virtue of equations (2) and (4) above, uncorrelated with the corresponding predictor LVs.

Model Estimation

The above equations and the accompanying set of assumptions constitute the structural or theoretical form of PLS models. The LVs, the inner model coefficients and the loadings are, of course, unknown and must be estimated. The PLS parameter estimation proceeds in two steps. The first step involves the iterative estimation of LVs as linear composites of their associated MVs. The second step involves the non-iterative estimation of inner model coefficients and loadings. The estimated LVs are defined as:

$$\text{est.}(\eta) = X = W_X x \tag{6a}$$
$$\text{est.}(\xi) = Y = W_y y \tag{6b}$$

where W_X and W_y represent $(h \times k)$ and $(g \times m)$ weight matrices, with non-zero weights corresponding to the grouping of MVs into $g + h$ disjoint blocks. The matrices X and Y contain estimated LV scores which are standardized so as to give each LV unit variance.

The estimated LVs defined above are in the second step of PLS estimation used to estimate the loadings and the inner model coefficients by means of standard least squares methods. The loadings are obtained by regressing each MV on its associated LV-estimate. That is, the PLS loadings are estimated as covariances or, in case of standardized MVs, as zero-order correlations between each MV and the corresponding LV estimate. The inner model coefficients are estimated using standard path analytical procedures. That is, for recursive inner models, the respective coefficients are obtained by ordinary least squares (OLS) regression applied to each inner model equation separately.

The core of the PLS procedure is obviously the determination of the weights defining LV estimates. These weights are obtained iteratively by a series of either simple or multiple OLS regressions applied to each block of MVs. The investigator has the choice between two modes of weight estimation, called *outward* mode and *inward* mode. It may be noted that the distinction between outward and inward blocks corresponds to the differentiation between reflective and formative indicators made by Hausser (1973). Reflective or outward indicators are assumed to "reflect" the corresponding latent construct. A typical example would be a set of attitude items assumed to reflect an underlying attitudinal dimension. Formative or inward indicators, on the other hand, are assumed to "form" or "produce" a latent construct. An example would be a set of teacher behaviors assumed to form a specific teaching style.

The specification of the inner model, the block structure (i.e., the grouping of MVs into $g + h$ disjoint blocks), and the estimation mode to be applied to each block together constitute what can be called the PLS iteration model. The iteration model specifies the way in which the estimation of a given PLS model proceeds.

Since it is not possible here to give a description of the PLS iteration procedure, the reader is referred to Wold (1982) for a detailed exposition of PLS weight estimation. Suffice it to say that the estimation of outward blocks is based on an iterative sequence of simple OLS regressions where the respective MVs are considered as dependent variables. The estimation of inward blocks is based on multiple OLS regression where the MVs are used as independent variables. It should also be noted that the PLS algorithm incorporates, as special cases, principal components and canonical correlations. As shown by Wold (1975), one-block PLS models estimated by the outward mode are numerically and analytically equivalent to the first principle component, while the first canonical correlation is obtained from two-block PLS models when both blocks are estimated by the inward mode. Since the general features of principle component and canonical correlation analysis can be expected to carry over to multi-block PLS models, it is a general advice to use the inward mode for exogenous LVs and the outward mode for endogenous LVs in order to increase the predictive power of the corresponding inner model and outer model relations. Such statistical considerations may occasionally overrule theoretical assumptions with regard to reflective and formative measurement relations.

Model Evaluation

PLS can be characterized as a "prediction oriented" approach. This is because the PLS procedure basically aims at optimal least squares prediction of endogenous LVs and MVs. It will also be recalled that predictor specification as applied to inner and outer model relationships constitutes an integral part of the structural form of PLS models. Hence, in addition to the examination of point estimates (i.e, loadings, weights, and inner model coefficients), an important part of model evaluation is the examination of fit indices reflecting the predictive power of estimated inner and outer model relationships. Three descriptive fit indices can be derived from the inner and outer model equations given earlier. (1) R^2 values can be computed for each inner model equation. (2) The squared correlations between MVs and their associated LV estimates can be used to assess the predictive power of outer model relations. Following factor analytic terminology, these indices are commonly called "communalities." (3) Similar to the computation of communalities, squared correlations can also be calculated from relations derived by substitutive prediction. These indices are called "redundancies" and can be interpreted as indicating the joint predictive power of inner and outer model relations.

The statistics referred to above can be used in essentially the same way as the familiar R^2 computed for multiple regression equations. They reflect the relative amount of "explained" or "reproduced" variance of LVs and MVs. The researcher will usually wish to go beyond evaluating predictive relations in purely descriptive terms, however. One option is to adopt the distributional assumptions on which the computation of classical estimates of standard errors and corresponding F-tests are based and to apply standard significance tests. This approach has been used by Noonan and Wold (1983), for example. It must be emphasized, however, that the classical distributional assumptions, notably normality and independence of residuals, do not constitute prerequisites of PLS estimation. It may therefore be inappropriate to adopt them *post hoc* in order to evaluate the model results. In practice, it is also often the case that the classical assumptions would appear highly unrealistic so that it would be nonsense to employ standard test statistics.

Since PLS provides estimated case values of LVs and estimated case values of inner and outer residuals, less demanding statistical techniques can be used. As an alternative to conventional statistical tests, Wold (1982) proposed the general use of the Stone-Geisser test (SG-test) of predictive relevance (Stone 1974; Geisser 1974). The SG-test basically produces jackknife estimates of residual variances while jackknife standard errors of point estimates can be obtained as a by-product. The general idea is to omit or "blindfold" one case at a time, to re-estimate the model parameters on the basis of the remaining cases, and to reconstruct or predict omitted case values on the basis of the re-estimated parameters. An adaptation of Ball's (1963) Q^2 can then serve as the test criterion. As applied to $i = 1, 2, \ldots, n$ cases and to the familiar case of multiple OLS regression, Q^2 is defined as:

$$Q^2 = 1.0 - \{ \Sigma \, n \, (Y_i - X_i b_{(i)})^2 \}/\{ \Sigma_n (Y_i - \overline{Y}_{(i)})^2 \} \qquad (7)$$

where Y_i denotes the ith case value of the dependent variable and X_i the row vector of the ith case values of, say, k predictor variables. $\overline{Y}_{(i)}$ represents the jackknife mean of Y (i.e., the mean when the ith case is omitted), and $b_{(i)}$ is the $(k \times 1)$ coefficient vector obtained when the ith case is exempted from estimation. From equation (7) it can be seen that Q^2 is nothing else than a jackknife analogue of the familiar R^2. The tested model equation has more predictive relevance the higher Q^2 is, and model modifications, such as the deletion of predictor variables, can be evaluated by comparing Q^2 values. It should be noted that, contrary to R^2, Q^2 values may increase when predictors are deleted. This indicates, intuitively speaking, that "noise" emanating from irrelevant predictors or instability of parameter estimation has been removed. Q^2 values may also turn out to be negative. The specified model is then said to be misleading because the trivial prediction in terms sample means is superior to the prediction derived from the tested model relation.

The SG-test allows straightforward extension to PLS models (see, for example, Lohmoeller 1981; Wold 1982; Sellin 1985a). The corresponding procedures provide indices of the predictive relevance of inner and outer model relations as well as jackknife standard errors of PLS parameter estimates that can be used for testing purposes.

Comparative Comments on PLS and LISREL

As pointed out by Wold (1982), PLS and LISREL are complementary rather than competitive estimation methods of the same type of path models. The LISREL approach assumes that observations are governed by a specified multivariate distribution and offers, on this basis, a general framework for (a) maximum likelihood estimation, (b) hypothesis testing leading to either rejection or non-rejection of the tested model, and (c) assessment of standard errors for the parameters. In practice, the most problematical aspect of LISREL concerns the distributional assumptions on which model testing is based. Least squares estimation, including PLS, is distribution free except for predictor specification. As compared with LISREL, the complementary characteristics of PLS are (a) least squares estimation by means of the PLS algorithm, (b) tests of predictive relevance leading to either non-relevance or some positive degree of predictive relevance, and (c) jackknife estimation of standard errors (see Noonan and Wold 1983, pp. 286-288). In general, PLS is useful in research situations where exploratory model analyses without restrictive distributional assumptions would seem appropriate. LISREL, on the other hand, is a powerful and highly flexible statistical tool in situations where distributional assumptions would seem justified and where theoretical knowledge is strong so that a confirmatory analysis strategy is in order. It should be noted, however, that PLS may still be operational in situations where LISREL can not be used. These include the analysis of large and complex path models where LISREL often fails to converge within reasonable time limits as well as model analyses based on small data sets where the sample covariance matrix is not positive definite (e.g., when the number of MVs exceeds the number of cases).

Appendix C

Examples of Exploratory Model Analyses

This appendix has three purposes: (1) to present a fairly detailed illustration of the application of PLS in the analysis of influences of schooling variables; (2) to illustrate the use of jackknife techniques for improving and evaluating PLS models; and (3) to highlight some general principles and problems of the analyses that were undertaken. The following presentation is based on data collected in the Netherlands although any of the other countries' data sets could have been used.

As used in multivariate analyses, the Netherlands' data set comprised 47 eighth-grade mathematics classes. Each class was observed on eight occasions resulting in a total number of 376 observed lessons. In what follows, several PLS models estimated on the basis of the Netherlands' data will be considered to illustrate different steps in exploratory analyses.

As a point of departure, however, it is instructive to examine a multiple regression example. Table C.1 displays the results of a multiple regression of the observers' rating of the percentage of academically engaged students (as derived from the SNAP) on twelve observational variables. All these variables have, in terms of standard statistical tests, significant correlations (at the 5 percent level) with the criterion. As with all analyses presented in this appendix, the multiple regression was undertaken using classes as units of investigation.

Table C.1 displays for each predictor variable the standardized regression coefficient (Beta), the corresponding zero-order correlation with the criterion variable (Corr), and the change in the value of R-square if the predictor variable would be included last in the multiple regression equation (Delta R-square). The table also displays so-called tolerance indices defined as the squared multiple correlation of a given predictor variable with the remaining set of predictors. These indices reflect the amount of collinearity within the set of twelve predictor variables. That is, the higher the tolerance indices the larger the amount of collinearity associated with specific predictors. As can be seen from the tolerance indices presented in Table C.1, a great deal of multicollinearity exists in the data. This multicollinearity is partly due to the small number of cases involved in the multiple regression (47 classes) and partly a consequence of analytical and empirical relationships among predictor variables. For example, the variables "redirecting question" and "acknowledge correct answer" must obviously be closely related to the variable "teacher to

317

TABLE C.1   *Multiple regression of SNAP rating of academic*
engagement on twelve observational variables
The Netherlands, $N = 47$ classes

Predictor	Beta	Corr	Delta R^2	Tolerance
Lecture/Explain/Demonstrate	203	392	018	577
Seatwork Written Assignment	121	− 495	002	838
Teacher Interacting	013	432	000	780
Social Interactions	191	− 275	024	345
Verbal Lecture	− 054	− 336	002	398
Lecture with Materials	124	317	003	784
Redirect Question	− 107	328	005	577
Acknowledge Correct Answer	147	394	012	463
Teacher to Student Questions	140	444	005	737
Student to Teacher Questions	− 077	− 331	004	356
Procedural Interactions	− 348	− 515	081	327
Disciplinary Activities	− 562	− 673	159	497
R-square	698			
Q-square	377			

Notes: The data displayed in this table and in all other tables and figures in this appendix were from the Netherlands, with 47 classes. All coefficients are multiplied by 1,000 in all tables and figures. The measure of academic engagement was taken from the Snapshot instrument. Beta refers to the standardized regression co-efficient. Corr refers to the zero-order correlation with academic engagement. Delta is the increase in R-square if a given predictor variable is added last to the regression equation. Tolerance is a collinearity index defined as the multiple correlation of each predictor variable with the other 11 predictor variables.

student question." The more questions asked, the more likely teachers will redirect questions or acknowledge correct answers. In fact, the corresponding zero-order correlations were 0.59 and 0.48, respectively. Primarily because of the high degree of collinearity among predictor variables, the multiple regression produced uninterpretable results. The data presented in Table C.1, then, constitute a superb example of possible multicollinearity effects in multiple regression.

It should be noted at this point that collinearity among observational variables was by no means unique to the Netherlands' data considered in this appendix. Although the multiple regression presented above constitutes a somewhat extreme case, much the same multicollinearity problems were encountered in all data sets when similar analyses were undertaken.

The multicollinearity problems referred to above were also reflected by the large difference between the R-square and the Q-square values included in Table C.1. The R-square value is equal to 0.698 and the Q-square value is equal to 0.377. As explained in Appendix B, the Q-square statistic can be interpreted as a jackknife analogue of the familiar R-square; it is obtained by re-estimating a given regression equation N times (that is, 47 times in the present case), each time omitting just one case. The ratio of Q-square to

R-square can be used to assess the relative amount of "noise" or instability in the regression. For the present example this ratio is equal to 0.54. This indicates that the regression involves about 46 percent "noise"" due to the instability of coefficient estimates when single cases are excluded from the estimation. In the present case, this noise was primarily due to the multi-collinearity among predictor variables, as can be illustrated by the statistics presented in Table C.2.

TABLE C.2 *Multiple regression of SNAP rating of academic engagement results of backward exploration*

Step	Deleted Predictor	R^2	Q^2	$D(R^2)$	$D(Q^2)$	Q^2/R^2
0	—	698	377	-	-	540
1	Teacher Interacting	698	408	000	031	584
2	Verbal Lecture	696	438	− 002	030	629
3	Student to Teacher Questions	693	451	− 003	014	651
4	Seatwork Written Assignment	687	468	− 006	017	681
5	Lecture with Materials	685	497	− 003	029	726
6	Acknowledge Correct Answer	674	506	− 011	009	751
7	Redirect Question	658	486	− 011	− 020	739
8	Teacher to Student Questions	645	487	− 012	001	755
9	Social Interactions	632	490	− 013	003	775
10	Lecture/Explain/Demonstrate	577	468	− 055	− 022	811
11	Procedural Interactions	453	346	− 124	− 122	764

Notes: D(R-square) and D(Q-square) denote the differences between the statistics at step $k + 1$ and step k. The single variable that remained the regression equation at the last step 11 was "disciplinary activities".

Table C.2 displays the results from an exploration routine designed to examine regression models in terms of changes of Q-square values if single predictors are deleted from a given equation. This routine operates in much the same way as the familiar stepwise regression procedure. The results shown in Table C.2 were produced using a "backward elimination" algorithm. At each step of the exploration the equation was evaluated in terms of the change of the Q-square statistic if just one predictor variable was deleted. The predictor variable which produced the minimum increase or maximum decrease of Q-square was eliminated at each step and the regression equation was then re-estimated. This elimination process was continued until just one predictor variable was left. For example, in Table C.2 it can be seen that the variable "teacher interacting" was excluded at the first step of the analysis because this resulted in the largest increase of Q-square (from 0.377 to 0.408). The variable "procedural interactions" was excluded at the last step (Step 11). At this point only the variable "disciplinary activities" remained in the equation.

In Table C.2 it can be seen that the Q-square values increased up to the sixth step when six predictor variables were excluded from the initial equation. The Q-square value at this step (0.506) was considerably higher than the initial Q-square value of 0.377. This increase of Q-square values when predictors are deleted is typical for regression models involving a great deal of collinearity. Furthermore, even at the tenth step the Q-square (0.468) is still higher than the initial value of 0.377. At this step, only the variables "procedural interaction" and "disciplinary activities" remained in the regression equation. Hence, a regression involving these two variables only is, in terms of predictive relevance as measured by Q-square, superior to the initial regression involving all twelve predictors.

To be sure, *automatic* explorative routines as used above can only be used to identify potential problems and not to generate theory. The above example, however, has been presented to illustrate two points relevant for further analyses. First, except for the variables "procedural interactions" and "disciplinary activities," all variables involved in the multiple regression are largely interchangeable as predictors of the variable "academic engagement." Second, and directly related to the first, empirically-derived exploratory analyses must fail to produce useful results because in situations such as illustrated above it is virtually impossible to distinguish between relevant and irrelevant predictors on purely statistical grounds.

Initial PLS Model

The remainder of this appendix is devoted to the examination of three PLS models which have been subsequently tested on the basis of the Netherlands' data. These analyses will serve as an example of the way in which the "final" PLS models discussed in Chapter 7 were obtained for each country.

Figure C.1 presents, in PLS terms, the path model that will be used as a point of departure. For convenience, this model will be referred to as model Neth.A.

The model shown in Fig. C.1 constitutes an intermediate model version derived from preliminary PLS analyses. It involves 9 constructs and 28 manifest variables. Figure C.1 displays the between-construct paths and the corresponding path coefficients (i.e., the direct effects). The diagram also indicates the number of manifest variables associated with each construct and the estimation modes used to estimate the constructs (see Appendix B, for details of PLS estimation). Arrows pointing from a block of manifest variables to the associated construct indicate "inward" estimation; arrows pointing from a construct to the corresponding block of manifest variables indicate "outward" estimation. In Fig. C.1 it can be seen that three constructs were defined as "inward," namely "teacher perception of class ability," "managing," and "quantity of instruction."

In general, it was deemed more reasonable to use "inward" rather than "outward" estimation for constructs comprising measures of instructional

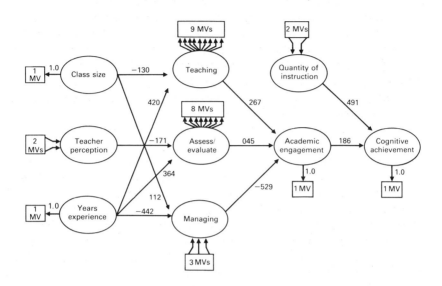

FIG. C.1 Between-construct and within-construct relationships of model Neth.A (path coefficients multiplied by 1,000).

events and teaching practices. This is because it would seem appropriate to assume that particular teaching behaviors "form" or "produce" constructs supposed to reflect specific domains of classroom instruction and teaching. That is, it would seem theoretically appropriate to assume "productive," or inward, rather than "reflective," or outward, relationships between these constructs and their manifest variables. However, since PLS inward estimation involves multiple regression, the choice between estimation modes was often constrained by statistical considerations concerned with multicollinearity within blocks of manifest variables. Such was the case for the constructs "teaching" and "assessing/evaluating" in model Neth.A. In order to avoid unstable or even uninterpretable PLS results, outward estimation had to be used for these constructs.

The model shown in Fig. C.1 also includes four constructs, each associated with a single manifest variable: "class size," "years of teaching experience," "academic engagement," and "cognitive achievement." As indicated in Fig. C.1, the associated loadings are in these cases always equal to unity irrespective of the choice of a particular estimation mode. That is, the construct is formally equivalent to its single manifest variable.

Table C.3 displays the within-construct results obtained from model Neth.A.

TABLE C.3   *Within-construct coefficients for Model Neth.A*

Construct/Variable	Weight	Loading	Tolerance
Teacher Perception (inward)			
High Ability?	509	640	029
Need Remediation?	−779	−865	029
Teaching (outward)			
Lecture/Explain/Demonstrate	243	492	570
Discourse/Discussion	264	395	333
Seatwork Written Assignments	−396	−808	440
Directives	−011	−024	276
Structuring Cues	219	234	238
Verbal Lecture	−186	−498	231
Lecture with Materials	230	662	554
Demonstration	111	282	440
Use of Examples	239	540	441
Assessing/Evaluating (outward)			
Teacher to Student Probes	148	591	642
Teacher to Group Probes	164	439	733
Teacher to Group Questions	240	510	669
Teacher to Student Questions	221	718	780
Redirect Question	280	720	543
Acknowledge Correct Answer	334	685	331
Teacher Says Student Answer Wrong	206	603	223
Effectiveness Questions	047	092	120
Managing (inward)			
Procedural Interactions	138	402	114
Disciplinary Activities	948	986	069
Uninvolved Teacher	078	127	050
Quantity of Instruction (inward)			
Teacher OTL Rating	884	910	004
Time Allocated to Instruction	415	472	004

Note: Constructs with single manifest variable omitted.

For each construct involving more than one manifest variable three coefficients—weight, loading, and tolerance index—are presented in Table C.3. Constructs comprising just one manifest variable are, for convenience, omitted because the corresponding weights and loadings must be equal to unity. As explained in Appendix B, the PLS weights are used to estimate the constructs as linear composites of their associated manifest variables while the loadings are defined as the zero-order correlation between each manifest variable and its associated construct. Both weights and loadings reflect the strength of the relationships between constructs and manifest variables. The tolerance indices reported in Table C.3 are defined as squared multiple correlations among the manifest variables belonging to a given construct. As such, they reflect the amount of within-construct multicollinearity. From the tolerance indices presented in Table C.3 the need to use the "outward" mode (rather than the "inward" mode) for estimating the constructs "teaching" and "assessing/evaluating" should be clear. Because of the high degree of collinearity within these two constructs, the use of the "inward" mode would have resulted in much the same stability problems as was illustrated by the multiple regression example presented earlier.

From a comparison between model Neth.A and the corresponding "final" model version described in Chapter 7, it can be seen that model Neth.A is fairly close to the Netherlands' "final" model. The major difference concerns the structure and composition of the intervening constructs "teaching," "assessing/evaluating" and "managing." Thus, the following discussion will be primarily concerned with the restructuring of these three constructs.

Within-Construct and Between-Construct Collinearity

The first modification considered concerns the variables "lecture/explain/ demonstrate," "discourse/discussion" and "seatwork on written assignments" belonging to the construct "teaching." These three manifest variables were derived from the Classroom Snapshot (SNAP) while the remaining variables associated with the "teaching" construct were derived from the Five-Minute-Interaction (FMI) form. As can be seen from the loadings displayed in Table C.3, the three SNAP variables had relatively high correlations with the construct "teaching." However, they were also found to be highly correlated with the constructs "assessing/evaluating" and "managing." If such correlations between blocks of manifest variables exist, the feasibility of eliminating some of the manifest variables should be considered for two reasons. First, large correlations between manifest variables across constructs indicate ambiguity in the definition of block structures. Second, these correlations imply relatively high intercorrelations among constructs which may cause stability problems in the estimation of between-construct paths.

Tables C.4 and C.5 present loadings and path coefficients resulting from the exclusion of the three aforementioned SNAP-variables from the construct "teaching." For comparative purposes, the tables also include the corresponding results of the initial model described above, and the results of the deletion of all FMI-variables (rather than the SNAP-variables) from the "teaching" construct. For convenience, the different model versions are denoted as Neth.A(1), Neth.A(2), and Neth.A(3).

Table C.4 displays the loadings of the construct "teaching." Table C.5 presents for each model version the direct effects on the construct "academic engagement" and the ensuing R-square and Q-square values. Since the construct "academic engagement" consists of just one manifest variable, the R-square and Q-square values can be directly compared. (Such direct comparisons would be inappropriate if the predicted construct would involve more than one indicator.) From Table C.4 it can be seen that there is not

TABLE C.4 *Loadings of the "teaching" construct*
obtained for three versions of model Neth.A.

Manifest Variable	A(1)	Model A(2)	A(3)
Lecture/Explain/Demonstrate	492	-	528
Discourse/Discussion	395	-	485
Seatwork Written Assignments	− 808	-	− 908
Directives	− 024	− 094	-
Structuring Cues	234	375	-
Verbal Lecture	− 498	− 521	-
Lecture with Materials	662	600	-
Demonstration	282	400	-
Use of Examples	540	746	-

Note: Table entries marked "-" correspond to manifest variables omitted from the construct.

TABLE C.5 *Direct effects on "academic engagement"*
for Models Neth.A(1) to Neth.A(3)

Predictor	A(1)	Model A(2)	A(3)
Teaching	267	213	197
Assessing/Evaluation	045	118	− 026
Managing	− 529	− 560	− 574
R-square	552	541	540
Q-square	398	397	368

much difference in terms of the corresponding loadings obtained from the three versions of model Neth.A. Specifically the signs of the estimated loadings are the same.

In Table C.5 it can be seen, however, that the model modifications introduced in versions Neth.A(2) and Neth.A(3) had remarkable consequences in terms of between-construct relationships. The Q-square values obtained for models Neth.A(1) and Neth.A(2) are almost identical; this indicates that the three SNAP-variables can be excluded from the "teaching" construct without loss of predictive power. That is, influences of these variables on "academic engagement" are covered by the FMI-variables included in the model. Version Neth.A(3), however, results in a lower Q-square and in a negative path coefficient for the construct "assessing/evaluating." This change is due to multicollinearity problems emanating from large correlations between the SNAP-variables and the manifest variables in the constructs "assessing/ evaluating" and "managing." The specification of model Neth.A(3) simply reveals more clearly the collinearity problems already involved in model Neth.A(1). On the basis of the results presented above, the model version Neth.A(2) was selected for subsequent analyses.

Restructuring of Constructs

The block structure results obtained from model Neth.A(2) suggested that the block structure specification of the intervening constructs "teaching," "assessing/evaluating," and "managing" should be examined for further modifications. Tables C.6 and C.7 summarize the results of six modifications that were undertaken. The corresponding model versions will be referred to as models Neth.B(1) to Neth.B(6).

TABLE C.6   *Models Neth.B(1) to Neth.B(6) R-square and Q-square of "academic engagement"*

Model	Modification	R^2	Q^2	Q^2/R^2
B(1)	"uninvolved teacher" dropped from construct "managing"; "effectiveness questions" moved to construct "teaching"	563	425	755
B(2)	"demonstration" dropped from construct "teaching"	557	410	736
B(3)	"directives" dropped from construct "teaching"	564	425	754
B(4)	"teacher to group probes" dropped from construct "assessing/evaluating"	571	434	760
B(5)	"use of examples" dropped from construct "teaching"	594	461	760
B(6)	"teacher to group questions" dropped from construct "assessing/evaluating"	597	466	781

The modifications introduced in subsequent steps of the PLS analyses are noted on the left of Table C.6, which displays for each model version the R-square and Q-square values of the construct "academic engagement." Table C.7 presents the loadings of the constructs "teaching" and "assessing/evaluating" obtained at each step. This includes a Q-square statistic called crossvalidated communality which can be used to evaluate the predictive relevance of within-construct relationships (see Lohmoeller 1981; Wold 1982). Both the Q-square values displayed in Table C.6 and those presented in Table C.7 need to be examined jointly in order to evaluate the corresponding model modifications. In Table C.6 it can be seen that the restructuring of the

TABLE C.7   *Models Neth.B(1) to Neth.B(6)*
Loadings and block Q-square (crossvalidated communality)
of constructs "teaching" and "assessing/evaluating"

Construct/Variable	B(1)	B(2)	B(3)	B(4)	B(5)	B(6)
Teaching						
Directives	−053	374	-	-	-	-
Structuring Cues	408	266	466	466	475	475
Verbal Lecture	−473	322	−445	−445	−430	−430
Lecture with Materials	576	−190	598	598	618	618
Demonstration	272	-	-	-	-	-
Use of Examples	600	672	530	530	-	-
Effectiveness Questions	525	276	573	573	705	705
Block Q-square:	093	050	183	183	242	242
Assessing/Evaluating						
Teacher to Student Probes	593	593	593	623	623	677
Teacher to Group Probes	439	439	439	-	-	-
Redirect Question	729	729	729	739	739	763
Acknowledge Correct Answer	679	679	679	720	720	722
Teacher Says Student Answer Wrong	604	604	604	609	609	593
Teacher to Group Questions	509	509	509	399	399	-
Teacher to Student Questions	719	719	719	793	793	857
Block Q-square:	322	322	322	382	382	481

Note: Entries marked "-" correspond to manifest variables eliminated from the construct.

constructs involved mainly the elimination of specific manifest variables. One manifest variable, "effectiveness questions," was moved from the construct "assessing/evaluating" to the construct "teaching." This modification was undertaken because the variable "effectiveness questions" was found to be more highly correlated with the construct "teaching" than the construct "assessing/evaluating."

An examination of Tables C.6 and C.7 indicates that, with but one exception, the Q-square values increase as a result of the modifications introduced. The exception occurs in version Neth.B(2) when the FMI-variable "demonstration" was deleted from the construct "teaching." The Q-square value associated with "academic engagement" decreases from 0.425 to 0.410, and the block Q-square associated with the construct "teaching" drops from 0.093 to 0.050. The within-construct relationships of the construct "teaching" change dramatically as a result of the deletion of the variable "demonstration" (compare the loadings obtained for versions Neth.B(1) and Neth.B(2) in Table C.7). These changes indicate some degree of instability within this subset of manifest variables.

Further examinations of the data revealed that this instability was primarily due to just one outlying teacher who not only had a large value for the variable "demonstration" but also an outlying value for the variable "directives." This finding suggested to drop the variable "directives" in addition to the variable "demonstration" from the construct "teaching." The structure of the "teaching" construct stabilizes as a result of the deletion of these two variables (see the results for versions Neth.B(3) to Neth.B(6) in Table C.7). It should be noted at this point that this sort of sensitivity to minor model modifications was typical for PLS analyses of influences of "schooling" variables. Based on the data presented in Tables C.6 and C.7, Neth.B(6) was finally selected as the most adequate version of the model.

As a matter of fact, the model denoted above as model Neth.B(6) represents what has been referred to earlier as the Netherlands' "final" model. The results of this model are discussed in greater detail in Chapter 7. To summarize the above presentation, the PLS analyses started with an intermediate model version with a Q-square of 0.398 for the construct "academic engagement" (see version Neth.A(1) in Table C.5). A series of subsequent analyses concerned with modifications of the intervening constructs "teaching," "assessing/ evaluating" and "managing" resulted in a Q-square of 0.466 (see version Neth.B(6) in Table C.6). In addition, the block structure modifications considerably increased the block Q-square values associated with the constructs "teaching" and "assessing/evaluating" (see Table C.7). These results indicate that it was possible to eliminate "noise" due to inadequate specifications of within-construct and between-construct relationships.

Alternative Ways of Analysis

A discussion of some alternative ways to analyze relationships between observational variables and student outcomes will conclude this appendix. For this purpose the results of analyzing the Netherlands' "final" model in four different ways will be examined. The different model versions, denoted for convenience as models Neth.C(1) to Neth.C(4), can be described as follows.

Model Neth.C.(1): Class Level Means of Instructional Events

Model Neth.C(1) will be used for comparative purposes and represents the Netherlands' "final" model analyzed on the basis of class mean percentages of observed instructional events and practices. That is, the percentages available for each lesson were aggregated to the class or teacher level in order to obtain variables indicative of what may be termed "average teaching behavior." In accordance with the general data analysis plans of the Classroom Environment Study, these class mean percentages were used in the PLS analyses presented above.

Model Neth. C(2): Class Level Medians of Instructional Events

One possible alternative to the examination of class mean percentages is the use of median percentages over observed lessons. Because some teachers exhibited particular instructional behaviors more frequently in just one or two lessons while these behaviors were virtually never observed and coded in the remaining lessons, medians may be more appropriate than means as summary statistics. Such skewed within-teacher frequency distributions may strongly influence the computation of means and statistical analyses based on these class level means. Since medians are more robust against seemingly exceptional or "outlying" lesson level frequencies, one may consider the analysis of median percentages as a potentially useful alternative to the analysis of mean percentages. Model Neth.C(2) was estimated on the basis of median percentages rather than mean percentages over observed lessons.

Model Neth. C(3): Nonlineaear Scale Transformations

In model Neth.C(3) the scales of all observational variables involved in the Netherlands' "final" model were transformed using the arcsine function. This nonlinear scale transformation was suggested by Mandeville (1984) and constitutes one possibility to cope with data analytical problems emanating from the fact that some variables in the SNAP and FMI observation schemes were quite rarely observed and coded. This often resulted in skewed frequency distributions that may invalidate correlational analyses. It should be noted that, apart from the arcsine transformation, so-called power transformations (see, for example, Emerson and Stoto 1982) also were considered, but they basically produced the same results. The use of power transformations has been discussed in Chapter 7 in connection with the examination of zero-order correlations between observational variables and outcome achievement.

Model Neth. C(4): Use of Lesson Level Observational Data

While models Neth.C(1) to Neth.C(3) employ observational data aggregated to the class or teacher level, model Neth.C(4) is analyzed on the basis of observational data defined at the lesson level. That is, the predefined class level aggregates of observed instructional events and practices used in models Neth.C(1) to Neth.C(3) are in model Neth.C(4) replaced by the set of eight lesson level indicators (defined as percentages of the associated total number of coded events) that were in the Netherlands available for each observational category. The diagram shown in Fig. C.2 can help to clarify the major difference between model Neth.C(4) and the remaining model versions.

The model depicted in Fig. C.2 is recognizable as a simple path model that can be estimated using PLS. The coefficients included in the diagram were, in fact, obtained using the PLS procedure. The model shown involves two

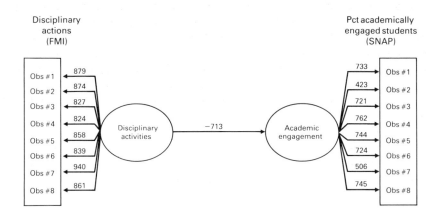

Disciplinary actions (FMI)

Pct academically engaged students (SNAP)

Obs #1	879				733	Obs #1
Obs #2	874				423	Obs #2
Obs #3	827				721	Obs #3
Obs #4	824	Disciplinary activities	−713	Academic engagement	762	Obs #4
Obs #5	858				744	Obs #5
Obs #6	839				724	Obs #6
Obs #7	940				506	Obs #7
Obs #8	861				745	Obs #8

FIG. C.2   PLS model for the bivariate relationship between disciplinary actions and academic engagement using lesson level indicators (coefficients multiplied by 1,000).

constructs denoted as "discipline" and "academic engagement" and 16 manifest variables representing the lesson level percentages available for each observational category. The coefficients linking the lesson level indicators and the constructs represent PLS loadings; the coefficient associated with the path from "discipline" to "academic engagement" (-0.713) is, in this case, equal to the zero-order correlation between the constructs (as estimated by the PLS procedure). The PLS "outward" mode was applied to both constructs.

In essence, the model shown in Fig. C.2 constitutes the PLS analogue of the bivariate relationship between the class level means of "disciplinary activities" and "academic engagement." Although rarely stated explicitly, the computation of class or teacher level means of instructional events is based on the well-known assumptions of classical measurement theory. It is specifically assumed that teachers possess some stable dispositions to exhibit particular instructional behaviors more or less frequently, and that the corresponding lesson level indicators constitute parallel measurements of these behavioral dispositions. Similar assumptions are made for variables reflecting student learning behaviors, such as attentiveness. The notion of parallel measurements corresponds to a factor analytic measurement model with identical error variances for all indicators. The errors of measurement are also assumed to be uncorrelated over occasions. It is this fairly restrictive measurement model that simplifies the estimation of teacher dispositions considerably. This is because, under the assumptions outlined above, the computation of means over occasions can be shown to provide reliable estimates of behavioral dispositions.

The model shown in Fig. C.2 constitutes an alternative to the use of pre-defined composites of lesson level measures of instructional events in that a principal component approach is used to obtain estimates of teacher dispositions as represented by the constructs included in the model. More precisely, the PLS algorithm as applied to the model shown in Fig. C.2 performs an eigenanalysis of the (non-symmetrical) intercorrelation matrix of the eight lesson level indicators available for each observational category. The weights used to compute the equivalent of a "grand mean" over occasions are derived from the eigenvectors associated with the largest eigenvalue of that matrix. That is, for the model depicted in Fig. C.2 the PLS procedure provides a least squares approximation to the intercorrelation matrix of the respective lesson level indicators of instructional events that has much in common with the familiar method of principal component analysis. The procedure corresponds to what van den Wollenberg (1977) refers to as "redundancy analysis." It does not require specific assumptions about the errors or residuals associated with the various indicators, except for the assumption that the residuals are uncorrelated with the constructs. It is also not necessary to assume that the residuals or measurement errors associated with a given set of lesson level indicators are uncorrelated with each other. In addition, the presumed relationship between the constructs "disciplinary activities" and "academic engagement" is incorporated in the process of estimating the constructs.

It should be noted that principal component analysis and factor analytic measurement models such as those underlying the computation of class or teacher level means of instructional events are similar to some extent but have different aims (see, for example, Jöreskog 1979). The computation of means across occasions presumes that the frequencies with which particular instructional behaviors are observed are governed by a specific measurement model. This model implies constraints for the covariance structure of observed events which are *a priori* considered as being fulfilled. The principal component approach, on the other hand, assumes no specific covariance structure; it rather aims at data reduction by means of a specific loss function which is minimized using least squares criteria. It will be noted that the computation of teacher or class level means of instructional events can, of course, also be viewed as being a data reduction technique that minimizes the squared differences between the composite scores representing estimates of teacher dispositions and the associated sets of lesson level indicators. Hence, ignoring the more complex issues involved in specific measurement models, the principal component approach and the computation of means over occasions may simply be seen as alternative procedures for data reduction.

The basic difference between both procedures, then, is that the covariances among indicators are discarded when means are computed while these covariances are incorporated in the computation of principal components.

Another aspect that should be noted in connection with the model shown in Fig. C.2 concerns Wold's theorem of "Consistency at Large" (see, for example, Wold 1982). This theorem states that PLS parameter estimates become better in the sense of being closer to the target parameter values with increasing numbers of cases *and* increasing numbers of indicators for each construct. For the PLS analyses presented in this appendix, it was of course not possible to increase the number of cases. The availability of lesson level frequencies of instructional events, however, provided an opportunity to increase the number of indicators or manifest variables considerably. For example, the model shown in Fig. C.2 involves 16 indicators rather than two manifest variables representing predefined class level means. The model in Fig. C.2 also permits an examination of the relative strengths of the relationships between the lesson level indicators and the constructs as indicated by the various loadings. As mentioned earlier, PLS loadings are defined as zero-order correlations between manifest variables and their associated construct. The presumed existence of stable teacher dispositions to exhibit specific instructional behaviors more or less frequently would suggest to expect relatively large positive loadings for all indicators. This is the case for the PLS model shown in Fig. C.2. It will be seen below, however, that somewhat less consistent results were obtained for other sets of indicators involved in the more complex model Neth.C(4).

Results for Models Neth.C(1) to Neth.C(4)

The PLS results related to models Neth.C(1) to Neth.C(4) are displayed in Tables C.8 and C.9. Table C.8 presents for each model version the loadings of the constructs consisting of observational variables. For convenience, the mean loadings over the eight lesson level indicators available for each observational category are reported for model Neth.C(4). Table C.9 displays for each model version the path coefficients associated with the direct effects on the constructs "academic engagement" and "outcome achievement." In addition, the jackknife standard errors and the ensuing R-square and Q-square values are given.It should be noted that the coefficients presented in Table C.9 may not be compared across the different model versions in terms of their numerical values. The same is true for the loadings presented in Table C.8. This is because the manifest variables and the constructs were in each model version defined in terms of different scales and because all coefficients presented in the tables are based on standardized data. Since standardization generally effects the magnitude of the ensuing coefficients, the loadings and the path coefficients obtained for the different model versions should only be compared in terms of the *relative* size of the corresponding

TABLE C.8   *PLS loadings of observational variables
for models Neth.C(1) to Neth.C(4)*

Construct/Variable	Model C(1) Means	C(2) Medians	C(3) Arcscine	C(4) Lesson
Teaching				
Structuring Cues	475	504	434	262
Verbal Lecture	−429	−519	−448	−347
Lecture with Materials	618	692	645	430
Effectiveness Questions	705	577	700	432
Assessing/Evaluating				
Teacher to Student Probes	677	744	683	437
Redirect Question	763	731	753	371
Acknowledge Correct Answer	722	763	730	412
Teacher Says Student Answer Wrong	593	651	582	278
Teacher to Student Questions	857	813	860	657
Managing				
Procedural Interactions	403	546	400	175
Disciplinary Activities	989	957	989	855
Academic Engagement				
SNAP Rating	1000	1000	1000	674

Note: Mean loadings over eight lesson level indicators reported for model Neth.C(4).

TABLE C.9   *Direct effects on the constructs academic
engagement and outcome achievement for models Neth.C(1)
to Neth.C(4). Jackknife standard errors in parentheses*

Criterion/Predictor	Model C(1) Means	C(2) Medians	C(3) Arcscine	C(4) Lesson
Academic Engagement				
Teaching	325 (130)	302 (150)	359 (172)	404 (112)
Assessing/Evaluating	189 (094)	167 (135)	212 (098)	303 (092)
Managing	−483 (132)	−497 (144)	−421 (150)	−366 (135)
R-square	597	586	566	667
Q-square	466	460	420	571
Outcome Achievement				
Academic Engagement	186 (154)	151 (158)	184 (139)	186 (158)
Quantity of Instruction	491 (109)	489 (111)	489 (109)	492 (108)
R-square	293	281	292	293
Q-square	176	158	189	173

effects. This caveat also applies to comparisons between models Neth.C(1) and Neth.C(4) where the manifest variables were defined in terms of similar scales (i.e., as percentages of the total number of coded instructional events), but where the constructs were estimated using different loss functions. It must also be noted that in model Neth.C(4) the construct "managing" was estimated using the PLS outward mode because this construct involved, in this model version, 16 manifest variables, namely eight lesson level indicators for each of the categories "procedural interactions" and "disciplinary activities." With 16 manifest variables and 47 cases, it is obviously not advisable to use the PLS inward mode (i.e., multiple regression) for estimating the construct "managing." In contrast, the "managing" construct involved in the remaining model versions Neth.C(1) to Neth.C(3) just two indicators so that inward estimation was possible.

Turning, first, to the results associated with model versions Neth.C(1) to Neth.C(3), it can be seen in Tables C.8 and C.9 that there is not much difference in terms of the corresponding PLS results. It will only be noted in Table C.9 that the magnitude of the jackknife standard errors (as compared with the magnitude of the associated path coefficients) obtained for models Neth.C(2) and Neth.C(3) was somewhat larger than the corresponding jack-knife standard errors obtained for model Neth.C(1). This was to be expected because the use of median percentages and the use of arcsine scale trans-formations will generally reduce the relative amount of between-teacher or between-class variance of the respective observational variables. This will also reduce the variance of the corresponding constructs. The smaller amount of variance will usually result in larger standard errors (jackknife statistics share this property with the classical estimates of the variance of point estimates).

The similarity of the PLS results for models Neth.C(1) to Neth.C(3) is partly a consequence of the model modifications described earlier in this appendix when observational variables with skewed frequency distributions such as "demonstration," "use of examples," and "directives" were eliminated. This is not to say, however, that the "final" model for the Netherlands would have been different in terms of the included constructs and manifest variables if medians or arcsine scale transformations had been used from the outset. Appropriate PLS analyses were, in fact, undertaken and the results of these analyses suggested the same modifications for the Netherlands' model as the PLS analyses discussed previously. The latter result was to be expected at least for the analyses based on class level medians of instructional behaviors since the computation of medians over observed lessons stresses the importance of seemingly "stable" behaviors to a greater extent than the computation of class level means. Indeed, extreme lesson level frequencies, that is, seemingly "outlying" frequencies for specific lessons taught by a given teacher are generally discarded when teacher level medians are computed. As a consequence, the teacher or class level variances of the medians of observational categories which typically had greatly skewed within-teacher frequency distributions were often found to be considerably smaller than the variances of the corresponding class level means.

As mentioned earlier, the use of arcsine scale transformations was considered in order to cope with data analytical problems associatd with skewed frequency distributions by reducing the relative distance between seemingly "outlying" data points and the rest of the data. Similar effects can be achieved by using other types of nonlinear scale transformations, such as so-called power transformations which have been discussed in Chapter 7 in connection with the examination of zero-order correlations. Depending on the shape of the data to be analyzed, such scale transformations may help to facilitate and improve linear analysis. For the present example, however, it can be seen in Tables C.8 and C.9 that the PLS results for model Neth.C(3), in which arcsine scales were used, are much the same as the results of model Neth.C(1).

Turning, finally, to the results related to model Neth.C(4), it can be seen in Table C.9 that the use of lesson level observational data had remarkable consequences in terms of the path coefficients representing the direct effects on academic engagement. That is, the relative magnitude of the estimated direct effects of the constructs "teaching," "assessing/evaluating," and "managing" on academic engagement changed as compared with the remaining model versions. Specifically, the largest direct effect on academic engagement is in model Neth.C(4) associated with the construct "teaching" while in models Neth.C(1) to Neth.C(3) the largest effect on academic engagement was associated with the "managing" construct. It can also be seen in Table C.9 that the relative size of the effect of the construct "assessing/evaluating" on academic engagement increased considerably when lesson level observational data were used. When interpreting these results, it is useful to examine the data presented in Table C.10, which displays for the constructs containing observational data the median, minimum and maximum loadings associated with each observational category involved in model Neth.C(4).

The data presented in Table C.10 should specifically be examined in terms of the range of loadings obtained for the eight lesson level indicators associated with each observational category. It can be seen that the largest shift in the magnitude of estimated loadings occurred for the category "procedural interactions" involved in the construct "managing;" the minimum loading was -0.138 while the maximum loading was 0.636. The minimum loading of -0.138 and, hence, the shift in the signs of estimated loadings was associated with just one observation where the frequency distribution of "procedural interactions" was found to be quite different from all other observations. This is an outcome of chance variation that might be expected specifically for instructional events which typically occur with low frequency and which likely depend on the specific contents of the lessons which are being observed. That is, fluctuations in the shape of frequency distributions for single observations and fluctuations in the magnitude of loadings associated with

TABLE C.10 *Median, minimum and maximum loadings*
for model Neth.C(4)

Construct/Variable	Median	Minimum	Maximum
Teaching			
Structuring Cues	298	026	516
Verbal Lecture	− 208	− 490	− 018
Lecture with Materials	483	255	559
Effectiveness Questions	497	250	604
Assessing/Evaluating			
Teacher to Student Probes	450	141	649
Redirect Question	432	230	564
Acknowledge Correct Answer	462	264	527
Teacher Says Student Answer Wrong	298	193	376
Teacher to Student Questions	680	530	680
Managing			
Procedural Interactions	206	− 138	636
Disciplinary Activities	867	803	934
Academic Engagement			
SNAP Rating	739	484	754

these observations may be expected at least for some observational categories and are, as such, not of particular concern. It might nevertheless be useful, however, to apply some differential weighting that takes such fluctuations into account. Such differential weighting is implemented in model Neth.C(4) using a principal component approach. As illustrated by the data presented in Tables C.9 and C.10, this can be expected to have two closely interrelated effects. First, seemingly "outlying" observations which do not "fit" into the overall correlational pattern presumed by the specification of a given model will generally receive weights and loadings reflecting this lack of fit. That is, such observations will generally be downweighted and will thus influence the model results to a lesser extent than is the case for prespecified composites, such as means, where all observations receive identical weights. Second, the use of lesson level indicators in connection with the use of a principal component approach can be expected to increase the overall stability and the predictive power of between-construct relationships. These considerations, and the results of detailed exploratory analyses such as those presented in the appendix, suggested to examine not only the results of models involving class mean percentages of instructional events, but also the results of analogous PLS models in which the means were replaced by the corresponding lesson level data.

Name Index

Subject Index